Ellis Island to Ebbets Field

ELLIS ISLAND

TO EBBETS FIELD

Sport and the American Jewish Experience

Peter Levine

New York   Oxford
OXFORD UNIVERSITY PRESS
1992

Oxford University Press

Oxford   New York   Toronto
Delhi   Bombay   Calcutta   Madras   Karachi
Kuala Lumpur   Singapore   Hong Kong   Tokyo
Nairobi   Dar es Salaam   Cape Town
Melbourne   Auckland

and associated companies in
Berlin   Ibadan

Copyright © 1992 by Peter Levine

Published by Oxford University Press, Inc.,
200 Madison Avenue, New York, New York 10016

Oxford is a registered trademark of Oxford University Press

Library of Congress Cataloging-in-Publication Data
Levine, Peter.
Ellis Island to Ebbets Field:
Sport and the American Jewish experience
Peter Levine.
p.   cm.   Includes bibliographical references (p.   ) and index.
ISBN-0-19-505128-9
1. Jewish athletes—United States.
2. Sports—United States—History—20th Century. I. Title.
OU697.A1L48   1992   796'.089'924'073—dc20   (B)   91-42016

Portions of Chapter 11 previously appeared as
"My Father and I, We Didn't Get Our Medals":
Marty Glickman's American Jewish Odyssey,"
in *American Jewish History* 77 (March 1989), 399–424.

This volume is one in the series, *Sports History and Society,*
edited by Peter Levine and Steven Tischler.

2 4 6 8 9 7 5 3 1

Printed in the United States of America
on acid-free paper

For Jack Lipson, 1943–1989

Acknowledgments

In February 1973 my father died. I met my older brother in Chicago and we flew home to Brooklyn to bury him and to share our grief with our mother. The night we arrived, we sat down on a bed in the room my brother and I had grown up in and looked through the hundreds of family photographs my parents had accumulated over the years. Although no doubt I had seen them before, scattered throughout the shoeboxes and albums were pictures of my father as a college athlete—playing basketball, posing with his lacrosse buddies, and alone, in his football togs, on the field at Lewisohn Stadium. These and other images provoked our laughter and tears, temporarily offering some relief from the reality of his death.

None of us could have known that this would be the last time we would be together to share our feelings about Sam. Seven months later, my mother and brother died within hours of each other in a hospital in Portland, Oregon. And seventeen years later, I finished this book, which in ways both obvious and hidden, is about fathers and sons, about generations in conflict and at peace, about memory and loss and ultimately about coming to terms with the past in ways that provide hope and optimism about the future. Although this book is not dedicated to Sam, Pearl, or Jon, my rich life with them and my desire to understand and appreciate it with all its love and conflict certainly influenced its course.

My father and I never talked about his days as a college athlete at CCNY (City College of New York), whether or not his Russian immigrant parents ever saw him play, or what they thought about his passion for American games. Over the last six years I have had the opportunity to ask these and other questions of men and women of his generation and also of others of my own. Without the sincerity and cooperation of the following individuals who talked to me on the phone, exchanged letters, or invited me into their homes and offices, this book could not have been written. This list is long, some names more familiar than others, but all are important for what they had to offer about themselves. It includes Phil Weintraub, Bobby Sand, Nancy Lieberman, David Sorkin, Cal Abrams, Mel Allen, Andy Cohen, Harry Danning, Marty Glickman, Marshall Goldberg, Mike Epstein, Allie Sherman, Hank Kaplan, Ben Bentley, Ed Krinsky, Irving Rudd, Jammy Moskowitz, Harold Juden-friend, Irving Bernstein, Red Sarachek, Goody Rosen, Haskell Cohen, Sonny Hertzberg, Bernie Riesman, Danny Schayes, Harry Glickman, Justin Kesten-baum, Paul Berns, Abe Gerchick, the late Moe Goldman, Red Barber, Cy Block, Davey Day, Sammy Kaplan, Irwin Shaw, Mort Plotnick, Ruby Benja-min, Harry Litwack, Vic Hershkowitz, Harold Zimman, Bernie Fleigel, Bill Jacobs, Seymour Brode, Bob Steinberg, Mickey Fishman, Bill Hertz, Gary Stol-lak, Mark Unger, Myron Milgrom, and some fifty members of a group called the Basketball Fraternity who you'll learn more about as you read on.

Many other friends and acquaintances also showed interest in what I was doing. Ken Waltzer shared his knowledge of American Jewish history with me and offered wonderfully critical evaluations of early drafts. Richard White read the entire manuscript, offered many rich suggestions, and shared with me his own insights into the interaction of different cultures. Peter Vinten-Johansen and Steve Tischler also read the entire manuscript and pushed me to think about my ideas and my writing. Larry Gerlach, Harry Reed, Warren Cohen, and the late Steve Botein also read portions of my work and offered important insights to me. In a myriad of ways—from sending me newspaper stories to sharing their own ideas about sport and the American Jewish expe-rience—Jeffrey Goldberg, Robert Peterson, Tilden Edelstein, Eric Solomon, Rabbi Morton Hoffman, Ellen Uffen, Bill Himmelman, Joseph Overfield, Charles Salzberg, Steven Riess, Bill Simons, Jules Tygiel, Randy Roberts, Bill Baker, John Hoberman, Paul Breines, Fred Roberts, Bob Lipsyte, Marc Lee Raphael, Louis Siegelbaum, Stephen Brumberg, Erwin Lynn, Louis Jacobson, and Jeffrey Gurock also enriched my work. At Oxford, Joellyn Ausanka pro-vided good counsel and conversation. Sheldon Meyer, my editor and friend, supported this project from the outset, reading drafts along the way, making a number of important suggestions, and sharing with me his own enthusiasm and knowledge of American sport.

Grants from both the American Philosophical Society and the Michigan State University Foundation facilitated my research. So too did the able assis-tance of Ruth Levine, Linda Werbish, Peter Berg, Carmen DiCiccio, David Stra-mecky, Stephen Mockabee, Anita Herald, and Edwina Johnson. Equally important were the staffs of libraries and historical societies throughout the country, who patiently responded to my requests. Especially helpful were the inter-library loan staff at Michigan State University, Archie Motley of the Chi-cago Historical Society, Tom Heitz at the Baseball Hall of Fame Library, June Steitz at the Basketball Hall of Fame Library, Arona Rudavsky at the American Jewish Archives, Norma Spungen at the Spertus Library, the staffs at the Jew-ish Division of the New York Public Library, the YIVO Institute for Jewish Studies, the New York University Library, the William E. Weiner Oral History Library at the American Jewish Committee, and the Smith College Library, Faye Leibowitz of the Historical Society of Western Pennsylvania, Steve Sie-gel, librarian at New York City's 92nd Street Y, Linda Schloff of the Minnesota Jewish Historical Society, Rose Biderman of the Dallas Jewish Historical Soci-ety, Marsha Lotstein of the Jewish Historical Society of Greater Hartford, Lora

Meyer of the Jewish Historical Society of Oregon, Eleanor Horvitz of the Rhode Island Jewish Historical Society, Lily Schwartz of the Philadelphia Jewish Archives Center, and Miriam Schwartz of the Jewish Historical Society of New Haven. I also want to thank Lynda Miller for helping me stay loose and Curt Munson and my friends at Playmakers for keeping me in running shoes and for providing a much-needed change of pace from my writing and research.

My wife, Gale, and my daughter, Ruth, provided their own special support. They helped me gather material at Cooperstown, accompanied me on an occasional interview, and listened to what I wrote. Gale also came up with this book's title. Most important, their love and understanding made the experience of writing this book one of the most pleasurable and important things I have ever done.

Writing this book has been a very personal intellectual and emotional journey; one full of potential problem and possibility. Both chronologically and topically, it removes me still another step from my professional beginnings as a Jacksonian historian. Obvious throughout, however, is my rich debt to the work of Eugene Genovese, Lawrence Levine, Herbert Gutman, and other historians who take seriously the voice and experience of everyday outsiders, in search of identity and survival, as they interacted with each other and an American majority culture.

This book relies on the memories, anecdotes, and impressions of Jewish men, many between the ages of 60 and 80, who, in one way or another, actively participated in sport. Garnered from autobiographies, interviews given to others, and personal conversations and questionnaires solicited by myself, they include the thoughts of well-known sports personalities such as Barney Ross, Hank Greenberg, Red Auerbach, and Dolph Schayes as well as the recollections of lesser-known but equally perceptive individuals for whom sport was an integral part of their lives. Problems of selective memory, their comparative status as exceptional athletes, and the place of sport in the overall context of their lives naturally arise from such an approach. Awareness of them has tempered but hardly diminished the richness of their contribution to understanding the Jewish experience in American sport.

Talking to men like Sammy Kaplan, Moe Goldman, Red Sarachek, Marshall Goldberg, and Marty Glickman also encouraged reconnection with my own past. Whether it was attending Lafayette high school football games on Saturday afternoons or going to a Free Sons of Israel "fathers and sons" outing to watch the Dodgers at Ebbets Field or the New York Knickerbockers at Madison Square Garden, sport was one of the few shared experiences my father and I enjoyed. My Brooklyn neighborhood was predominately Jewish, but contained enough Irish and Italian Catholics to warrant St. Edmond's Church, whose illuminated cross, an avenue block away, was clearly visible from my fourth-floor bedroom window on winter nights when the backyard trees on one of the few blocks along Ocean Avenue not filled with six-story apartment houses bared their leaves. Part of the "majority" culture in my neck of the woods, my friends and I even let an occasional Catholic join the East 19th Street Spartans as we played every street and schoolyard sport imaginable. Sundays rarely permitted such pleasure. Until I turned thirteen, my family always traveled to the house on Sackman Street where my father was born and where his parents still lived. My fondest memories of those reluctant visits that I increasingly resented, were sitting with my Zaide, in front of his small Dumont television in the parlor, as he followed the exploits of the great "professional" wrestler of those days—"Gorgeous George."

My interest in sport continued as an adult, long before I decided to write about it. This book is dedicated to the memory of one of my favorite Jewish athletes and friends—Jack Lipson. We met in college when we both tried out for the very "un-Jewish" sport of crew. He remained one of my closest friends—someone who truly appreciated a good stickball bat and "spaldeens." Our visits to Cooperstown, both to work on this book and to share his passion for baseball, became ritual.

While this book emerged directly out of my previous work on that famous baseball giant and Gentile A. G. Spalding, it clearly became an opportunity for me to understand more clearly who I am and where I come from. Historians, I believe, regardless of what they write about and however much they may seek to avoid it, always bring to their work their own values, interests, and beliefs. I am not uncomfortable with this fact. Hopefully, my own personal quest has enriched rather than diminished what follows.

East Lansing, Michigan   P.L.
September 1991

Contents

Introduction, 3

1. The Promise of Sport, 11

2. Basketball and Community, 26

3. Jews and Professional Basketball, 1900–1950, 52

4. "Allagaroo, Garoo, Gara": The College Game, CCNY, and the Scandals of 1950, 74

5. America's National Game, 87

6. Cohen at the Bat, 100

7. "Mantle, Schmantle, We Got Abie": Jews and Major League Baseball Between the Wars, 117

8. "Oy Such a Fighter!": Boxing and the American Jewish Experience, 144

9. "Fighting for All My People": Jewish Champions and American Heroes, 170

10. "Der Yiddisher Vildkat" and the "Hebrew Hillbilly": College Life and College Sport Between the Wars, 190

11. "My Father and I, We Didn't Get Our Medals": Marty Glickman's American Jewish Odyssey, 216

12. "Where Have You Gone, Hank Greenberg?": Sport and the American Jewish Experience Since World War II, 235

13. Conclusions, 270

Postscript: The Jewish Experience in Comparative Perspective, 281

Bibliographic Note, 286

Notes, 291

Index, 319

Ellis Island to Ebbets Field

Introduction

IN 1923, the *Sporting News* denied claims of dissension on the Philadelphia Athletics ostensibly caused by the membership of some of its players in the Ku Klux Klan. As the "bible of baseball" put it, religious and ethnic differences were not issues in America's National Game. With the exception of the "Ethiopian," all players were valued strictly on the basis of ability. "The Mick, the Sheeny, the Wop, the Dutch, and the Chink, the Cuban, the Indian, the Jap or the so-called Anglo-Saxon—his nationality is never a matter of moment if he can pitch, or hit, or field."[1] Despite its own ethnic slurs, the *Sporting News* announced longstanding views about the role of baseball and sport in the American experience that are still pronounced today. Baseball earned the label as America's National Game supposedly because it personified American values and character and transmitted them to its participants. Sport in general, an activity lauded as open to all based solely on talent, still garners attention as a metaphor of American democratic ideals and a pathway to assimilation.

But was it? What part has sport played in the process by which people became Americans? Informed by the experiences of other immigrant groups and minority people, this book explores this question by looking at part of the rich culture of everyday life created by East European Jewish immigrants, and especially their children, during the first half of the twentieth century. Relying on their stories and experiences rather than on intellectual debate and elite perspective, it seeks to recreate something of their world and of the active and critical role they played in shaping it. Mindful of their struggle to find a meaningful balance between ethnic values and traditions and the promise of American life, it also ponders the legacy of their experience for the continual survival of Jewish identity in the United States.

Sport as culture, and Jewish culture at that? As my grandmother might have said, "What are you, meshugah?" Nice Jewish boys and girls don't enjoy or participate in sport. Don't you know that Jewish culture and tradition emphasizes intellectual accomplishment and the life of the mind and has no place for sport or the physical? How could such frivolous activity reveal anything important about how immigrant Jews and their children lived, worked,

3

and struggled with each other and with a larger American world in search of survival, a future, and themselves?

Jewish voices better known than my grandmother's are even ready to counter claims that recognition of Jewish athletic achievement, however rare, might challenge stereotypes of Jewish physical weakness or soften the hostility of those Americans who view Jews as alien and unacceptable. As Mordecai Richler warns, even focused on these limited concerns, sport is risky business for Jews. Commenting on one encyclopedic compendium of Jewish sport accomplishment, written, as its preface states, "to challenge the curious belief that the Jew is nimble in the head but not too nimble with his feet," he indicates that while such books might make wonderful Bar Mitzvah presents, they do not effectively make their case. Detailed in its pages, he reminds us, is the fact that for every Sandy Koufax, there are a dozen Hy Cohen's and Steve Hertz's. While Koufax, the incomparable Dodger lefthander, enjoys membership in baseball's Hall of Fame, Cohen never won a game in his seven appearances with the Chicago Cubs and Hertz went hitless in his lifetime five at bats with the Houston Astros. What might happen to attitudes about Jewish physical prowess, Richler wonders, should such information fall "into the hands of an anti-Semite sportsman?"[2]

Richler's cautionary tale and my grandmother's imagined admonitions rehearse a popular view of Jews that in its most vicious form depicts them as inferior, physically incompetent, and in milder versions as a people who are repulsed by anything physical. Determined to show Jews were ill-fit to be true Americans, Henry Ford, America's best-known anti-Semite and automobile king, for instance, proclaimed in 1921 that "Jews are not sportsmen. . . . Whether this is due to their physical lethargy, their dislike of unnecessary physical action or their serious cast of mind, others may decide. . . . It may be a defect in their character, or it may not; it is nevertheless a fact which discriminating Jews unhesitatingly acknowledge."[3]

Although hardly for the same purpose, Jewish intellectuals, from Abraham Cahan to Irving Howe, have contributed to popular images of Jews as people of the book rather than as people of the hook, right cross, or home run. Nowhere is this more apparent than in their description of first-generation East European immigrants to the United States. Describing the fictional work of a new Yiddish writer that focused on the conflict between a first-generation "rabbinical scholar" and his American-born son who had become a local boxing champion, Cahan, legendary socialist publisher of the *Jewish Daily Forward,* emphasized the "bewilderment and despair" this news was to a father who belonged to "the Yiddish-speaking old generation" that grew up in a world "in which athletic sports [were] utterly unknown."[4] Writing about that same generation in *World of Our Fathers,* Irving Howe emphasized that "suspicion of the physical, fear of hurt, anxiety over the sheer pointlessness of play: all went deep into the recesses of the Jewish psyche. It was a price, hardly the largest, that Jews paid for the conviction of specialness. They no longer could suppress their true feelings about the frivolities of street or gymnasium than they could deny the shudder that passed through them walking past a church." Decades would have to go by," he insists, "before the sons and daughters of immigrants could shake off—if they ever could—this heritage of discomfort before the uses and pleasures of the body."[5]

Drawing on an historical tradition of Jewish aversion to sport and physical violence connected both to Jewish life in antiquity and to life in 19th-century Eastern Europe shtetls, both Cahan and Howe evoke pictures of devout orthodox Jewish men with long beards, yarmulkes, and prayer shawls who spoke only Yiddish and Hebrew, valued the intellect over the physical, and devoted their lives to God and the Talmud.[6] Clearly, these descriptions reflect an important part of the reality of the American Jewish experience. Scholars and rabbis devoted to formal religious orthodoxy and the life of the mind certainly were among the two million immigrants who came to the United States between 1881 and 1924. And the vast majority of these new arrivals, regardless of their religious beliefs, initially shared similar East European customs, spoke Yiddish, observed the Sabbath and kept kosher.

But as Abraham Cahan knew full well and as historians are beginning to appreciate, not all of the first generation, and certainly not their children, fit stereotypes that in varying degrees depicted Jews as a physically weak, devoutly religious people tied to Old World custom and tradition that included disdain and rejection of sport and physicality. The vast majority of these people eagerly embraced American opportunity and experience. For many, this included a love of sport.

By their very decision to come to America, East European Jewish immigrants set themselves apart from relatives and friends left behind. Comprising 15 percent of all East European Jewry and roughly 8 percent of the almost 26 million immigrants who entered the country in these years, these Russian, Polish, and Rumanian Jews, like Gentile immigrants from other places, chose migration as one alternative to dramatic changes taking place in Europe. Confronted by the commercialization of agriculture that forced many off the land, the rise of industry that undermined traditional patterns of work, and a population boom that exacerbated competition for limited possibilities, a large, displaced population faced poverty and diminished opportunity. In search of economic survival, many Europeans responded by internal migration on the continent. Others came to America. Although not the primary factor in their decision, the reality of violent anti-Semitic repression and specific economic restrictions based on religion further influenced those Jews who chose to emigrate.

Adventurous and, by definition, more willing to risk the loss of old ways in the hope of finding a better life, they shared a vision of America as a promised land. According to a recent student of the first-generation experience on New York's Lower East Side, East European Jews so eagerly grasped the image of the United States as the "Golden Medinah" that they immersed themselves in a passion of material consumption as symbolic mark of their American status. For every "Tevye" who struggled as a peasant dairyman while he dreamed of the life of the learned rebbe, there were far more "Yekls" and "David Levinskys"—hard-working immigrants eager to establish themselves as Americans.

Nor did they arrive empty-handed in pursuit of their quest. Although many did come from rural Russian villages, they also included substantial numbers of skilled, urban workers who were well prepared to take advantage of this country's economic needs. Popular images of the "people of the book" notwithstanding, whether skilled worker or peasant farmer they shared a lack of education and no deep attachment to Jewish religious orthodoxy. Migrating most often as families with little thought of returning to homelands that threatened their very existence, East European Jewish immigrants hoped for a better life for themselves and their children in the United States.[7]

Remarkably, within two generations, they achieved their goals, but not without struggle and conflict among themselves and with a majority American culture about what it was to be an American and a Jew. For many of these people, participation in American sport became both a measure of that success as well as a source of such conflict. Understanding that story and the role of sport in it forms the larger purpose of this book.[8]

The exploration of both the sportive experiences of everyday people and the significance of the careers of elite Jewish athletes, both for themselves and for others, offers enticing possibilities for understanding questions of ethnicity, assimilation, generational conflict, and the meaning and future of an American Jewish identity. The mass migration of East European Jews to the United States marked the beginnings of a major Jewish presence in this country. Their arrival coincided with the emergence of a modernizing, industrial society and the development of organized sport as both an important social institution and an increasingly significant part of 20th-century American leisure consumer culture. The growth and acceptance of sport as a new way of spending leisure time hinged on its promotion as an activity full of social purpose, one even capable of transforming immigrants into competent workers replete with new American values and character. Consciously employed as a mechanism of Americanization, especially for the children of Jewish immigrants and other outsiders, it was, from the outset, a critical meeting point where majority and minority peoples intersected and, as such, a special place for illuminating the ongoing process of assimilation.

It was also a meeting point for immigrant parents and their children. Identified both as American activity and as physical pursuit worthy of Jewish disdain, it became one area capable of illustrating the wide range of response of both generations to their new American situation. Although not the major preoccupation of a people struggling to survive in a new land, where the demands of the workplace and anti-Semitic restrictions at times severely limited opportunity and choice, increasingly sport, as part of leisure time, also became one part of their lives over which they exerted real control. Despite the best efforts of settlement house workers, organized play reformers, and educators to impose their own order on how immigrants should participate in sport, both as participants and as spectators, second-generation children and young adults, within the bounded space of their ethnic world, shaped these opportunities to their own purpose.

The diversity of 20th-century Jewish community, from the teeming, over-crowded, totally Jewish world of New York's Lower East Side, to scattered pockets of Jews throughout the United States from El Paso, Texas, to Portland, Oregon, often makes it difficult to generalize about the American Jewish experience. As part of an American national culture, however, Jewish involvement in sport bridged differences in size and geography, often evoking similar purpose and response.

As unfolded in these pages, sport emerges as a middle ground—a complex experience shaped by interaction between generations of Jews as well as between ethnic and majority cultures that involved both the adaptation of traditional practice to new American settings and the transformation of American experiences into ethnic ways.[9] More than a simple agency of assimilation, sport, both as actual experience and as symbol, encouraged the active participation of immigrants and their children in shaping their own identities as Americans and as Jews. In a society far more free and open than anything their immigrant parents ever experienced in Europe, the second generation, both as adolescents and adults, participated most fully in the opportunity to define for themselves who they were and how they would live. In their hands, sport became an activity capable of nurturing communal beliefs tied closely to Jewish tradition and culture while at the same time reinforcing mainstream American values. Periods of severe anti-Semitism and real restrictions on opportunity certainly caused some of them to anguish either as "marginal men" or to expunge all attachment to things Jewish in order to make their way. For many, however, control of their sport and leisure world helped counter feelings of helplessness and alienation in ways that encouraged their claims to legitimacy and full participation while at the same time providing a sense of ethnic solidarity and identity.

Despite the diverse cultural and religious backgrounds of East European Jewry and the different kinds of communities they and their children established in the United States, a Gentile majority dismissed distinctions of class, culture, and religious practice in their perception that a Jew was a Jew by matter of birth. By participating in a common American experience, Jews, both consciously and inadvertently, helped dispel beliefs that they were alien and unacceptable in ways that did not deny their special importance to their own Jewish communities or their own Jewish identity. Competing against non-Jewish athletes in settings that attracted public attention—boxing arenas, major league baseball parks, or college gridirons—the achievements of Jewish athletes encouraged assimilation by subtly altering the ways in which different groups understood each other.

Potentially able to alter the meaning of quintessential American events into ethnic experiences, participation in sport both confirmed a meaningful Jewish identity while promoting assimilation and American acceptance. Rich and complex, full of conflict and reconciliation, encompassing questions of economic goals, class, family and community, this story of the Jewish experience in American sport demands rejection of any simple model or any one theory of assimilation. It does not depict the destruction of some idealized European Jewish or first-generation-immigrant past in exchange for inclusion into an homogenized American world. Rather, it recounts both the flowering of a new American Jewish present out of the crucible of cultures that assimilation was all about and its legacy for the future of American Jewry.

Prior to 1881, some 250,000 Jewish-Americans, primarily of German descent, lived in the United States. Scattered throughout the country, they established congregations in virtually every state, with largest settlements in New York, Philadelphia, and other cities throughout the Northeast, South, and Midwest. Although our story primarily concerns the experiences of East European Jewish immigrants and their children, these German Jews occasionally come into play; especially in terms of how they responded to the arrival of two million "brethren" that, to them, threatened to overwhelm their own sense of security and place in the American mainstream. Determined to include a sense of the diversity of American Jewish community and the role that sport played as common experience, New York City, nevertheless, remains a special focus of what follows. The simple fact that by 1920, almost half of all American Jews lived there, comprising almost 30 percent of the population of the nation's largest city, demands it. So too, does the almost exclusive attention given to the athletic involvement of Jewish males. Jewish women certainly appear throughout these pages, but their participation in sport, especially prior to World War II, remained severely limited. When they did engage in sport, gender rather than ethnicity gave primary definition to how they participated and the meaning it carried.

Although it does include accounts of individual athletic careers and accomplishments, this book makes no attempt to offer sport-by-sport coverage of Jewish participation. Initial chapters offer insight into early debate within the Jewish immigrant community about the propriety and purpose of sport and establish its attraction to second-generation youth. The heart of the book follows. Large sections on basketball, baseball, and boxing recreate the sense of Jewish community and the place of sport in it prior to 1950, with special attention to the years between World War I and World War II. Richly informed by the reminiscences of former athletes, both nationally known and those more obscure, they illuminate the role of sport, both as symbol and actual experience, in the ongoing process of assimilation.

While these chapters all explore the role of sport as middle ground, the nature of each sport and patterns of Jewish participation in them allow each one special connection to particular themes. In settlement houses, school yards, colleges, or in loosely organized, regional, professional leagues, basketball was a game dominated by Jewish players and always closely connected to the local, everyday, social and economic life of Jewish communities. No activity more clearly shows the important connections between sport and Jewish community than James Naismith's American invention. The experience of participating as the majority in an American game also carried special meaning for participants and spectators alike, especially for second-generation youth who found in the game opportunities of freedom, mobility, and choice not always available to their fathers and mothers.

In a time before television and sports capitalism as we know it today, only baseball emerged as a truly national professional team sport. Loaded with symbolic value by those who promoted it as America's National Game, it appeared as a sport that underlined competition, fair play, and American opportunity. For Jewish boys who played it on the sandlots and in the streets and who followed the exploits of major leaguers, at times with their fathers, it became a special way of connecting to a larger American community. Simply buying a ticket to a game, learning its rules, following the sport in newspapers or on the radio, trading baseball cards, or rooting for a favorite team or player made a person a participant in America's consumer culture and "American" by the very act of making such choices. The opportunity to follow the exploits of the occasional landsman who made it to the major leagues enhanced this connection in special ways. Particularly in the years between the two world wars, when American Jews faced increasing anti-Semitism at home and Nazi atrocity abroad, the triumphs of Hank Greenberg and other Jewish sons of immigrants carried special symbolic import for American Jews concerned both with American acceptance and with Jewish survival.

If baseball lends itself to exploring the symbolic importance of sport and basketball provides better opportunity for understanding everyday community experience, boxing, more so than either, combines both concerns in special ways. Brutal and bloody, no sport evoked more strongly admonitions about Jewish disgust for physical activity or conflict between generations about Jewish and American attachments. Whether in championship fights that demanded national attention or in local contests involving neighborhood champions, boxing, especially between the wars, remained dominated by second-generation Jews and Italians. In the hands of fight promoters and managers, many of whom were Jewish, it became a public arena that provoked strong ethnic passions and loyalties. Vicarious celebration of the achievements of local and national Jewish boxing heroes—from Benny Leonard to Barney Ross—even underlined the emergence of a reshaped American Jewish identity in the 1920s and 1930s that emphasized the defiant, strong, tough Jew capable of surviving, regardless of the horrors of historical reality.

Chapters on Jewish involvement in intercollegiate sport between the wars and the special story of one second-generation American Jewish athlete, Marty Glickman, selectively embellish stories and themes concerned with anti-Semitism and the possibility of American acceptance and the importance of historical memory for Jewish survival. They set the stage for appreciating connections between past, present, and future.

American Jews today are culturally assimilated, so much so that serious doubts exist about the survival of a meaningful Jewish identity, a casualty, some would argue, of the very process by which succeeding generations of American Jews relinquished first their religious orthodoxy and then even cul-

tural manifestations of their Jewishness in exchange for American acceptance. The ways in which they participate in sport are also clearly different
from their forebears. Jews today are more involved in sport on the community
and recreational levels than ever before. Although there are still successful
professional Jewish athletes, there numbers increasingly diminish. And rarely
does the public or press pay much attention to them as Jews. The chapter
"Where Have You Gone, Hank Greenberg?" explores this contemporary
American Jewish experience in sport both as continuance and counterpoint
to the rich story of the second generation. Informing the important discussions of Herbert Gans, Herbert Feingold, Irving Howe, Arthur Hertzberg, Steven Cohen, Charles Silberman, and others who are concerned about the
meaning of Jewish identity and the future of American Jewry, the concluding
chapter makes clear that this story of the Jewish experience in American sport
offers a rich legacy to future generations of American Jews concerned about
their survival both as a distinct people and as Americans.

The Promise of Sport

ASSESSING the impact of the great migration of East European Jews to America at the turn of the century, sociologist Edward Ross unfavorably contrasted the physical attributes of Jewish immigrants to those of white Protestant native American stock. "On the physical side," he noted, "the Hebrews are the polar opposites of our pioneer breed. Not only are they undersized and weak-muscled, but they shun bodily activity and are exceedingly sensitive to pain. Says a settlement worker: 'You can't make boy scouts out of Jews.'"[1]

Not that settlement house workers, boy scout leaders, sociologists, public school officials, and social reformers didn't try. Responding to the arrival of millions of East European Jews and other immigrants to the United States, a wide range of groups and individuals attempted to make them into new Americans, complete with the character and values required for success in the "American Century."

Nourishing these efforts were the very facts of America's transformation into a modern state and the fears it engendered among those who benefited most from it. Taking their cues from an army of secular and religious spokesmen, middle- and upper-class Americans applauded their own contributions to national progress—the growth of industry, the large corporations they developed in order to maximize profits, and especially the increase in their material comfort, opulently displayed in their homes and new urban surroundings that made consumption and accumulation appear as basic American rights.

But progress had its darker side. Convinced that self-reliance, the work ethic, and aggressive individualism forged in the crucible of America's frontier experience had been key ingredients in the country's forward march, many wondered what would sustain such traits in a 20th-century world marked by the growth of large cities and the close of the frontier. Even the very symbols of success—sedentary life-styles and a conspicuous consumption—caused concern that "overcivilization" was sapping American character.

Also a problem were immigrants. A source of cheap, industrial labor, their presence was essential to the country's rapid economic expansion. Yet their rapidly increasing numbers crowded together in city neighborhoods, the willingness of some to protest violently their economic circumstances in struggles as dramatic as Haymarket and in lesser-known battles that never made national headlines, and their attachment to Old World traditions of work that often conflicted with the efficient organized plans of American capitalism all caused concern about continued American progress. With no more western frontier, lauded both as a cultivator of American values and as a safety valve for the frustration and discontent of those packed into the more settled regions of the nation, where would immigrants or, for that matter, new generations of Americans learn how to be? What would be done to prevent immigrants from diluting the purity of an already endangered American stock?

While not the only solution offered, organized sport emerged as one possible antidote to these problems. Whether measured by the rise of professional baseball, the popularity of college football, the bicycling craze, or by the proliferation of organizations like the Young Men's Christian Association (YMCA) and the Playground Association of America, sport promised to revitalize the individual's physical and moral fiber. Depicted as an "artificial frontier" by a host of social reformers, popularizers, and entrepreneurs, in the hands of skilled professionals it would transform and prepare immigrants and their children for full participation in a new modern age.

Much of this story is well told, usually from the perspective of white Anglo-Saxon Protestant reformers who dominated efforts to appropriate sport as a social and political force.[2] But there was also a distinctive Jewish voice that spoke to the role and purpose of sport and physical recreation. Understanding it provides initial access to the richness and complexity of Jewish assimilation and the place of sport in it.

I

Not surprisingly, articulate voices of a prosperous American German-Jewish population were most vociferous in urging Jewish involvement in sport. Although hardly without incident or discrimination, by the turn of the century, German-Jewish immigrants and their descendants scattered throughout the country found a good deal to applaud about their own American experience. Successful in business, taken by Reformed Judaism, and well assimilated into American life, they had mixed reactions to the influx of East European Jewry. News of pogroms, anti-Semitic restrictions on economic opportunity, and the dire poverty experienced by Jews in Russia encouraged German-American Jewish philanthropy on their behalf. Be it the individual influence of a Jacob Schiff or an Oscar Straus or the collective efforts of a variety of committees and organizations, they lobbied to make the United States an open sanctuary. Concern about their own American place along with contempt and compassion for their co-religionists, however, also compelled German Jews to work just as hard to change these "unwashed" Europeans into "normal," acceptable Americans.

The onset of East European Jewish migration punctuated German-Jewish fears about their own American status. Their successful participation in the country's urban and industrial growth increasingly made them the targets of those less enamored by such change and less able to enjoy its rewards. Confronted in the late 19th century by a popular resurgence of anti-Semitism and new restrictions on their participation in organizations, clubs, and schools, German-American Jews feared that the sudden appearance of hundreds of thousands of Russian Jews, publicly linked to them by a common religion, threatened to undermine their own precarious security as Americans.[3]

Critical here were first impressions of these new immigrants, often shared by Gentiles and German Jews alike. Poor and without initial prospect, crowded together in unhealthy, dirty, working-class ghettos, depicted as a devout people attached to orthodox religious beliefs, speaking a language and practicing customs that underlined their separateness—such description only reinforced longstanding Christian stereotypes about Jewish inferiority and difference. German Jews, several generations removed from their own American beginnings, practiced a Judaism far different from strict Sabbath observance and daily attention to Jewish law that supposedly characterized East European orthodox Jewish religious practice. Accustomed to American middle-class comfort and consumption, they too were appalled by images of immigrant Jewish life, captured most frequently in depictions of New York's Lower East Side.

Even a more accurate appraisal of these East European immigrants would not have markedly altered initial impressions or responses. Although historians still find it difficult to agree on the character and composition of this mass migration, clearly a large proportion never fit the stereotypes that in part first motivated the German-American Jewish community to embrace Americanization plans. Many, in fact, eagerly looked forward to becoming Americans.[4] Still, German-American Jews, confronted with their presence, were not sanguine about such prospects. Connected to them as Jews but set apart by class and custom, moved both by embarrassment and by compassion, they adapted existing Jewish institutions and created new ones in order to make them into acceptable American citizens. Over time, increased awareness among German Jews of the immigrants' desire to become American, especially obvious among second-generation adolescents and young adults, only redoubled their efforts to determine how assimilation unfolded. Only by doing so could they hope to maintain their leadership and place, despite the fact that they no longer comprised a numeric majority among Jews in America. Although never the centerpiece of their elaborate educational programs that included English-language and civics classes, vocational training, and a variety of social activities and social welfare services, organized sport and physical recreation increasingly occupied essential places in their plan.

II

Located on New York's Lower East Side at East Broadway and Jefferson Street, the Educational Alliance, organized in Manhattan in 1891 by prominent members of New York's German-Jewish community, clearly had such purpose in mind. As Isidore Straus, one of its founders put it, its goal was "to help immigrants understand American ideas . . . the dignity of American citizenship," and "to appreciate an American atmosphere of obedience to law."[5] In 1905, a special committee concerned with reorganizing the institution emphatically reaffirmed that its "first aim and object . . . is to Americanize the recently arrived immigrant and to socialize him in the sense of making him better able to do his share in the work of society." In this spirit the committee urged continuation of the Alliance's preparatory school for immigrant children and its School of Physical Culture.[6]

While Alliance leaders did not make a special case for "the athletic field" as the only means of transforming immigrant into American, they had no doubt of its potential, especially for children. Critical here was not only physical activity but the context within which it took place. The Alliance urged its young immigrants to join together into small clubs—arranged by activity and age. Here, guided by detailed rules and leaders trained by a professional staff of social workers, impressionable youngsters would be "instilled gradually and unobtrusively into . . . right thinking and right feeling" and become "good American citizens."[7]

The Young Men's Hebrew Association (YMHA) also participated in this work. Begun in 1874 as a cultural organization concerned with the moral, social, and educational life of young German Jews, by 1900 its many branches scattered throughout the country offered an array of sport and physical recreation activities. Although still catering to its German clientele with the hopes of keeping it fit for the ardors of life and business, these programs also sought to teach newly arrived East Europeans how to be good Americans. Noting that "many a moral lesson may be learned on the athletic field and in the gymnasium," one editorialist in a 1912 Y newspaper urged all members to take part in athletics because "athletics and morality go hand in hand."[8]

Sharing a basic faith in the ability of trained professionals and the power of environment to alter and reshape human character, these German-Jewish prescriptions sounded very much like those offered by other Progressive reformers concerned with immigrants. Settlement house programs also emphasized sport as one means of easing the transition from immigrant to American. Jane Addams, the founder of Chicago's renowned Hull House, declared that teamwork and cooperation learned on the ballfield would well serve immigrants in the industrial workplace. In New York, where the University and Henry Street settlements on the Lower East Side served a predominantly East European Jewish clientele, an Inter-Settlement Athletic Association, formed in 1903, sponsored inter-house competition in basketball, boxing, and wrestling.[9] Especially in cities with large immigrant populations, settlement house workers also allied themselves with the Playground Association of America in urging municipal governments to provide more play space and trained supervision in crowded immigrant neighborhoods. The goal of these efforts was clear. As one play activist put it, "by means of proper recreation, thousands of young men and women are learning a spirit of comradeship, a truer humanity and a higher standard of civic duty" that instills them with "a broad patriotism."[10]

Connected by class and aspiration to mainstream American culture, it is not surprising that American German-Jewish reformers also believed that sport, properly controlled by experts, might revamp East European Jews into acceptable Americans. Rarely, however, did they make this case without specifically Jewish concerns in mind. Inextricably tied to Jewish prescription about the power of sport were attempts to counter arguments that these new Jewish immigrants and, by implication, German Jews too, were unassimilable because they belonged to a weak and alien race whose people historically rejected physical pursuit in favor of religious and intellectual study. Mixing both apology and explanation, celebration of Jewish athletic accomplishment and encouragement for participation aimed at eliminating doubts about the potential of Jews to become normal, productive Americans.

William Mitchell, superintendent of New York's 92nd Street YMHA, suggested these themes in the blessing he gave its Atlas Athletic Club when it broke official ties with the organization and established itself independently in 1907. Begun in 1898 under the auspices of the Y as a club for elite Jewish athletes, its stated goal was to help "Jewish athletes gain recognition and merit as Jews have done in other areas of life."[11] Hampered by the Y's lack of outdoor track facilities, club members, all of German background, severed formal ties and leased their own building on 162nd Street and Jerome Avenue (where Yankee Stadium now sits) adjacent to an outdoor track in Macombs Dam Park. Speaking at the club's opening on May 4, 1907, Mitchell wished its members good fortune and urged them to "stick to your resolution to do purely athletic work, to the end that you may draw to your club the many young Jewish athletes who at present are barred from other clubs." Even more direct were his comments in the Y's 1908 Annual Report. Talking about the athletic achievements of its own membership, Mitchell urged Y athletes to strive for the highest goals in sport, hoping "some day to see some of our own boys take a prominent part in athletic competition and thus disprove that our own people do not give proper attention to physical development."[12]

Yiddish newspapers catering specifically to East European Jews also carried a similar message. Urging its East European Jewish audience to support the drive to build a gymnasium for Chicago's Hebrew Institute (CHI) in 1909, the *Jewish Messenger* remarked that only now are Jews "awakening to the advantages of physical culture" and that "provision on a large scale must be made and opportunity offered for a race to accomplish its physical rejuvenation." "The Jew," the *Messenger* concluded, "has left behind . . . lands of oppression" and in the "free country" of America "desires to improve his physical equipment to meet adequately the demands of the strenuous life."[13]

Whether the *Messenger's* goal to prepare Jews for full participation in Teddy Roosevelt's concept of the American future helped build a new gymnasium, the task was accomplished. In 1918, the CHI's weekly newspaper, the *Observer*, celebrated the gymnasium's tenth anniversary by declaring it as "second to none in the country." After cataloging the achievements of its athletes over the years, it insisted that "the record of . . . athletic possibilities set by members of the Gymnasium refutes forever the charge of Jewish physical disability and lack of courage." The *Observer* also provided explanation for this recent outburst of Jewish athletic excellence. Turning the tables on a Gentile world that censured Jews for their supposed physical inferiority, it declared that the charge was not grounded in any Jewish trait but rather in the reluctance of mainstream society "in swinging the doors of opportunity open to all alike."[14]

Even more emphatic in urging Jewish participation as a way of demonstrating normalcy, gaining respect, and even reducing prejudice were the pages of Chicago's Yiddish *Daily Jewish Courier*. A 1923 editorial, "Do Jews Value Physical Culture?," encouraged interest in sport as a mark of both their freedom and their acceptance as Americans. Directly confronting popular stereotypes of weak and cowardly Jews, it demanded Jews refute them as matters of self-respect and even survival:

> We have been branded as weak and physical cowards. That is a dangerous point of view for people to hold of us. . . . we can clarify the atmosphere and assure our saftey better by making it unmistakably clear that we are a people that are decadent in no sense. . . . While we are proud to emphasize our interests in matters intellectual, we must not brand ourselves as physical weaklings, but by displaying an all-around development, we will best gain the respect of the world.[15]

Although not as direct as late 19th-century European cries for "muscular Jews" as critical to Jewish survival, the *Courier's* appeal anticipated American Jewish voices in the 1930s that called for tough, physical Jews able to defend themselves against anti-Semitism at home and Nazi horror abroad.[16]

Another *Courier* piece of the same year went even further in praise of Jewish muscle. Referring to Benny Leonard, the world's lightweight boxing champion between 1917 and 1925, one writer observed that in the United States, "Jewish strength" commands more respect than "Jewish intellect." As he put it:

> The Benny Leonards will never arouse any hatred or envy among their non-Jewish colleagues; they will receive honor and respect from their American admirers. American youth always respects the brave sons of their homeland; they will even respect Jews who are of foreign birth because their physical prowess is in conformity with one aspect of American culture and increases the prestige of the nation.[17]

In short, Jewish acceptance of physicality not only challenged claims of deviancy or abnormality. It was a mark, itself, of becoming comfortable with being an American.

Predictably, the *American Hebrew,* a New York Jewish paper catering to the tastes and views of its middle- and upper-class German-Jewish audience, consistently added its own voice to such sentiments. Commenting on the domination of New York public high school basketball by Jewish boys who learned the game in settlement houses and after-school playground centers, a 1917 "Melting Pot" column took notice of the "evolution of the Jew in this country from a shrunken, wizened creature afraid of its own shadow into a being unafraid, buoyant and erect." "How splendidly resilient the Jews!" it concluded. "Two generations ago he cowered timidly in the ghettoes of the dark countries; now he leaps toward the light like a young god of the sun." Eleven years later, with pagan imagery absent, the paper reiterated similar claims of Jewish interest and physical well-being in its annual survey of Jewish athletic accomplishment. Success in American sport taught American Jewish youth that they could "play on an equal footing, and this has earned them added respect from a world which formerly patronized their athletic indulgence."[18]

III

Be it Benny Leonard, basketball players from New York City high schools, or the vast majority of names dotting the *American Hebrew*'s list of outstanding Jewish athletes, the cast of characters offered as proof of Jewish normalcy were predominately the children of East European immigrants. Nor is this surprising. Aspiring immigrants eagerly embraced obvious and accessible avenues that permitted immediate identification as Americans, even as they tackled more formidable barriers of language, livelihood, and prejudice. Indeed, central to our concerns is the importance of appreciating that, like other outsiders—the Irish before them, Italian immigrants who arrived in the United States when they did, and American blacks who followed—enthusiasm for sport, both as participants and spectators, provided one such route for Jewish immigrants. Obviously those who encouraged Jewish athletic involvement were also aware of such possibility.

Jewish reformers who argued for their brethren's participation in sport at times, however, feared that they had been too successful in their efforts. Originally troubled by the exotic appearance and culture of East European Jews, German-Jewish leaders worried increasingly that the children of immigrants, whether born in the European Pale or in the United States, threatened to discard all attachments to Jewish religion and culture in their fervor to become Americans. Anxious about an American Jewish future and their own precarious place as its leaders, they hoped to foster assimilation without denying Jewish connections by encouraging it in settings that they could define and control. If sport enthralled immigrant youth, nurturing it in managed Jewish environments would be part of such design.[19]

Whether in Seattle, Chicago, Detroit, or New York, regardless of the size of their East European immigrant populations, YMHAs in these cities offered messages entwining Jewish and American purpose almost as often as they championed a strict Americanist line. Typical were the remarks of Manhat-

tan's borough president Marcus Marks, who in 1917 described the purpose of
the Washington Heights YMHA "in two words—Judaism and Citizenship."
Declaring "patriotic American citizenship" as "fundamental," he insisted that
no Y "member may properly claim to be a good Hebrew unless he is at the
same time a good American."[20] Reiterating the same message a few months
later in an editorial on the "Influence of YMHAs," the *American Hebrew* praised
them as "vital community centers" that solved "local Jewish problems" by
providing educational and recreational facilities "in a wholesome Jewish
environment, making for a finer American manhood and womanhood."[21]

Similar sentiments invariably accompanied announcements of the massive expansion of Jewish community centers in the 1920s. In Philadelphia,
for example, dedication ceremonies for a new YMHA emphasized a commitment to provide a Jewish setting for the recreational interests of the city's Jewish youth. Sol Stroock, who that same year took over as president of New
York's 92nd Street Y, urged its youth to proudly declare their Jewishness, for
only through "a proper appreciation of their self-respect as Jews" could they
be "worthy exponents of America and all that America means to the world."
Even more to the point were the remarks of Joseph Proskauer, Stroock's successor, on the eve of ceremonies in 1929 marking the laying of a cornerstone
for a new $2.5 million facility. "Twenty years ago," he noted, "the communal
problem of Jewish youth had largely to do with the Americanization of newly
arrived immigrants to our shores. Today," he continued, "we have in marked
contrast to deal almost entirely with the needs of a young American manhood
. . . entitled . . . to facilities and leadership which will enable them to maintain
their ties with the religious and social traditions of their forefathers and at the
same time . . . enjoy those activities of mind and body which will give spice
and zest to healthy youth."[22]

Proskauer's observations about the changing nature of immigrant life
underline what had become obvious to many observers by World War I. As
the second generation embraced American prospects, concern about preserving Jewish identity for its own sake and as a way of exerting control over how
they became American increasingly became part of the arsenal of argument
encouraging Jewish participation in sport. Along with apologizing for alleged
race weakness, demonstrating normalcy as prelude to American acceptance,
and defining physical strength as necessary both to American success and to
Jewish survival, they indicate the complex and often contradictory pulls East
European immigrants, their children, and reformers experienced as they
struggled to come to terms with America.[23]

These prescriptions for Jewish participation in sport are also tantalizingly
suggestive about different models of assimilation available to Jewish immigrants, including the provocative notion of the benefits of assimilation taking
place within a Jewish environment and the potential role of children as agencies of social and cultural change. But they are only prescriptions. It remains
to be seen both how they were translated into opportunities for Jewish participation in sport, and most important, what that participation meant as East
European Jews became American Jews.

New York also provided athletic activities as part of their efforts to accom-modate immigrant needs.[33] Public schools, with their own agendas for social-ization and assimilation, additionally satisfied Jewish interest in sport. The "young god[s] of the sun" who illuminated the *American Hebrew*'s praise of high school Jewish basketball players in 1917 were more than matched by counterparts who participated in a full range of scholastic sports programs. One study of extracurricular activities in New York City high schools in the 1930s and 1940s, for instance, shows that Jews more than held their own compared with other ethnic groups when it came to athletic participation. While not privy to such statistical documentation, anyone who read the sports pages of the city's daily newspapers, the *American Hebrew,* and even Abraham Cahan's Yiddish *Jewish Daily Forward* could find reports of the exploits of Jew-ish schoolboy athletes and their accomplishments.[34]

So too could readers of Chicago's newspapers, which often featured accounts of Jewish athletes who represented the Chicago Hebrew Institute. Commenting on the success of his athletes in his 1918 annual report, Philip Seaman, the institute's superintendent, offered a litany of triumph: 13 victo-ries by the women's basketball team, 64 victories in 70 games by senior and junior basketball teams, an undefeated indoor baseball team, and 260 prizes captured in various competitions by the gymnasium department. "Wherever they go, in whatever competition they may enter," Seaman exalted, CHI ath-letes ". . . are not the *average,* they are at the *top.* This statement is not an *exag-geration.* It is a *fact* that is recognized throughout the city by all amateur asso-ciations."[35]

Much of this success was attributed to the fine instruction offered by the Institute and to the large pool of young men and women who participated in its programs. In 1912, for instance, 944 boys, girls, men, and women regis-tered in the gymnasium department, producing an aggregate attendance for the year of 17,231. Excluded from this count was the 78,365 aggregate atten-dance figure, up some 20,000 from 1911, of those boys and girls who used the Institute's six acres of outdoor athletic and playground facilities in organized summer programs. The dedication of a new gymnasium in 1916, advertised as "one of the finest gymnasiums in the country," did nothing to diminish its constituency's interest in sport.[36]

As in New York, the 1920s and 1930s witnessed an expansion of athletic opportunity for Chicago's second-generation youth. Scrapbooks of Chicago's Jewish People's Institute (JPI), the renamed CHI, for these years are full of clippings from every Chicago daily that recount the exploits of its teams in virtually every sport against both Jewish and Gentile competition. Occasion-ally, women even received equal attention. Highlighted in 1927 and 1928, for instance, were the triumphs of the JPI's girl's varsity basketball team, billed by the Chicago *Daily News* as "one of the best in the country."[37]

The JPI was not the only Jewish organization in Chicago to offer athletics. Commenting on its athletic department in 1923, the city's Sinai congregation noted that its physical recreation programs, with 2000 active participants, was by far the most popular of all temple activities. One year earlier, the Northwest

YMHA noted that 50 men planned to try out for its elite baseball team that will play "the best teams" in the area.[38]

Chicago and New York hardly provided unique opportunities for Jews to participate in sport. In Pittsburgh, Philadelphia, Boston, Portland, Dallas, Providence, Detroit, Los Angeles, and other cities, athletic programs offered through some Jewish agency remained an important part of organized Jewish activity and proliferated after World War I. In Pittsburgh, for example, young Jewish boys and girls made physical education programs the most popular offerings of the Irene Kaufman Settlement House. IKS athletes consistently won prizes for athletic competition among the city's youth, a fact well announced in the settlement house's own weekly bulletin and also in the pages of the *Pittsburgh Press*.[39] Weekly sports columns in the California *Jewish Voice* and the *B'nai B'rith Messenger* reported on the daily exploits of local Los Angeles Jewish athletes in competition sponsored by a variety of local Jewish organizations as well as news of Jewish boxers, hoopsters, and baseball players throughout the nation. Whether or not, as the *Messenger's* Harry Glantz insisted, Jews participated in sport "to bring glory to the race," it is clear that Los Angeles Jews clearly took advantage of the opportunities offered to them.[40]

V

Jewish participation in sport was not limited to programs crafted by Jewish social reformers intent on controlling assimilation and building character. Other Jewish agencies with different agendas also appreciated the powerful attraction of sport to immigrants and their children. Prominent here were Jewish labor organizations which established formal athletic programs to provide relaxation and community for its members.

The International Ladies Garment Workers Union (ILGWU) and the Amalgamated Clothing Workers, labor unions led by Jews and with predominately Jewish membership that approached 500,000 by the 1920s, not only spearheaded the politics of immigrant Jews who toiled in the textile trades but also served as centers of their social and cultural life. Sports figured prominently here. In New York, for example, the ILGWU fielded a varsity basketball team in the 1930s that played in the Eastern Jewish Center League. Amalgamated workers in Chicago, Milwaukee, and Rochester participated in a wide range of athletic contests, from baseball games organized along craft lines (cutters versus tailors) to less serious competition for all ages, including sack races and wheelbarrow races at annual summer picnics.[41]

Although the *Advance* occasionally carried stories about European trade union sports activity and even international efforts to establish "proletarian sports societies as distinct as those under the control of the bourgeoisie," Jewish labor organizations in the United States rarely approached sport in such political terms.[42] In one instance, however, operating much like other Jewish advocates concerned about the rapid Americanization of the second generation, Jewish labor leaders attempted to use sport to revitalize and expand a Jewish labor constituency increasingly susceptible to American customs and political traditions that drew them away from their European socialist roots.

The socialist Workmen's Circle (WC), established in New York in 1892 and organized nationally by 1900, tried to help immigrant Jewish workers adjust to American life without losing touch with traditional customs or Jewish identity. Providing mutual aid, death and disability benefits, and even health insurance to its members, the Circle resolved "to remain Jewish while [it] made America into the society they believed it ought to be . . . an equitable society committed to social justice for all." At weekly meetings conducted in Yiddish, members participated in cultural programs, took stands on international issues involving Jews, and supported the activities of Jewish labor organizations by giving money to striking workers. By 1911, a national membership of almost 39,000 took advantage of these opportunities. Fourteen years later, celebrating the 25th anniversary of its national organization with a New York convention that attracted Abraham Cahan and Eugene Debs as featured speakers, the WC boasted a peak membership of 84,000.[43]

Even in the midst of this seeming prosperity, however, Circle leaders recognized that the decline of East European immigration, the gradual movement of Jews from the working class to the middle class, and the introduction of social welfare services by labor unions threatened its existence. Essential to maintaining its numbers was a calculated effort to attract second-generation youth by offering activities and programs popular among young men and women far more acclimated to American society than their parents. The purpose of what became known as the Young Circle League (YCL), as one of its leaders put it, was to attract "the children of radical parents [who] are leaving us." While the defeat of fascism and the triumph of socialism through the "ceaseless efforts of Labor" was at the heart of the YCL effort, it recognized that "if we want Jewish children in America to come to us in large numbers, we must provide for them the social activities and entertainments which they find in conservative centers."[44]

Sports was a significant aspect of the "social activities and entertainments" provided by the YCL. From its outset, its newspaper, the *Call of Youth,* featured a weekly sports column that reported on the activities of its members. YCL youth participated in intramural athletic competition and also against organized teams in their own leagues and against teams affiliated with the Worker's Sports League of America. In its very first issue, the *Call* announced the formation of a YCL basketball team in New York and the formation of a soccer team that would compete in the Eastern District Soccer League, a group composed of teams representing socialist organizations. Circle elders who believed sport was frivolous may well have been comforted two months later when the *Call* reported not only the YCL's second consecutive victory over the Young People's Socialist League team but also the fact that all gate receipts went to the Kentucky Miners Defense Fund.[45]

Similar stories prevailed elsewhere. Renting out public school gymnasiums and using public parks, YCL clubs in Chicago and Philadelphia partici-

pated in baseball, basketball, soccer, and track. Despite its best efforts, however, the YCL never attracted numbers significant enough to bolster a dying
labor organization that had outlived the first-generation Jewish immigrants it
endeavored to serve. At its peak, in 1937, the organization boasted a total
youth membership of 4000. Even this small total was misleading as only 1700
were regular dues-paying members.[46] The rest, it appears, were like the boys
who made up the YCL's varsity basketball team in New York—Jewish youngsters who took advantage of its athletic programs while eschewing any interest in its politics.

Red Sarachek, who served as athletic director and basketball coach for New
York's YCL for several years in the late 1930s, confirms that the socialist organization tried to attract children and adolescents to its programs through
sport. Especially through its senior team, the Circle hoped to enhance its reputation, thus attracting new members. The players, however, as Sarachek
recalls, came to play ball and to enjoy each other's company rather than to
embrace the Circle's politics or goals. Circle members "flooded the place" to
see the team play. Their enthusiasm for sport, however, no more than that of
the young men they came to cheer, was not sufficient to maintain an organization whose goals and values no longer seemed relevant to second-generation American Jews.[47]

Employing a variety of arguments and providing a myriad of opportunities,
YMHAs, the Educational Alliance, settlement houses, even Jewish labor organizations all hoped to use sport as one means of directing and shaping the process by which East European Jewish immigrants became Americans. Jewish
immigrants, especially the children, eagerly embraced every bat and ball
offered to them, challenging stereotypes that depicted them as physically
weak and uninterested in sport.

But what did their participation mean and how did it help shape the inevitable process by which immigrants became Americans? Did they succumb,
with little resistance, to the press of arguments and the control of play
demanded by Jewish spokesmen and social workers who ran the settlement
houses, Ys, and playground programs? Did they passively imbibe American
values and culture just as quickly as they discarded their past? Did they accept
prescriptions on how to be both an American and a Jew? Or did they participate on their own terms, in order to meet their own ethnic and class needs,
contributing to the shaping of "a culture of everyday life," as John Bodnar
calls it, that mediated between the past and the present while never fully
embracing the new order?[48] Or were these the only alternatives? Only by turning things inside out, only by taking seriously the voice and experience of
everyday people as they participated in sport can we truly answer these questions.

Clearly, a variety of groups, with varied purpose, encouraged sport as a
means of assimilation. Reality also tells us that over time the goal was
achieved—immigrants themselves and especially the generations that fol-

lowed them did become Americans even as many proclaimed their Jewishness. But, as Red Sarachek's recollection of the Workmen's Circle suggests, prescriptive design did not guarantee control of the process. Imbedded in his story is the failed attempt of an organization to use sport as a means of shaping how the children of immigrants became Americans and Jews. That failure, however, does not mean that assimilation did not take place within a Jewish environment, as many reformers hoped. But that environment encompassed far more than YCL meetings, YMHA gymnasiums, and settlement house activities. Nor was it only the constructed domain of social workers and religious leaders.

Set within the rich life of ethnic Jewish communities, everyday people making their way through the daily routines of household and community acted on their own behalf in determining what it was to be an American and a Jew. Seizing opportunities provided by others and creating their own in their streets, playgrounds, and school yards, the children of immigrants turned sportive experiences to their own ends in ways that paid attention both to traditional Jewish communal purpose and mainstream American values. Adapting Jewish tradition to new American settings and transforming American sporting activity into ethnic moments, both as experience and as symbol, they transformed sport into a middle ground—altering and adapting a significant American cultural institution to serve ethnic community ends while encouraging their own enthusiasm for full integration into American life.

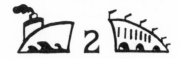

Basketball and Community

I spent a good part of my adolescence watching and playing basketball. Kelly Park in Brooklyn, on the corner of Avenue S and East 15th Street, was my second home. Fat, slow, but a good outside shooter, I made it into half-court games with my friends, played one on one with Kenny Hammerman, and, leaning against school-yard fences, watched the likes of Connie Hawkins, Billy Cunningham, and other high-school stars do battle. From an early age, armed with my trusty public school G.O. card, I took the BMT subway to the old Madison Square Garden on 49th Street and Eighth Avenue to watch the erstwhile exploits of the New York Knickerbockers. Unaware that I was witnessing the professional game's transformation into integrated sport, I marveled at "Sweet Water" Clifton's hands, the height of Ray Felix and Walter Dukes, Harry Gallatin's wide body, and the shooting ability of the Santa Clara stick, Kenny Sears. Once a year, my father even took me to a game—father and son night for the Flatbush Lodge branch of the Free Sons of Israel—but we always left early to avoid the crush on the subway that for some reason he feared. Today, as my middle-aged body resists the physical demands I make on it to keep my blood pumping and my adrenalin flowing, my basketball dreams—on the court, taking over for Bill Bradley or Earvin "Magic" Johnson, scoring, passing, and dominating the action—provide solace from the inevitable physical deterioration that awaits us all.

Growing up in America as a third-generation Jewish-American male, both my past and my fantasy do not seem unusual. What may be surprising, however, is that they are not very different from what my father and many other second-generation Jewish men experienced. Born to orthodox Russian Jewish immigrant parents in 1908 on Sackman Street in the Brooklyn Jewish enclave of Brownsville, he won a basketball medal playing for Evening Recreation Center 184 at the age of 17 before a brief career at guard for Brooklyn College. Unlike my fantasies, however, any dreams he might have had of glory on the hardwood likely found him taking over for one of the "Heavenly Twins," Max Friedman or Barney Sedran, or for the incomparable Nat Holman—smallish, white, Jewish men like himself who grew up in urban, Jewish neighborhoods and who established basketball, especially in the eastern United States, as the sport of Jews. Both as spectators and as participants, Jewish involvement in basketball, especially between 1900 and 1950, was greater than in any other sport. A rich part of second-generation community life, both as experience and symbol, it served as a middle ground in which the children of immigrants took advantage of opportunities provided by themselves and by others to determine their own identities as Americans and as Jews.

I

While hardly all Jews embraced basketball as valid enterprise, by the late 1930s, certainly sportswriters identified it as the "Jewish" game. Paul Gallico, longtime sports editor for the New York *Daily News,* explained the intimate connection between Jews and basketball. "Curiously . . . above all others," Gallico wrote, "the game appeal[s] to the temperament of the Jews." While "a good Jewish football player is a rarity . . . Jews flock to basketball by the thousands," he insisted, because it placed "a premium on an alert, scheming mind . . . flashy trickiness, artful dodging and general smart aleckness," traits naturally appealing to "the Hebrew with his Oriental background."[1] One year earlier, in 1936, Stanley Frank, former varsity trackman and campus sports editor at the City College of New York (CCNY), offered his own version of Jewish attachment. Rejecting the implicit anti-Semitism of Gallico's remarks, nevertheless Frank insisted that no other sport so required "the characteristics inherent in the Jew . . . mental agility, perception . . . imagination and subtlety. . . . If the Jew had set out deliberately to invent a game which incorporates those traits indigenous in him . . . he could not have had a happier inspiration than basketball." Describing Jewish domination, Frank concluded, "ever since Dr. James A. Naismith came up with a soccer ball, two peach baskets and a bright idea . . . basketball players have been chasing Jewish athletes and never quite catching up with them."[2]

Providing slightly different spins on the same biological deterministic ball, Frank and Gallico offer no more satisfactory explanations of Jewish involvement in basketball half a century ago than similar arguments sometimes offered to explain black domination of the game today. But they were right in one respect. Although you didn't have to be Jewish to play basketball, especially in large eastern and midwestern cities containing substantial numbers of first-generation East European immigrant Jews, Jewish children flocked to the sport, making it a significant part of everyday community life and ultimately earning some of them local and national reputations for their exploits in the cage and on the court.

Not surprisingly, in urban, ethnic working-class neighborhoods, a game open to improvisation and requiring little space or equipment proved attractive to children. As early as the turn of the century, in the streets and on the school yards, at settlement houses and YMHAs, their imagination and control of their own turf along with more structured opportunities for sport shaped their introduction to the game.

Certainly that's how Nat Krinsky and Harry "Jammy" Moskowitz, my high-school gym teachers, remember it. Harry was born in 1904 and Nat in 1901 in Brownsville to Russian immigrant parents. They went to local high schools and attended respectively the Savage School for Physical Education and CCNY. Later, they became good friends and neighbors as well as colleagues at Brooklyn's James Madison High School, where for some forty years "Jammy" coached basketball and Nat track and field. They were also competitors, teammates, and stars of amateur, college, and professional basketball teams in the New York City area.[3]

"Jammy," who got his nickname in high school not because he could dunk but because he always ate jam sandwiches before a game to settle his nervous stomach, first played basketball on Bristol Street when he was nine years old. As both he and Nat recall, aschans placed on brownstone stoops served as baskets, roughly simulating the more formal game where backboards did not exist in any form and baskets were freestanding. A bunch of rolled-up rags, an old stocking stuffed with them, or a woolen stocking cap sufficed as balls. Neither running nor dribbling were allowed; instead playmates tapped the ball to each other. As Macyln Baker, Jewish captain of New York University's (NYU) 1921 basketball team put it, "rags didn't bounce."[4]

Three years apart in age, Krinsky and Moskowitz moved their street skills to the gym and school yard of P.S. 84 where they played on class teams and also on clubs like the Mercurys, the Beavers, and the Invincibles—teams defined by age and weight that represented the local evening recreation center. Enthusiastically recalling his boyhood at the age of 83, Jammy remembers watching Nat play for the senior Invincible team which matched its skills against opponents from the Educational Alliance, the College Settlement House, and even professional teams; all at a time when the professional game was in its unorganized infancy and when little distinction was made between professional and amateur. Jammy himself starred for the Invincible Cubs, a team composed of high-school freshmen who weighed no more than 140 pounds. The Cubs, composed of Gelman, "Slippery" Plotnick, Cohen, "Sissy" Hut, and "Fat" Moskowitz, made their own schedule and dominated similar teams throughout the city as newspapers like the *Brooklyn Citizen* carried news of their triumphs in its sports pages.[5]

Barney Sedran and Max "Marty" Friedman, among the first Jewish basketball players elected to the Basketball Hall of Fame, recall similar childhood experiences. Born two years apart on the New York's Lower East Side, they first became teammates in their early teens when they played in 1903 for the "midget" team of the University Settlement House located on Eldridge and Rivington streets. Coached by Harry Baum, a Jewish settlement house worker who migrated from Austra in 1883, their team, "the busy Izzies," won settlement house and metropolitan American Amateur Union (AAU) championships. Fondly, they remember the importance of their settlement house days. Growing up in a neighborhood which simply had no space for baseball diamonds, Sedran, who learned the game at University Settlement and in Hamilton Fish Park, recalls that basketball was "the only sport I could play with little trouble." Marty Friedman, who bypassed college and became a professional ballplayer at the age of sixteen, remembers that when his friends joined him as professionals, the newspapers nicknamed them the "Clark University alumni," not because they had attended that distinguished Massachusetts university but because they had "graduated" from the Clark and University settlement houses.[6]

Even more direct is Nat Holman, without question one of the most celebrated and well-known basketball players of all time. A member of the Basketball Hall of Fame, head basketball coach at CCNY for 36 years, athletic director of the 92nd Street Y, Holman, whose career demands attention in a variety of contexts, grew up on the Lower East Side and attended P.S. 72, P.S. 62, Commerce High School, and the Savage School of Physical Education. He learned the sport that made him the best-known professional basketball player of his generation in the streets, school yards, and settlement houses of his youth. Commenting on his early basketball days, Holman credits the "inspirational qualities" of his elementary-school physical education teacher for attracting him to the game. Also critical were the games he and his friends played at settlement houses and Ys scattered throughout New York. As he put it, "there is no question in my mind that the settlement houses were instrumental in popularizing the game of basketball as well as developing some of the most outstanding players in the history of the sport." Games there, he recalled, "were the most spirited and hard fought . . . that I ever witnessed. Basketball was THE GAME on the Lower East Side and every youngster tried to excel at it."[7]

Outside of New York, other men of the same generation repeat similar stories. Joseph Weiner, who grew up in New Haven, Connecticut, in the 1890s and went on to become Yale's first Jewish basketball player, remembers that for himself and his five brothers the Edwin Bancroft Foote Boys Club, run by Yale Divinity students, was a "haven" for the children of Jewish immigrants where "we gathered to play, learn and develop." Isadore Frieberger, who graduated from Western Reserve University in 1901, recalls learning basketball and organizing teams at a settlement house in Cleveland. Rube Risewerg, born in Indianapolis in 1912 to Russian immigrants, grew up on the south side of town in a neighborhood he describes as overwhelmingly Jewish. A former professional basketball player in the National Basketball League and today a kosher butcher in an Indianapolis suburb, his shop's walls are lined with old team photos from the Kaufman Settlement House and the local YMHA where he first played the game. And Harry Litwack, Temple University's legendary basketball coach, born in Poland in 1907 and who arrived in America at the age of five, first played basketball in his Philadelphia school yard and at St. Martha's, a church-affiliated settlement house, where his club team, comprised of second-generation Jewish kids like himself, competed in church and settlement house leagues. As he recalls his South Philadelphia childhood, "when I was a kid . . . every phone pole had a peach basket on it" and "every Jewish boy played basketball."[8]

Not surprisingly, social reformers concerned with using such settings as agencies of assimilation emphasized the positive role of basketball in turning immigrant youth into solid American citizens. Consistent with his position as a senior physical education instructor at the Brooklyn YMHA where basketball was the most popular sport, Nat Krinsky, writing in 1923, made the connections quite clearly. Writing for the Y's newspaper, he emphasized that "the gymnasium and the athletic field are ideal places to develop . . . the qualities of courage, respect for authority, co-operation, unselfishness, and a desire to play cleanly and in a sportsmanlike manner."[9] Such rhetoric served as code words for organized play advocates, settlement house workers, and YMHA enthusiasts who hoped that the ability to inculcate these traits into the children of immigrants would ease their entrance into the American mainstream.

Whether or nor Krinsky's remarks reflect his own childhood experiences at settlement houses and in evening recreation programs, other men who first became involved in basketball in similar ways certainly remember their power and persuasion. Red Sarachek was born in the Bronx in 1912, and raised in the Williamsburgh section of Brooklyn. Workmen's Circle coach and also mentor in the American Basketball League as well as coach and athletic director at Yeshiva University for 39 years, he clearly recalls efforts to use sports as a means of acculturating the children of immigrants. As he put it, "they expected it to grow on them and it did grow on them. After all, they gave them a home, a place . . . the incentive to do something would carry over."[10]

Even more impressive for Sarachek and the many others who joined Ys, settlement houses, the Educational Alliance, and evening recreation programs was their own part in determining their participation. Joining because of their enthusiasm for sport or, as Ruby Benjamin, a longtime Sarachek friend who played for him remembers, to get free milk and cookies, even within these organized programs they often maintained control of their own activities.[11] On their own but within the framework of Jewish family and community, they learned more about "American" values and survival skills than what they absorbed from the actions and words of social workers and physical education teachers. Though not without conflict between themselves and their parents, their early basketball experiences illuminate the role of sport as middle ground in all its many versions.

Certainly that's how Sammy Kaplan remembers the Dux. The Dux took shape in the summer of 1925 when a bunch of high-school freshmen and sophomores in Sammy's Brownsville neighborhood got together and won a basketball tournament at a summer recreational program in the school yard of P.S. 184. Veterans of punchball, stickball, hide and seek, kick the can, and johnny on the pony played in "Nanny Goat" Park and their local streets, they decided to form a club in order to play basketball at their school's evening recreation center. As Kaplan recalls, they chose the name "Dux" because it meant leader in Latin and for the more practical reason that it only contained three letters, making it cheaper to sew the name on uniform shirts and jackets.[12]

Recreation center rules required the club to hold weekly meetings, collect dues, and keep minutes, all in the spirit of a philosophy well articulated by youth organizations at this time which insisted that such practices would teach good citizenship and respect for authority. The Dux dutifully followed procedures, independently turning the experience to their own ends. Establishing ten-cent weekly dues, they used the money to promote their basketball. One member acted as a booking agent, arranging games with other clubs around the city. Visiting teams received as much as $2 for participating. Occasionally, the Dux even rented out the main school gym for $5 to host their opponents, money recouped by charging five-cent admissions to the games and by betting club dues on the outcome.

Sammy joined the club in 1926 at the age of fourteen, on the recommendation of his life-long friend Dudie Lynn that he was a good punchball player. As best as I can reconstruct, he missed by one year playing with my father—who, in 1925, won his own Evening Recreation Center 184 basketball medal. A growth spurt during the summer of 1927, which made Kaplan the tallest member of the club, moved him into the Dux starting lineup. The team relied on Sammy to win the center jumps held each time someone scored.

In 1928 the Dux represented P.S. 184 in a city-wide evening recreational basketball league and won the city championship, defeating P.S. 171 of Manhattan by a score of 33–15. To celebrate their success, the club put out a single issue of its own newspaper. Appropriately called *The Leader,* it proclaimed the Dux as city champions and detailed the exploits of the team, giving due credit not only to its young Jewish stars but also to Alvin Borten, who ran the center and coached the team. Edited by Kaplan and Lynn, the paper also included accounts of other center activities, taking great care to mention as many participants as possible by name. Although the paper's editorial noted that the Dux had issued the newspaper not for financial gain but to "demonstrate that the organization does not thrive on sports alone," as Sammy told me, the inclusion of so many names assured that neighborhood children and their parents would buy the paper at its five-cent price and turn a profit for the club. Paid advertisements from the Steinberg Studio, "official photographers of Thomas Jefferson High School," and from Englander's Candy Store on the corner of Christopher Street and Newport Avenue, the place to go "after the game," enhanced the profit margin.[13]

The paper also included praise from P.S. 184's principal, one Patrick J. Murray, who made clear the connection between the role of sport run by professional educators and reformers and the Americanization of immigrant youth. Congratulating a team composed entirely of second-generation Jewish adolescents, he noted that "success and failure are elements calculated to try the souls of men. . . . The man or boy who achieves success and still remains unspoiled is a true American. . . . When the time comes that you will leave the portals of the Recreation Center [and] you are called upon to face the more stern realities of life, may the same success be yours."[14] An anonymous poem written by one of the Dux suggests that at least one of the club's members absorbed Murray's sentiments:

> Who are we—The Dux A.C.,
> The Club we've pledged to honor 'til eternity.
> Dux stands for Leader, The Leader leads the rest.
> We'll put the Basketball of Life in the Basket of Success.
> We play to win, but when we take it on the chin,
> We take it with a grin you will agree.
> Thru fair and stormy weather, we will always stick together,
> We're the Pals of the Dux A.C.[15]

The internal workings of the Dux and Kaplan's own recollections of the club suggest, however, that of far greater importance in becoming Americans was how they shaped their own world. Much as David Nasaw describes the street and work life of turn-of-the-century immigrant children in cities throughout the United States, the Dux control over their own fortunes, both literally and figuratively, gave them a sense of independence, optimism, and a taste of success that made them more comfortable and accepting of a new American environment than many of their parents.[16] In love with a city that offered all kinds of possibilities for fun and adventure, Kaplan remembers the freedom and opportunity involvement in basketball gave him and his friends. As he put it, "the street, the school yard and the candy store was [sic] our second home. It may have been our first home, according to my stepmother. She would always point out that I only came home to sleep, eat, and use the bathroom."

Collecting dues, booking games, betting on the outcome, and selling their own celebratory announcements gave them a sense of independence and taught them first hand about American capitalism and the pleasures of success within it. Building on their growing reputation, after 1928 the Dux left the evening recreation league and moved over to Hopkinson Avenue to represent the Hebrew Educational Society (HES), primarily because it had a bigger gym. Although Meyer Landesman, its head, tried to get the boys interested in the society's religious, educational, and social activities, basketball remained their focus. After two years the club broke its affiliation and freelanced throughout the city, playing college and professional teams as well as fives in established leagues. As Kaplan remembers, the "city was teeming with YMHA's, YMCA's, settlement houses, temples, Educational Alliances, Boys club, Harlem Hebrew Institute. . . . All the institutions were trying to get the immigrant children and their parents into the American mainstream and off the streets. They had all kinds of athletic programs, arts and crafts, drama, night classes which taught English and trades. And the immigrants seeking only a chance, grasped these opportunities with both hands. . . . We played them all. We played three or four times a week and demanded more expense money. . . . The city was alive for us."

By 1930 the Dux played throughout New York's five boroughs and also in upstate New York, New Jersey, and Pennsylvania. Successful on the court and at the gate, they "were even able to shower more than once a week," a mark, for Kaplan, of their separation from their immigrant parents. Occasionally, when they traveled outside the city limits, the boys would hire a bus and charge their friends $1.50 for the opportunity to accompany them. Charged by their love of the game and "their own incentive to do well," Kaplan asserts the Dux took reponsibility for their own lives and never wanted "somebody to give us a handout or do something" for them.

Basketball provided the Dux and other clubs like them opportunities for learning American ways. Whether playing in their own neighborhood or representing other Jewish communities, their games also became an integral part of the social life of Jewish neighborhoods, especially for other second-generation friends and neighbors. Cheering their own to victory, they chose to be caught up in a web of assimilating experiences, both by deciding as American consumers how and where to spend their leisure time and by vicariously identifying with modern values of competition and meritocracy that victory on the court demanded.

So intense were basketball rivalries and fan loyalties among New York's Jewish communities that, during the 1933–34 season, the Staten Island Jewish Community Center hired the Brooklyn Dux to represent them in the YMHA league. Led by Sammy Kaplan, the Dux by this time were already established as one of the best independent clubs in the New York area. As the JCC Dux, they played a schedule that included other Y and Jewish center teams, local college teams such as NYU and CCNY, and a host of professional clubs including the New York Jewels, the Jersey City Reds, and the Chicago Studebakers. The schedule also included games with independent barnstorming teams that took on Jewish names to heighten crowd appeal. The Hebrew Cyclones, the House of David, and the Jersey City Hebrews, a team of former college and professional ballplayers that included Hank Greenberg, baseball's emerging Jewish star, described by one reporter "as a replica of Primo Carnera" and "as fine a basketball player as he is a polished performer on the diamond," all did battle with the Dux.[17]

The Dux were unabashedly billed as the Brooklyn club. Nevertheless, the Staten Island *Advance* praised the boys as their own. In graphic prose the paper described a March 1934 victory over a previously undefeated Holman-coached City College club, noting how the "Dux went beserk in the final two periods as their passing attack . . . suddenly began to click on all cylinders—a quickening tempo that hypnotized" the jam-packed crowd of over 600 "into taut silence for a while and then into a wildly exuberant mob as shots repeatedly went in."[18] Despite the fact that the Dux were clearly earning expenses and appearance money, the paper billed them as the "city's best amateur team" and emphasized the "tremendous local interest" they generated. In part this was due to a 17-game home-court win streak which ended when the JCC Dux lost to eventual national collegiate champions NYU by a 32–24 score before 500 fans. The same issue of the *Advance* that reported this despairing news to the Staten Island faithful also offered a column headlined "Jewish Centers Click on Court" which ranked the Dux among the top of the current crop of New York Y teams. Commenting that the teams were generally composed of ex-college stars and younger players of "college timber," the *Advance* suggested that "never before in the history of Jewish centre basketball has the interest been widespread and attendances so good."[19]

The story of New York's 92nd Street Y varsity five underlines basketball's popularity and its potential for encouraging American connections. Regaling its senior team's Thanksgiving triumph over a visiting team from the Brooklyn YMHA in 1917, for instance, the 92nd Street Y's *Bulletin* reported that "hundreds of Brooklyn rooters" accompanied their team to the game. In a gymnasium "packed to the doors" with 570 paying customers, the largest crowd in the history of the Y applauded the spectacular feats of "Spike" Spunberg and the Goldstein boys, "Schmuley" and "Ouchey," as they "crushed the boys from across the river" by a 37–25 score. Two weeks later, after the team posted its eighth straight victory by defeating the Ozanam Oradales by a 63–34 score, the *Bulletin* jokingly suggested that its many fans were considering a novel way, first introduced by the Y's cross-country runners, to get into games without buying a ticket. According to the paper, before each game the runners take a five-mile run around Central Park and then "shoot up the back entrance" without paying. "Big crowds are now expected to join the cross-country team."[20]

The Y's senior team consistently packed its home games throughout the 1930s. At a meeting of the Y's Athletic Council in September 1930, Nat Holman, in his capacity as physical education director, urged that new bleachers be installed in the gym and that ushers be hired to handle crowds at their games.[21] Gate receipts and attendance figures for the 1930s indicate that Nat had reason for concern. Exclusive of its participation in Jewish Welfare Board and AAU tournaments, the Y's senior five usually played on the road on Saturday nights and at home three times a month on Sunday nights from mid-October to mid-March. Home game admissions were 50 cents for members and ladies and a dime extra for non-members, with higher admissions for especially attractive teams like the all-black Harlem Renaissance, or Rens, as they were commonly called. Although figures varied somewhat from year to year depending on the number of home games played and the number of free passes given to visiting teams and special guests, some 450 to 500 people typically came to watch the team play. Attendance reached a high in the 1936–37 season when an average of 534 fans turned out for the Y's 18-game home schedule, paying some $3600 over the course of the season.[22]

Reporting on a drop-off in game revenues after the 1941 season during which the basketball program generated only $2,464, the Y's Athletic Council emphasized how important basketball revenues were to the Y's athletic program. According to the report, even after covering the expenses and guarantees for teams like the Dux and the Rens, basketball revenues helped outfit and finance its competitive varsity sports program that included soccer, baseball, swimming, wrestling, walking, handball, tennis, and cross-country. It also helped purchase awards, pay AAU dues, and contribute to charity programs such as the Old Timers Fund, Keren Ami, and the Y's summer camp.[23]

Although opponents varied from year to year, like the Dux, the majority of games were played against other local YMHA and Jewish community center teams with occasional games against local college and professional fives. During the 1934–35 season, for example, the 92nd Street boys dotted their home schedule with games against Brooklyn College, the Harlem Rens, and the Dux. The biggest draw, however, was its home encounter with the Bronx YMHA, which drew a paying crowd of some 530 fans.

People who watched the 92nd Street Y varsity and the Dux came to enjoy good basketball, cheer their friends and neighbors, and also to see each other, catch up on local gossip, and socialize. Invariably, the price of admission also included refreshments and dancing to live music after the game. Fans attending a basketball carnival at the Port Richmond Community Center on Staten Island in December 1933 to raise money to supply Christmas food baskets to Staten Island's needy could see two games, one featuring the Dux, and dance afterward to midnight to Charles Bischof's Brownies eight-piece orchestra, all for 50 cents. Over in Paterson, New Jersey, anyone attending a 1934 game between the Dux and the local Y team could also count on dancing to the music of Natey Platt's orchestra, regardless of whether their local heroes triumphed on the court. At least some members of New York's 92nd Street YMHA Athletic Council blamed poor attendance during the 1940–41 season on the lack of opportunity for dancing after Sunday evening games. Although some noted that no one wanted to dance after midnight because they had to go to work the next morning, others insisted that a rule prohibiting all music and dancing after midnight so as not to disturb people living in the neighborhood's many apartment houses cut into attendance.[24]

Although not all stories are as well documented as that of the Dux or the 92nd Street Y, in Jewish communities large and small, scattered throughout the United States, the children of East European Jewish immigrants, as players and as spectators, took up this American game and made it their own. Twenty years before the Dux began, Joseph Weiner and a handful of New Haven Jewish boys, after learning the sport at the local boys club, formed their own organization, the Atlas Club. Holding weekly meetings, collecting dues, even publishing a club newspaper, over the next quarter-century this Jewish social athletic club participated in a wide variety of sports but excelled most prominently in basketball. In the early 1920s, its varsity team not only won city, state, and regional amateur championships but also played for pay against professional teams scattered throughout Connecticut and nearby states. During the 1919–20 season, for instance, the team, often referred to as "the Jewish boys" by the New Haven press, went undefeated over a 24-game schedule that included games with YMHA teams from Bridgeport and Waterbury as well as contests with the New York Collegiates and the Invincible Deaf Mutes of Lexington, New York.[25]

Even though many of its members came from orthodox Jewish homes—its founders included sons of a rabbi, a shammos, and a schochet—basketball games often were scheduled for Friday nights. As one member recalls, that evening turned out to be the most profitable, attracting large numbers of youthful Jewish supporters interested both in basketball and the dance at the Music Hall that followed. Violation of Sabbath observance, however much it might have upset their parents, did not diminish the club's own sense of Jewish purpose. Playing in cities which had never seen a Jewish athlete, Joseph Weiner recalls that club members "looked upon ourselves not simply as another team of players but as a group of goodwill representatives on behalf of the Jewish community. We were shattering the stereotype of the nebbich Jew." Or as Maurice Bailey, an original Atlas member and coach of the team between 1917 and 1928, put it, "throughout Connecticut we made them respect us." Harry "Pookie" Alderman, who played for the club in 1921 and 1922 before becoming its president, also recalls its symbolic importance for Jews. In his mind, Atlas's basketball prowess not only "earned respect for the Jewish people," it also "established ethnic pride which overrode fear."[26]

No doubt their athletic success also made other Jews both proud and hopeful of their own chances for success in America. Certainly the club's victory over the Yale varsity basketball team in a 1922 exhibition game which raised $2100 for the Jewish Relief Fund encouraged such sentiments. Playing before 2800 spectators at the Meadow Street Armory, the largest crowd ever to see a basketball game in New Haven up until that time, the Atlas, led by "Mickey" Botwinik and George Greenberg, crushed the Elis by 42–22.[27] So too did the fact that many of the boys who played for the Atlas Club over the years went on to Yale or other colleges and then to careers in business and the professions. Celebrating its 20th anniversary in 1926, the club highlighted such success by offering capsule biographies of its alumni along with a brief history of the club. Collected in its Jubilee Book, the emphasis throughout is on the Atlas boys' strong identification as Americans and as Jews, all shaped by their own efforts and choices and underlined by the American accomplishments of "the finest of the younger Jewish men in our community."[28]

The young men who organized the Talmud Torah Athletic Club in Minneapolis in 1922 also attempted to balance similar American and Jewish concerns through their interest in basketball. With bylaws modeled after the United States Constitution and a slogan proclaiming "a sound mind in a sound body," the club announced its intentions as a social and athletic enterprise open to Talmud Torah graduates over the age of seventeen interested in continuing their study of Jewish concerns.[29] Throughout the 1920s, the club sponsored a basketball team, known as "the Fighting Rabbis," participated in the Emanuel Cohen settlement house basketball competition, put out a newspaper that, among other things, kept track of its members' activities at the University of Minnesota and in the community, and held meetings, often in Hebrew, to discuss such issues as the Jewish-Arab conflict in Palestine. Staying committed to Jewish tradition as its members excelled in American universities and in American sport was not always easy. A 1929 newsletter that proudly announced the "Fighting Rabbis'" victory in the senior champion-ship basketball game for the Emanuel Cohen League also questioned if they had accomplished as much intellectually as Jews. The remedy proposed was daily Bible readings aimed at reminding club members of "the fascinating events of Jewish history." Although there is no way of knowing how many boys took up the call, two months later, a brief poem appearing in their *ACC News* confirmed the club's strong Jewish sense even as it members established themselves as Americans:

> Oh, A.C.C, the all embracin,
> The standard bearer of our race,
> Where all the virtues are embellished
> Where every T.T. graduate finds a place.
> Thru the midst of Anti-semites, Thru the fog of disbelief
> Comes the shining light of Judea,
> The A.C.C. in bold relief.
> Oh people close your hearts of treason,
> Oh, open up your hearts of joy,
> The A.C.C. will find its promise,
> Will make a Jew of every T.T. boy (perhaps goy).[30]

Whether in areas surrounding Brooklyn's HES, the Bronx's YMHA, Chi-cago's Jewish People's Institute, Detroit's Jewish Community Center, Cleve-land's Jewish Center, or in Los Angeles and Philadelphia Jewish neighbor-hoods, similar stories unfolded. Most popular in the years between the wars but beginning as early as 1902, second-generation Jewish youth on Philadel-phia's south side organized and played ball in the Jewish Basketball League. Teams in the league represented a variety of Jewish organizations, including temples, Jewish community centers, YMHAs, and settlement houses. By the 1920s, Tuesday-night league doubleheaders at the YMHA on Broad and Pine streets attracted crowds of up to 1500 to witness the exploits of Eddie Gottlieb, Chicky Passon, Cy Kaselman, "Inky" Lautman, and other prominent local stars who went on to successful professional and college careers. Both former players and neighborhood people who came to cheer and dance afterward still gather annually in Philadelphia to remember those days when basketball in Philadelphia was a Jewish game.[31] Pages of the Detroit *Jewish Chronicle* throughout the 1920s and 1930s daily recounted the exploits of elite Jewish basketball teams in city and even national competition before large, enthusi-astic neighborhood crowds. Weekly, through the winter months, it carried reports of games in the city's Jewish league complete with standings and attendance figures which usually averaged some 300 people a game. Aside from games against local YMHA and YMCA teams, competition included the senior teams of the Jewish centers in Akron and Cleveland, Ohio, as well as contests with the Flint, Michigan, YMHA and Chicago's JPI. Scrapbooks of newspaper clippings from local Chicago newspapers that record the history of the JPI replicate the same tale. Here and elsewhere, organized leagues for older, elite players existed side by side with those for younger boys and occasionally girls, all eager to enjoy the sport. Even growing up among Portland, Oregon's small Jewish population in the 1920s and 1930s, Harry Glickman, today president of the Portland Trail Blazers, fondly remembers his adolescent playing days with his Jewish center's community team, the B'nai B'rith Cardinals, another group of second-generation Jewish boys whose team excelled in local competition.[32]

Basketball, then, all within the setting of Jewish community, provided second-generation participants and spectators opportunity to experience dominance and success in an American enterprise. In community centers and gymnasiums, neighborhood people also participated as American consumers by purchasing a ticket and choosing to root for whomever they pleased. They became fans of an American invention and more "American" in turn, by watching their own kind transform it into a Jewish majority sport. These Americanizing experiences unfolded in ways that encouraged ethnic pride and identification. Although this dynamic was to receive far greater publicity with the success of Jewish boxers and major league baseball players, the achievements of local boys in local settings carried a most immediate, palpable sense of American possibility for all Jews.

Witnessing friends excel in American sport while socializing in settings distinctly Jewish even provided opportunities for maintaining Jewish tradition. Whether raising money to buy Passover matzoh for poor Brownsville residents or for the Jewish Relief Fund in New Haven, or using basketball revenues, as the 92nd Street Y did, to send children to summer camps or to supplement its Keren Ami Fund which raised money for a host of Jewish charities, those who participated in basketball both as players and as spectators also expressed collective concern for community welfare consistent with the long-standing Jewish tradition of tzedakah—God's directive to help others less fortunate than yourself. Engaging sport as a middle ground, participants in this world of basketball and Jewish community acquired American ways while absorbing Jewish sensibilities, even as they moved inexorably away from the Jewish world of their immigrant parents.

II

Not everyone was happy about this transformation. Harry Glantz, who glowingly reported on the success of Los Angeles Jewish community basketball teams for his *B'nai B'rith Messenger* readers, chastized the local B'nai B'rith lodge for sponsoring league games on Friday nights. Players certainly have the chance to be home for the "Shabbus feast." But as soon as the meal is over, he lamented, "they bundle their athletic trunks and shoes in their grips and they're away as fast as they can—to uphold the fair name of a Jewish club on a basketball court," in violation of the true meaning of "our most important holy day."[33]

Fathers and mothers also voiced disapproval. Even those eager to see their children make their mark as successful Americans were often appalled by their children's passion for basketball and other sports. Talking about his boyhood Brownsville street life, William Poster, a poet and writer, remembers parents "who assured us as we came streaking in from a punchball game covered with sweat and grime" before rush[ing] off to one of a hundred feverish nocturnal activities that we were all bums, gangsters, boolvans and paskudnyaks." Poet and teacher Milton Klonsky, who also grew up in the late 1920s and early 1930s a little further south in the Jewish neighborhood surrounding Brooklyn's Brighton Beach, recalls similar memories. Proudly he remembers his loyalty to his club, the Trogans, and their inventive use of streets and sidewalks in their all-consuming love and interest in sport. "We played hard with a will to win so strong it willed itself," he remembers. "Sometimes we became so engrossed by a punchball or a stickball game that night would fall without anyone's being aware of it." Their passion, however, was not shared "by mothers who complained because they had to complain and even more by the old ones, those zaidas with embroidered yamelkas and their white beards worn like orders upon their chests. They wondered whether we were Jews or a new kind of shagitz. . . . They painted a picture of our decline and fall stage by stage . . . until someday we would be eating pig and pulling beards on the streets of New York."[34]

Reminiscing about his experiences in basketball and how they shaped his identity, character, and independence, Sammy Kaplan offers his own contribution to the question of how first-generation immigrants responded to their children's involvement in basketball. "Our parents," he notes, "shouldn't be disappointed."[35] Many were; others weren't. Yet, even for those fathers and mothers most critical of their children's fascination with sport, daily tasks of work and survival preoccupied parental concern, often leaving children free to decide how to spend their time and what to do with their lives.

This theme dominates family recollections of second-generation men for whom basketball was a critical part of growing up. Separated by the boundaries of a full generation—from second-generation children born at the turn of the century to those who passed through adolescence in the 1920s—they document a rich Jewish family life full of conflict, occasional resolution, and also love and warmth in which parents and children attempted to balance their desire to become American with their attachment to ethnic and religious tradition.

"Jewish" obviously included William Poster's "zaidas"—elderly, Old World, religiously orthodox men, for whom America and sport remained anathema. But as we know, it also encompassed a wide variety of people of different ages and religious beliefs, with varying committments to the old and the new, all bound together in the same geographic space and all identified as Jews by a majority of Protestant culture. In such places, as one chronicler of American Jewish life observes, "Jews knew they were Jewish." Although the world of their fathers and mothers was not especially religious, memories of growing up in familiar ethnic neighborhoods where Jews were the majority, of common cultural traditions, and of an inherent sense of feeling different, strongly colors their reflections of parental reaction to their involvement in basketball.[36]

Parents, they remember, caught up in their own struggle between new American desires and traditional East European ethnic ways, often expressed displeasure with their sons' love of sport. More important, however, they were too preoccupied with making ends meet to devote time and energy to the daily direction of their children's lives. When they did raise objections, it had little to do with fears that children were abandoning any sense of traditional Jewish life but rather that they were squandering opportunities for education and economic opportunity offered by a new American world. For some parents, over time, their children's accomplishments in this American game softened their disappointment, even serving as a common ground between generations both caught up in learning how to be American.

When asked if his parents objected to his playing basketball, Harry Litwack recalls that they were too busy trying to survive to worry about how he spent his time. Although not orthodox, his Polish parents kept kosher, observed the high holidays, and spoke only Yiddish in the home. Noting the difficulties they experienced in coming to terms with America, he mentions that his mother never learned English and that his father struggled with it. Harry's father repaired shoes, putting in hours from 6 a.m. until his day's work was done. Only on Sunday afternoons did he take time off from his labors, when after a tub bath he went out to buy his supplies for the following week. In such a setting, there was no time for outside interests or for worrying about his son's participation in athletics. Not once, through his playing days at Philadelphia's Southern High School, Temple University, or even with the renowned Philadelphia SPHAs, did his parents come to see him. "All the parents in the ghetto," Harry remembers, had no interest in sport. "All they understood were books, books, books, knowledge, knowledge, knowledge." His parents' only concern, as Harry recalls it, was that "I came home at night."[37]

Left to his own devices, basketball provided Litwack with a ticket to college, a sense of empowerment and independence as an adolescent, and ultimately a highly successful career in basketball, all unfolding in the Jewish world of South Philadelphia. Several thousand miles away and almost a generation later, Harry Glickman offers a somewhat different version of family and community. Born in Portland, Oregon, to immigrant parents from Russia and Poland in 1924, he grew up in Portland's small East European Jewish neighborhood that he remembers as distinctly "Jewish." His parents divorced when he was five and Harry was raised in an orthodox, kosher home by his mother, who worked as a finisher in the garment trade to make ends meet. Although not an outstanding basketball player, his childhood memories remain dominated by his days spent at the local Jewish community center where he played basketball with his Jewish friends—friends he still sees regularly today. His mother, he recalls, encouraged his interest, worrying only that he might be injured. Today, president of the National Basketball

Association's Portland Trail Blazers and long active as a sports promoter, like Litwack, he fondly recalls a childhood in which basketball provided a sense of freedom and independence within the framework of Jewish family and community.[38]

Not surprisingly, New York, the city where most Jews lived and where basketball was the dominant organized community sport, offers its own rich contributions to discussion of basketball, family, and childhood. Typically, Jammy Moskowitz recalls growing up in a "Jewish neighborhood." By the time he became a teenager on the eve of World War I, Brooklyn's Brownsville, a two-mile square bounded by Livonia Avenue, Junius Street, and the intersection of Pitkin Avenue and Eastern Parkway, was even more solidly Jewish than the Lower East Side, populated by Jewish working-class and lower-middle-class families successful enough to move to new Brooklyn apartment houses and brownstones in an area that another former resident remembers as a "Jewish island." Although Sammy Kaplan may well be exaggerating when he asserts that as a child he never heard of Christmas or saw a Christmas tree even in public school, Brownsville defined a world in which it was rare to meet someone who was not Jewish and in which Yiddish, especially among adults, was the common language. Whether shopping from pushcart peddlers, buying groceries, vegetables, or meats from local merchants on Pitkin Avenue, "the Fifth Avenue of Brownsville," or purchasing the *Jewish Daily Forward*, cigarettes, or two cents plain at the corner candy store, a Jewish ambience prevailed.[39]

Sammy Kaplan's remembrances of his Brownsville childhood remain focused on recollections of the Dux and of a loving, orthodox Jewish father who took pride in his son's accomplishments even as they led him away from his own traditional world. Sammy's parents both came from Steppin, Poland. His father, Gershon, worked in a millwork factory in a neighboring town but returned home each week to spend the Sabbath with his wife and her family. In 1907, Gershon, who Sammy insists was "more religious than the rabbi," left for America in search of a new life, leaving behind his wife and five children. Working as a carpenter, in three years he saved enough money to bring his family to New York, one person at a time. Sammy was the only member of the family born in the United States.

Sammy's mother died when he was two. Raised by his older sisters and then by a stepmother who his father married because he wanted a woman to "run a religious orthodox home," they lived in the first floor of a brownstone and rented out the upstairs. Sammy shared a bed in the living room with his father while three of his brothers slept together in one of the two small bedrooms. His father added on a closed porch where the family ate meals during Succoth, drinking wine made from grapevines that grew in the backyard. Every Friday night the floors were washed and newspapers spread over them for the coming of the Sabbath, a day his father spent in shul while Saturday's dinner cooked on the stove where it had been set the night before. As he grew older, less observant, and more independent, Sammy, afraid of explosions, turned the burner off before he went to bed and relit it in the morning.

Growing up in a strictly orthodox home, Kaplan went to Hebrew school and had a melamed tutor him at home for his Bar Mitzvah, an event celebrated back at the house where his father and his friends shared herring, cake, and tea at the only birthday party Sammy recalls having. Although he put on tefillin for the year after his Bar Mitzvah, Sammy, like his brothers, moved further away from formal Jewish observance. Even as Sammy began spending his Friday evenings and Saturdays with the Dux, his father never protested or tried to impose his religious views on his son. "I was the apple of his eye," Sammy recalls of the man he describes as a "good-natured, sensitive person."

Like many men of his generation, Gershon Kaplan's lack of insistence about his son's religiosity carried over to concern about Sammy's education and career. His father, and other immigrants like him, Sammy insists, wanted their sons to be "a doctor or a lawyer or a musician or something like that." Athletes, in their minds, were "bums." Parenting, however, for men and women caught up in the Great Depression, revolved around issues of economic necessity and survival, not career counseling. Sammy graduated from Thomas Jefferson High School in 1930 and then attended evening college at CCNY for five years, where he studied accounting. Playing professional basketball helped pay for his education. College and career choices were his decisions. "College was up to you. There wasn't any extra money to pay for college. If you wanted to go, you had to find a way."

Similar memories belong to Moe Goldman, the first Jewish All-American at CCNY and a successful professional player who was born three years after Kaplan. Moe grew up in the same Brownsville neighborhood on Hopkinson Avenue, across the street from the HES, which he and his friends joined so that they "could play ball." His parents both came from Odessa. Living in a neighborhood where people rarely could afford to buy new furniture, his father worked as a repainter of beds in his own store while his mother, a housewife, helped her mother sell chickens. Although his parents welcomed the opportunity to become Americans, they also kept a strictly kosher home, spoke both English and Yiddish, and were observant Jews. His father went to shul on the holidays and to an occasional Friday evening service. Escorted by his grandson, Moe's blind grandfather attended services every day at his shul on Pitkin Avenue. Moe went to a neighborhood cheder and also to a rabbi to prepare for his Bar Mitzvah.

Attention to family duties, schoolwork, and religious training, however, hardly defined Moe's adolescence. Active in neighborhood sports with his Jewish friends at HES, P.S. 184, and the streets, Moe became fully involved in basketball in his junior year at Franklin K. Lane High School. A growth spurt that saw him gain almost a foot over the summer suddenly found him playing center for a Lane five that went on to win the city championship. Although he did not go to City College on a basketball scholarship, he became the star of Holman-coached City teams that lost only three games in his three-year varsity career, including a senior year record of 14–1 when Goldman, the squad's captain, was named All-American.

Moe's parents' initial reaction to their son's infatuation with basketball was clear. Frivolous activity that interfered with their son's future simply made no sense to them. "At the beginning," he recalls, with a sense of comic timing that is God's gift to Jews, "they thought I was nuts. What is this? You go out with short pants and go running around with a round ball?" Once Moe assured them that basketball would not interfere with his college education, they made no issue of his interest and "were happy for [him]." Although they never once saw him play either in college or in the pros, they did listen on the radio each night to see if his team won or lost, in their own way participating in his American success.[40]

A few miles to the north, hugging the shores of the East River and under the shadows of the Williamsburg Bridge, another Jewish ballplayer also remembers a father who did not share his passion. Red Auerbach, best known as the coach who led the Boston Celtics to nine National Basketball Association championships between 1956 and 1966 before becoming the club's general manager and then president, grew up consumed by basketball and by a fervent desire to become a physical education teacher and a coach. His father, Hymie, came from Minsk and was sent over to America with his brother when he was thirteen to escape anti-Semitism and to "have a shot at a better life." A hard-working man who married an American-born office worker and who eventually came to have his own dry-cleaning business, Hymie did not appreciate his son's love for basketball or his career plans. As Red recalls, it simply did not reverberate with his own past or his reasons for coming to America:

> My father didn't know what it was to be a kid in this country. He never had a moment of youth here. It made no difference what your age was—10, 12, 14—when you stepped off the boat as an immigrant in those days, you were expected to be a man. There was no such thing as going to school for people like my father. He had come here to work . . . to create a life that wouldn't have been available to him back in his homeland. That was what America was about; it wasn't playing games and having fun. It was to someday start a family and be able to provide security for your kids. Those were my father's goals in life and to his credit, he achieved them.[41]

Although Auerbach's father questioned the amount of time his son spent on basketball and assumed that he would never go to college, Red remembers that "he knew enough to take his kids to watch Ruth and Gehrig play every once in a while; he realized that was part of being an American father." Regardless of his father's disapproval, Red pursued his dream. Unable to make it to CCNY because his grades were not high enough, he eventually earned a basketball scholarship to George Washington University, completing his B.A. as well as a master's in physical education. To his father's credit, "once he saw that I had made up my mind, he didn't try to hold me back. In fact," Red recalls, "he sort of came over to my side and encouraged my ambitions."[42]

Hymie Auerbach lived to see his son become one of the most successful coaches in the history of professional basketball and an American basketball legend. Although his son's dreams were not his own, the fact that he witnessed their fruition was important to Red. "[It] meant a lot to me because he never approved of all the time I spent playing the game as a kid. It wasn't that I wanted to prove him wrong; I just wanted him to see that I was right, that my time hadn't been wasted."[43]

As they describe them, both Moe Goldman's and Red Auerbach's parents found little in their East European upbringing or in their reasons for coming to the United States to offer support for their boys' American passions. Focused on hard work and economic survival, these parents viewed preoccupation with sport as potential obstacle to their children's futures. Eventually, however, the Goldmans and the Auerbachs took pride in the athletic accomplishments of their sons. In so doing, they suggest the possibility that sport could even mediate sharp generational differences about how to succeed in America.

The potential of sport as middle ground between immigrant parents and American children emerges most clearly in the stories of Harold "Judy" Judenfriend and Max Zaslofsky. Harold, born in 1920 to Polish immigrant parents who first came to America as young children, grew up in Brownsville on Sackman Street in a tenement apartment shared by his parents and his sister. A member of Nat Holman's City College teams in the early 1940s, Harold also played in the American Basketball League and coached high-school basketball before embarking on a successful career as a university professor and administrator. He remembers his neighborhood as a place of lower-middle-class and working-class Jews struggling rather unsuccessfully with the economics of the Depression. Judenfriend's father, a furrier, lost his own business when the demand for fur coats disappeared. Although he continued to work in the trade, Harold's mother took a job as a dress finisher in the garment district to help "keep the family in food and shelter." As he tells it, neighborhood women like his mother were not supposed to work outside the home. Embarrassed that her neighbors might find out that she was working, she insisted that no one in the family tell anyone.[44]

Whether or nor the Judenfriends kept this secret is not clear. Living in a neighborhood that Harold describes as a "Jewish ghetto" where most people were unemployed and where "it was very difficult to make a living," it seems unlikely. What is certain, however, is his strong sense of growing up in familiar Jewish surroundings despite the fact that his family was not especially religious. Although his parents spoke Yiddish and Polish when his grandparents visited, English was the main language in the Judenfriend household. They did not observe the Sabbath or the high holidays and did not attend shul or belong to any congregation. Harold did not go to Hebrew school and was not Bar Mitzvahed. Nevertheless, he recalls immersion in a Jewish, Yiddish culture encapsulated by the sounds of language, the smell of foods, and the practice of custom that, in his words, provided "a commonality which [was] very comforting."

Also providing comfort was a warm family circle whose members did not question his interest in sport. Harold's father and uncle had both been ama-

teur wrestlers, prominent enough at one time to have their pictures in the
Police Gazette. Although too busy working to watch his son develop his basketball skills in school yards, community center gyms, or playing for teams representing such diverse groups as Franklin K. Lane High School, the Furriers
Joint Council, and the Workman's Circle (where he played for Red Sarachek),
his father always accepted his son's involvement in a variety of sports as a
normal part of growing up.

Max Zaslofsky's Russian immigrant parents also found reason to be proud
of their son's athletic accomplishments. Born in Brownsville in 1925, Max's
recollections of his youth and family reverberate with positive memories of
athletics and of growing up Jewish. Although aware of the "tough times" the
Depression had on his father, who got by as a painter and "trader of merchan-
dise," he insists that "as a youngster it never really bothered me too much
because I wasn't aware of it. I was playing basketball."[45] Max was intrigued
by the game from the age of six when his father gave him a ball as a present.
"By the time I was eight or nine," he recalls, "I wanted to be a professional
player. This is what I always dreamed of and wanted." He nurtured his game
in school yards, high school, and at the Brownsville Boys Club among Jewish
boys like himself, who like the Dux and countless other adolescent groups,
joined together to form organizations centered on sport, especially basketball.
After a fine college career at St. John's, he went on to play eight years as a
professional, primarily for the Chicago Stags and the New York Knickerbockers. Known as "the Touch," he retired in 1956 as the NBA's third highest all-
time scorer.

Max retained positive memories of Jewish family life. Both of his parents,
who he describes as "loving," were orthodox Jews who spoke Yiddish, kept
kosher, observed the Sabbath, and went to shul every Friday and Saturday.
Although he went to cheder for three years and was Bar Mitzvahed, Max's
attachment to religion and ritual quickly waned.

His parents, who knew little about sports, did not discourage his interest
in basketball. In part, they saw it as a healthy alternative to other options open
to Brownsville's Jewish boys in the midst of Depression—after all Murder
Incorporated, a notorious band of Jewish gangsters and hitmen who occasionally took over a local street or Betsy Head Park for stickball or basketball,
was always in the market for new recruits. Most likely, their own struggle for
economic survival that included putting food on the table and a roof over the
heads of Max and his two brothers, precluded constant attention to how their
son spent his time.

Talking about their reaction to his basketball career, Zaslofsky captures
both the cultural distance between his own generation and his parents and the
potential for sport as common ground in their search for American acceptance. Although his parents came "from the Old Country and . . . didn't know
anything about sports," his mother recognized that for him, basketball "was
a labor of love." She also knew that "if she ever needed me, she could find me
in the school yard. So this is what made her happy." Later, when Max established himself as a well-known college and professional player whose name

appeared frequently in the press and on the radio, his parents became avid fans. His mother, he remembers, "was very proud of how her son 'Maxie' did." According to one sportswriter, she so enjoyed hearing Max's name on the radio that she took to listening to hockey broadcasts, a game even more foreign to her than basketball, because announcers occasionally reported basketball scores and "sometimes speak of Max."

Whether listening to Harry Litwack describe his early-20th-century Philadelphia childhood or Max Zaslofsky reminisce about his Brooklyn neighborhood twenty years later, these stories of second-generation children and their immigrant parents are richly repetitious about the place of sport in their upbringing. Memories of childhoods in Jewish settings, of parents both disapproving and occasionally supportive, but generally too busy to demand obedience to their views, of the ability of sport as a bridge between generations, and, most important, of a sense of empowerment, independence, and drive to determine their own destiny that involvement in basketball imparted predominate.

Clearly it would be unfair to suggest that these stories about basketball and Jewish life, offered by exceptionally talented athletes, were typical of the experience of all other men of their generation. Well-marked Jewish enclaves like Brooklyn's Brownsville, Chicago's Maxwell Street, or Philadelphia's south side, where everyone and everything seemed "Jewish," did not describe the situations of Jews growing up in places like El Paso, Texas, or Montgomery, Alabama. Moreover, neither in Brownsville nor on Maxwell Street did all young boys find basketball and sport their all-consuming passions.

Still, in neighborhoods located in eastern and midwestern cities where most Jews lived, for those who played the game and for friends who offered their support, basketball provided a large segment of second-generation Jewish youth from urban East European working-class backgrounds opportunities to relish what was most exciting about being an American. Social reformers and religious leaders certainly tried to impose their own definitions of propriety and citizenship on them, even using sport as one means of cutting their own versions of Americans out of immigrant cloth. But through basketball, these children of immigrants became active participants in the process of deciding what it was to be an American and what it was to be Jewish. For them, it was never a choice between remaining part of some idealized version of European immigrant culture or blending into an American Gentile world. Rather, in the context of their own ethnic world, they shaped their own sense of Americanism, one that ultimately fused what they considered to be ethnic and mainstream values. In short, these people recognized an incredible feature of American life totally alien to their parents' European beginnings. Here, public definitions of community, of Americanism, of Jewishness, and of the place of sport in it all were not dictated by secular or religious authorities. Even in the face of opposing views from within and without their own communities, they were free to determine what assimilation meant for themselves.

III

Members of the "Basketball Fraternity" who gather annually in Miami Beach each December to share memories of basketball and childhood appreciate these connections. Initially, a small dinner for eight arranged by Sammy Kaplan and Harold Judenfriend in 1977, this event now attracts over 300 men and women to the Inverray Country Club in Miami Beach each Christmas. About half of those who attend these reunions are second-generation Jewish basketball players from the community, college, and professional ranks. Although some represent Philadelphia, the overwhelming majority of them grew up and played ball in New York. Others in attendance include old neighborhood buddies who fondly remember the court exploits of their more talented friends and a small group of wives who, with few exceptions, sit in the back of the ballroom at their own tables, perhaps reliving in their own way the separation of men and women familiar to orthodox shuls in Brownsville or on the Grand Concourse where they grew up.[46]

And what about the men? Their reasons for coming are as clear as the way in which they seat themselves. At the 1987 dinner which I attended, tables defined by neighborhood and school predominated. Sammy Kaplan and the surviving members of the original Dux sat together. Several tables full of CCNY graduates every so often spontaneously broke into City's famous "Allagaroo" cheer. Jammy Moskowitz and his wife held court amid a number of his former Madison High School ballplayers. I found myself at a table with a group of men who also shared a similar sense of nostalgia and celebration for a way of life that defined their identities. It included Moe Goldman, among the most celebrated ballplayers in attendance and also among the oldest; Irv Torgoff, All-American and captain of a national championship Long Island University Team in 1939 who played professionally in the late 1940s; Norm Nathanson, a successful businessman, by his own account a school-yard ballplayer who proudly recalls watching Moe Goldman play; and myself, who possessed his own link to the assembled crowd in the form of his father's basketball medal earned in the same school gymnasium that produced the Dux.

Members first observe a moment of silence for recently deceased brothers—Shikey Gotthifer and Abe Bidane. The evening then unfolds in the able hands of Abe Gerchick, who grew up on my father's block in Brownsville and who played basketball at Brooklyn College in the 1930s. Abe emcees the affair as if he is at a Jewish Catskill Mountain resort on a Saturday night. Comic timing is everywhere as he introduces one speaker after another who embellish and celebrate "the small, little secular world of basketball they all belong to." Abe establishes the rhythm by reminding his appreciative audience of the difference between a City College and a Brooklyn College ballplayer. In a story at least as old as the "Borscht Belt," he tells of a bathroom encounter with Babe Adler, who played for CCNY, at half-time of a game between the two schools. City boys, Gerchick notes, always made Brooklyn players feel like "second-class citizens." The example? As he tells it, after both he and Adler urinated, "I wash my hands and he walks out. I tell him that at Brooklyn College they taught us to wash our hands after we piss. You know what this hussum says? At City College they taught us not to piss on our hands."

Then, although they don't mention the word "tzedakah," several speakers announce projects that connect them to that longstanding Jewish tradition. Although they no longer live in a neighborhood that now is mostly working-class black, a group of former Erasmus High School ballplayers from Brooklyn's Flatbush section who played for Bidane between 1932 and 1945 pay special tribute to their former coach by announcing that a college scholarship fund in his name has been established at the school. Next, Herb Gershon, who grew up in Manhattan and played for the Bronx YMHA and several professional teams, tells of efforts to raise over $10,000 to help pay the medical costs of an absent friend who is suffering from Parkinson's disease. Finally, Mat Miletzok, another New York boy who played briefly for CCNY, Hofstra, and Cornell and then professionally in the late 1940s and early 1950s, details plans to establish the Basketball Fraternity as a non-profit organization in order to establish a permanent emergency relief fund to help fellow members in time of need. As a change of pace, Norm Drucker, who learned to play at Brooklyn's HES, Erasmus, and CCNY before becoming one of the premier officials in the National Basketball Association, invites his friends to try out for the World Basketball League, a new professional circuit limited to players 6'4", which he directs.

And so the evening goes—patterned reminiscences of neighborhood, basketball, and present accomplishment interspersed with informal schmoozing, hugging, and kissing—men recreating for a moment a world with few exceptions that was distinct from their parents. This American world of play, responsibility, and accomplishment forged in a distinct Jewish environment gave them a sense of independence, pride, and identity that was critical to their discovery as Americans and as Jews, and one, despite the conflicts it certainly produced, they now remember with obvious warmth and affection. Here, as Moe Goldman told me, there are no special awards. The banquet is a place where everyone is of equal importance, regardless of their basketball ability, precisely because what is being honored is the world that produced Jewish ballplayers, not the players themselves.

A somewhat smaller gathering that includes many Basketball Fraternity members held in Sammy Kaplan's backyard in Kendall, Florida, each March continues the celebration. Depending upon who can make it, up to 140 friends and family gather to wish Sammy happy birthday and to remember the Dux at "Kaplan's Kamelot." In his invitations and at the party, Kaplan consciously recreates the world of his childhood.[47] The invitation to the 61st anniversary of the founding of the Dux, held on St. Patrick's Day, 1986, for instance, reminded recipients "that once there was a spot, Brownsville; for one brief shining moment that to us was Kamelot." Instead of traditional St. Paddy's day fare of "corned beef and cabbage, green lime pie, and Irish coffee," Sammy warns his guests that leprechauns may well surprise you with a menu of "matzoh ball soup, gefilte fish, strudel and a glessele tay and Manischewitz wine instead."

Although it is doubtful that anyone missed the message of a menu that invoked a familiar Jewish ethnic world, the following year, Sammy marked the tenth Dux reunion with a very clear definition of what the gathering was all about. Upset that Stone Avenue in Brownsville had been renamed Mother Gaston Boulevard in honor of a community worker for black residents who now populated the Jewish streets of his youth, Kaplan announced, "with equal chutzpah," the naming of a dirt lane on his three Kendall acres as Stone Avenue. Selectively recalling the world of Stone Avenue and the Dux, Kaplan noted:

> *There on Stone Avenue* at P.S. 184 we went to school, played in the playground, met, got acquainted, formed athletic clubs, and joined the ERC neighborhood program. There, in 1927–28, the DUX, representing the school, won the city-wide championship under the guidance of teacher-coach Alvin Borten— there they taught us how to run a meeting, keep minutes and become a "mensch."
> *There on Stone Ave.* at Sherman's Candy store we drank 2 cents plain, egg creams, ice cream sodas, malted milks and ate Charlotte Russes and penny candy. There we socialized, dated, and dreamed; and went to war.
> *There on Stone Ave.* and in the surrounding neighborhood streets we lived with our immigrant Parents and Grandparents who struggled and hoped their children would have a better life in the "Golden Medina." Affluent America fulfilled their hopes and satisfied their dreams. So come, come. To the reunion. Bring your memories, your pictures, your mementos, and your tears.

Kaplan's prose encapsulates much of the experience of second-generation lower-middle-class and working-class youth who found in basketball an experience that provided enjoyment, physical vigor, camaraderie, and their own chance to shape American identities that emphasized success, independence, opportunity, and choice without denying strong Jewish ties. Irving Bernstein, who, in his youth, belonged to an East Bronx athletic club also known as the Dux, emphasizes similar sentiments in calling such clubs "the unifying experience" in the lives of his generation. Growing up as "the sons of immigrant parents" whose struggle "to feed, clothe, and house their children and at the same time close the gap between their European experience and the American dream" left them "little time for us," the Dux of Brownsville and the East Bronx," Bernstein concludes, "found the kinship, security, and confidence to reach beyond the physical horizons of their neighborhoods to join the mainstream of American life."[48]

This sense, so palpable at their reunions, is confirmed by a collective profile of Basketball Fraternity members. Much like New Haven Atlas Club members in the 1920s or Philadelphia's Jewish Basketball League or the Brownsville Boys Club alumni who today hold their own annual reunions, they are proud Americans who recall the self-sufficiency, independence, manliness, and sheer enjoyment that basketball and American freedom brought them.[49] Time

and again, these are the words that define their American sensibility, one reinforced by the fact that 34 men, or 70 percent of those who responded to interviews and questionnaires, proudly served in the military during World War II,
with assignments ranging from combat action in every theater of the war to
stateside duty as physical education instructors. For many, basketball played
on the community level also brought a chance for college and career, the kind
of American success immigrant parents hoped for their children. Forty
attended college, where partial or full basketball scholarships helped many
pay the way. Playing at a time when professional basketball was a part-time
profession, 39 played professionally for at least one year while 22 also either
coached or owned a professional basketball team.[50] More secure and substantial careers followed for all. Of the 47 men who responded about their occu-
pations, 20 identified themselves as businessmen, 10 became either professors, doctors, lawyers, or accountants, two worked as labor organizers, and 15
became public-school teachers, often combining coaching with their classroom duties.

Proud identification as Jews also defines these men. Although their
responses defy easy quantification, the vast majority indicate that they did not
come from particularly observant families nor have they had much interest in
encouraging such practice for themselves or for their children. Nevertheless
they strongly feel their Jewishness. Most often displayed by simple assertion
of pride, it includes a sense of being different, fond attachment to the ethnic
culture of their childhoods, philanthropy, and concern about Jewish survival
conditioned by recent world history.

Despite the fact that he sees his own life as proof that the United States is
"a great country," Sammy Kaplan, for example, insists that it is impossible for
him to feel totally comfortable as an American. Growing up in an immigrant
home in an "insulated Jewish community" and remembering the occasional
anti-Semitic taunts of opposing fans and players when the Dux played on the
road condition his response.

So, too, do memories of the Holocaust and of the creation of the state of
Israel. Although he has never visited Israel and offers no comment on its internal politics, Sammy strongly identifies with its survival. Only here, he
believes, can Jews feel totally secure. In that spirit, along with other members
of the Dux, he dedicated their 75th anniversary party to raising money for the
Jewish Nation Fund of Israel. Harry Litwack, honored by the B'nai B'rith for
his contributions of time and money to Jewish causes and coach of the U.S.
basketball teams to the Maccabiah Games in 1957 and 1973, talks equally
strongly about his commitment to Israel's survival and the honor he feels it is
to be a Jew. Now in his late seventies, and clearly past his physical prime as a
basketball player or pugilist, this legendary coach and player who experienced
his own share of anti-Semitic encounters on the court is ready "to put his fist
up" to anyone who passes a derogatory remark about Jews.[51]

Sonny Hertzberg, who grew up in Brooklyn and went on to a successful
career as a stockbroker after his playing days with the New York Knicks
ended, also recalls his physical response to several instances when opposing

players ridiculed his Jewish identity. Refusing apologies, Sonny retaliated with his fists. As he put it, "I've had my share of fights and I've stood up and I'm proud of the fact that I'm Jewish." For him, that identity includes philanthropy, involvement in temple activities, and pride in the committment of Israel to "stand up and fight" for its survival. Louis Lefcourt, a New York accountant who grew up in Brooklyn and played for CCNY in the mid-1930s, captures similar themes while highlighting his own sense of Jewish specialness. "Being Jewish," he notes, "keeps reminding me that I am a member of a most extraordinary race who have contributed greatly to the entire world." For him, concern about "our struggles and our problems to survive throughout history," rather than formal religious practice, define his Jewishness.[52]

The stories of these men span the full chronology of the second generation. They are proud Americans, many of whom served their country during World War II and who all went onto successful careers after basketball as businessmen, stockbrokers, educators, and coaches. Regardless of their religious backgrounds or patterns of observance, they are also proud Jews who are aware of their people's past. Connected to an historical memory that includes the Holocaust and the survival of Israel, their own lives are also part of a Jewish-American historical memory that is just as significant in shaping their identity. Growing up as the children of East European immigrants in communities that were overwhelmingly Jewish, they created for themselves, sometimes with parental approval, often without it, their own world within a world—a meaningful life in which sport and physical activity played an important role. Here, with basketball at its center, both at Jewish community centers, public schools, and settlement houses, they learned about American values, tried out new identities, thought new thoughts, challenged their roots, and made choices—all within Jewish bounded space. Their story demonstrates the possibilities for living in the United States as Americans in ways that do not deny a real Jewish presence and a fierce pride in being Jewish. It is a heritage worth the attention of those who worry about the future of American Jewry.[53]

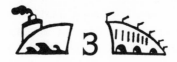

Jews and Professional Basketball, 1900–1950

ON January 7, 1948, the Chicago Stags came to New York's Madison Square Garden to play their Basketball Association of America rivals, the New York Knickerbockers. Loyal Knick fans who subscribed to the club's monthly *Knick Knacks* and daily readers of the *New York Times* and the Brooklyn *Eagle* knew full well that the game carried special import for at least one Chicago ballplayer, Max Zaslofsky. As Ben Gould reported in the *Eagle*, "it's Zaslofsky night in the Garden"—a gala testimonial sponsored by the Brownsville Boys Club to honor "as great and outstanding an athlete as his community ever produced." Noting that Max, a charter member of the club, "is a hero to Brownsville Boys club kids," Gould recounted his career from his days at Lewis Wallace JHS, Thomas Jefferson High School, and St. John's University, adding that his teammates and opponents over the years have included other neighborhood greats such as Hy Gotkin, Harry Boykoff, and Sid Tannenbaum.[1] George Sullivan, who repeated much of the same story for his Knickerbocker subscribers, reported that more than "1500 neighbors and friends from Brownsville" were expected to turn out for the game to honor the 6'2", 175 lb. "Chicago Ace." Max's "Brooklyn pals" were looking forward to a good time. As the Stags' leading scorer, averaging almost 15 points a game, their old friend was ready to oblige. Without question, Sullivan concluded, Zaslofsky "is putting the Brownsville section of Brooklyn on the basketball map."[2]

Obviously Sullivan hadn't heard of Jammy Moskowitz, Nat Krinsky, Sammy Kaplan, Moe Goldman, and a host of other Jewish boys from Brownsville, outstanding amateur and professional ballplayers who Max doubtless thought of when he contemplated his own basketball future. In fact, rather than putting Brownsville "on the basketball map," Zaslofsky's night in the Garden represents a watershed of several overlapping experiences—the decline of a significant Jewish presence in professional basketball, its transformation from local affair to national entertainment spectacle, and the waning of tightly knit ethnic communities that produced its Jewish ballplayers. While it lasted, playing professional basketball brought them the opportunity to earn a living and contact with a larger Gentile world. Depending upon time and circumstance, such experiences both heightened prejudice and helped mitigate it. Regardless of the outcome, along the way they became culture heroes in their own communities for people both proud of their Jewish connections and eager for American acceptance.

I

In 1910, Max "Marty" Friedman, a product of New York's Lower East Side, began playing professional basketball for a team in Newburgh, New York, franchised in the Hudson River League. Although we know that Friedman received $5 for his first league game, he left no account of the action. A recent history of professional basketball allows us to recreate the scene. Friedman, at 5'7½", did not look short when he took the court with his fellow professionals, none of whom were taller than six feet. The court, approximately two-thirds the size of a standard basketball court today and temporarily lined on whatever flooring existed, was located in an armory or town hall. The baskets may have had backboards, instituted to keep spectators from interfering with the ball, or they may have been freestanding affairs. The court likely was surrounded by a wire or rope cage from 10 to 35 feet high. Designed to keep spectators and players apart, cages assured that the ball was always in play. Although this innovation meant that the game proceeded with few interruptions (a 40-minute contest typically took an hour to complete), it did not assure a fast pace. Without 24-second clocks and with no rule requiring an offensive team to cross mid-court within ten seconds, teams prided themselves on their ability to hold on to the ball until a sure shot—either a one-handed lay-up or a two-handed set shot—was available. Center jumps held after each free throw or field goal also dictated a slow game. Although the local Newburgh newspaper may well have reported the game's outcome, it's unlikely that Friedman's debut, his team, or even his league received any additional coverage by the press. Two years later, when the Hudson River League folded and Marty went to play elsewhere, only those people closely connected to the sport would have noticed.[3]

Well into the 1920s, professional basketball, as Friedman experienced it, a local sport, poorly financed and publicized and predominately centered in the Northeast, attracted young Jewish men from New York, Philadelphia, and other eastern cities who first learned the game in neighborhood settlement houses and playgrounds. Although hardly as dominant as Jews were to become in the game in the 1930s, their experiences in this world of independent barnstorming teams and loosely organized, unstable leagues brought them local attention, contact with a Gentile world, loyal ethnic followings, and the opportunity to earn a living, all accomplished while playing a game they loved.

The careers of basketball's "Heavenly Twins," Marty Friedman and Barney Sedran, typify the itinerant and ephemeral nature of early professional basketball. Much like the early days of professional baseball, the lure of better money and the inability of leagues to prevent contract-jumping or guarantee satisfactory year-long contracts encouraged players to move from team to team. Over the course of a fifteen-year professional career, often with Friedman at his side, the dimunitive Sedran, at 5'4", a perennial scoring leader and playmaker, labeled by Nat Holman as "the brainiest player I ever saw," played for ten different professional teams in six different leagues. Teams he played for won league championships ten times, including four New York State league titles with the Albany club. Sedran also found the time to play for four independent clubs, including the renowned New York Whirlwinds. No different was the peripatetic Friedman, who played for at least eight teams during his seventeen years as a professional.[4]

Quite frequently, Marty and Barney played for more than one team at a time. During the 1920–21 season Friedman played for five different teams. On two, he teamed with Sedran to win the championships in the New York State and Interstate Leagues. Sundays found him with Sedran and Holman and the New York Whirlwinds. So complicated were the lives of these itinerant ballplayers that, in one instance, scheduling confusion rather than their reputation for graceful play resulted in their nickname. Already playing on two teams in different leagues who had coordinated their schedules to avoid conflicts, they were advertised to appear with a third team. Unaware of the situation, they didn't show up. As Friedman remembers, the promoter who tried to use their names to attract customers told newspaper reporters that they had reneged on their committment. Although they denied the charge, one reporter sarcastically named them the "Heavenly Twins" who could do no wrong.[5]

By their own accounts, these two stars of the early professional game made reasonable livings as ballplayers. Playing virtually every night of the week and sometimes twice on Sundays and usually paid by the game, Friedman's top salary averaged about $125 a month. Sedran recalls doing substantially better, pulling down close to $200 a month even in his first years as a professional. Eventually he became the game's highest paid player, once earning $12,000 in a single season. More typically, their teammates, like the majority of those men who played professionally, found the $15 to $75 they earned a game a substantial supplement to income from their regular jobs.[6]

Whenever they took the court, whether in or out of cages, and regardless of the pay, professional basketball's pioneers played a rough brand of basketball. Sedran, for instance, insisted that his contemporaries certainly thought of shooting jump shots but decided that the style of play simply made attempting them too dangerous. "It was suicide," he remarked, "to shoot for the basket with your feet off the ground because you'd be lucky to come down alive." Two-handed set shots were less risky. "That way," as Sedran put it, "it was much safer to take the belt you knew you were going to get."[7] According to one account, so popular was rough play that, on more than one occasion, boisterous spectators joined the battle. During one road game for the Wonder Workers, a Carbondale, Pennsylvania, team, Friedman recalled that Sedran, his backcourt partner, was being particularly harassed and punched by an opposing player. In retaliation, Marty told Barney to run by him at full speed and "as the bully boy came alongside me I stepped in front of him and down he went." Incensed by the tactic, avenging fans rushed the court. "By some miracle," Marty noted, "someone pulled the light switch and turned off the lights. I grabbed Barney and pulled him down on the floor and there we were on our hands and knees" until the police came and restored order.[8]

While cages prevented such incidents, they did not reduce the game's violent quality. Although most of his career was not played in the cage, Nat Holman's description of the early game provides a vivid sense of its roughness that explains why he and other players wore steel-lined pants especially designed for professionals by A. G. Spalding and Brothers:

> When chicken wire was used to enclose a court instead of rope netting, the game was even rougher. I wore the heaviest pads I could get. It got so bad that one sporting goods company designed special metal reinforced trunks to protect the players. To keep the wire from giving way, there were two by four timbers around the court about three feet from the floor. It was a common practice to hit an opponent hard and drive him into the boards to slow him down. . . . Then with the cage shaking and the floor swaying and the fans in the gallery tossing peanuts and pop bottles on the court and their language searing you on both sides, you would step up and try to shoot a foul. Surprisingly, we had no bad injuries—nothing worse than somebody getting most of his teeth knocked out.[9]

Rough play on the court and the "searing" rantings of home-town fans occasionally were accompanied by anti-Semitic outbursts. Friedman remembers experiencing ethnic slurs especially when he barnstormed through the midwest. Nat Holman recalls only infrequent occurrences, always instigated by opposing team fans and never by any players. Ira Streusand, however, one of Marty and Barney's settlement house teammates who played college ball for NYU and professionally in the Hudson River and Eastern leagues, found prejudice quite prevalent. "I ran into anti-Semitism everywhere, from my first collegiate game until I retired from basketball. I don't know how many times I heard, 'get the little sheenie.'"[10]

It is difficult to assess the meaning of these scattered reminiscences about anti-Semitism. Although Sedran, Friedman, and Holman were among the game's best players, they and other second-generation Jewish ballplayers who participated in professional basketball prior to 1930 were a distinct minority of those who made a living playing the sport. Playing alongside men from different ethnic and religious backgrounds and, for the most part, on teams representing small towns scattered throughout the northeast or on barnstorming teams that traveled throughout the country, basketball brought them into contact with peoples and places far different from the urban Jewish enclaves where they first learned the game. Neither their recollections nor the brief newspaper accounts of their careers tell us if their appearances in Carbondale, Newburgh, Turner Falls, Massachusetts, or Trenton, New Jersey, reinforced the popular anti-Semitic ravings of a Henry Ford; or the prejudice evidenced by colleges and universities that restricted Jewish admissions; businesses and professions that limited opportunities; or the United States Congress that enacted restrictive immigration laws, stopping the steady flow of East European Jewish migration to America. Nor do we know whether their hard play, skill, and talent unconsciously challenged racist stereotypes and subtly contributed to a lessening of prejudice, especially for people who may have had no personal contact with Jews before they came to watch a basketball game.

Depending upon time and circumstance, both outcomes were likely. More certain, however, is the adulation and pride other Jews took in the success of their own kind. Although these men rarely publicly declared their attachment to Jewish culture or religion (Sedran, in fact, shortened his more ethnic sounding name from Sedransky), their exploits on the court filled the dreams of Jewish youngsters. They also made good copy for Jewish spokesmen, eager to encourage assimilation without denying ethnic connections, who appropriated them as symbols of Jewish possibility. Nat Holman's professional basketball career clearly illustrates this reality.

A dominating player from his days in the settlement houses and at Commerce High School, the 5'11" Holman became professional basketball's superstar in the 1920s. Like Sedran and Friedman he began his career playing for a number of different teams, even occasionally suiting up with the "Heavenly Twins" on teams representing Bridgeport, Connecticut, in 1917 and Albany, New York, in 1920 and 1921. During his last year at Albany, all three spent their Sundays with the New York Whirlwinds, a team put together by Tex Rickard, the famous sports promoter who hoped to bring the professional game to New York's Madison Square Garden. Rickard's experiment failed, but a two-game series split between the Whirlwinds and another independent professional barnstorming team based in New York, the New York Celtics, brought out professional basketball's largest crowds to that date. Two weeks later, Holman signed on with the Celtics, the only Jewish player on a team that dominated the sport for the next decade and that became one of the few teams selected for membership in basketball's Hall of Fame.[11]

Full-time basketball coaching responsibilities at CCNY, which he assumed in 1919, no doubt complicated any plans Holman might have had to play for teams other than the Celtics. In one instance, he even found it difficult to juggle his careers as player and coach. Scheduled to play with the Celtics against a Northampton, Massachusetts, team that had recruited Sedran and Friedman for the occasion, Holman was abruptly called back to New York to attend to his collegiate duties. Luckily the "big crowd of over 600 fans" who turned out for the game witnessed a brilliant display by the "Heavenly Twins" as the home-town team pinned a rare loss on the New York five. More likely, how-ever, the fact that Holman and the other Celtics, including Joe Lapchick, Johnny Beckman, Dutch Dehnert, and Chris Leonard, earned guaranteed yearly salaries up to $10,000 assured their loyalty.[12]

Playing for only one team hardly cut Holman's court time. Dressed in green tops that prominently displayed a large shamrock, Holman and his Celtic teammates barnstormed throughout the country and also participated as a franchise in several eastern professional leagues that came and went in the early 1920s. During the 1922–23 season the team began as an entrant in the Eastern League, switched over to the Metropolitan League centered in New York, and then, when that circuit floundered, pulled out and went on the road. Between September and April the Celtics toured 13 midwestern and northeastern states, winning 193 of 205 games. Wherever they played, they brought out the crowds. By one estimate over 500,000 people saw them play on this tour. So well known were the Celtics that the 1925 *Reach Basketball Guide* declared that every game against them "is for the world champion-ship. . . . [I]f a team beats them they claim to be the new champions." In 1926, the Celtics made a southern swing through Florida and Tennessee, playing in places like Jacksonville and Chattanooga and, according to one account, "giv-ing southern lovers of the game a sight of the quintet they had often heard about but had never seen." Closer to home they played everyone from the Harlem Renaissance to Brooklyn's Nonpareils, dazzling fans with their sharp passing and tight defense and giving local Jewish boys ample opportunity to follow Holman's exploits.[13] That same season the Celtics joined the first truly national professional basketball league, the American Basketball League (ABL), which in its brief five-year history fielded teams in Detroit, New York, Boston, Washington, Chicago, Philadelphia, and Buffalo. Both in that year and in the following campaign, the team swept to league championships before disbanding. Holman briefly joined the New York Hakoahs, the ABL's new franchise in New York, for his last full season as a professional.[14]

Known for his shooting ability, defense, and passing skills, Nat was described by one sportswriter as "an arresting and tense figure . . . an artist . . . direct[ing] the short passing, weaving, meshing, game" who "revolution-ized basketball."[15] Nowhere was he more "arresting" or popular than among contemporaries and young Jewish boys growing up in neighborhoods like the one that had produced basketball's best-known player. When I asked mem-bers of the Basketball Fraternity if they had any heroes when they were grow-ing up, invariably Nat Holman led the list.[16] Reporting Nat's accomplishments as the "scintillating star of the Celtics and noted coach of the basketball team at CCNY" for readers of the *National Jewish Monthly* in 1928, Irving Weiner pointed out that "it is on the East Side, where he was born, that Holman finds his most fervent and loyal supporters. Among the schoolboys downtown . . . where basketball is the foremost sport among our boys," Weiner continued, "he is a greater idol than any athlete. . . . Let his name be mentioned in the auditoriums of the school where he went and the boys will raise the roof with their shouts and cheers."[17]

For Weiner and others concerned with the image of immigrants and their children as Americans, Holman was idolized for more than his basketball brilliance. Equally important to the *Monthly* was his status as an "intellectual," defined by his love of the theater and his particular interest in the works of Ibsen and Molière. Holman's accomplishments on and off the court, Weiner hoped, made him an appropriate symbol for those who understood the possibilities of sport as a middle ground. Comparing him to athletes of classical Greece, he pictured Nat as a role model capable of breaking down anti-Semitic stereotypes that characterized Jews as unfit for American life because of their supposed physical weakness. Holman, Weiner implied, helped mitigate prejudice and encourage American acceptance. For Jews, Nat's success became inspiration for their own dreams. Able to balance intellectual pursuits traditionally associated with Jews with athletic excellence in a sport especially suitable to "Jewish lads whose quick and alert minds prove sufficient to triumph over muscle and brawn," he became a symbol of American Jewish possibility.[18]

Similar themes emerge in a story about Holman that appeared in the *American Hebrew*. Written by Elias Lieberman, one of Nat's elementary-school teachers and the magazine's chief writer on assimilation, "The Holman Family of Athletes" located Nat's success in his ability to fuse ethnic and family values with distinctly American traits. Describing the exploits of Nat, Morris, and Aaron Holman, Lieberman exclaimed that "this is the story of three brothers, Jewish young men, whose careers are an example to the youth of America for clean living, fair-playing, bull-dog tenacity on the athletic field and a militant idealism in pursuit of cultural and civic aims as well." Impressed not only by his athletic ability but by his "dignified bearing" as "a man of culture," his "well-enunciated speech" and "poise," Lieberman attributed Nat's development into a Jewish version of America's muscular Christian to his people's inherent "love of learning," their "endurance under stress," and also to the Americanizing experiences of the settlement house. Instrumental here were not only Nat's own involvement but also the influence of the oldest of the four Holman brothers, Jacob, who, according to Lieberman, played sports for club teams at the Educational Alliance and became "the guide, philosopher, and friend" to his younger brothers and "helped them plan their lives successfully." "It is through his wise leadership," Lieberman concluded, "that each of them made a mark not only in athletics but in scholarship. His influence may also be traced in the clean, high-minded Americanism of each young man."[19]

In Lieberman's hands, Holman appears as a fully assimilated American Jew, transformed by his own effort, Jewish tradition, and American reform into a quintessential American man capable of serving as a role model not simply for Jewish immigrant children but for any American boy. This prescriptive imaging is not surprising in a paper like the *American Hebrew,* an organ representing the views of respectable, middle-class German Jews who were intent on assimilating their East European brethren as quickly as possible, thus assuring themselves and a larger Gentile world that these recently arrived

Jews posed no threat. Although Harry Litwack, Babe Adler, Dudie Lynn, and others who remember Holman as their hero neither read the *Hebrew* nor spoke of Nat in such specific terms, their own lives are testimony to his appeal as a model of assimilation for second-generation youth who yearned for American success.

Holman's status among a particular segment of second-generation Jews emerged at a time when he and other Jewish ballplayers were a distinct minority in professional basketball; only occasionally playing on teams located in communities with large Jewish populations. In fact, prior to the late 1920s, club and community basketball provided far more opportunity to watch Jewish ballplayers than the professional game. Still, the very fact that professional basketball was minor-league sport rooted in local urban neighborhoods and small towns made Holman's success seem accessible to others with similar dreams. Originating during Holman's heyday and extending into the 1930s when professional basketball, at least in the East, truly became a Jewish sport, the stories of Jammy Moskowitz and the Phildelphia SPHAs illustrate these possibilities while also providing entrance into the last period of significant involvement of Jewish players in organized professional basketball.

II

Jammy Moskowitz's professional basketball career is detailed in his memory and the scrapbooks he kept as a young man.[20] Like Holman, one of his heroes, Moskowitz first established his basketball reputation in neighborhood school yards and in the gymnasiums of Jewish community organizations. Brownsville residents were able to follow his exploits in local newspapers from his early days with the Junior Invincibles. By 1923 they knew that Jammy had led Commercial High School to the city's Public School Athletic League title while being named by the Brooklyn *Eagle,* along with four other Jewish players, to its all-borough team. Playing for the Labor Lyceum Center five against such teams as the Brownsville YMHA or Brooklyn's Hebrew Educational Society (HES) at the Lyceum's home court on Sackman Street or at the HES on Hopkinson Avenue, Jammy led his team to one win after another during the winter of 1923. The Brooklyn *Eagle,* the New York *Daily Mirror,* and other local papers carried the results of such contests in their daily sports pages and even the story of how Moskowitz acquired his nickname.

When Jammy started playing for pay in 1924, then, he already possessed a public identity with local Jewish fans who appreciated his "nerve . . . and wicked eye." Over the next eight years, he plied his talent for a host of professional teams in and around the New York area. Some, like Lou Gehrig's All-Stars, barnstormed up and down the East Coast. Others, like the Knights of St. Anthony's and the New York Hakoahs, participated in organized professional leagues. Jammy even found the time to play for teams in a department-store league. Jammy got paid for every game he played, making from $15 to $75 an evening, depending upon the size of the crowd and on whether his team won or lost. Along the way he pursued a degree at New York's Savage School for Physical Education and then taught and coached basketball at Brooklyn's James Madison High School while also acting as mentor for the Brooklyn College of Pharmacy five.

Through it all, Moskowitz attracted a loyal following of Jewish fans who eagerly applauded his exploits on the court. So popular was he that in March 1924 the Knights of St. Anthony's, a Metropolitan League team representing Brooklyn's mixed Italian and Jewish neighborhood of Greenpoint, asked Jammy to join them. As he recalls it, the Knights sought him not only for his talent, but because they wanted a "Jewish fellow" to attract Jewish people to their games. One local paper confirmed Jammy's memory, reporting on the eve of his debut that "tomorrow evening will be a big night for the Jewish basketball fans of Greenpoint as their season's pride, Harry Moskowitz, known on the court as 'Jammy'. . . lines up with the Knights against McDowall Lyceum at the Greenpoint court." So impressive was Jammy's start with the Knights that a later article, on a game with a team from Mount Vernon, noted that Moskowitz, "will again be the center of attention for the Knights. He made such a great showing in his initial appearances that practically everyone will have their eyes on the new sensation. The Jewish fans throughout Brooklyn are enthusiastic over the great showing of the young Jammy and a great following will be out to root for him."

Jammy played a few more games for the Knights, including a smashing victory over the Cleveland Rosenblums, a team sponsored by a Jewish businessman which soon was to become the premier team in the newly formed ABL and which featured a lineup that included Marty Friedman and Benny Sedran. Less successful was a 34–17 loss to the famed Celtics. Nevertheless, one reporter noted the significance of the encounter for Jewish fans. On the court at the same time were Holman, "the greatest Jewish sensation in basketball and the young 'Jammy'. . . who bids to some day hold the crown of being the greatest of Jewish stars."

Over the next few seasons, Jammy asserted his claims to royalty. During the 1925 season, he joined the Nonpareils, a Jewish club team from Brownsville, first organized in 1922, that made the move to big-time basketball in 1925. The Nonpareils, who established themselves as one of the game's best independent professional squads, also included Nat Krinsky and Davey "Pretzel" Banks, the son of a Lower East Side pretzel maker who eventually became one of Holman's Celtic teammates. Although his commitments to other teams allowed him to play in only 18 of the team's 31 games, Moskowitz was the team's fourth highest scorer.

Anticipating the Nonpareils' success for the 1925–26 season, one newspaper reporter tabbed the squad as one of the best in New York. Playing as an independent, the "Nons" expected to take on the usual local fives in the Metropolitan League, independents like the Celtics, the Harlem Rens, and Lou Gehrig's All-Stars, as well as every club comprising the new ABL. By March, the "Nons" had posted a 20–2 record, including two wins over the Rens, one over the Celtics, and a victory over the Visitation Triangles, noteworthy less for the 39–24 thrashing the Italian neighborhood squad received than for the fact that the proceeds of the game, attended by 2000 fans, went to the Matzoh Fund established by the Nonpareils to help "the needy of Brownsville during Passover."

Jammy put in his minutes for the "Nons," not always in a starting role. At a time when distinctions between amateur and professional status were less critical than they are today, he also starred for the Greenpoint YMHA Hebrews, touted as "one of New York State's leading amateur teams." Somehow he even found an occasional free evening to play for Lou Gehrig's team, although obviously not on nights when "Columbia" Lou led his charges against the Nonpareils. Recognized by one reporter as "one of the leading professional basketeers in the East," Jammy so impressed Marty Friedman, then in his first year as player-coach of the Cleveland Rosenblums, that the Jewish basketball legend tried to sign him up.

Jammy turned down the opportunity, postponing his ABL debut while pursuing the typical vagabond life of professional basketball players. During the 1926–27 season, he continued his duties as a part-time teacher, assistant football coach, and head basketball coach at Madison while playing on seven different teams, including the Springfield, Massachusetts, YMHA. Hired for a game against the Howitzer Athletic Association of Bennington, Vermont, Moskowitz led his new teammates to a 52–24 victory, scoring a game high of 18 points. As one Springfield paper reported, although local fans could not expect to see Jammy every Saturday, "it's a lead pipe cinch that when the Hebrews [Springfield] are tackling a tough one . . . the Brooklyn boy will be in a local uniform." Later in the season, Jammy led Springfield to nine straight victories, including a Christmas day triumph over his own Greenpoint Hebrews before 1500 fans, the largest crowd ever to watch a game at the Springfield YMHA.

Jammy's last five seasons as an active player were highlighted by his appearances for various ABL teams, most prominently in 1928–29 for the New York Hakoahs. Coached by Nat Holman, who also played, and Davey Banks, both of whom joined the club after the Celtics disbanded, the Hakoahs played a full league schedule and a host of independent teams. The ABL was not dominated by Jewish players. Only 19 of 101 players on club rosters for the 1927–28 season were Jewish. But the Hakoahs were invariably referred to as its "Jewish" team.[21] Reporting on an Hakoahs' victory over the Richmond Association in Richmond, Indiana, for instance, the local paper applauded the play of Banks, Holman, and Moskowitz in the "all Jewish professional league basketball team's" victory over the home team.

Crowds outside of New York came to see the Hakoahs because of Holman, including a monstrous outpouring of 4500 fans who filled Chicago's Broadway Armory to watch the hometown Bruins defeat the New York squad by a 25–22 score. Still, Jammy had his moments. According to 1928–29 league statistics, Jammy played in 25 league games and scored 99 points, putting him among the top third of the league's scorers.[22] Playing one of its many games outside the league, the Hakoahs, led by Jammy, defeated Vic Hanson's All-Americans 31–20 before a Syracuse crowd of over 2000. According to one account, Moskowitz was the architect of the victory. Obviously unaware of the jam-sandwich origins of his nickname and oblivious of the fact that he was only 5'7", one Syracuse sportswriter put it this way: "'Jammy' they call him. And jam them he did. Straight down the throat of the basketball rim." And in a league game against the Trenton Bengals, played on the Hakoahs' Brooklyn home court at Arcadia Hall, one partisan reporter, testifying about Moskowitz's "proven play," noted that Jammy was the only "Brownsville boy on the team" with a "large personal following," which desires "to see [him] in the line-up at all times."

Moskowitz played with the Hakoahs for one season and then switched over to the independent Newark Hebrews. Although he remained an active player for club and YMHA teams through 1932 and still grabbed an occasional headline in local sports pages as "one of the greatest Jewish players in the game," more and more he devoted his time on the court to coaching. On his way to becoming one of the legendary coaches of New York high-school basketball at Madison, where many of his players were second- and third-generation Jewish boys, Jammy also piloted the Brooklyn College of Pharmacy from 1929 to 1938. Long before stories about steroids and cocaine began sharing the sports page with accounts of basketball games, Jammy received billing as the "chief druggist" as he led his all-Jewish five to victories over local college fives and to the championship of the Eastern States Intercollegiate Pharmacy League in 1930 and 1932. One New York Jewish paper recognized the 1932 championship by publishing a picture of Jammy and his team with a caption that proudly proclaimed, in both Yiddish and English, the achievements of "a sporting club of Jewish students."

Although Jammy Moskowitz received his share of basketball awards and honors, he is not in the Basketball Hall of Fame. In part, that's what makes the rich detail of his story so important for understanding both the involvement of young second-generation Jews like himself in the game and the attention they received in Jewish communities. Moskowitz never made as much as Holman or Sedran, but he played a game he loved and earned a good, if erratic, salary, supplementing his regular employment as a school teacher. Although he was not in any traditional way a practicing Jew, he retained a strong sense of cultural and historical Jewish attachment, both as a young man and as an adult. Clearly, here was a man whose very presence reminded loyal second-generation Jewish fans from aspiring working-class neighborhoods that it was possible to succeed in America without denying obvious and proud connections to one's ethnic roots.

Philadelphia's Jewish fans who flocked to watch their SPHAs vicariously shared similar experiences, cheering for a team that began as a South Philadelphia Jewish social club and that became one of the dominant teams in professional basketball. Much like the Dux, the Nonpareils, and countless other semi-professional clubs, the SPHAs took shape in 1918 when a group of South Philadelphia Jewish boys who had joined together as youngsters in settlement house games and at South Philadelphia High School continued to play together. Named for the South Philadelphia Hebrew Association, a neighborhood social club that sponsored them, the SPHAs quickly broke affiliation with the club but kept the handle. Wearing uniforms that brazenly announced their Jewishness—tops embroidered with the six-pointed Mogen David and the Hebrew letters samech, pey, hey, and aleph—the team, also known for a short time as the "Wandering Jews" because they had no home court, played against all comers and participated in the Philadelphia League.[23]

A collection of local community professional teams similar in composition to New York's Metropolitan League, Philadelphia League clubs played each other for small guarantees based on paid admissions from friends and neighbors who came, as they did in New York, to watch young men they knew play basketball and to dance afterward. The SPHAs dominated the competition. Harry Litwack, who later played for them, recalls that he first became interested in the game that shaped his life by watching his boyhood heroes. Fourteen years old in 1921, Harry's first job was to set up the chairs in Auditorium Hall, two blocks from his house, where the team played their Thursday-night home games. Harry received 25 cents plus free admission for his labors. As he remembers, neighborhood loyalty to the team was strong and every young Jewish kid in the neighborhood aspired to be on it.[24]

Part of this attachment was due to the fact that the SPHAs were always winners. Throughout its history, Eddie Gottlieb made sure of that. Gottlieb was born in the Ukraine, came to New York as a child, and moved to Philadelphia in 1907 at the age of nine. Although never known as an outstanding basketball player, Eddie learned the game in Jewish neighborhoods on Philadelphia's south side, went to South Philadelphia High School, and in 1918 organized, played, and coached the SPHAs. Sometimes called "Gotty's Goal Gatherers," the SPHAs, under Gottlieb's direction and led by Chick Passon, Babe Klotz, Davey Banks, and "Doc" Lou Sugerman, overwhelmed their competition, winning three consecutive Philadelphia League titles between 1922 and 1925.[25]

The Philadelphia League collapsed after the 1925 season but the SPHAs continued their winning ways. Gottlieb, sometimes called the "Mogul," and by all accounts a basketball visionary who would later coach and eventually own the Philadelphia Warriors of the National Basketball Association, reorganized the team for the 1925–26 season. Adding two non-Jews to the lineup, 6'7" "Stretch" Meehan and Tom Barlow, the SPHAs played in the newly formed professional Eastern League and continued to barnstorm against independent clubs. Highlights of the season included a league championship, two wins in three games against the Original Celtics, two victories over the Harlem Rens, and a series of triumphs against teams in the fledgling ABL, marred only by a loss to the league's eventual champions, the Cleveland Rosenblums. Although somewhat biased, Abe Radel, a SPHA member, writing in the 1926 *Reach Basketball Guide,* correctly declared the SPHAs as "one of the greatest, if not the greatest combinations in basketball history."[26]

Over the next few years, Gottlieb renamed the SPHAs the Philadelphia Warriors and entered them as a team in the ABL. When that league collapsed at the close of the 1931 season, he revamped the SPHAs again, staffing them solely with Jewish players from Philadelphia and New York including Cy Kaselman, Harry Litwack, and Moe Goldman. This team dominated eastern professional basketball for the next sixteen years. After winning championships in still another version of the Eastern League during the 1932 and 1933 seasons, the SPHAs joined a newly reconstituted ABL. Primarily consisting of eastern teams, the ABL, along with the midwestern National Basketball League (NBL), passed for what was major league professional basketball until the advent of the Basketball Association of America (BAA) in 1946 and the NBA in 1949. During its heyday, the SPHAs, also called the Philadelphia Hebrews when on the road, played from 75 to 100 games a season. Barnstorming all over the East, they won six league championships while never finishing lower than third in the ABL. Each year at Christmas, they packed into Gottlieb's nine-passenger Ford and headed off on a brief midwestern tour that took them to such places as Oshkosh, Wisconsin, Akron, Detroit, and Chicago. Several times they returned to the Midwest in March to participate in Chicago's World Tournament, open to all professional basketball teams.[27]

While success on the court brought out the fans, ethnic connections intensified their loyalty. From their inception, the SPHAs, by their uniforms and their personnel, were always strongly identified and promoted as a Jewish team from a Jewish neighborhood. Never was this identification more powerful than in the 1930s and 1940s. Harry Litwack, who says "it was an honor to play with the SPHAs," asserts that the team consistently sold out its home games to loyal fans who followed the team "like it was a religion." As he recalls, "it wasn't just a South Philadelphia team. It was the team for all Jewish people in Philadelphia. We were the best around and we were Jewish. It was an amazing combination." Moe Goldman, who joined the SPHAs in 1934, one night after completing his last game as a City College All-American, confirms that Gottlieb successfully built and promoted his team to bring out Jewish crowds. "Shikey" Gotthoffer, a New York boy who grew up first on the Lower East Side and then in the Bronx, and who was an SPHA teammate of Goldman's in their championship ABL days, insists that the team became "the darlings of Philadelphia." "Even William Penn's statue on top of City Hall," Gotthoffer suggests, "used to bow to us . . . everytime the SPHAs came by." Less dramatic but just as sincere, Yock Welsh, who began play with the team in 1930, recalls that "it was pinnacle of athletic achievement just to be able to wear that jersey with those four Hebrew letters on it. The money meant nothing. The goal was to play for the greatest basketball team in the world, the South Philadelphia Hebrew Association."[28]

As with Jammy Moskowitz, the SPHAs' success and their open identification as Jews provides another example of the power of sport as middle ground in the ongoing process of assimilation. Jewish fans who attended their games relished the triumph of ethnic heroes who symbolically served as manifest signs of their own American possibilities. They did so in a familiar setting that reinforced ethnic attachments and connections to American consumer culture by the social opportunities offered by a night at the gym. Playing at the Broadwood Hotel on Broad and Wood streets, the SPHAs, like other amateur and professional teams, always offered dancing as part of the 65-cent admission price for men and the 35 cents charged women. For at least one season, team member Gil Fitch also doubled as the bandleader. After finishing the typical 45-minute game played in three 15-minute periods, Fitch hurried back to the dressing room, threw on a tux, and joined his ten-piece orchestra that featured Kitty Kallen, a young singer just beginning her career. Dave Zinkoff, who earned a national reputation as the game announcer for the NBA's Philadelphia 76'ers in the 1970s, recalled that sometimes the demand for music was so great that Fitch occasionally didn't have time to shower, making for a "very pungent orchestral leader."[29] "The Zink," one of Gottlieb's lifelong friends, was the public address announcer and publicity man for the SPHAs. Above all, he remembers them as a rich community experience that bound people together in common affection for a Jewish basketball team. Even the game programs he put out, "The SPHAs Sparks," reflected it. Each one included basketball statistics, player profiles, and also birth, engagement, and marriage announcements of SPHAs players and their fans. For those who required additional incentive to purchase a copy, Sam Gerson, a local clothier, offered a free $19.95 suit to the person who bought one with the lucky number on it. Zinkoff, who drew the winning number at half-time, fondly recalls that "the big deal back then was to come to a SPHAs game, meet a nice girl at the dance, win the suit and get married." "It was," as he put it, "our own little society."[30]

III

What the SPHAs provided for Philadelphia's Jewish community also existed in other cities that fielded professional basketball teams in a revived ABL. Faced by collapsing franchises and the financial difficulty of maintaining any semblance of a national schedule in the face of the Depression, the original ABL suspended operation after the 1931 season and reopened in 1933 with franchises only in eastern cities. In this new version, centered in New York, New Jersey, and Pennsylvania, no team had to travel further south than Washington, D.C., further west than Scranton, further east than Boston, or further north than Harrisburgh to play league opponents. Down through 1946, when the league ceased to exist as a major professional circuit, the majority of its franchises remained centered in the metropolitan New York–New Jersey area. It was in this league, playing for teams close enough to their homes while they held other jobs, that Jews dominated professional basketball.[31]

An ABL scorekeeper's account of a 1935 game between the Philadelphia SPHAs and the Brooklyn Jewels played in Brooklyn's Arcadia Hall suggests just how thoroughly Jewish the league was in these years. From Goldman to Gotthoffer, the SPHAs coached by Eddie Gottlieb fielded an all-Jewish team. Led by Mac Kinsbrunner, the Jewels, coached by Barney Sedran, matched them virtually man for man, fielding a Jewish team that had played together at St. John's University where they had earned the reputation as the "Wonder Five" by helping the Redmen compile a 68–4 record between 1929 and 1931. Scoring the game on an official ABL program that encouraged fans to buy their clothes at Abe Stark's, "Brooklyn's finest clothing store," located in the heart of Brownsville on Pitkin Avenue, was Abie Koenig. Keeping time, as Abie's notes reveal, was Bob Greenberg.[32]

Although Koenig did not provide attendance figures, it's a good bet that the vast majority of those who came to cheer for the Jewels were loyal, local Jewish community people much like those who supported the SPHAs in Philadelphia. Between 1933 and 1942, fans in both places had much to cheer about. During these years, the SPHAs and the Jewels dominated league play, together winning seven league championships and playing in all but two title series. Although these teams consistently fielded the greatest number of Jewish ballplayers, they were not alone. A list of the league's top scorers for the 1940–41 season, for instance, shows that 36 of the 61 names listed are clearly identifiable as Jewish. Heading the list were eight Jewish players, including the league's leading scorer, the SPHAs' Petey Rosenberg. Seventeen of the 36 Jewish names on the list comprised the full rosters of the Jewels and the SPHAs. Even more telling, club rosters for the seven ABL teams that participated in the 1937–38 season show that 45 of 91 players, or almost 50 percent, were Jewish. Only two teams, the Brooklyn Visitations and the Jersey City Reds, fielded squads that were significantly under that figure. As late as the 1945–46 season, things hadn't changed very much. In that year, 71 of the league's 159 players, or almost 45 percent, were Jewish.[33]

This Jewish presence, particularly on teams located in Jewish neighborhoods, guaranteed the support of loyal Jewish fans. But it also provided opportunity for anti-Semitism, especially when teams like the SPHAs or the Jewels played on the road against teams with their own ethnic followings. Not surprisingly, those who played for the SPHAs, a team that blatantly displayed its Jewish connection, most often remember such incidents. Uniforms with Hebrew letters and Jewish stars fueled anti-Semitic taunts; especially when the SPHAs took on the Brooklyn Visitations in their tough Irish Catholic neighborhood. Eddie Gottlieb remembers Prospect Hall, the Visitations' home court, as the roughest place his team played. As he describes it, "they made the fans check their guns at the door there. They used to have a balcony that hung over the court where the spectators sat, and they'd serve the fans bottled beer and sandwiches. Whenever something would happen down on the court those Brooklyn fans didn't like, they'd send those bottles down at us." Although neither Harry Litwack nor Moe Goldman remember guns, both recall that beer bottles, occasional burns from fans who sat in the front row and touched players' legs with their lighted cigarettes as they ran by, and pin pricks from ladies' hat pins were invariably accompanied by anti-Semitic remarks. Both remember Union City as another tough place to play. On one occasion, Litwack was clubbed over the head with a Coke bottle while he and the SPHAs sat under the basket resting after the first third of an ABL game with the Union City club. Although bleeding from the head, Litwack and his teammates fought back with their fists until order was restored. Harold Judenfriend, who played briefly for the Wilmington, Delaware, Bombers when he came out of the service in 1944, recalls how uncomfortable it was to sit on the bench while his hometown fans rained anti-Semitic remarks on the visiting SPHAs.[34]

Although these stories do not suggest that professional basketball mitigated ethnic conflicts and encouraged mutual acceptance, it is important to remember that, on balance, they do not figure prominently in the remembrances of those Jewish men who played in the ABL or NBL. More so than their friends and neighbors who worked and lived solely within the confines of ethnic communities, professional basketball required them to participate in a larger American world. For the most part, their memories of that experience are positive. Invariably, they focus on the game itself, the excitement and love of competition, and the opportunity to make extra money in trying times. They also emphasize the mutual respect players of all backgrounds had for each other. Playing against the all-black Harlem Rens or teams like the Southern Collegians, an all-star team composed of former black college stars, even encouraged sympathy for the plight of American blacks. For most of the players, participation clearly diminished prejudice. Nat Miletzok put it best. Reminiscing about his playing days on the Scranton Miners, a team composed of Jews, Italians, and blacks, he recalls that there was "really love between teammates. . . . We were one big happy family. There were no blacks, no Jews, no Italians—they were just our friends." "We loved to be together," he concludes. "I wouldn't trade that experience for anything in the world."[35]

Today the decision to become a professional basketball player involves an organized, nationally televised draft of college players, financial agents, multimillion-dollar contracts, and a full-time commitment to the business of basketball. In the ABL, however, things were much simpler. Unlike professional basketball's pioneers, most ABL players, especially the Jewish ones, had attended college. But like their predecessors, they still led a vagabond existence that intertwined the itinerant life of professional basketball with pursuit of more permanent careers. Moe Goldman, who graduated from CCNY as an All-American in 1934, recalls that he was first approached about the possibility of turning pro after he played a CCNY–Temple game in Philadelphia by an emissary of Eddie Gottlieb, who arranged a meeting with the SPHAs' owner. Promised $35 a game by "the Mogul" if he would play for the Philadelphia entry in the ABL, Goldman accepted. As he put it, "it was good money, comparatively speaking." Returning to New York, CCNY closed out the season with a Saturday night game with NYU. Moe showed up the next night at Arcadia Hall in Brooklyn, where the SPHAs were scheduled to play the Brooklyn Jewels. When he attempted to enter the building as a player, the attendants refused to let him in until Gottlieb came to the door and told them that Goldman was an SPHA. Goldman picked up a uniform and warmed up with the team, fully expecting to spend the game on the bench. Gottlieb, however, had other ideas. Moe started the game at center where he became a fixture until his retirement in 1942.[36]

Although a darling of Philadelphia's Jewish basketball fans, Moe lived in Brooklyn, pursued a master's degree from CCNY, and became a public school physical education teacher, first at P. S. 41 and Boys High School and then at Tilden High School in Brooklyn where he also helped coach the basketball team. His first team there included Abe Gerchick of Basketball Fraternity fame. Along with Red Wolfe and Joel "Shikey" Gotthoffer, other New York boys who also played for the SPHAs, Goldman traveled to Philadelphia by train on Saturday night, played on Sunday, and returned to Brooklyn in time for his Monday morning classes. Since ABL teams usually played on weekends, Moe also found time to play for Wilkes-Barre in the Pennsylvania State League. After completing his day as school teacher, Moe took the Lackawanna Railroad to Wilkes-Barre, played the game, and traveled on a sleeper back to Hoboken, New Jersey, arriving in time to catch a train to New York and a subway to work. No doubt the incentive of making $75 a game plus expenses— good money during the Depression—plus his love of the sport, gave Moe the energy to manage life out of a gym bag.[37]

"Shikey" Gotthoffer recalls similar ABL experiences. Born in the Bronx and a high-school teammate of Hank Greenberg on a James Monroe basketball squad that won city championships in 1926, 1927, and 1928, "Shikey" ended up at Providence College after being heavily recruited by a number of colleges. As he tells it, revelation that he had once earned $5 playing for an independent semi-professional team when he was in high school cost him his scholarship and the chance to play college ball. Still, Gotthoffer kept his hand in basketball, helping to coach NYU's varsity and playing for $15 a game with the Yonkers Knights of Columbus. In 1932 Eddie Gottlieb bought his contract from Yonkers for $2500 and "Shikey" became an SPHA. Like Goldman, Gotthoffer played for the SPHAs on weekends and for other teams during the week. By the time he left the SPHAs, a team where he was voted the most valuable player for six consecutive years, "Shikey" topped the club's pay scale at $100 for an evening's work.[38]

Gotthoffer was among the ABL's most high-priced talent. Still a bargain by today's standards, the pay he and other Jewish ballplayers earned in the league's heyday often surpassed income from their full-time jobs and made professional basketball during the Depression attractive for those who had the ability to play. Even after World War II, before the coming of the NBA dramatically changed the professional game's structure, itinerant professional ballplayers found the game profitable. Sonny Hertzberg, for instance, one of a handful of ABL players who made it to the NBA, began his professional career in 1946 with the ABL's New York Jewels, then moved to the New York Gothams, an all-Jewish team coached by Barney Sedran, where he earned $50 a game. He and his teammates played two or three times a week, sleeping on

the road only on weekend trips. All made more playing ball than in their regular employment. As Hertzberg recalls, in a game replete with former college
players who had no time to practice together or keep in shape, the incentive
to hang on to this outside income made for extremely rough contests.[39]

One ABL ballplayer even found that his reputation as a basketball player
improved his off-the-court opportunities. Sammy Kaplan, who first reached
basketball prominence with the Dux, played for several ABL teams in the
1930s and 1940s, finishing his career in 1946 with the Wilmington, Delaware, Bombers. Urged by Dudie Lynn, chairman of the Brownsville branch of
the American Labor Party and former Dux member, to run for the New York
Assembly, Kaplan took up the challenge. His own politics, like many in his
Brooklyn neighborhood, he remembers, moved dramatically to the left in the
midst of economic depression and Nazi atrocity. Running on a platform that
called for a return to "the program of F.D.R." and as a candidate "for the people," Kaplan won both the Democratic and American Labor Party primaries
and then the general election, becoming the only state assemblyman elected
as an American Labor Party candidate. Some party officials opposed his can-
didacy because he was an athlete, yet Sammy recalls that his reputation as a
basketball player figured prominently in his campaign by providing instant
recognition with neighborhood people who were proud of his accomplishments on the court. Although lack of any party base in the legislature limited
his effectiveness, Kaplan dutifully reflected the concerns of his working-class
Jewish constituents by taking stands in support of day-care center legislation,
repeal of the Taft-Hartley law, retention of the five-cent New York subway
fare, and aid to Palestine.[40]

Between the time Kaplan played his first ABL contest in 1935, and 1946,
when he left basketball, the professional game underwent important changes.
The cage disappeared, games consisted of three fifteen-minute periods, teams
played a split season with the top finishers in each half vying for the championship, and the center jump had been eliminated after each basket. Players,
however, still saw basketball as part-time employment, managed to play for
several teams at the same time, and participated in a financial enterprise at
best described as a shoestring operation. As others have recounted in detail,
by 1949 the emergence of the NBA as the truly dominant national professional circuit reduced the ABL and NBL even further. The best players moved
on to BAA and NBA teams while ABL and NBL franchises left cities where
these new major leagues situated themselves. So precarious did the ABL
become, that in 1951, although his team had won consecutive league titles,
"Speed" Maloney, the Scranton Miners owner, attempted to solve his franchise's constant financial woes by cutting his club's roster to eight players and
reducing player salaries to $40 a game. Implementation of this plan midway
through the 1951–52 season precipitated a brief player's strike led by the
Miner's coach, Red Sarachek. Red, who was busy coaching Scranton, a team
in the New York State League, as well as serving as Yeshiva University's basketball coach and athletic director, proposed an alternative plan which called

for both visiting and home-team players to share game gate receipts. Angered by it all, Maloney traded away three players, all New York Jewish boys who commuted with Red to Scranton, and fired Sarachek.[41]

The appearance of three Jewish players on the same ABL team in 1951 was itself an oddity. By the late 1940s Jewish dominance of the ABL was in clear decline. Scoring statistics kept during the 1950 season, for instance, show that although Irv Rothenberg of the Paterson Crescents led the league in scoring, only ten of the top 36 point-getters were Jewish. Five of them, including Hank Rosenstein and Nat Miletzok, played for the league champion Scranton Miners. League rosters for the following year indicate that only 9 percent, or 11 of the ABL's 121 players, were Jewish. Nor were any of the six franchises located in New York, Philadelphia, or any large city with an appreciable Jewish population.

A scattering of Jewish players, including Max Zaslofsky, Red Holzman, and the incomparable Dolph Schayes did appear in the NBL, the BAA, and the NBA in the late 1940s and 1950s. All of these men, along with Red Auerbach, continued their association with the game as coaches, scouts, and general managers of NBA teams. By the 1960s, Jews were more likely to be found in NBA boardrooms than on the hardwood. Following an entrepreneurial tradition in basketball established by the likes of Abe Saperstein, Frank Basloe, and Eddie Gottlieb, men like Maurice Podoloff, Ben Kerner, and, more recently, Harry Glickman, William Davidson, and David Stern have played critical roles as club presidents and league commissioners in establishing the NBA as profitable capitalist enterprise.[42]

The professional game awaited the advent of the 24-second clock, the influx of black talent, and television to become mass entertainment spectacle. Its emergence as a national sport with a reasonably stable organization, year-long player contracts, a player draft, and new demands on athletes to devote all of their energies to their sports careers helps account for a diminishing Jewish presence. Sonny Hertzberg, for example, who began his professional career in the waning years of the ABL, found its part-time nature compatible with his planned career in his father-in-law's optical business. Believing that he could continue this way when he moved into the NBA, Sonny turned down an offer from the Washington Capitols and signed instead with the New York Knickerbockers, allowing him to stay close to his wife and business. After a few years, however, he gave up basketball because the full-time commitment to playing and traveling that life in the new league demanded limited his business opportunities and family life.[43]

Even more important for understanding the end of Jewish basketball, however, was the gradual disappearance of second-generation ethnic Jewish neighborhoods that produced the players and the very fruits of assimilation itself. Although Brownsville fans still made their pilgrimage to Madison Square Garden in 1948 to honor Max Zaslofsky, their world was in clear decline by 1950. Not only in New York but in Chicago, Detroit, Cleveland, and even smaller cities with Jewish populations old, ethnic neighborhoods filled with familiar reminders of an East European cultural and religious Jewish heritage slowly gave way to the forces of aging and assimilation. The incredible degree to which second-generation American Jews moved into the middle class and beyond—a phenomenon tied both to post–World War II boom and to the drive and determination of individuals, which has caught the eye of anyone who has examined assimilation in America—figures prominently here.[44] Fulfilling beyond expectations the dreams and hopes of their parents, these children of immigrants, as Sonny Hertzberg made clear, less and less looked to sport even as a supplementary means of subsistence. Increased economic opportunity coupled with suburbanization and the simple passage of time eroded inner-city Jewish enclaves that had been at the heart of the assimilation experience for the vast majority of first- and second-generation East European Jews. First-generation immigrants died. Their children, who became American Jews in the vibrant ethnic world that existed between the wars, slowly but clearly moved away from that world—both geographically into the suburbs and culturally into a mainstream materialistic society that they had helped shape. The process, well under way by the late 1940s, was not completed overnight. By the end of the 1950s, however, gone were the tightly knit ethnic communities full of immigrant parents and grandparents and the bustling energy of their American-born children—a world of extended family and secular Jewish life in which young men played basketball and carved out their American futures within a Jewish setting—the kind of world needed to support basketball clubs like the SPHAs or the Jewels.

Recounting the saga of the SPHAs and the days when Jews were an important part of professional basketball, Dave Zinkoff, Eddie Gottlieb, Moe Goldman, "Shikey" Gotthoffer, and others, in the tradition of other great Jewish storytellers, display a sense of timing and hyperbole that make us laugh about and envy the experience they enjoyed. As part of the larger story of Jewish involvement in basketball from the turn of the century through World War II, they help capture a sense of the close attachment and pride a significant segment of working-class Jewish communities had with the sport and its Jewish practitioners.

Ethnic pride in sports heroes was hardly unique to Jews. And as we will see, the occasional college Jewish football star, the Jewish boxer, or the Jewish major-league baseball player provided other opportunities for such adulation that carried special significance. But always more immediate, familiar, and tied to community were the Atlas Club, the Dux, the SPHAs, and the Jewels. These local teams, easily accessible on an everyday basis to neighbors, family, and friends, provided an opportunity to witness a Jewish majority dominate an American game. For Nat Holman, the "Heavenly Twins," Sammy Kaplan, Jammy Moskowitz, Harry Litwack, and others, basketball also encouraged assimilation and provided an opportunity to experience the fruits of American capitalism and a taste of materialism and freedom that so intoxicated the second generation. Even in the onset of the Depression, when their fathers may well have been selling fruit on the corner, play for pay provided substantial supplements and at times the main income of ballplayers who were their sons.

In its own way, America's truly "national game" also provided Jewish fans similar opportunities. Long before basketball became a national entertainment vehicle it was local sport, operating on amateur and professional levels, that provided a cheap and available form of amusement totally integrated into the local community's social fabric. The chance to cheer on your friends, dance with each other, and take part in festive weekly rituals that applauded participation and enjoyment for its own sake encouraged Jewish fans to enjoy leisure time in ways that marked their own assimilation into the American mainstream. Yet they did so often in settings that reminded them of their Jewishness—by the very names of the players they cheered, by the neighborhood gyms in which games were played, and occasionally by the anti-Semitic taunts they heard. Although hardly the only events on the Jewish community social calendar, basketball played by Jewish men on neighborhood clubs and professional teams was an integral part of the assimilation experience of second-generation American Jews.

Obviously, however, involvement in basketball, either as participant or spectator, was not a critical experience for everybody. And in a society increasingly enveloped by a consumer ethic, there were many ways to spend money set aside for entertainment and leisure other than buying a ticket to watch Jewish boys play amateur or professional basketball. Curiously, one of those choices, the movies, by its contrast highlights the particular attraction basketball may have held for people involved in the complexities of becoming American.

From the days of the nickelodeons on through the talkies, Jewish immigrants and their children were especially fond of going to the movies, an art form made possible and popular by filmmakers and movie moguls who, with few exceptions, were also first- and second-generation East European Jews. Ironically, however, men like Louis B. Mayer of MGM, Adolph Zukor of Paramount, and Harry Cohn of Columbia offered cinematic images of America to landsmen that underlined the distance they tried to put between themselves and their own East European Jewish roots.[45]

The Hollywood Jews, as critic Neil Gabler calls them, "embarked on an assimilation so ruthless and complete that they cut their lives," and most important, their movies, "to the pattern of American respectability as they interpreted it." Although the visions of each filmmaker were different, only rarely did they involve any sense of the struggle of ethnic outsiders trying to survive in a "genteel America." Instead, moviegoers thrived on Cohn's homogenized American world populated by stars like Ronald Coleman, Jean Arthur, and Barbara Stanwyck, "where houses were spacious, money plentiful, style abundant, values reasonably clear, and Jews absent." They also watched Zukor's tales of sophistication and respectability and Mayer's ideal, sentimental versions of the American family brought to life in the Andy Hardy movies where Mickey Rooney, that "all-American teenager," lived in "an all-American town with his sage father and tolerant, loving mother." In short, their silver-screen depictions of American reality and fantasy, despite occasionally portrayed by Jewish actors who had changed their names, in no way, shape, or form bore any resemblance to the ethnic world from which they came.[46]

For those Jews eager to discard all remnants of their own ethnic past, these images may have reinforced their own determination to become as fully assimilated into mainstream America as possible. More likely, most were attracted to the fantasy provided by silver-screen spectacles that allowed them to escape temporarily their daily routines. Either way, exposure to idealized depictions of American life far removed from the realities of their own existence suggested the distance to be traveled before Jews could obtain full integration. Basketball, too, provided a vision of assimilation. Unlike the movies, here Jewish spectators found a familiar and even attractive version of themselves uninhibitedly on display for all of the world to see. For roughly the same price as going to a movie, they could enjoy themselves by watching people they knew play an American game well enough to achieve local and even national attention—all in a totally familiar environment. A young Jewish boy's fantasies of becoming a Nat Holman or a Jammy Moskowitz may have been just as elusive as that of a black ghetto youngster of today aspiring to be the next Michael Jordan or "Magic" Johnson. But in the local, neighborhood context in which he watched them play, it was certainly a more realistic fantasy than any he might have imagined at a local movie house. For both adults and children, appreciation of and connection to Jewish basketball encouraged assimilation to unfold within the rich fabric of the ethnic, Jewish world in which they lived.

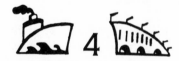

"Allagaroo, Garoo, Gara": The College Game, CCNY, and the Scandals of 1950

IN its catalogue of Jewish athletic achievement for 1935, the Detroit *Jewish Chronicle* took special note of the accomplishments of Jewish collegiate basketball players. Announcing a long list of hoopsters that included "Teitlebaum of Michigan" and the New York University's (NYU) national championship team, confidently it concluded that, "as in almost every year, basketball and Jewish stars are synonymous."[1] The *Chronicle*'s claim about the college game was not an exaggeration. Our own story of Jewish participation in both amateur and professional basketball contains scattered evidence of this fact. We know that the likes of Nat Holman, Jammy Moskowitz, Nat Krinsky, Harry Litwack, and Moe Goldman, who first learned basketball in neighborhood school yards and Jewish community centers before becoming professional stars, also played college ball. At a time when the college version was more popular than the professional, especially in the East and most notably in New York, college basketball played by the children of East European Jewish immigrants provided another outlet for Jewish identification with this American invention. In a special way, the triumphs and tragedies of one college team offer fitting postscript to this story of Jewish involvement in basketball during the first half of the twentieth century.

I

Allagaroo, garoo, gara
Allagaroo, garoo, gara
Ee-yah, Ee-yah, Sis Boom Bah
Team! Team! Team!

For more than 75 years this college cheer has been the battle-cry of the athletic teams of the City College of New York (CCNY). Between the wars, when the school's student population was overwhelmingly Jewish, this familiar chant echoed largely from the voices of Jewish crowds of students and fans. Whether watching the Beavers take on other New York college teams, an occasional YMHA team, or a professional five loaded with Jewish talent, loudly they proclaimed their loyalty to basketball teams coached by Nat Holman, a Jewish basketball legend, and dominated by Jewish ballplayers.

Jewish newspapers across the United States dutifully lauded the accomplishments of this "Jewish" team in ways that emphasized both ethnic pride and American possibility. Most emphatic was the *American Hebrew*'s Elias Lieberman. Reporting on a City victory over a Yale team in January 1917, he informed readers of his "Melting Pot" column that the game was "a striking example of real American democracy" in that it pitted a Yale team that included a son and a grandson of former presidents of the United States against a City quintet "who were either immigrants themselves or the sons of immigrants—kings of endeavor and emperors of progress." "It was a royal tussle, indeed, for supremacy of brawn, speed and skill," Lieberman concluded, "and victory, ever in league with the most powerful battalions, finally rested with the immigrant boys, the red-blooded aristocrats of America's future."[2]

Although the Jewish press took care to elicit such connections, the regular press did not always follow suit. Writing about City's 1921 squad led by Nat Krinsky, Willie Ball, Irv Lipton, and Hy Fliegel, one Brooklyn paper attributed the success of the squad to this strong contingent of "Brooklyn boys." More concerned with emphasizing community pride than ethnic heritage, the paper declared their success as proof that "Brooklyn can produce the best basketball players and that the Brooklyn lads are the most active wherever they go." Although all four ballplayers happened to be Jewish, there was no need to belabor the point to the newspaper's subscribers, who recognized these Jewish names or who knew them as neighborhood children growing up in a city with the heaviest concentration of Jews in the United States.[3] Almost two decades later, a reporter for the Staten Island *Advance,* offering an account of a 1939 game between CCNY and the Staten Island Jewish Community Center team represented by the Brooklyn Dux before a "packed Jewish Center" crowd of 600, did not have to mention that the "huge . . . widely exuberant crowd" that cheered the Dux to a 35–26 victory and the players on both teams were Jewish.[4]

Led by Krinsky and Fliegel, Holman's 1921 Beaver squad won 13 of its 16 games, many played before capacity crowds of 2000 screaming fans that packed into the school's bandbox gymnasium on 139th Street and Convent Avenue. Only a season-ending defeat at the hands of NYU, a squad also replete with Jewish players, prevented the team from playing the University of Pennsylvania for eastern college supremacy and the right to compete for the national college championship. Ticket demand for the season's finale was so great that the game was moved from City's gym to the 22nd Engineer's Armory at 168th Street and Broadway to accommodate the standing-room-only crowd of 10,000—the largest number of people to that date to witness a college basketball game in New York. Again, however, stories about the game focused on basketball, not ethnicity.[5]

By the 1930s, City, NYU, St. John's University, Long Island University (LIU), and other New York schools played many of their home games before even larger crowds at Madison Square Garden. Although professional teams attracted their own local followings, in New York and throughout the country the college game was far more popular. And although not all the fans who flocked to the Garden were Jewish, it's a good bet that on nights when City or NYU played, many were. Certainly the teams from both schools, the neighborhoods they came from, and a high proportion of the student bodies claimed Jewish connections. By the mid-1920s, over 85 percent of City's student population was Jewish. According to one estimate, almost 30 percent of all New York Jewish youth who attended college in 1918–19 went to the school. So predominant were Jewish students at NYU, that the school earned the derisive sobriquet "N. Y. Jew."[6]

Not surprisingly, both schools fielded basketball teams loaded with Jewish talent. From its very first team in 1907, NYU was led by Jewish basketball players. Joseph "Gid" Girsdansky, the son of Max Girsdansky, one of the founders of the Socialist party in the United States, played on that team. Later he became its first Jewish captain and helped the 1909 squad to a 12–0 mark. Down through the 1930s, Ira Streusand, Alfred Levy, Maclyn Baker, George Newblatt, Sammy Potter, Sid Gross, Willie Rubenstein, Milt Schulman, and Robert Lewis helped NYU consistently field nationally ranked teams. Rubinstein, Gross, and Irwin "King Kong" Klein led the 1934 Violets to an undefeated 16–0 season. Joined by Len Maidman and Milt Shulman the following year, NYU went on to post an 18–1 record en route to a national championship. CCNY proved even more impressive in its number of Jewish players. Over Nat Holman's 38 years there as a coach, 438 of his 518 players—some 83 percent—were Jewish. Jewish concentration peaked in the 1930s when over 90 percent, or 142 of 157 names listed on team rosters, were Jewish. Only in the 1950s did the percentage of Jewish ballplayers fall below 85 percent.[7]

At schools populated by the children of Jewish immigrants who dominated not only its athletic life but also its significant cultural and intellectual pursuits, there was no apparent need for those closest to it to announce such involvement as self-evident proof of Jewish physical prowess, reason for Jewish pride, or evidence of successful assimilation. Year after year, throughout the 1920s and 1930s, the pages of NYU and CCNY student newspapers and yearbooks extolled the achievements of Jewish student-athletes with never a mention of what was obvious to anyone who attended the college or followed its athletic teams—these were Jewish boys playing sports for schools full of Jews. When Nat Krinsky graduated from CCNY in February 1921, for instance, newspaper articles praised his athletic and scholastic achievements, noted his presidency of his senior class, his charter membership in Lock and Key, the senior honorary society, and his fine record as a student without ever mentioning his religious or ethnic identity. Announcement that he was planning to return to his alma mater, Boys High, to teach history, implicitly under-lined for anyone reading the story the Jewish roots and background of "one of the most versatile and gifted athletes that Brooklyn ever sent to City Col-lege."[8]

Every generalization has its exception but here it simply underlines the Jewish milieu offered by City College. One of Nat's teammates, Willie Ball, had entered City College as Willie Bolowtofsky. By the end of his freshman year he had changed it to Barlow and in his junior year to Ball. Although there is no way of knowing why Willie changed his name, his classmates at City took notice of it when he graduated. Next to his picture in the *Microcosm,* the editors wrote: "First Bolowtofsky, Barlow, then Ball/ A few more years/He'll have no name at all." Whether or not Willie's name-changing signified, as it did for others, distaste for one's ethnic identity and a commitment to rapid assimilation or a practical step to counter discrimination in the workplace, among his Jewish friends in the Jewish world of CCNY it provided opportu-nity for jest.[9]

Although no school could boast as high a percentage of Jewish basketball players or students as NYU or CCNY, other colleges also showcased Jewish talent.[10] Noting the fourth consecutive victory of New York's St. John's Uni-versity over Holman's Beaver quintet before an enthusiastic crowd of 12,000 at New York's Madison Square Garden in January 1931, Harry Glantz calmed any fears his West Coast *B'nai Brith Messenger* readers might have had that the Catholic sons of Irish and Italians playing for a Jesuit school had achieved dominance over their Jewish boys. Three of the five St. John's players "who starred" in the game, Shuckman, Posnack, and Begovitch, were "our lads," he informed them. Actually, Harry's count was off by one. Although Begov-itch was not Jewish, St. John's other four starters were. Between 1928 and 1931, led by Max Posnack, Max Kinsbrunner, Albert "Allie" Shuckman, and Jack "Rip" Gerson, the Redmen posted a 68–4 mark. During the 1931 season, this "Wonder Five" went 21–1. After leaving college, this same quintet, as we know, became the professional New York Jewels, following the lead of other Jewish collegians who went on to play in the American Basketball League and in other professional leagues.[11]

Whether they formed the core of Claire Bee's celebrated LIU teams in the late 1930s, starred for the University of Southern California and the University of California at Los Angeles (UCLA), led the University of Syracuse Orange-men to a national championship in 1920, or, like Eddie Wineapple, played well enough for the Friars of Providence College to be the first Jew to be named an all-American, it seemed, as one reporter predicted at the outset of the 1932 season, that "every school in the country will have one or more out-standing Jewish boys on their basketball team." Litanies of their names and accomplishments appearing regularly in the Jewish press, along with the accounts of Jewish achievement in other sports, announced Jewish success in American games and reminded readers by example after example that the children of immigrants were fully assimilable.[12]

Occasionally these stories provided more than opportunities for Jewish pride or proof of American credentials. The collegiate career of Sam Balter, for instance, who played ball for UCLA between 1927 and 1929, encouraged one writer that better relations between Jew and Gentile were possible. Commenting on the college graduation of this Detroit native who went on to play on the U. S. Olympic team that won a gold medal in basketball at the 1936 Olympics, Harry Glantz remarked that his departure from UCLA "will bring to a close the sensational record that has been such a source of pride to Los Angeles Jewry." Balter's brilliance on the court and his election as the first Jewish captain of a major sports team at UCLA were only part of the reason. His outstanding academic achievement as an English major also played a part. Most important, however, Balter had consciously worked to better relations between Jews and Gentiles while proving Jewish ability to participate fully in all that American life had to offer. As Glantz put it:

> . . . Balter has devoted his college career toward the establishment of friendly relationships between Jews and Gentiles by showing that a member of the Mosaic race can excel in a number of activities. "Captain Sammy," as he is affectionately called both by students and faculty because of his outstanding athletic record, has also distinguished himself in other lines, and has demonstrated that a Jew can readily rise to a position of prominence, prestige and affection, and attain real Gentile friendship and respect.[13]

Such appraisals of the significance of Jewish collegiate basketball players rehearsed themes about assimilation and ethnic pride also apparent in the accounts of Jewish professional basketball players and even of those athletes who never ventured past the hardwood and concrete courts of local school yards, gymnasiums, and community centers. By the 1950s, however, such accounts became rare as Jewish boys playing college basketball diminished and as assimilation proceeded apace. The story of CCNY's last great team underlines this fact.

II

In many ways, Nat Holman's 1949–50 CCNY basketball squad was typical of other teams he had put on the court in previous years. Like them, they prided themselves on tenacious defense, hustle, and a precision passing, fast-break game. In the tradition of CCNY athletics, these players were acclaimed as students first and athletes second; young men who recognized college as the necessary steppingstone to American success and acceptance. Echoing City's own publicity releases, a 1951 New York *Herald Tribune* editorial reminded its readers that students went to City College to get an education. Its athletes received no special privileges nor athletic scholarships. Although players regularly missed practices to go to classes, the *Tribune* reported the sacrifices were worth it as "the scholastic record of CCNY athletics is unsurpassed." Noting the academic and professional achievements of past basketball players, the paper concluded that Holman's present group was following in a "tradition that combines athletic success with scholastic honors that had its start back in the days when Bernard Baruch played baseball at CCNY."[14] As in those days, most of the players were Jewish. Although two black ballplayers, Ed Warner and Floyd Lane, played key roles on the team, the rest of the squad, led by Eddie Roman, Al "Fats" Roth, Herb Cohen, Irwin Dambrot, and Norm Mager, came from ethnic Jewish neighborhoods that dotted the city's five boroughs.

Finally, like all Holman-coached teams, the 1949–50 Beavers were winners. Playing an independent schedule against other New York City schools and inter-sectional contests with UCLA, Oklahoma, and the University of California, the squad compiled a regular season record of 17–5, good enough to be ranked among the nation's top thirty college teams. Here similarities end. In the space of one year, this City team experienced both the greatest success and the worse despair that any college basketball team has ever known. Over a three-week period in March and April 1950, City became the first and only college basketball team to win both the National Invitation Tournament (NIT) and National Collegiate Athletic Association (NCAA) basketball championships. Less than twelve months later seven of its players were indicted for taking bribes to fix basketball games in the most famous gambling scandal ever to hit college sport.[15] Public interpretations of these events offer interesting perspectives on the situation of American Jews and their quest for assimilation.

First, the Beavers conquered the NIT. Today a competition confined to second-tier college teams unable to qualify for the NCAA tournament, in 1950 it was *the* post-season college basketball tournament at a time when the college game was the most popular version of the sport. Long before the National Basketball Association became the centerpiece of basketball spectator interest, the NIT—scheduled at the mecca of college basketball, Madison Square Garden—was the single biggest attraction in the world of organized basketball. In existence since 1938, the tourney had expanded to a twelve-team field by 1950, including the unseeded Beavers and four of the nation's top-ranked teams: Bradley, Kentucky, Duquesne, and St. John's. Needing four victories to win the title, City, led by Warner and Roman, barreled past San Francisco by 19 points and then astonished Adolph Rupp's third-ranked Kentucky squad by a score of 89–50. The consistent scoring of Dambrot and Warner and the fine defensive play of Eddie Roman were key factors in handing Kentucky its worst defeat in the school's history. Although the margin of victory was far less, City also contained Duquesne, its semi-final opponent, setting up a championship game against the nation's number-one ranked team, the Bradley Braves.

Buoyed by a capacity home-town crowd, an unheard-of day off from Friday classes, and a city radio audience tuned into Marty Glickman's play-by-play account the Beavers took the floor of the "old" Garden on Eighth Avenue between 49th and 50th Streets to do battle with their midwestern foes. For Stanley Cohen, whose semi-autobiographical account of this City team best captures its meaning and spirit, the Garden itself, City's other "home" court, symbolized New York and the neighborhoods that produced its basketball players. "The old building," as he describes it, with its steep bank of stairs, its steel posts that often obscured full view of the court, its theatre marquee and massive size, "resembled the maw of the city in which it was built. It was a hard, gray, angular structure as rugged and as tough as the streets of Harlem or the back alleys of the Bronx."[16]

At the outset, even the Garden didn't seem enough to counter the smooth Bradley attack. Led by its All-American forward Paul Unruh and a fiery guard named Gene Melchiorre, the Braves raced to a 14-point lead. When Norm Mager took over for Al Roth, however, the game began to turn. By half-time, the Beavers were within three. With five minutes to go City took the lead for good. The final score was 69–61, earning the Lavender squad its first NIT title and a bid to the NCAA tournament.

In 1950, only eight teams, chosen from different parts of the country, played for the NCAA championship. Once again City had the luxury of playing all of its games in Madison Square Garden. Opening against the nation's second-ranked team, the Ohio State Buckeyes, City prevailed by the slim margin of 58–57. Two nights later, it made it past North Carolina State, ranked fifth in the nation, by a 78–73 score. All that was left between the team and destiny was a rematch against the Bradley Braves, who had won the western half of the draw in two hard-fought games in Kansas City.

Tired but determined, the Braves surprised the Beavers before a capacity Garden crowd by opening in a zone defense. Although Bradley took an early lead, City, led by Mager and Roth, put the Beavers ahead at half by a 39–32 score. Ahead by five with two minutes to go, City's Cinderella season hung on the brink as the Braves' press, engineered by Gene Melchiorre, brought Bradley to within one, at 69–68, with 40 seconds left in the game. Only a last-second shot by Irwin Dambrot sealed the victory for New York's most famous public university, a triumph engineered by young men born and bred in its neighborhoods.

Victory celebrations not only connected the city to the team but also emphasized a vision of assimilation that extolled the promise a free and open democratic society offered all those who asked no favors and who were willing to work hard to achieve their goals. Before a spontaneous celebration of over 6000 students at City's campus at 137th Street and Convent Avenue, the school's president, Harry Wright, introduced the players to their adoring fans and praised them as boys "who came here to study, not to play basketball." Observing that Norm Mager was unable to attend the rally because he was taking a midterm exam, Wright noted that he was "proud of the team and what it has done for the college. I want to emphasize that the players have been given no scholarships to play ball. They are not imported mercenaries. I am particularly proud of their high scholastic ratings." Quite simply, the *New York Times* called City's victories "a vindication of the democratic process."[17]

Although local newspapers noted that Ed Warner was the first black ballplayer ever to win the NIT tournament's most valuable player award, no mention was made that it had been a predominantly Jewish squad that had twice taught midwestern Gentiles a thing or two about basketball.[18] In a city with a large Jewish population, in a college known for its high proportion of Jewish students, and in a sport where Jewish success had been commonplace, perhaps there was simply no need to belabor the obvious. Just as likely, the absence of attention to ethnicity, especially in contrast to the constant mention of race, suggests something about public perceptions of Jews and blacks in 1950. Although blacks still had a long way to go to achieve full integration in sportsworld, let alone mainstream society, second-generation Jews and their children already had made substantial progress. The sons of seltzer-truck drivers and tailors, these young men from ethnic Jewish neighborhoods who availed themselves of the fine and free education City College offered, appeared destined for better things. However they might have felt about themselves, implicitly they stood as symbols of the fulfillment of all that America supposedly offered their grandparents and their parents before them. Winning the NIT and NCAA tournaments were marks of that accomplishment.

Stanley Cohen, then a high-school junior with basketball dreams of his own, poignantly recalls that his own sense of celebration emphasized similar themes. At City College, Cohen's own immigrant father, ten years earlier, without "a word of English on his tongue" and "without a dollar in his pocket" gained admission to a school "that had produced its full share of Supreme Court justices and scientists and writers." Cohen believed that "so long as there was a City College, every kid in New York knew he had a chance . . . only New York chose to offer free education to sons of immigrants and grandsons of slaves." The Beavers' victory over the Bradley Braves symbolized the success made possible by such opportunity. As he put it, how else to understand the importance of what transpired on the Garden floor, where "five street kids from the City of New York—three Jews and two blacks . . . whale[d] the shit out of middle America"?[19]

The fact that they were coached by Nat Holman, a man whose very style, speech, dress, and reputation demonstrated the seemingly endless possibilities for creating one's own version of the American Dream, encouraged such perceptions. Praised for his coaching achievements by Manhattan's borough president, Robert F. Wagner, who made him an honorary Deputy Commissioner of New York, Holman, rumors had it, already was dreaming of taking his boys to the 1952 Olympic Games as the United States basketball team. More immediately, Howard Hobson of Yale, head of a committee to choose the basketball team that would represent the United States at the 1951 Pan American Games, asked Holman and his best seven players to form the core of that squad. Clearly such dreams and reality only fueled beliefs that anything was possible in America, even for those whose ancestors came from Russia and Poland.[20]

The Beavers never made it to Brazil. Aware that the Pan American games conflicted with 1951 NIT tourney dates and pressured by Ned Irish, the owner of Madison Square Garden, who was concerned about losing his top draw, CCNY president Wright rejected Hobson's offer, claiming that his students would miss too much schoolwork if they made the trip. As it turned out, more serious concerns intervened that made both international travel and tourna-ment basketball problematical for "Nat's boys."[21]

Unaware of what was to transpire, Holman looked forward to the upcom-ing season. In a letter to Ed Hickcox, secretary of the National Basketball Hall of Fame, Nat acknowledged that the key to success for the 1951 season relied on his ability "to put the emphasis on team spirit and pride in accomplish-ment." "I hope," he concluded, "the boys will do as well for me next year as they did this year." Certainly, the school's sports information department that produced the Beavers' basketball guide expected more of the same. Replete with a cover picture of a beaming Holman being carried off the Garden court after the NCAA title game, it also contained optimistic appraisals of the young team's chances to repeat. A 21-game schedule with only five away games and 14 dates at Madison Square Garden certainly figured in these forecasts. But well past the midway mark of the 1950–51 season, City boasted only an 11–7 record. Returning home by train from a solid win against the Temple Owls in Philadelphia on February 17, Holman learned what he may well have sus-pected was the cause of his team's inconsistency. A New York City detective informed him that when the train pulled into Pennsylvania Station, Eddie Roman, Al Roth, and Ed Warner would be arrested for conspiring with gam-blers to "fix" basketball games against Missouri, Arizona, aned Boston Col-lege.[22]

Anyone familiar with the history of big-time college athletics knows that only a month earlier several Manhattan College players had been arrested on similar charges. Those close to the college basketball scene knew of rumors that had persisted since the early 1940s about players "dumping" games for money. Paid by bookmakers and gangsters for their services, players "shaved" points in order to keep the margin of victory within the boundaries estab-lished by bookmakers. Several Brooklyn College ballplayers had been found guilty of such practice as early as 1945.[23] And at least one person close to the CCNY team worried that some Beavers might also be involved. Bobby Sand, who played for Holman in the late 1930s and who became his chief assistant coach in 1944, recalls that rumors of a fix for the Missouri–CCNY game filled the Garden as the Beavers took the court on December 9, 1950. Heavily favored by 14 points, City fell apart in the first half and trailed by 31–14 at the intermission. Concerned that members of the first team were purposely not playing their game, Sand urged Holman to put in his second-string in order to press Missouri into mistakes. Holman, however, stayed with his frontliners. City lost 54–37. Roth, Warner, Roman, and Layne collectively shot only 18 percent from the floor. According to Sand, so certain was he that gamblers had reached his players that he asked Frank Thornton, an economics professor and a member of the college's Intercollegiate Athletics Committee, to launch an investigation. As he tells it, however, and as others have confirmed, Holman and Sam Winograd, the school's athletic director, stifled any inquiry on the grounds that there was no hard evidence to warrant one.[24]

By February, however, the truth about the Missouri game and many oth-ers became everyday news. In a story well told elsewhere, over the next eight months college basketball players from all over the country were implicated

Kutsher was not alone in suggesting broader explanations for what had occurred. Part of the reason commentators paid little attention to Jewish connections lies in the Cold War concerns of that era. At a time when Joseph McCarthy claimed that American strength was under attack from internal Communist infiltration, others wondered whether the country had the moral strength and determination to fight Communist threats abroad, be they in Korea or elsewhere. In the face of such problems, no area of American life, including sports, was immune from scrutiny.

The dismissal of 96 West Point cadets from the military academy in August 1951, including virtually the entire football team, for cheating on exams underlined concern that America's youth lacked the moral strength and integrity to face up to perceived international threats. Similar concern was echoed by those closest to the basketball scandal. Frank Hogan took no joy in his achievement. Noting how "disagreeable and sickening" the whole investigation had been, he told one reporter, "It just makes you wonder what has happened to our moral values."[31] Nat Holman, who, along with Bobby Sand and other CCNY officials was eventually investigated by the New York City Board of Higher Education, found culpable in not taking steps to stop corruption, and eventually reinstated, offered a similar appraisal in an article that appeared in *Sport Magazine* in November 1951. Although Holman acknowledged that corrupt recruiting and admission practices were part of the problem, he blamed the involvement of his players on "a relaxation of morals in the country." Noting that the affair had "been like a death in the family," Holman himself took no part of the blame, arguing that he repeatedly warned his boys about gambling and point shaving. His City players, Nat concluded, were "all basically good boys." "Unfortunately," however, "when they were asked the big question, they were not quite strong enough. They needed toughness!"[32]

The simple fact that the scandal was national in scope also helps explain the lack of specific attention to Jewish involvement. One former City player recalls that after Kentucky and Bradley players were indicted, earlier press attention to Jewish connections that he remembers disappeared. Clearly one didn't have to be Jewish or grow up in New York to be a participant. As Judge Streit and others argued, the pressure on athletic programs throughout the country to produce winning teams both to raise money and to attract alumni support created an atmosphere of corruption which implicitly encouraged athletes to participate as well.[33]

Although these explanations sufficiently account for the lack of discussion of Jewish involvement in the scandal, other matters that touch directly on the question of Jewish assimilation also deserve attention. Anti-Semitism hardly disappeared in the United States in the 1940s, in the world of sports or elsewhere. During a 1946 Wyoming—CCNY game at the Garden, Nat Holman had to be restrained by his players from going after Wyoming coach Everett Shelton, who was directing anti-Semitic remarks toward City's Jewish players.[34] Still, World War II softened its edges. Jews, Irish, Italians, all Americans—even blacks, albeit in segregated units—were needed to repel fascism and preserve democracy. No less a united effort seemed required to turn back the supposed new menace of Communism, as it appeared in the late 1940s. While such sentiments did not mean the end of discrimination, especially for black Americans, nevertheless a more tolerant public perception toward ethnic groups certainly existed. For the most part, Jewish conspiracies no longer served as viable explanations for either international politics or athletic corruption.

These were also the years when the struggle of second-generation Jews to make a better world for themselves and especially for their children yielded obvious signs of fruition. While places like Brownsville and the Grand Concourse, which produced City's Jewish ballplayers, still maintained an obvious ethnic flavor, they were already in decline. In New York and elsewhere, economic success and social mobility propelled many Jewish residents out to the suburbs and away from close, everyday reminders of where they and their ancestors had come from. In short, as the ethnic world of the second generation began to disappear and Jews became more fully assimilated, they became less vulnerable to attacks that set them apart on the basis of religion or ethnicity.

Not surprisingly, when the United States Committee Sports for Israel (USCSI) decided to honor their president, Nat Holman, on the occasion of his 80th birthday in 1976, the program of his testimonial dinner did not mention the 1950–51 scandal. Instead, Nat was proclaimed as "a rare person—a Jew, an American, an individual who has enriched us all." Especially noted were his efforts to introduce basketball to Israel and to help the USCSI raise money in order to send American Jewish athletes to compete in the Maccabiah Games.[35] That same year, similar praise was bestowed on Holman at the 25th annual awards ceremony of the Max Kase Sports Lodge of the B'nai B'rith in New York. Here, among New York City officials, lodge members, and a host of sports celebrities including Hank Greenberg, Moe Goldman, and Whitey Ford, Nat received the Founder's Award. In a tribute written for Holman, Haskell Cohen, past president of the lodge and active as a sports publicist and journalist for the Jewish Telegraphic Agency, compared him to King Saul. Quoting from First Samuel 9:2, Cohen suggested that what was said of the biblical figure was also true of "King Holman": "And there was not among the children of Israel a goodlier person than he; from his shoulders and upward, he was higher than any of the people."[36]

Sanitized versions of Nat Holman's past were neither surprising nor inappropriate at Jewish banquets honoring his life accomplishments. Proclaimed as successful American and proud Jew, Holman epitomized what many East European Jewish immigrants had hoped for their children. Even the stain of the scandal could not diminish what his own experiences in basketball, from his childhood days on the Lower East Side to his achievements as one of basketball's greatest players and coaches, signified for those who applauded the successful assimilaton of American Jews.

America's National Game

ON August 6, 1903, Abraham Cahan devoted part of his daily advice column for New York's growing East European Jewish immigrant population in his Yiddish-language *Jewish Daily Forward* to America's National Game. "A father wrote us," Cahan's "Bintel Brief" began, "that he thinks baseball is a wild and silly game. His son, who is in the upper grades, loves to play. Most of our immigrants agree with this father. But he does not make his point in an effective or interesting way." As the "father" put it:

> It makes sense to teach a child to play dominoes or chess. But what is the point of a crazy game like baseball? The children can get crippled. When I was a boy we played rabbit, chasing each other, hide and seek. Later we stopped. If a grown boy played rabbit in Russia they would think he had lost his mind. Here in educated America adults play baseball. They run after a leather ball like children. I want my boy to grow up to be a mensh, not a wild American runner. But he cries his head off.

Cahan's reply may well have surprised the "father" and others like him who were less quick than their children to adjust to the rhythms of American city life, which included new attitudes about time and play and new opportunities for both formal and informal leisure at the ball park, nickelodeons, or in the streets. Noting that "half the parents in the Jewish quarter" have the same problem, he advised, "let your boys play baseball and play it well, as long as it does not interfere with their education or get them into bad company. . . . Bring them up to be educated, ethical, and decent, but also to be physically strong so they should not feel inferior." "Let us not so raise the children," Cahan concluded, "that they should grow up foreigners in their own birthplace."[1]

Cahan's view that baseball encouraged confidence and taught immigrant children about being American echoed the words and actions of Yekl, his fic-

tional creation of the novella of the same name, published in 1896. Yekl, a
Russian immigrant to New York, proclaims his love of boxing and baseball as
badges of his new American identity. Chided by one fellow sweatshop worker
that professional boxers and ballplayers are uneducated, Jake, as he calls himself in America, reminds his critic that while most boxers "are not ejecate,"
baseball players were. As for his love of American sports, Jake is clear of its
significance. "Once I live in America," he asserts, "I want to know that I live
in America. Dot'sh a' kin a man I am. One must not be a greenhorn. Here a
Jew is as good as a Gentile. How then, would you have it. The way it is in
Russia, where a Jew is afraid to stand within four ells of a Christian?"[2]

Anyone familiar with Yekl's battle to balance his love of America with his
Russian Jewish past knows that Cahan was well aware that picking up a bat
and ball or becoming acolytes of Christy Mathewson or Babe Ruth did not
guarantee an easy path toward assimilation. Enthusiasm for baseball as una-
dulterated American experience was quite capable of provoking real conflict
between immigrant parents and their children who disagreed about how to
live in America. Baseball, however, Cahan understood, also provided immigrant children acceptance and identity as Americans. Whether playing it in
neighborhood streets and school yards or following the exploits of major-
league heroes, baseball, by its vary status as America's National Game, symbolically permitted an immediate sense of belonging to a larger American
community in ways that few other sportive experiences provided. It is this
theme that defines the game's special contribution as middle ground in the
process of becoming American.

I

Although Abraham Cahan and the "father" he addressed in his Bintel Brief
column had different opinions about baseball, both recognized that the children of Jewish immigrants in turn-of-the-century New York avidly played the
game. Although basketball remained the most popular participatory team
sport and the one rooted deeply in the social and community fabric of Jewish
neighborhoods, in New York and elsewhere, baseball, both informally played
in the streets and in more organized settings, always attracted its share of Jewish youth.

Encouraging this interest were capitalists of leisure and social reformers.
Of all the sports offered to immigrants as vehicles of assimilation, baseball
received special attention.[3] Magnates like A. G. Spalding, eager to promote the
country's only truly national professional sport, declared baseball America's
immaculate conception—a game invented by Americans that personified "all
the attributes of American origin [and] character." Touting baseball as democratic sport, a game open to all, that combined teamwork and individual
excellence in pursuit of victory, he proclaimed its ability to teach "American
Courage, Confidence, Combativeness; American Dash, Discipline, Determination; American Energy, Eagerness, Enthusiasm; American Pluck, Persis-

tence, Performance; American Spirit, Sagacity, Success; American Vim, Vigor, Vitality."[4] Sportswriters like Hugh Fullerton offered their own contribution, arguing that baseball was "the greatest single force working for Americanization," the game most loved by "foreign born youngsters," and more capable even than schools for teaching "the American spirit so quickly." Organized play reformers and settlement house workers who saw baseball as one of a number of opportunities for reforming the character and values of immigrant children also encouraged their charges to take up bats and balls. As one settlement house worker in a Jewish immigrant Chicago neighborhood put it, "we consider baseball one of the best means of teaching our boys American ideas and ideals."[5]

Whether baseball actually carried the American freight its promoters claimed is doubtful. Any young black man, for example, could well have questioned rhetoric that announced the sport as open to all based on merit and competition when professional major league baseball remained closed to members of his race until Jackie Robinson broke the color line in 1947.[6] Even so, immigrants and their children who read about the game in their daily newspapers or who played it in streets and school yards could not escape rhetoric that told them it did or news of major league players whose success on the diamond in a game glorified as distinctively American seemed to underscore values deeply rooted in the national mythology. This American attraction and children's own control over the game predominates in reminiscences about baseball and Jewish immigrant life prior to 1920.

Especially in large cities, where most Jewish immigrants settled, young Jewish boys found more organized opportunities to play basketball, a game that required less space than baseball. Undaunted, they improvised their own game. Reflecting on his childhood years on Rivington Street, in the heart of New York's Lower East Side, George Burns, Jewish comedian and entertainment legend, unintentionally recreates this informal world of street play. "Our playground," Burns remembers, "was the middle of Rivington Street. We only played games that needed very little equipment, games like kick-the-can, hopscotch, hide and go seek, follow the leader. When we played baseball we used a broom handle and a rubber ball. A manhole cover was homeplate, a fire hydrant was first base, second base was a lamp post, and Mr. Gitletz, who used to bring a kitchen chair down to sit and watch us play, was third base. One time I slid into Mr. Gitletz; he caught the ball and tagged me out."[7]

Not every young Jewish boy was so fortunate to have a Mr. Gitletz on the block, but scattered through the autobiographies of individuals who spent their youth as the children of immigrants is ample testimony of the sense of freedom, opportunity, and participation in something distinctly American that baseball provided. Reminiscing about his childhood, Morris Raphael Cohen, philosopher, scholar, teacher, and son of devoutly orthodox Russian Jewish immigrants, recalled the significance of his family's move from Manhattan's Lower East Side to Brooklyn's Brownsville in 1893. Although his new neighborhood did not have a public library, "the lack of reading matter" for his fertile mind was "fully balanced by the opportunity to play with the Jewish boys of the neighborhood, far more than I had done in New York or even in Minsk. It was in Brownsville that I was introduced to the various forms of boy's baseball. Sometimes we played with only two forming a side or even with three of us playing what was known as 'one o' cat.' . . . I played for a considerable time in the fall of 1893, and I began again early in the spring of 1894—the first year of my life in which I had anything like a proper share of exercise and outdoor existence."[8]

Cohen's interest in baseball went beyond informal participation in the streets. At a time when the Brooklyn "Trolly" Dodgers played not far from his home, at Eastern Park at Pitkin Avenue and Powell Street, he recalls going "almost every afternoon to watch part of the game through the various cracks in the fence." Known to his friends as "Giant" because of his loyalty to the New York team despite his new residency in Brooklyn, he recalls the thrill of sneaking into a game between Brooklyn and New York and watching his "hero, Jouett Meekin, pitch and hold the Brooklyn team down."

Although he attended less than a dozen major league games in his lifetime, Cohen admits that he never was "able to get over [his] early emotional loyalty" to the Giants.[9] Uncharacteristically for a philosopher, he does not delve deeply into his adolescent fascination with baseball or any connection it might have had to his gradual break with the religious orthodoxy of his parents. But it is not unreasonable to imagine that both playing the game and passionately following it provided Cohen immediate entrance into an American world. Like many other children of immigrants, baseball helped him become American by affording participation in a sport that enjoyed universal acceptance as the American game.

Similar testimony comes from men who became professional baseball players. Al Schacht, whose passion for the game troubled his orthodox Jewish mother, recalls a boyhood in which baseball encouraged his American connections. A journeyman major leaguer whose diamond antics as "The Clown Prince of Baseball" would put the "San Diego Chicken" to shame, Al was one of six children born to Russian immigrants Sam and Ida Schacht. Born in 1892 in a two-room tenement apartment on New York's Lower East Side, he remembers that his mother, whose father was a rabbi, ruled the family and was not happy about his American aspirations to become a major league baseball player. Like Eddie Cantor, the legendary vaudevillian and movie star who grew up on the Lower East Side and who remembers that the worst name his grandma called him was "you baseball player you," Schacht notes that his mother "didn't know nor did she care much about baseball. Since my life-long dream was to be a baseball player," he recalls, "my mother was sure that I would grow to be a bum or loafer. Baseball was not an honorable profession to a woman with such a background." Nor did "names like Honus Wagner, Christy Mathewson and Ty Cobb," Al's American heroes, impress her.[10]

If Ida wasn't impressed, Al surely was, especially after his family moved to the Bronx, where he spent his childhood. Like many other Jewish immigrant families who first settled in overcrowded, inner-city ghettoes, the Schachts escaped to new neighborhoods where Jewish builders constructed apartment houses for their own kind in places where there were more open spaces for youngsters to play. Here, Al discovered baseball.

"My love for baseball began," he recalls, "when I was a kid growing up in the Bronx. I was always crazy about the game." Using makeshift baseballs—including smaller versions of the sock, wool, and twine balls that often passed for basketballs—Al played the game with his friends in school yards, in vacant lots that made "the Bronx much like a wilderness," and in city streets. As he grew older, his ability as a pitcher, honed in these informal ways, advanced him to the sandlots, where he played for semi-professional teams. Receiving $5 for one such effort, he turned the money over to his mother, keeping only 25 cents for himself. "After that," he remembers, "she never said too much about my playing ball."

Nurturing his love of the game was the opportunity to follow the New York Giants. "I used to walk from where I lived . . . up to the Polo Grounds with two cents in my pocket to buy a frankfurter." Standing on Coogan's Bluff overlooking the Polo Grounds, Al followed the exploits of his heroes, "Turkey" Mike Donlin, a Giant outfielder, and especially the incomparable Christy Mathewson.[11] Blond-haired, blue-eyed, and college-educated, the Giants' righthander from Factoryville, Pennsylvania, renowned for his pitching ability, was hailed as baseball's muscular Christian—in appearance and character, as one student of the game puts it, "just about everything that clean-cut young American manhood was supposed to be."[12] By the time he was 15 Schacht moved inside the Polo Grounds, selling pop and peanuts in the stands. Eventually he worked out with the Giants, occasionally pitching batting practice. With a screwball learned from Mathewson himself, Al even earned a try-out with his beloved team.[13]

You didn't have to grow up in New York or follow the New York Giants to have similar experiences. Most explicit is Harry Danning, New York Giant catcher in the 1930s, who was born in Los Angeles in 1911. For him, his brother Ike, and his father, baseball was important for defining their American identities. Danning, whose father owned a small used-furniture store, grew up in a Mexican neighborhood. His family did not observe the Sabbath nor speak Yiddish, and he was not Bar Mitzvahed. "My father," Danning recalls, "said we are not going to live as Jews. We're going to live like Americans. That was his belief." And it included a love of baseball. As Harry remembers, his father was always playing ball with the neighborhood children, making balls out of old stockings and repairing windows broken in local street games. His father's love of the game and the enthusiasm with which he applauded his sons' interest in it were for Danning critical factors in their decision to try to make it as professional baseball players. Baseball bound them together as Americans.[14]

Andy Cohen, whose career with the Giants was shorter but far more dramatic, also found in baseball common bond with his father and a fantasy of American opportunity. Andy's parents left Europe to escape the pogroms. They met and married in Baltimore and settled in Petersburgh, Virginia, where Andy was born in 1904. Born there as well was his younger brother Syd, who also attempted a career in professional baseball.

Cohen's father, a cigarmaker by trade, loved baseball. Good enough to earn a tryout with the Baltimore Orioles, he enjoyed playing catch with his boy. Unfortunately, day-to-day involvement with his son's upbringing ended when Andy was only seven. In 1911, his mother moved to El Paso, Texas, because of respiratory problems, taking her children with her. Five years later, Cohen's parents divorced.[15]

Andy grew up in a community far removed from the intensely Jewish surroundings familiar to the vast majority of East European Jewish immigrants living in eastern and midwestern cities. His memory recreates an American childhood focused on sports, school, Horatio Alger novels full of rhetoric about the self-made man and American opportunity, and dreams of becoming a major league baseball player. Although his mother was not enthusiastic about her son's goal—"What Jewish mother doesn't want her son to be a doctor or a lawyer?" Andy explains—she did support both himself and his brother as they made their way in professional baseball.[16]

Although he made his mark as the voice of the New York Yankees rather than as a ballplayer, Mel Allen's upbringing in the deep South combines elements of a number of these stories.[17] Allen came from a family that managed to maintain its orthodox Jewish background even in the wilds of Alabama. Baseball, however, linked him with his father and marked him as American.

Mel's maternal grandparents came to the United States from Russia to escape persecution, bringing his mother, Anna, when she was seven years old. Her mother came from a family of rabbis and her father, a cantor and a rabbi, continued his work in America. Allen's paternal grandfather, also a Russian émigré, settled in West Blocton, Alabama, in the late 1880s. Nestled in the heart of Klan country, this rural coal-mining town, located in Bibb County some 35 miles outside of Birmingham, was populated by Russians, Poles, Italians, and blacks. Like the few other Jewish immigrants to the area, he worked first as a peddler. Eventually he earned enough money to open his own store.

Allen's paternal grandparents were hardly as devout or centered in a Jewish community as his maternal grandparents were, but they were no less serious about maintaining their Jewishness. Remembering her grandfather as a black-bearded, imposing man who stood 6'4", Esther Kaufman, Mel's sister, recalls the efforts he made to practice his religion. When he peddled his wares from farmhouse to farmhouse, for example, he often shared the supper table with his Gentile customers, making a point to bring his own glass dishes and to eat only their dairy products. Concerned that the few Jewish families in Bibb County could not obtain kosher meat, he arranged for a schochet to come from Birmingham once a week for ritual killings of a few chickens and a steer. And, along with the other Jewish men in Blockton who at times needed another man to make a minyan, he would think nothing of hopping into his horse and buggy and driving ten miles to find a tenth man for services in a small synagogue attached to his house and store that he built. Here, on the high holidays, Bibb's Jewish families camped out in the yard and the house to celebrate the Jewish New Year together.

Mel's father, Julius Allen Israel, born and raised in this setting, helped his father peddle wares and eventually became successful selling fashionable ladies' clothing. His children described him as a "Jewish yokel," who as a young man drove their grandfather mad by spending his time fishing, playing baseball, and even dating Christian girls. Julius, along with his wife, who was more knowledgeable about Jewish custom and law, nevertheless was serious about his religion and about raising his children as Jews. The Israels kept a strictly kosher home, attended orthodox synagogue regularly, and celebrated all the Jewish holidays. As Mel recalls, they even held Purim balls, no matter "if there were only half a dozen Jewish families around." At one point, when they lived in a small town in Walker County, Alabama, Esther remembers that each Sunday her father would pick up all of the Jewish children in the area in his car and take them to Jasper or to Birmingham for Sunday school. As any good southern Jewish mother would do, her mother would pack a lunch of fried chicken, potato salad, and chocolate cake for a picnic on the way home.

Mel, who changed his name reluctantly at the insistence of network executives when he began doing radio because they felt that Israel was "a little too all-inclusive" (he used Allen because it was his father's middle name), grew up in a religious home and was Bar Mitzvahed in 1926. His Jewish upbringing, however, posed no obstacle to his interest in baseball, and sport in general. Allen recalls playing versions of the game, including "one hole cat" as a youngster. Fondly, he remembers that his father "loved baseball," and encouraged his own interest by taking him to ballgames when he was as young as three years old. Baseball, he asserts, was "something that I grew up with."

Baseball, however, as other Jewish major leaguers who grew up in the first decades of the 20th century remember, could also produce conflict between parents and children. Phil Weintraub, who was born in Chicago in 1907 and who spent most of his seven years in the majors playing the outfield and first base for the New York Giants, received little encouragement from his family. His father owned a small butcher shop and wanted him to continue in the business. Much like Al Schacht and Eddie Cantor, Phil recalls that his "parents thought baseball players were bums." Only after he threatened to run away from home at 17 did they relent and co-sign his first professional contract. Some ten years later, Phil's fiancée introduced him to her mother for the first time. When she asked what he did, Phil proudly told her he was a ballplayer. "That's nice," she replied, "but what do you do for a living?"[18]

Better known is Moe Berg's story. Born on the Lower East Side in 1902, Moe and his family moved to Newark where his Russian immigrant parents, Bernard and Rose, struggled successfully to find a better life for themselves and their children. Moe's father opened his own drugstore. Constantly he encouraged his children to improve their minds in hopes that one day it would lead them to success.[19]

Although Moe proved himself to be a brilliant student, his intellectual pursuits went hand in hand with his love of athletics, especially baseball. After graduating from Newark's Barringer High School, he went on to Princeton, an unusual achievement for a lower-middle-class Jewish boy in a time of open quota restrictions for Jews at elite colleges. Moe worked summers as a camp counselor and Christmas vacations in the post office to earn part of Princeton's $600 annual fee. He also relied on and appreciated his parents' financial contribution. Asking for $31.90 to help cover the cost of books and supplies for his first semester, Moe began by telling his "Pa" not to "spoil your eyes on account of me" and expressed his regret in having to ask for help. "I hate like the dickens to write to you to do this but I have to, . . . My expenses are curtailed now to a minimum. If I could leave to make the money I would. Goodbye and don't work too hard."[20]

Bernard and Rose's sacrifices did not go unrewarded. Moe mastered seven languages and graduated magna cum laude. He also played a fine shortstop for an outstanding Princeton baseball team. Upon graduation, he was offered a teaching post in the school's Romance Languages department. Although he later found time to graduate from Columbia Law School and to study language at the Sorbonne, professional baseball, in the form of a contract with the Brooklyn Dodgers, won out.

Moe played for five teams over a 15-year major league career, mostly in the role of back-up catcher. His best year was 1929, when he appeared in 106 games for the seventh-place Chicago White Sox, and batted .288. Although a reliable if unspectacular player, Berg received far greater attention in the press for his mind than his baseball talent. A column by F. C. Lane, for example, proclaimed that by the age of ten the precocious Berg could read the Torah in Hebrew. Invoking New Deal rhetoric, another columnist referred to him as "baseball's one man brain trust" while still others acknowledged that Moe was an "erudite scholar" and "a ball player who had studied at the Sorbonne." Berg enhanced his reputation as baseball's resident genius when he appeared on the popular radio show "Information Please" in February 1938. On it, he stunned a nation-wide audience with his wide-ranging knowledge, naming, for example, the Seven Sleepers, the Seven Wise Masters, the Seven Wise Men, the Seven Wonders of the World, and the Seven Stars.[21]

Baseball players, if apocryphal tales have any merit, knew of Moe's exceptional brilliance long before he went on the air. While with Washington between 1932 and 1934, one of his teammates, Sheriff Harris, supposedly complained to Berg that he was feeling rather ill. As one sportswriter recounted the tale, Moe asked Harris to stick out his tongue and Harris did, "because for all anyone knew Berg had a degree in medicine too." "You have a touch of intestinal fortitude," Moe informed his uneducated teammate. "Go upstairs to your room, take it easy, don't eat anything heavy and you'll be fine." Lo and behold, the next day Harris pronounced himself healthy and thanked the amused Berg for curing his illness.[22]

Attention to Berg's intellect must have fueled Bernard Berg's disappointment in his son. Although his proud mother occasionally attended her son's games, his father never saw him play. According to Moe's brother, Samuel, their father believed that "Moe's pursuits should be elsewhere. He wanted Moe to devote his mind and energies to a profession; total commitment to law or teaching languages in a university." Recalling how strongly his father felt about Moe's baseball career, Samuel remembers talking to Bernard outside his Newark pharmacy during the Depression. "We were discussing income and how difficult it was for everyone in the country. And then we referred to Moe. I said, 'Well look, Pa, after all Moe's making a living. He's a baseball player.' And my father said, 'A sport,' then turned his head and feigned spitting."[23]

Moe keenly missed his father's approval. According to one account, as he entered his last major league season in 1939, he told his friends that his "greatest joy would be to see his father in the stands, a joy far greater than breaking Babe Ruth's home run record." "No matter how much I entreat the man," he concluded, "my father will not see me play."[24] As best as can be constructed, father and son never reconciled. Ironically, the elder Berg died of cancer on January 14, 1942, the same day that Moe announced his official retirement from baseball to continue a career in espionage and government work, that, by all accounts, he had begun in secret while a ballplayer.[25]

These vignettes suggest a variety of meanings. Children's participation in a sport universally accepted as the American game could obviously be a source of conflict between immigrant parents and their children, who did not embrace their new American life with the same enthusiasm. Parents also worried that their children's preoccupation with the sport distracted them from acquiring the education they felt necessary for success in America or from putting it to its best purpose. Baseball, however, as an American activity, also provided an experience shared by generations which strengthened their American identities and their connection to a larger American community. Certainly Irwin Shaw, a Brooklyn-born second-generation Jewish novelist who played the game as a youth, understood the game's power in this way. Talking about Israel Federov, the father of the central character of his favorite novel, *Voices of a Summer Day,* Shaw describes how his character became an American. Arriving at Ellis Island at age six from Kiev, Federov, he writes, "was made into an American in the slums of New York City, in vacant lots along the East River where they played with taped baseballs, homemade bats, and without gloves." "Israel Federov," Shaw insists, "was made into an American catching behind the plate bare-handed in the years between 1895 and 1910."[26]

II

Interest in baseball only increased as Jews moved out of urban ghettoes like Chicago's Maxwell Street or New York's Lower East Side into so-called secondary areas of settlement. Between the wars, the game became even more accessible to second-generation Jewish youth. Unlike Eddie Cantor or George Burns, whose baseball exploits primarily remained confined to the streets, second-generation youngsters who came of age in the 1920s and 1930s also played the game on regular baseball diamonds. Many of them as well availed themselves of any number of organized baseball programs sponsored by Jewish organizations.

Even a brief survey of Jewish participation in the game during these years confirms these patterns. By the 1920s, baseball teams representing Jewish organizations were commonplace. In cities like New York and Chicago, with large Jewish populations, settlement house and Y teams played each other in organized Jewish leagues. Places with smaller Jewish populations found teams playing Gentile opponents. The YMHA in Dallas, for instance, eager to promote support for its team that played in the city's Merchant League against the likes of Texas Furniture and the Sanger Brothers, even devoted a whole issue of its monthly bulletin to baseball, encouraging Y members to come out and cheer for "our boys" who are "fighting for you and me" and "the fundamental elements of this great institution."[27]

More typical, however, were games played among neighborhood kids. Bernard Reisman, now a professor in American Jewish communal service at Brandeis University, recalls that, in his Bronx neighborhood, baseball, or one its many variations, including stickball, "off-the-wall," and stoop-ball was the "spring sport" played by members of the Trojans, an "athletic club" founded by himself and his friends in 1938. At their clubhouse on Wheeler Avenue and only a block away from Hymie's candy store and the vacant lot near Bassow Brothers junkyard where they played baseball, the Trojans held regular weekly meetings, established rules and a judiciary committee, wrote a formal constitution, elected officers, and collected dues. The club's first purchase was baseball caps, custom-made black ones with a yellow T on the bill.

Much like Brooklyn's Dux or New Haven's Atlas Club, for Reisman and his friends, participating in sport gave them a sense of independence and opportunity that nurtured their American sensibilities. The Trojans' day-to-day life revolved around sports. In the spring this meant baseball. So successful were they that when the local synagogue formed a community center, the center's staff urged them to affiliate to enhance its own status, offering them a professional "group leader" as the enticement. As Bernie recalls, the Trojans politely demurred. "What the center professionals viewed as a benefit . . . the Trojans viewed as a liability," preferring to "do things by ourselves and in our own way."[28]

Similar memories belong to Trojan contemporaries who made it to the major leagues. Marv Rotblatt, a lefthander for his hometown Chicago White Sox in the early 1950s, grew up on Chicago's north side and honed his skills as pitcher for a team he organized to play in the Neighborhood Boys' Club league at River Park. Raised in Brooklyn, Cal Abrams, who later played for the Dodgers between 1949 and 1952, remembers growing up on a block where everyone, "except for the old Italian who had the grape vines two doors down," was Jewish. Recalling that he rarely went into Manhattan because his neighborhood had all he wanted, including movies, Chinese restaurants, handball courts, and baseball fields, Abrams lived for baseball. He nurtured these loves at Ebbets Field and on the sandlots with his friends, and also with his father, a truck driver and frustrated ballplayer who pushed his son to become a professional.[29]

Adults elsewhere also found baseball accessible, in ways reminiscent of the way in which basketball, as part of Jewish community life, encouraged assimilation with an ethnic setting. In Columbus, Ohio, while Jewish adolescents played baseball in youth leagues at the Schoenthal Center and informally in the city's parks, their fathers, the children of East European working-class immigrant parents, played fast-pitch softball in their Sunday morning league. Less orthodox than their first-generation parents but not sufficiently liberated from the traditions of the past to play on the Jewish Sabbath, these middle-class men, denied admission to the exclusive German Jewish country club in Columbus, played ball on Sundays for themselves and their families. Championship games brought out hundreds of fans from the local Jewish community, and the Ohio *Jewish Chronicle* religiously reported the scores and doings of the league in a regular column called "Shmoos." One observer of the Columbus softball scene recalls that the league was "a major Jewish community matter. There were personalities involved as well as the desire for accomplishment and competition. For somebody who's in religious school, like myself, to go out to the park and watch the games, it was really and extraordinary kind of social event. Part of it was not just playing the game but the kibitzing going on and the socializing around the sidelines."[30]

Although our Columbus commentator did not spell out the significance of his experience, a number of second-generation Jewish writers and novelists who invoke baseball as metaphor for their American Jewish experience give meaning to such reminiscences. None does it more powerfully than Philip Roth, whose fascination with the game helped forge his own American identity.

Born in Newark, New Jersey, in 1933, along with other children of "first-generation offspring of poor turn of the century immigrants from Galicia and Polish Russia" and raised, like them, in the Yiddish-speaking homes of lower-middle-class families, Roth evokes a male childhood world in which sport was prominent. Two blocks from his home, across from the local candy store at Chancellor Avenue, was a playing field where, he tells us, he "virtually evolved as a boy," playing pick-up football, shagging fly balls, and "where my friends hung around on Sunday mornings, watching with amusement as the local fathers—the plumbers, electricians, and produce merchants—kibitzed their way through their weekly softball game." Most important, however, it was where Roth played baseball:

My larger boyhood society cohered around the most inherently American phenomenon at hand—the game of baseball, whose mystique was encapsulated in three relatively inexpensive fetishes that you could always have at your side in your room, not only while you did your homework but in bed with you while you slept if you were a worshiper as primitive as I was at 10 or 11—they were a ball, a bat and a glove. The solace that my Orthodox grandfather could be expected to have taken in the familiar leathery odor of the flesh-worn straps of the old phylacteries in which he wrapped himself each morning, I derived from the smell of my mitt, which I ritualistically donned every day to work a little on my pocket. I was an average ballplayer, and the mitt's enchantment had to do less with foolish dreams of becoming a major leaguer, or even a high school star than with the bestowal of member-ship on a great secular nationalistic church from which nobody had ever seemed to suggest that Jews should be excluded. The softball or hardball teams we organized and reorganized obsessively through our grade school years—teams we called by unarguably native names like the "Seebees" and the "Mohawks" and described as "social or athletic clubs"—aside from the opportunity to compete against one another in a game we loved, also oper-ated as secret societies that separated us from the faint, residual foreignness still clinging to some of our parents' attitudes and that validated our own spot-less credentials as American kids.[31]

Baseball as "secular nationalistic church" provided Roth and his friends proof of their American identities even as it separated them still further from parents in his mind not totally cleansed of traditional European ways. Remembering baseball in this way, he dismisses the possibility that watching his friends' fathers play softball, much like similar games played by Columbus adults, also allowed baseball to serve as a middle ground—a shared American experience that helped mitigate conflict between generations.

Either way, the ability of sport to facilitate immigrant connection to Amer-ican ways was not limited to baseball or to Jews. The same Jewish boys who played baseball in the spring most likely, as Roth reports and Reisman remem-bers, played football in the fall and basketball in the winter, gaining from them the same sense of independence, physical competence, and accomplish-ment that baseball provided. These overlappping sportive experiences rein-forced their acceptance of American ways and values. Irish immigrants who flocked to bare-knuckle boxing in the late 19th century also became Ameri-cans, Eliot Gorn argues, by participating in a sport that emphasized American values of success, meritocracy, and competition and that glorified "the Amer-ican dream of personal achievement and unlimited individual opportunity." Be it boxing, baseball, or, as we know, basketball, purchasing a ticket to a sporting event was one of many ways to participate in an American consumer society. At the same time, rooting for the home team or local boxing cham-pion underlined the freedom of choice that made American life seem unique while developing loyalties to new American surroundings.

Baseball, however, symbolized the connection between sport and being American most forcefully. Whether in Blocton, Alabama, the Bronx's Grand Concourse, or a field on Newark's Chancellor Avenue, the game guaranteed second-generation Jewish boys admission to an American childhood and con-firmed their American identities. Baseball also provided something else. Long before television made basketball and football national sport and entertain-ment spectacles, major league baseball was America's only national sport. By virtue of the game's reputation as the quintessential American game and because of the attention the major-league variety received, its athletes, more so than in any other sport, became available as national symbols of American achievement. Although never many in number, the story of those Jewish men who made it to the majors and the way they were viewed by Jew and Gentile alike underlines the importance of baseball for understanding Jewish assimilation in America.

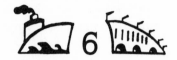

Cohen at the Bat

WHEN "Giant" Morris Raphael Cohen conjured up images of American baseball heroes, Jouett Meekin, a Dutchman born in New Albany, Indiana, came to mind. Al Schacht fulfilled his fantasies by playing with his idol, Christy Mathewson, a Protestant from Factoryville, Pennsylvania. Andy Cohen's heroes also included Mathewson as well as Horatio Alger's fictional characters—none of whom was a baseball player and none of whom was Jewish. In fact, not until Cohen himself received national attention as the first prominent Jewish major leaguer did Jewish fans proudly identify with Jewish major leaguers as symbols of their own struggle for American acceptance. Arnold Rothstein, changes in the professional game dictated by scandal and the bottom line, and the simple passage of time made it all possible. What happened to Andy Cohen in 1928 and 1929 set the stage for even more meaningful displays of ethnic loyalty in the decades that followed.

I

Numbers alone offer partial explanation for the lack of identification with Jewish baseball heroes prior to Andy Cohen's appearance. Throughout the history of the professional game, there have not been very many Jewish major league baseball players. Latest counts indicate that 115 Jewish individuals, from Lipman Pike to Steve Stone, played major league baseball between 1871 and 1980. These players represent approximately 1 percent of the some 10,000 men who made it to the big leagues in these years. Of this total, far fewer played the game prior to 1930 than after.[1]

Before 1900, only occasionally did a Jewish ballplayer appear on the roster of a major-league club. Between 1900 and 1930, an average of 4 Jewish ballplayers made it to the majors each year, compared with the period between

1930 and 1955, the peak years of Jewish participation, when an average of 8 Jews played for major league teams each year, or 1955 through 1980, when 6 to 7 Jewish players competed each year in the bigs. The 1930s witnessed the greatest involvement: 9 to 10 players per year with no less than 10 in consecutive seasons between 1935 and 1939. Twelve players, the most in any single season, played ball in the majors in 1936.

By this count, not Morris, Al, nor Andy should have been expected to "think" Jewish when images of professional baseball players danced in their heads. Nor did the exploits of those who played the game prior to 1930 encourage them to identify with the few landsmen who made it to the majors. With few exceptions the average career of the 35 men who played in these years, all of whom were born before 1901, was a brief 4.4 years. Only 15 of them lasted more than three years and 12, including Bob Berman and Lou Brower, stayed with a major league team for less than one season. Typical was Berman's "cup of coffee," two games with the Washington Senators during the 1918 season. In neither did he bat. His only full inning came on June 12 when he caught his idol, Walter "Big Train" Johnson.[2]

There were occasional Jewish players with careers more distinguished than Bob Berman's. "Silent George" Stone played seven years in the majors, six with the St. Louis Browns between 1905 and 1910 as an outstanding left-handed hitter on at best a mediocre club. Stone was born in Lost Nation, Nebraska, in 1876. In his first full season in the majors, he led the American League in total bases and hits and came in second in home runs with seven. Although his .296 batting average was not good enough to lead the league, it was some 50 points better than another rookie who broke into the majors that year, Ty Cobb. In 1906 Stone enjoyed his best season in a career that left him with a lifetime batting average of .301. That year he led the league in batting average (.358), slugging percentage (.501), total bases (291), and came in third in home run production (6) and in hits (208).

Also impressive was Johnny Kling, another midwesterner, born in Kansas City in 1875, who had a distinguished career with the great Chicago Cubs team at the turn of the century. In an eleven-year career in the Windy City between 1900 and 1911, Kling's prowess behind the plate helped the Cubs win four pennants and two World Series. Altogether, Kling played in 1,260 major league games and compiled a lifetime batting average of .272. According to all accounts, his ability as a catcher was even more important than his batting skills to the Cubs' success.[3]

But Stone and Kling, along with almost half of the men identified as Jews who played the game before 1930, came from midwestern and southern towns far removed geographically and culturally from Jewish immigrant constituencies and with no obvious affinity to them. Even their names did not sound Jewish. Those who grew up in cities with growing Jewish immigrant populations—ten players alone were born in New York City—generally lacked the talent and staying power that would have encouraged identification with them. Exceptions like "Broadway" Alec Smith, born and raised in New York, who spent much of his nine-year career between 1897 and 1906 with local teams, did not carry a moniker that struck a familiar chord with the Cohens of the Lower East Side.

Compounding matters further, a number of Jewish ballplayers changed their names to mask their Jewish backgrounds. Phil Cooney, who played one year with the Yankees in 1905, Sammy Bohne, an outfielder with Cincinnati and Brooklyn in the 1920s, Reuben Ewing, who played in the National League for St. Louis in 1921, and Harry "Klondike" Kane, who pitched for St. Louis, Detroit, and Philadelphia in the early 1900s all changed their names from Cohen when they became professional baseball players. None of them indicated whether they took on new names to counter anti-Semitic stereotypes about physically weak Jews that might have limited their opportunity, to keep the news from mothers and fathers who might have disapproved of their career choice, or because they had renounced their Jewishness. Al Schacht, who has left the most extensive accounts of any of these early players, recounts tale after tale of harassment and pranks of which he was both victim and perpetrator, but never does he suggest that they were anti-Semitic or outside the bounds of what ballplayers naturally do to each other to break the boredom of a long season. Jacob Atz, a journeyman infielder for Chicago in the American League between 1907 and 1909, claimed to have changed his name from Zimmerman to Atz in order to be first on the payroll line. Whatever the reason, any young Jewish fan looking for ethnic heroes in baseball would not have had an easy time finding these men.[4]

In some instances, the lack of obvious Jewish credentials may have contributed to the problem. For instance, Jacob Atz's biographical file at baseball's Hall of Fame makes no mention of his religion, indicating only that he was of German and Irish ancestry. Jewish encyclopedias of sport, all published after 1960, while listing him as Jewish, also note that he was buried as a Roman Catholic. No more convincing is the evidence for Johnny Kling. Although every listing of Jewish athletes celebrates Kling's Jewishness, not one provides any evidence for the assertion. Newspaper coverage, both during and after his career, makes no mention of his religion. The most telling evidence about his faith challenges all claims that he was Jewish. Writing to Cooperstown in 1969 to clear up "erroneous reports" about her husband's religion, Kling's wife informed its director that "Johnny was baptised in the Lutheran Church." Confusion about his Jewish credentials, she continued, centered on the fact that she was Jewish and that they had been married by a rabbi. "I often tried to get Johnny to deny rumors that he was a Jew," she concluded, "but he said he didn't care what was written about his religion."[5]

For both Atz and Kling, claims of their supposed Jewish connections came from a host of Jewish writers in the 1930s and after who, for a variety of reasons still to be explored, found it useful to herald the accomplishments of Jewish baseball players, however questionable some of their credentials might have been.[6] In fact, whether from Manhattan or from Kansas City—whether a Berman, a Stone, or a Kling—one thing all early Jewish major leaguers had in common that complicated public identification with them as Jews was that prior to the late 1920s neither the American nor Jewish press paid much attention to the ethnic identity of professional baseball players. Fueling its "hot stove league" columns with less-than-hard news, the *Sporting News* of November 1, 1890, did quote from the *Philadelphia Item* that "Dan Stearns of the Kansas City team is said to be a Hebrew. He is the only one of the Chosen People engaged in professional ballplaying." The *News* added: "What is the matter with Billy Nash of the Bostons? He is, we believe, a Hebrew."[7] By all counts, "baseball's bible" was on the mark. A decade later, sportswriters occasionally referred to Barney Pelty, a good fielding pitcher for the St. Louis Browns from 1903 through 1912, as "the Yiddish Curver." For the most part, however, these references were exceptions to newspapers' general lack of interest in the Jewish identity of baseball players. Nor, for that matter, did a Jewish public pay much attention to the participation of their own kind in America's National Game. The impact of the Black Sox scandal, business decisions of baseball executives, and the ongoing process of assimilation, however, altered matters dramatically.

II

In 1919, members of the Chicago White Sox agreed to throw the World Series to the Cincinnati Red Stockings. Erskine Mayer, a Jewish boy of German descent born in Atlanta, and the first Jewish hurler to win 20 games in two consecutive seasons, appeared in one inning of the fifth game of the series for Chicago. Mayer, however, was not involved in the conspiracy. His name does not appear in the *Baseball Encyclopedia's* White Sox team roster for the 1919 season nor was he mentioned in contemporary accounts of the "fix" or in studies of a scandal that rocked baseball and a hero-worshipping American public to its foundations.[8] Instead, Jewish involvement of a different sort brought attention to the connection between American baseball and American Jews in ways that Mayer and other Jewish ballplayers before him had never been able to accomplish. Arnold Rothstein and Abe Attell made sure of that.

Arnold Rothstein did not come up with the idea to fix the 1919 World Series. Chick Gandil, the White Sox's tough first baseman, deserves the credit. He also convinced seven other teammates to join him and contacted gamblers to finance the operation. Charlie Comiskey, the tight-fisted owner of the White Sox who was unwilling to pay decent salaries to treat his players equitably, helped provoke the eight into action. Yet without "the big bankroll," as Rothstein was sometimes called, or Abe Attell, popularly known in his days as featherweight boxing champion of the world as the "Little Hebrew," it is unlikely that it would have occurred. The labyrinth story of intrigue, deception, and double-cross involving ballplayers and gamblers has been well told elsewhere and needs no full recounting here. Its bare outline makes clear their critical role in the scandal.[9]

By 1915 Arnold Rothstein was one of the best-known of New York's underworld figures. Like other Jewish criminals, he learned the business on the streets of the Lower East Side from the likes of Monk Eastman, Big Jack Zelig, and Lefty Louie Rosenthal and their gangs who robbed, killed, gambled, and arranged for protection and prostitution in their Jewish ghetto. Much like the Irish before them and the Italians who arrived in America when they did, the criminal careers of Rothstein's "teachers" grew out of ghetto poverty and the opportunity for quick success that illicit activities provided. Many of these Jewish immigrants kept kosher and spoke Yiddish while they plied their illegal trade among their own kind. Rothstein, however, sought a different image.[10]

Born in 1882, Arnold was a third-generation American, the son of an American father whose own father had fled Bessarabia to avoid persecution. Raised in a well-to-do Upper East Side New York orthodox Jewish family by a father who was a well-respected religious and business leader, Rothstein rejected his religion and family at a young age, preferring instead the rough company of immigrant Jewish gangsters.

By his own account, Rothstein suffered from a severe case of sibling rivalry that fueled feelings of hate toward his brother and father and that separated him from his family at an early age. While his brother studied for the rabbinate, once Bar Mitzvahed, Rothstein ignored religion and his family, choosing to spend his time perfecting his billiards game and gambling skills. For him, generational conflict had little to do with the familiar cultural clashes that marked the battles of first-generation East European Jewish immigrants and their American-born children. A life of crime was not a ticket out of the ghetto and quick access to American riches but an act of defiance against his father.

Rothstein, who rarely found himself depicted as a Jew in the press, married out of the faith (his father declared him dead and sat shiva for him—a Jewish mourning ritual—when he heard the news), preferred the company of high society and Big Tim Sullivan, a Tammany Hall politician and mentor, and made his money outside of the Jewish ghetto where he had apprenticed. By 1919, his reputation as a professional gambler, race-track owner, and criminal with special talents for organization, efficient operation, and ready cash for big ventures was so well known that mere mention of his name persuaded Gandil and his teammates to "fix" the World Series.

Abe Attell didn't discourage them. Attell grew up in San Francisco, made his way through its rough street world along the city's docks, and reigned as featherweight boxing champion of the world between 1900 and 1912. While in the ring, he was often billed as the "Little Hebrew" in promotional efforts to attract immigrant Jewish fans to his fights. Throughout his career Attell consistently dodged allegations that he conspired with gamblers to throw fights. When he retired from the ring he joined their ranks, making his living as a small-time operator and sometime bodyguard of Arnold Rothstein.

Hoping to capitalize on that connection and to make it big on his own, Attell assured Gandil that Rothstein would bankroll the World Series fix by providing a $100,000 bribe demanded by the players even after Rothstein rejected the idea. Rothstein learned of Attell's duplicity, but kept quiet about it. Instead, working through a different middleman who had also been contacted by Gandil, he agreed to support the scheme, promising an $80,000 pay-off to the players for their efforts with $40,000 up front to show his good faith.

Ultimately, the fix was successful, the Series thrown, and Chicago humiliated by an underdog Cincinnati team in eight games. Through it all, two sets of gamblers and White Sox players played games with each other, all trying to gain as much as possible for themselves and often cheating and lying to each other in the process. Rothstein himself remained aloof. Although he laid down judicious bets and made good money on an affair that probably would not have happened without him, he never made personal contact or discussed it with any of the White Sox. While Rothstein might well have rejected F. Scott Fitzgerald's characterization of him as the thin-lipped nervous Jew Meyer Wolfsheim in *The Great Gatsby*, he no doubt would have been pleased with the exchange between Nick Carraway and Gatsby after Carraway has just learned that the man he has had lunch with "fixed the World Series." Staggered by the idea that "one man could start to play with the faith of fifty million people—with the singlemindedness of a burglar blowing a safe," Carraway asks Gatsby how he managed it. "He just saw the opportunity," Gatsby replies. "Why isn't he in jail?" Carraway demands. "They can't get him, old sport," Gatsby declares. "He's a smart man."[11]

Over the course of a Chicago grand jury investigation of the scandal during the fall of 1920 and the subsequent trial of the ballplayers and gamblers indicted for fixing the World Series in July 1921, Rothstein denied involvement and escaped prosecution. Testifying before a Chicago grand jury to vindicate himself from charges that he had masterminded the affair, he fingered Abe Attell and "some other cheap gamblers" as the culprits. Although he admitted being approached by them he asserted that "I turned them down flat. I don't doubt," he continued, "that Attell used my name to put it over. That's been done by smarter men than Abe. But I wasn't in on it, wouldn't have gone into it under any circumstances, and didn't bet a cent on the Series."[12] Charlie Comiskey and other baseball officials, eager to keep their game from any taint of association with one of America's best-known criminals, supported Rothstein's claims of innocence.

In the end, Rothstein arranged for Attell's legal defense. When the grand jury confessions of Eddie Cicotte, Joe Jackson, and Claude Williams—three Chicago players who had admitted their guilt—mysteriously disappeared after the case came to trial, charges against all the ballplayers and gamblers were dropped. Rothstein denied accusations that he paid $10,000 to have the confessions stolen.

The Black Sox scandal remained front-page news in 1920 and 1921. Rothstein and Attell received their fair share of attention. The Chicago *Tribune, New York Times,* and other papers all referred to Rothstein as "the big New York operator," "the wealthy race track man," "gambler," and even as "Arnold the Juan" while never failing to note Attell's former career as a "pugilist and former featherweight champion" and his present status as small-time "gambler." No references to their Jewish backgrounds, however, accompanied any coverage in the regular press. Not surprisingly, American Jewish newspapers that eagerly sought full Jewish assimilation avoided all coverage of possible Jewish connection to a scandal that threatened to undermine America's National Game. But suspected Jewish involvement evoked virulent response from at least one newspaper publisher known better for his inventions and marketing skills than for his acumen as a reporter or editorialist. Henry Ford's claim that Jews were intent on destroying a great American pastime, set in the climate of anti-Semitism and nativism that marked the early 1920s, made Andy Cohen seem a messiah even for those American Jews who were not usually enthusiastic about Jewish participation in sport.[13]

By 1922, every other car in the world was a Model T Ford and Henry Ford relished public acclaim as "one of the twelve greatest living Americans." Both in the press and among politicians, he drew favorable attention as a potential presidential candidate. Revered as a real-life Horatio Alger hero who had risen from "simple mechanic to industrial giant," the Michigan native who helped popularize American consumer culture and who revolutionized social mores by offering the automobile to everyday Americans became equally known in the 1920s as an active advocate of restrictive immigration policies and as America's best known anti-Semite.[14]

Ford was not alone in his beliefs. In 1919, two years after violent revolution brought the triumph of the Bolsheviks in Russia, A. Mitchell Palmer, United States attorney general, used the FBI to round up hundreds of Russian Jewish immigrants, accused them of planning "to rise up and destroy the government in one fell swoop," and quickly deported many of them back to Russia. Although the "Red Scare" did not reveal a Communist conspiracy to overthrow American democracy, it did underline strong sentiments shared by Ford and other Americans who remained unconvinced that the activities of settlement house workers, social reformers and public educators satisfactorily reshaped European immigrants in ways that guaranteed the preservation of American character and American institutions. Many of Ford's sympathizers came from small towns and farm communities. Reared in fundamentalist Protestant beliefs, they felt uncomfortable with a modernizing society that seemed to take control of their daily lives and with an urbanizing, industrial economy that relied on millions of European aliens. Their attempts to preserve their sense of American life combined the extra-legal and violent activities of a refurbished Ku Klux Klan that sought out blacks, Jews, and Catholics with equal vigor in all parts of the country as well as more respectable organizations that eventually lobbied successfully for the enactment of restrictive immigration laws instrumental in virtually cutting off the influx of East European Jews and Italian Catholics after 1924.[15]

Through it all, both in the pages of his own newspaper, the Dearborn *Independent,* which he distributed through his dealerships, and in a collected edition of his newspaper articles, Ford provided his own contributions to these efforts. He railed at American Jewish bankers and financiers who, he claimed, were carrying out the plans of the so-called "Protocols of the Elders of Zion," a supposed international conspiracy to establish a Jewish world dictatorship quite popular with anti-Semites in the United States and elsewhere. Attacking

Jewish influence in the United States wherever he found it, he hoped to convince his readers that Jews were "the conscious enemies of all that Anglo-Saxons mean by civilization."[16] Arnold Rothstein and other Jews involved in American baseball were not spared.

Aware of the game's popularity and its reputation as a sport that personified American character and democracy, Ford gave special attention to baseball, presenting his invective in two long articles appropriately titled "Jewish Gamblers Corrupt American Baseball" and "The Jewish Degradation of American Baseball." Displaying little knowledge of the history of the game but an unfortunately good grasp of racist stereotyping and anti-Semitism, Ford bluntly asserted that "if fans wish to know the trouble with American baseball, they have it in three words—too much Jew." Blithely ignoring any mention of Harry Wright, William Hulbert, or A. G. Spalding, who had first capitalized on the commercial possibilities of baseball, Ford proclaimed that this "clean and helpful" American sport had been corrupted by Jewish investors and exploiters who had taken it over and turned it into a business. Whether analyzing the problems of baseball, horse-racing, or wrestling, the issue for Ford was clear. Jews who naturally spurn physical activity and sport for its own sake "saw money" in these sports "where the sportsman saw only fun and skill. The Jew set out to capitalize rivalry and to commercialize contestant zeal" in ways that "have been most instrumental in corrupting and nearly destroying our cleanest, most manly public sports."[17]

In baseball, the guilty included that "slick Jew," Arnold Rothstein, and his underworld lackey, Abe Attell, who turned the White Sox into "Jewish dupes." Also culpable were Arthur Austrian, a Jewish Chicago lawyer who represented the Chicago Cubs and served as Comiskey's legal advisor during the Black Sox scandal, Harry Grabiner, the White Sox club secretary, Barney Dreyfuss, the owner of the Pittsburgh Pirates, and Albert D. Lasker, a prominent Chicago businessman "reputed to be the second richest Jew in Chicago," a member of the American Jewish Committee, and a leading stockholder of the Chicago Cubs. Although Ford provided no detail, he asserted that in one way or another all of these men had been responsible for forcing organized baseball to accept the so-called Lasker Plan, "a widely heralded blueprint for the reorganization of baseball, which practically took the sport out of non-Jewish control." Blaming even rowdyism, "the razzing of umpires, hurling of bottles, [and] ceaseless shouting of profane insults" on eastern Jewish baseball fans, Ford concluded that if "baseball is to be saved . . . the remedy is plain. The disease is caused by the Jewish character which spoils everything by ruthless commercial exploitation. . . . [T]here is no doubt anywhere, among either friends or critics of baseball, that the root cause of the present condition is due to Jewish influence." Get rid of the Jews and their money-grubbing character and baseball and the world in general would be a better place.[18]

Ford's comments provoked both criticism and support. The Federal Council of the Churches of Christ, other Protestant organizations, and many prominent Americans including Woodrow Wilson and William Howard Taft condemned his attacks, while nativists who supported anti-immigration legislation applauded his efforts.[19] Either way, his anti-Semitic harangues, by focusing national attention on the place of Jews in American life, provided good reason for them, regardless of their position or background, to reflect on the negative effects of Jewish involvement in the Black Sox scandal.

Arnold Rothstein certainly did. Upset by accusations that he had been responsible for the fix, he announced his retirement from gambling, claiming that "real estate" and his "racing stable" would occupy his time. Criminal activity, however, still preoccupied Rothstein, who kept his reputation as "czar of the underworld" until his gangland assassination in 1928.[20] Jews in more respectable circles also voiced their concern by challenging Ford's accusations of Jewish conspiracies in and out of baseball. Be it through individual congregations, a meeting of the Union of American Hebrew Congregations, individual spokesmen such as Samuel Untermeyer, or the attempts of one New York State senator to refuse Ford water power rights in his state because of his attacks on Jews, a chorus of Jewish opposition countered the capitalist's anti-Semitic claims.[21]

Although Henry Ford was wrong to interpret Atell and Rothstein's involvement in the Black Sox scandal as evidence of an international Jewish conspiracy to corrupt Anglo-Saxon institutions, he was right to insist on their complicity in the affair. Wrong about the responsibility of Jews for turning baseball into commercial enterprise, Ford was correct in noting that America's national pastime was big business. While the professional game's reorganization under a new National Commission with a commissioner of baseball to keep the sport clean had been proposed by Albert Lasker and supported by the Jewish men that Ford mentioned, it was adopted by baseball executives as a way to restore public confidence in their business rather than, as Ford proclaimed, as part of a larger Jewish conspiracy to corrupt America.[22] In fact, the keen awareness of the sport's commercial possibility by Gentile baseball men in the aftermath of the Black Sox scandal helped focus national attention on Jews and baseball in ways that made both Jews and Gentiles forget about the "Little Hebrew" and the "big bankroll." Andy Cohen's brief moment as American baseball star and Jewish folk hero figured prominently here.

III

Baseball officials earnestly hoped that the appointment of Judge Kenesaw Mountain Landis as the major leagues' first commissioner with unlimited power to maintain the sport's purity would help its tarnished image. In that spirit, they applauded his decision to ban the eight White Sox players accused of throwing the 1919 World Series from the major leagues for life. Far more influential, however, in restoring professional baseball to popular favor was the emergence of Babe Ruth as the game's greatest star—as one sportswriter called him, "the uncrowned king of the diamond, the master figure of baseball, the big noise in the biggest game on earth."[23]

   Ruth's numerous and prodigious home runs ushered in a new era of power baseball and made the New York Yankees the game's dominant team in the 1920s. Known as much for his excesses off the field that included his love of fast automobiles and his insatiable appetite for food, women, drink, and gambling, Ruth personified a culture that encouraged Americans to believe that it was possible and permissible to partake of a new world of affluence and plenty. In a decade often celebrated as the "golden age of American sports," the Sultan of Swat was *the* sports hero in the first American age of sports celebrities, ranging above a cast of characters that included Bobby Jones, Red Grange, Jack Dempsey, and "Big" Bill Tilden. As one historian has put it, Ruth was "the ideal hero for the world of consumption" that was the 1920s.[24]

   Ruth's ability to attract fans to the ballpark was not lost on the Yankees' competitors, especially New York Giants manager John J. McGraw. Although the Giants won National League pennants and two World Series against their cross-town rivals in the early 1920s, the team began to slide after 1924. Even when successful on the field, increasingly they were no match for the Yankees at the gate. Anxious to bolster the Giants' sagging financial fortunes, McGraw sought new ways to capture the hearts of New York's baseball fans. Good Jewish ballplayers who might attract Jewish fans to the Polo Grounds became a central part of his scheme.

   McGraw's efforts to find Jewish players were no different from the Yankees' attempt to sell "Poosh 'Em up Tony" Lazzeri as an Italian hero to New York's second-generation Italian population or attempts in St. Louis and Cincinnati to attract German audiences to the ballpark by advertising their clubs in German-language newspapers. The Giants' manager was not even the only man who suggested that specific attention be paid to Jewish audiences. In 1926, Eddie Reulbach, a Jewish boy who grew up in Detroit and who emerged as one of baseball's outstanding pitchers for the Chicago Cubs between 1905 and 1913, lamented the presence of only one Jewish player, Sammy Bohne, in the major leagues. "If I were a [baseball] magnate in Greater New York at least," he told F. C. Lane in a *Baseball Magazine* story titled "Why Not More Jewish Ball Players?," "I would send scouts all over the United States and Canada in an effort to locate some hooked-nose youngster who could bat and field. Then I would ballyhoo him in all the papers. The Jewish people are great spenders and they could be made excellent fans. You could sell out your boxes and your reserved seats any time in Greater New York."[25]

   Reulbach's characterization of Jews as "great spenders" and potential baseball fans aptly recognized that large numbers of East European immigrants and their children were as taken by the fruits of American consumption as any one else. By the 1920s, in cities like New York and Chicago, many immigrants had managed enough economic success to move out of ghettos like the Lower East Side or Maxwell Street into new apartment buildings and brownstones in neighborhoods like Brooklyn's Brownsville or Chicago's Lawndale. They, too, were American consumers who fully participated in what society had to offer, including playing baseball, going to the movies, and riding in Ford automobiles.[26] McGraw, whose sole concern was the bottom line, recognized better than anyone else that they were ripe for their own hero.

McGraw's first experiment, unwise as it turned out to be, was a Solomon, not a Cohen. In 1923, on the advice of Giant scout Dick Kinsella, he signed Mose Solomon, a native New Yorker who had learned the game in Columbus, Ohio, to lead the Giants to the promised land. According to the *Sporting News,* Mose was a powerful home-run hitter who had hit 42 home runs in the minors during the 1923 season. The *News* also noted that this tough kid had punched out several ballplayers who had impugned "his ancestry as a Jew." Nicknamed the "Rabbi of Swat" and "the Jewish Babe Ruth" by the New York press, Solomon came up at the tail end of the season, played in two games, and managed three hits in eight at bats. According to his brother, his future with the Giants ended when McGraw asked Mose to stay in New York without pay for the World Series even though he wasn't eligible to play. Solomon refused, choosing instead to play professional football for an Ohio team, even though McGraw made it clear that if he left New York his career with the Giants was over. McGraw made good on his word and this Giants' answer to Babe Ruth never returned.[27]

Enter Andy Cohen. Early in the 1926 season, McGraw brought the young Texan to the Polo Grounds. Announcing his debut on June 18 as a pinch hitter for Frankie Frisch, the "Fordham Flash," the *American Hebrew* described him as "a pleasant faced youth of twenty with rugged features of an unmistakeably Jewish cast." Cohen's "clear single on the first ball pitched," according to the *Hebrew,* "started Andy off on a career which is very likely to make his name a household fixture." No less auspicious was his play at second base where Cohen cooperated nicely with George "Highpockets" Kelly, the Giants' first baseman, much like the Cohens and Kellys who had "worked side by side for years" on stage and screen. Hopeful that Andy's future success on the diamond might "stimulate the interest of the Jew in America in our great national pastime," the *Hebrew* proclaimed that "baseball is the great American sport and as the Jew is thoroughly Americanized there is no reason why his name should not be prominently found upon the baseball roll of honor." Aware of McGraw's search for a good Jewish ballplayer, the paper concluded that "if Cohen comes through as the manager expects him to, it is felt that he will rival Babe Ruth as a drawing attraction."[28]

Committed to the full assimilation of East European Jewish immigrants into American culture and society, the *Hebrew* hoped that Jewish success in baseball would provide a public, national expression of that possibility. Here, and in its Cohen-Kelly vaudeville version of Irish and Jewish harmony, it presented a view of society consistent with the ideas of Horace Kallen and others at the time who hoped for an American society in which ethnic groups maintained some sense of group identity while living in harmony with each other. Although such a vision was more hope than reality for most American Jews in 1926, its persistence helps explain Andy Cohen's popularity.

Not, however, until 1928. After appearing in 32 games in 1926, McGraw sent Andy to the Buffalo Bisons in the International League where he remained through the 1927 season. Cohen had a spectacular year. He hit .355 and was named as the shortstop of the league's All Star team. Just as important for McGraw's plans, Buffalo's Jewish population embraced him as their hero.[29] Faced with competition from the Yankee team that dominated baseball in 1927 with a "Murderer's Row" led by Babe's record-breaking 60 home runs, McGraw brought Andy back to New York for the opening of the 1928 season.

The early months of the 1928 season confirmed the Giant manager's hunch about the ability of a Jewish ballplayer to bring out his own kind. Opening day at the Polo Grounds set the tone. Cohen started the game at second base, taking over for the legendary Rogers Hornsby, who had been traded in the off-season to the Boston Braves, the Giant's opening day opponent. Before 30,000 fans, Andy led the Giants to a 5–2 victory. He scored twice, knocked in two runs, and put out Hornsby on grounders to second twice.

So overwhelming was the crowd's reaction to Andy's exploits that the young second baseman barely escaped with his life. As Andy remembers it, thousands of Jewish fans rushed the field, lifted him to their shoulders as they would a new Jewish bridegroom, and literally carried him around the Polo Grounds until he was rescued by teammates who escorted him to the steps of the Giant's center-field clubhouse. McGraw called it "the greatest ovation . . . given any player in all my life." James Harrison of the *New York Times* concurred, noting that "Andy Cohen took New York by storm. He captured the hearts of 30,000 fans as only a Ruth or a Walter Johnson could grip them."[30]

Other sportswriters added their own testimony, paying special attention to Cohen's Jewish fans. Not surprisingly, the *American Hebrew* extolled Andy as "the hero of the day," took note of fans "a thousand strong" who carried him off on their shoulders, and destined him to become "the greatest Jew in organized baseball." Grantland Rice, the nation's best-known sportswriter who covered the season opener for the New York *Herald Tribune,* declared that "it was Andy Cohen, the young Jewish ball player . . . the Tuscaloosa Terror, who drove in two Giant runs, scored two more on his own hook, and covered the infield sod of the Polo Grounds like a ball-playing centipede, to send the giants to victory" that "lifted 30,000 frozen spectators to their frost bitten feet. . . ." Outside of New York, Westbrook Pegler explained to his Chicago *Tribune* readers why Cohen's debut was so important to McGraw's Giants. "From Mosholu Parkway on the north down to Central Park," Pegler began,

there are thousands of restaurants and herring stores with Yiddish lettering on the windows. The tailor shops, the meat markets, the groceries, dry goods stores—almost all the places of business . . . bear such names as Levkowitz . . . Levy, Levitch, Myer, Mandelbaum, Katz, Jacobs . . . and Schanz. In the tall apartment buildings, which stand in solid rows for miles the names on the door bells are Jewish by a vast plurality.

With over one million Jews living in these New York neighborhoods, he reported, no wonder McGraw "desired a Jewish ball player, preferably an infielder, because an infielder plays closer to the customers." Based on the crowd's reaction to Cohen's opening-day heroics, Pegler concluded that if he succeeded at second base, "the Giant firm could do business in the Jewish trade alone. . . . If Mr. Cohen will stand up, the Giants will have the offset of Jake Ruppert's Babe Ruth, who will have to hit home runs against Cohen's singles."[31]

Although hardly free of ethnic slurs, an anonymous parody of *Casey at the Bat*, offered in the aftermath of Andy's debut, also captures the excitement of the day and explicitly makes clear the connections between Cohen and his Jewish constituency:

Cohen at the Bat

The outlook wasn't cheerful for the Giants yesterday
They were trailing by a run with but four innings left to play.
When Lindstrom flied to Richbourg and Terry weakly popped,
It looked as though those Bostons had the game as good as copped.
But Jackson smacked a single over Eddie Farrell's pate
And from the stands and bleachers the cry of "Oy, Oy" rose,
For up came Andy Cohen half a foot behind his nose.
There was ease in Bob Smith's manner and a smile on Hornsby's face,
For they figured they had Andy in the tightest sort of place.
It was make or break for Andy, while the fans cried "Oy, Oy, Oy,"
And it wasn't any soft spot for a little Jewish boy.
And now the pitcher has the ball and now he let's it go.
And now the air is shattered by the force of Casey's blow.
Well nothing like that happened, but what do you suppose?
Why little Andy Cohen socked the ball upon the nose.
Then from the stands and bleachers the fans in triumph roared.
And Andy raced to second and the other runner scored.
Soon they took him home in triumph amidst the blare of auto honks.
There may be no joy in Mudville, but there's plenty in the Bronx.[32]

Clear in the adulation New York's Jewish fans gave their new hero, the poem also evokes other potential. Both for Jews and for American blacks, baseball's power to bridge the gap between minority and majority peoples and bring them together awaited later times and different sets of historical circumstances. But even with its obvious anti-Semitic overtones, cloaking Cohen with the mantle of Casey, that immortal American icon, cast Andy as an American hero capable of appealing to both Jew and Gentile at the same time.

Andy's play during the opening months of the 1928 season fueled these possibilities. The Giants did so well at the gate that Harry M. Stevens, the famed concessionaire, instructed his Polo Grounds vendors that they were "no longer selling ice cream cones, but ice cream Cohens."[33] However much he may have been exploited by the Giants' management, Jewish audiences took advantage of his presence and turned it to their own ends. Everywhere Cohen played, they feted him with special "days" and demanded his appearance at their synagogues and organizations, seizing the moment to identify themselves with a young Jewish man making good in a very visible American way. The Giants even hired a secretary to handle his fan mail and, according to the *Sporting News*, put him up in a hotel suite so that he could meet his "mobs of worshipers, [t]he thousands of Jewish fans who have waited a long time to see one of their own race make good as a Giant regular." Even Gentiles got into the act. When the Giants feted their new star with a "day" in June, the Knights of Pythias gave Andy 1500 silver dollars.[34]

Although his hot bat cooled off during the summer months, Cohen batted a respectable .274 in 129 games, made only 24 errors in 126 games at second base, and helped the Giants to a second-place finish, two games behind the St. Louis Cardinals. Eager to cash in on his popularity, he made personal appearances for Nat Berler's Clothes Shop in the Bronx and played in a baseball game that pitted "All-Stars" led by "New York's idol, Andy Cohen," against a team captained by his Giant teammate Lefty O'Doul at the Bronx's Dyckman Oval. The Giants also recognized their new player's success by raising his salary to $11,500 for the 1929 season, a substantial increase from the $7,500 he earned the previous year.[35]

Cohen also benefitted from his status as Jewish folk hero in other ways. Like John L. Sullivan, Babe Ruth, and other celebrity athletes, he pursued a brief vaudeville career during the winter months of 1928 and 1929. Put together with ethnic audiences in mind, Cohen joined his Irish teammate Frank "Shanty" Hogan, the Giants' catcher, in an act that consisted of baseball skits and parodies of popular songs. They billed themselves as "Cohen and Hogan" in New York to attract Jewish audiences and as "Hogan and Cohen" in Boston to please an Irish majority. Typical of the repertory, as Andy recalls, was a parody of "Get Out and Get Under the Moonlight." Assisted by two girls from the audience, he and Hogan would croon: "We just bought a car, a second hand moon/ The thing was always out of tune./ We looked out and saw John J. McGraw/ We got out and got under the moon." "Crap like that," according to Cohen, "used to bring the house down."[36]

Not surprisingly, the close of Andy's vaudeville career coincided with his failure to return to the big leagues for the 1930 season. Andy posted decent numbers in 1929 for a Giant team that finished in third place. He batted .294 and made only 20 errors in 101 games at second base. Although the *Sporting News* commented that "the young Jewish boy"'s play had dropped off both in the field and at the plate during his second year, they fully expected him to be back in 1930. "McGraw, the master baseballman, is sweet on Andy," the *News* commented. "He sees in him that of which great players are made. He can hit, field, and run. He has dash and courage. He is aggressive and ambitious. . . ." Perhaps. But 1930 found Andy back in the International League, this time with the Newark Bears. Although he was to have a good career as minor-league player and coach, he did not return to the majors until 1960, when he spent one season as a coach for the Philadelphia Phillies.[37]

One historian who knows Cohen's story well suggests that his brief stay in the major leagues reflects the situation of any member of an American minority group competing for position or place with members of the majority culture. Simply put, one has to be better, not just competent or equal, in order to keep one's job. Harry Edwards and others who have studied American black history, especially the struggle of black athletes for equal opportunity, might well concur in this explanation of Andy's Giants' moment.[38] More telling, however, are explanations offered by Andy and his contemporaries that illuminate both the promise and the problems of investing symbolic purpose in sports heroes as ethnic groups stuggle to come to terms with American life.

Sportswriters responsible for making Cohen a folk hero recognized that he provided a national, public expression of the ability of Jews to make their mark as Americans. They also understood that this role put real strains on the young ballplayer's ability to perform on the diamond. Writing at the time of Cohen's opening-day heroics in 1928, Paul Gallico of the New York *Daily News* prophesized that McGraw's greed and the insatiable demands of loyal Jewish fans would take their toll on this baseball career. As he put it:

> It seems to me a shabby trick to play on young Cohen to send him up onto the diamond to play the Jew in public as well as the ballplayer. Finesse and tact have been lacking in the entire handling of the affair. If Andy Cohen makes good—and it's too early to say that he has done so—he will have surmounted more obstacles than any other big leaguer ever faced. . . . Andy is forced to parade his religion and commercialize it whether he wants to or not. . . . Every time Andy comes to bat he feels he must make a hit, not only for John McGraw, his teammates and the City of New York, but for the Jewish race as well, which is a large order. . . . It looks to me as though these days the baseball magnates are enslaving not only the bodies of their hired help but their souls as well.[39]

Other observers also recognized that Cohen's role as a national symbol for people eager to assert their own claims of Jewish pride and American possibility became a personal burden for the young ballplayer. One was Dan Daniel, the son of East European Jewish residents of New York's Lower East Side, who had changed his name from Daniel Margowitz to further his own career as one of baseball's best-known reporters. Commenting on the constant demands made on him for appearances before Jewish organizations, Daniel wondered if Andy's popularity with Jewish audiences destroyed his baseball talents. Too many "matzoh balls and gefilte fish" were responsible for the ballplayer's woes, Daniel gibed. Once "the upper Broadway herring-tearers got the big series of banquets under way, Cohen couldn't run around the bases without finishing the last quarter on his hands and knees." Harry Glantz of the Los Angeles *B'nai B'rith Messenger* echoed similar sentiments. Reflecting on the ups and downs of Cohen's 1928 season prior to the opening of the 1929 campaign, Glantz wrote that "everywhere he went among his own people he was feted and ballyhooed to the skies." Sportswriters complicated matters by placing "the future of Jewish ballplayers" and "the Giants' hope of every cap-

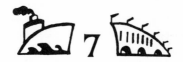

"Mantle, Schmantle, We Got Abie": Jews and Major League Baseball Between the Wars

In 1936, following a failed attempt to mount an American boycott of the Nazi Olympics, Stanley Frank, who often penned columns on the Jewish sporting scene for the Anglo-Jewish press, wrote a book called *The Jew in Sports*. Determined to disprove claims that Jews were weak, cowardly, and disdainful of physical activity, Frank challenged the racial theories of Nazism by demonstrating American Jewish physical toughness. He began by noting that Jews were not part of a race defined by a specific and fixed set of inherited traits but rather were a people with common religious beliefs who adapted their way of life to place and historical circumstance. Nowhere was this more apparent than when examining Jewish physical strength and athletic potential. "Segregate him in the Polish or German ghetto," he wrote of the Jew,

> and the chronic pogroms, constant persecutions, economic misery and the continual strain on his nervous system leaves pronounced marks on his organism. He has a bent and stunted body, a narrow chest, feeble muscles, and a pale complexion. But take him to America . . . give him half a chance to expand, and the Jew in one generation grows in height [and] gains the weight and strength which enables him to participate in the most strenuous activities of the new community. . . . No group of individuals . . . demonstrates this better than the Jewish athlete. He, above all others, has blasted the legend of physical weakness. . . .[1]

Eager to demonstrate Jewish physical prowess both to put the lie to Nazi propaganda and American anti-Semites as well as to show how comfortable Jewish immigrants and their children had become with their new American identities, Frank produced a litany of Jewish-American athletic achievement. The exploits of Jewish boxers, basketball players, and football players dominated his discussion. Baseball, however, was another story. Although he did include chapters on several Jewish major-league ballplayers, Frank argued that baseball was unsuited to Jews, who, for the most part, grew up in urban environments that nurtured "Jewish" traits of intelligence and imagination. Professional baseball, played by men who came from the country rather than the city, simply had no place for "the imaginative athlete"—read Jewish— who "broods over mistakes . . . magnif[ies] the loss of games." Instead, Frank explained,

> the major leaguer seems to take his tempermental cues from the environment in which he was raised. Our country cousin . . . can station himself under a high fly and be entirely oblivious to the fact that the catch can mean the difference between the pennant and second place. . . . The city bred man, whose mental response has been stepped up by the mad rush of his environment, will allow himself to think of the consequences if he should muff the ball and tends to tighten up physically in an effort to make his body keep pace with his mind.[2]

Jews, it seems, were not suited to the tedious pace and long season of the professional baseball player. Better to have the mechanical, slow-witted country bumpkin than the quick-thinking, intelligent, brooding Hebrew. For Frank, the lack of Jewish participation in the big leagues proved his point while also throwing the intelligence of the Jew "into bold relief." By his count, only 30 Jewish players had made it to the majors between 1900 and 1935. Of these, only a dozen had possessed the mechanical ability to stay long, and "very few of them have been labelled stupid or dull players."[3]

Frank's assumptions about race, environment, and "Jewish" characteristics were off-base, but his numbers were close to the mark. Numbers, however, can be deceiving. Although far more second-generation Jewish men gained prominence in football, basketball, and boxing, the success of those few who made it to baseball's major leagues carried special meaning in the 1930s and 1940s.

For Jews in the United States these were especially troubled times. Like all citizens, the Great Depression called into question their own hopes for American success. Be it reports of increasing anti-Semitism at home, the plight of Palestinian Jews, Germany's Nuremberg Laws or stories of Nazi oppression, legitimate concern about preserving and protecting Jewish existence in an increasingly hostile world heightened their anxiety.[4] Hank Greenberg's home runs and Harry Danning's sterling play behind the plate did not put an end to their fears. But at a time when all Americans looked to heroes of one kind or another for promise of better days or for simple relief from daily travail, the presence of Jewish ballplayers in the country's only true national sport provided American Jews comfort and hope that they too would make it through hard times and succeed. Jewish ballplayers, by dint of their sheer physical strength and their willingness to challenge anti-Semites with their fists, also helped shape a changing American Jewish identity, even as they became proud symbols of Jewish survival in a world that daily seemed to threaten Jewish existence. Especially as the United States drew closer to its own conflict with Nazi Germany, they became American heroes for Jew and Gentile alike, helping to soften racial and ethnic tensions at home at a time when all Americans were urged to unite in a common struggle against fascist terror. Set in the midst of economic depression and world war, their stories dramatically illustrate sport's symbolic power in the Jewish-American struggle for identity and acceptance.

I

Reporting on the 1942 Yankees, Dan Daniel told his New York *World Telegram* readers that the Bronx Bombers might go with Ed Whitner Levy at first base. Daniel cautioned "the Levys and Cohens" not to arrange testimonial dinners in Ed's behalf. "He is no more Hebraic," the reporter observed, "than George M. Cohan—and George doubtless knows more Yiddish than Eddie." As Daniel told it, club management urged Whitner, an Irish Catholic, to use his Jewish stepfather's last name as a means of appealing to "the numerous Jewish clients of the Bombers." Shirley Povich, another Jewish sportswriter, writing in the *Washington Post,* was even more precise on this point. As he reported it, Ed Barrow, president of the Yankees, told the young outfielder, "You may be Whitner to the rest of the world, but if you are going to play with the Yankees you'll be Ed Levy."[5]

Although the Yankees' ruse failed, the pursuit of Jewish ballplayers by baseball's establishment first announced by John McGraw in the early 1920s continued apace in the following decades and helps account for the increased presence of Jewish major leaguers. Not surprisingly, New York baseball teams led the way. In 1930 and 1931, when Jimmy Reese, whose real name was James Hymie Solomon, played an occasional second base for the New York Yankees, the team made little of the fact that he was Jewish. Babe Ruth and Lou Gehrig were more than enough to pack Yankee Stadium. By 1935, however, with Ruth in decline and attendance sagging, the Bronx Bombers sought 31-year-old Buddy Myer, the Washington Senators' second baseman who led the American League in batting that year with a .349 average. According to Dan Daniel, in a column headlined "Yanks Hope to Dress Myer as Tailor-Made Jewish Star," the club's interest centered on Myer's hot bat and fielding skills as well as his potential to attract Jewish fans. In the end, Yankees owner Jacob Ruppert, was unwilling to pay Clark Griffith's supposed asking price of $500,000. Although confident of his potential as ethnic hero, Daniel was pleased that Myer never put on the pinstripes. "As a Jewish player he may be worth more to the Yankees than to any other club in the league," but, he argued, Buddy's aging body made him a poor risk.[6]

Although John McGraw never found a Jewish player who matched Andy Cohen's appeal, it was not for lack of effort. In 1930 "the Little Napoleon of

Baseball'' settled on Harry Rosenberg as his "latest Jewish rose." According to one paper, the young, though inexperienced San Francisco outfielder, who had spent the previous summer as a shovel operator for a construction company, was a colorful character who would be popular with Jewish fans. Harry lasted only nine games and went hitless in his five at bats in the majors.[7]

McGraw left the Giants as manager at the tail end of the 1932 season and died two years later of cancer. But the Giants kept up their search for Jewish talent. Phil Weintraub and Harry Danning both arrived at the Polo Grounds in 1933. Harry stayed longer—a career that lasted through 1942 and that marked him as one of the premier catchers of his time. Over a ten-year career Harry the Horse, as he was called, played in 890 games, batted .285, and appeared in two World Series and two All-Star games. Phil played the outfield and an occasional first base for the Giants in the mid-1930s and then came back to the club in 1943 for several more years. In a major-league career that also included stops at Cincinnati and Philadelphia, he played in 444 games and batted .295.

Although Danning's career sustained more public attention over time, it was Weintraub's arrival in New York at the end of the 1933 season that first evoked the Jewish connection. "Again the Giants have reached out for that will-o'-the wisp of baseball, a great Jewish player," reported Daniel when Bill Terry brought Phil up. Although Weintraub had a good spring training in 1934, the Giants farmed him out to Nashville, much to the dismay of New York's Jewish baseball fans. As the *Sporting News* reported in a story headlined "Oi Gewalt! Make Way for the Weintraub Boy," Jewish patrons of the game "beseiged" the Giants' front office with letters criticizing the club's failure to call up the "big Jewish lad" who was tearing up the minors at a .400 clip. By August, Phil was in New York. Stories tracing his exploits that summer rarely failed to mention his Jewishness, wondering if this "Star of David" would become "New York's long awaited Jewish baseball star."[8]

Unfortunately for Weintraub and his Jewish audience, Phil appeared in only 46 games during the 1934 and 1935 seasons and in 1937 was traded to Cincinnati. By then, however, Harry Danning had become New York's Jewish star. Throughout his career, the appearance of Danning's name in the New York press invariably was accompanied by reference to him as a Jew—most often by phrases such as "Jewish catcher" or "Jewish lad" and occasionally by comments about his "hawk nose" or his "schnozz."[9]

Whether or not Branch Rickey realized the potential Jackie Robinson had to bring out black baseball fans by participating in the pursuit of Jewish ballplayers, the Brooklyn Dodgers also joined the hunt. Representing a community of 3 million people, almost half of whom were Jewish, Rickey and Larry MacPhail, the Dodgers' general manager whom he succeeded, made it their business to find Jewish players. Although the Dodgers missed out on Sid Gordon, a Brooklyn resident who grew up and lived in the shadows of Ebbets Field while playing for the New York Giants in the 1940s, Fred Sington, Max Rosenfeld, Goody Rosen, Harry Eisenstat, and Cal Abrams all took turns as the Dodgers' Jewish drawing cards. After 1947 until they deserted Brooklyn for the

West Coast ten years later, the club could always count on Jake Pitler, one of their coaches, as their continual "Jewish presence."[10]

New York teams were not alone in seeking out ballplayers whose ethnic identities might attract paying customers. Baseball's master entrepreneur and showman Bill Veeck, for instance, openly insisted that as Cleveland's general manager he sought to sign a "representative of every group of the city's population."[11] Such conscious admissions were not lost on *The Sporting News,* which reported in 1936 that a New York Giant scout, in search of "Hebrew players," had rejected Wally Moses as a prospect to lead the Giants out of the wilderness when he found out that he wasn't Jewish.[12] This claim notwithstanding, religion was never a substitute for ability when it came to selecting ballplayers. Still, the stories of virtually all Jewish ballplayers who played ball in the major leagues between 1930 and 1955 underline the real effort to attract Jewish baseball customers by looking for competent ballplayers who happened to be Jewish.

II

Like those who played before them, the careers of these Jewish ballplayers were mixed. Some, like Buddy Myer, Harry Danning, Sid Gordon, Al and Goody Rosen, and, of course, Hank Greenberg, had long and distinguished stays in the major leagues. Others, like Harry Rosenberg and Cy Block, barely survived a season or two. Baseball owners gave them the chance to play because their Jewish names and baseball talent meant good business. In New York, Chicago, and in other cities that fielded teams with Jewish players as well as in places where people's only connection with major league baseball was through the press, Jewish fans avidly followed the exploits of Jewish major leaguers and turned them to their own purpose.

Whether sons of rabbis or butcher-shop owners, Bar Mitzvahed or not, steeped in traditional European ways or born into eagerly assimilating American families—regardless of their baseball ability or their own feelings about their Jewish identity—Jewish ballplayers all experienced open expressions of Jewish pride and became visible symbols of ethnic identity and American accomplishment. Set in the context of the Great Depression, which often cast doubt on immigrant expectations for American success, their very presence kept alive in special ways a wider sense of Jewish possibility. In his own Chicago Jewish immigrant family, sportswriter Ira Berkow remembers baseball as the symbol of American experience, "a wholly American game" in which "it was as tough to succeed in as it was to succeed in the country at large." For his father and uncle who idolized Hank Greenberg, more than anything baseball also demonstrated that in America, with "sweat and brains and imagination . . . anything was possible."[13] Pride in the accomplishments of major-league Jewish ballplayers gave a special poignancy to these connections.

At a minimum, expression of these sentiments appeared in Jewish newspaper columns that kept track of baseball owners' search for Jewish talent, stories of Jewish players that appeared at the beginning and end of each base-ball season, or year-end summaries of Jewish accomplishment in sport that religiously recorded the names and exploits of Jewish amateur and profes-sional athletes. Harry Rosenberg's signing with the New York Giants in 1930, Phil Weintraub's acquisition by the same club three years later, and Morrie Arnovich's arrival in Philadelphia in 1936, for instance, all made the pages of the *American Hebrew,* the Philadelphia *Jewish Exponent,* and the California *Jew-ish Voice.*[14] In a May 1935 column titled "Highlights in Jewish Sports," the *Voice* offered a typical example of columns that informed readers of the where-abouts and expectations of Jewish major leaguers. Focusing on the prospects of Phil Weintraub, Milt Galazter, Joe Greenberg, Harry Danning, and Izzy Goldstein, it noted that with Weintraub, "the Giants are blessed with a col-orful Jewish player." "Harry Danning, Giants catcher, and Izzy Goldstein, Tiger pitcher," it concluded, "are two more rookies of Jewish faith who are destined to carve their names in the hall of big league fame."[15]

In matter-of-fact fashion, annual summaries of Jewish athletic accom-plishment provided further evidence that Jews were as American as anyone else by detailing the exploits of Jewish baseball players. One such column appeared in the Philadelphia *Jewish Exponent* in 1939, after the New York Yan-kees swept the Cincinnati Reds in four games to win the World Series. Although no Jews participated in the Series (the paper warned its readers not to be misled by the name of the Cincinnati reserve catcher, Hershberger, who was not Jewish), nevertheless it found it "appropriate . . . to review the rec-ords compiled this year by Jewish players in the big leagues," most notably because the 1939 season witnessed "a new high insofar as Jewish participa-tion in big league baseball is concerned."[16]

These compilations rarely went beyond the simple listing of Jewish ball-players. Other newspaper coverage, in both the Anglo-Jewish and the regular press, left no doubt of what these men meant to Jewish audiences. When Mor-rie Arnovich, a small-town boy from Superior, Wisconsin, became a regular outfielder with the Philadelphia Phillies in 1937, he found himself constantly referred to as "the son of Israel" or the next "Jewish star" whose success in "the great American pastime," as one writer for the *American Hebrew* put it, would make his people proud. Dan Daniel, writing for the New York *World Telegram and Sun,* linked Arnovich to Phil Weintraub of the Giants and Harry Eisenstat, a new Dodger pitcher, in musing that these three Jewish players may well "give the Chosen People something to talk about in a baseball way."[17]

Even more emphatic about such possibilities was Henry Levy. In a 1937 column for the *American Hebrew,* Levy pointed out that "Greater New York, the largest Jewish community in the world," had been "singularly unfortu-nate in its selection of Jewish ball players." Hank Greenberg had escaped to Detroit, Jimmy Reese "couldn't make the grade with the Yankees, and the stories of John McGraw's efforts to develop a Jewish star are legion." Now, however, Levy announced to his readers, the Dodgers had discovered Brook-lyn-born Eisenstat, a right-handed pitcher who managed to last seven innings in his major-league debut before being relieved by Van Lingle Mungo. Those who cheered Harry as he walked to the dugout left no doubt that he was already "the white haired boy of the Jewish fans."[18] In the same spirit, Harry Glantz of the Los Angeles *B'nai B'rith Messenger* noted what "a sight for the sore eyes of Jewish baseball fans" it had been to watch a St. Louis–Cleveland series in which the shortstops for each team, Jim Levey and Jonah Goldman, were both Jewish. Levey gave Glantz and his Jewish audience further cause for celebration when the shortstop refuted a sportswriter's claim that he was not Jewish. Glantz gleefully informed his readers that the young twenty-three-year-old from Pittsburgh openly denied the charge. "You tell him and everyone else who cares to know," Levey proclaimed, "that I am a Jew . . . and mighty proud of it."[19]

Jews did more than simply follow the exploits of their heroes in the sports pages. Be it at B'nai B'rith lodge meetings or father-and-son synagogue banquets, Jewish ballplayers received and honored countless invitations to talk about their achievements, their Jewish connections, or how to hit a curve ball.[20] Just as Italian fans honored Tony Lazzeri and Joe DiMaggio with "days" at the ballpark, Jewish faithful bestowed similar tributes on their local ethnic favorites. Morrie Arnovich found himself the object of such displays during the 1939 season. In his best major-league season, playing for a last-place Phillies club, the right-handed outfielder appeared in 134 games, batted .324, fifth best in the majors, and led his team with 67 RBIs. Several times during the season representatives of Philadelphia's Jewish community honored Morrie. In the middle of a 17-game hitting streak during a doubleheader with the Chicago Cubs, the Springfield, Pennsylvania, YMHA presented their hero with a radio and traveling bag at home plate. Morrie responded by going five for nine in the two games.[21] Far more elaborate, however, was a July 16 celebration at Shibe Park. "Morrie Arnovich Day" brought some 13,000 paying customers through the turnstiles. Predominant among them were members of the Jewish War Veterans, the YMHA and the YWHA, local synagogues, and the B'nai B'rith. Also present was Morrie's father, who had come all the way from Superior to see his son play in the majors for the first time. Together the groups presented Arnovich with new fishing gear and honored him after the games with a banquet.[22]

Morrie stayed hot through July. Wherever he played, the league's leading hitter was showered with gifts and presentations by Jewish fans. Much like Andy Cohen, however, he discovered that being a Jewish hero was not always easy. Even the little piece of material his mother sewed on his sweatshirt for good luck before the start of the season could not prevent an August slide which saw Arnovich go 21 at bats without a hit. Doc Protho, the Phillies' manager, benched his star, explaining:

> there have been too many presentations at the plate, too many handshakes, too many delegations telling him to "bear down for us today.". . . Down in Cincinnati he was called to the plate three times to receive gifts and as the season has progressed his popularity has grown so that our trips have been

triumphal tours. He's still the best hitter in the league but all this has finally made him tighten up . . . so I decided to give him a rest.[23]

Although neither Cal Abrams nor Jake Pitler ever had seasons as successful as Arnovich's 1939 campaign, they too had their "days" and "nights." Brooklyn's Jewish fans honored Cal with a "night" during the 1951 season, his last full year with the Dodgers. Similar festivities were held in 1948, when he played for the Dodgers' Baltimore farm club, and again in 1954, when he was traded from the Pittsburgh Pirates to the Baltimore Orioles. Baltimore's small Jewish community, centered around the Jewish Progressive Club, embraced Abrams and his wife. Its members invited them to weddings, holiday celebrations, and suppers at the club. As his wife Mae recalls, "Cal Abrams night . . . was just their way of saying what a source of pride it was for them to have a Jewish ballplayer."[24]

Jake Pitler, the Dodger's first-base coach when Cal came up to Brooklyn, received two "days" at Ebbets Field. On one occasion, Rabbi Joseph Wise of the West End Temple in Neponsit, New York, made clear why local Jews honored Pitler as one of their own. Wise praised Jake for his sportsmanship, his devotion to humanitarian causes, and most important, his visible statement of Jewishness by refusing to coach for the Dodgers if games fell on Rosh Hashonah or Yom Kippur.[25] Such connections were not lost on Brooklyn's Jewish population—as Jews, as loyal members of the Flatbush community, and as Americans for whom baseball was both symbol and passion. Michael Ebner, today an historian, fondly remembers Vin Scully and Red Barber carefully explaining to their radio audience the religious reason for Pitler's absence. "Jake Pitler," he recalls, "always made me proud as a youngster because he connected two things that were important to me: being Jewish and rooting passionately for Brooklyn to eclipse the Yankees in next year's World Series."[26]

Ebner's attachment to his Dodgers, his Jewishness, and to Brooklyn evokes a world in which second-generation American Jews and their children could comfortably participate in American society while maintaining a strong and enduring sense of Jewish identity. As Deborah Dash Moore describes Brooklyn between the wars, it was a place where Jews lived in vibrant ethnic neighborhoods full of constant religious and secular manifestations of Jewishness. Surrounded by their own kind in their apartment houses, stores, movie theaters, clubs, temples, and schools, for the most part they served each other's economic and social needs. Despite living in a country where Jews made up an insignificant part of the total population, in Brooklyn, Jews were a majority—proud and unafraid to announce themselves as Americans and as Jews.[27]

In such a setting, particularly for children of East European working-class immigrants struggling to outdo their parents in pursuit of the American dream, a Pitler or an Abrams only confirmed the legitimacy of their own desires. How else to explain the reaction of Brooklyn's Jewish fans when Abrams, whose proudest moment in baseball came when he put on a Dodger uniform, joined the club in 1949? When this son of a Russian immigrant and the product of the Jewish neighborhood surrounding Brooklyn's James Madison High School moved his ballplaying skills from the corner of Quentin Road and Bedford Avenue up the street a few miles to Ebbets Field, the *New York Post,* speaking for its Brooklyn Jewish constituency, proclaimed: "Mantle, Schmantle, We got Abie."[28]

III

Not all Jews lived in Brooklyn. Nor did Jews there or elsewhere necessarily experience assimilation as a smooth process, with little conflict between parents and children. Still, the *Post*'s celebration and Ebner's recollection suggest that Jewish major leaguers were a visible source of pride for Jewish-Americans and that the game itself contained the power to unite different generations of Jews caught up in becoming Americans. Those Jewish ballplayers who confronted anti-Semitism in the 1930s and 1940s also enhanced ethnic pride and unity by contributing to a public Jewish identity of a strong, tough people able to resist any challenge to their survival.

There is no evidence to suggest that Jewish major leaguers were aware that East European Jewish immigrants who came to the United States in the first decades of the 20th century received encouragement from some of their leaders to become physically strong in order to protect themselves and to insure a continued Jewish presence. Coming of age and playing ball in an era bounded by the anti-Semitic charges of Henry Ford and Father Coughlin on one end and news of the Holocaust and Israel's violent struggle for national survival on the other, however, they and other American Jews experienced constant reminders of the precarious nature of Jewish existence. As professional baseball players, they also encountered anti-Semitism from teammates, opponents, and fans. Some of them, like Harry Danning, Phil Weintraub, and Cal Abrams, interpreted these jibes and taunts as part of the sport—typical distractions designed to throw them off their game—rather than examples of overt and conscious anti-Semitism.[29] The majority, however, recognized prejudice as part of their baseball experience and vigorously challenged it.

Typical is Cy Block, a Brooklyn boy born in 1919 who went on to become a successful life-insurance salesman and an active supporter of Jewish organizations and causes such as the B'nai B'rith and the Maccabiah Games. Block played in the minor leagues in the late 1930s and eventually made it to the Chicago Cubs for a brief major-league career spanning 17 games during the 1942 and 1946 seasons. Talking about his entire professional baseball career, much of it spent in places like Paragould, Arkansas, and Macon, Georgia, he insists that every Jewish ballplayer he know "w[as] the butt of anti-Semitic jibes, remarks and obscenities." His experiences ranged from dealing with headlines in Jonesboro, Arkansas, that encouraged locals to "Come See the Jewish Second Baseman" to name-calling and spiking by opponents. At least on one occasion, Block retaliated by putting a tag on an abusive player as he tried to steal second base. As he describes it, "I got the ball and planted it squarely in his mouth, knocking out six teeth. He wasn't in too much of a position to call me a Jew bastard."[30]

Block's visceral challenge certainly contributed to his personal sense that Jews were willing and able to defend themselves against a hostile world in whatever guise it appeared. Ultimately, however, the significance of such incidents in terms of their impact on the shaping of an American Jewish identity rests with how others interpreted them. The experiences of Charles Solomon "Buddy" Myer, Goody Rosen, and Al Rosen suggest how private confrontations became transformed into public symbols of the proud, tough Jew.

"Buddy" Myer was one of the premier baseball players of his generation. Born in Ellisville, Mississippi, in 1904, he graduated from Mississippi A and M in 1925 and immediately began a major-league career that spanned 17 seasons, all but two spent with the Washington Senators. In 1935, the same year a young Hank Greenberg was chosen as the American League's most valuable player, Myer won the batting crown with a .349 average, some 46 points better than his lifetime mark of .303. A participant in two All-Star games and two World Series, the feisty second baseman retired in 1941 with 2,131 hits, the most ever by a Jewish ballplayer. Many of these details appeared in the *Sporting News* announcement of the end of his career in October 1941. Included as well was a brief reminder of his involvement in one of the more celebrated fights in major league baseball history—his altercation with the Yankees' Ben Chapman.[31]

Early in the 1933 season, the Yankees and Senators met at Washington's Griffith Stadium. Over 7000 fans, including John Garner, the Vice President of the United States, watched the Yankees club the home team 16–0. Newspaper accounts of the game, however, paid less attention to the score than to a riot that erupted after Chapman successfully broke up a double play by taking out "Buddy" Myer at second base. As reported by Shirley Povich, Myer retaliated by kicking Chapman in the back. An ensuing fistfight between the two players escalated into a full-scale twenty-minute battle between players from both clubs and some 300 fans who rushed onto the field. After a police riot squad ended the fight, Myer and Chapman were ejected from the game. On the way to the dressing room, "Buddy" threw a punch at the Yankees' Earl Whitehall. Whitehall fought back and was also tossed out. After reviewing accounts of the incident, American League president Will Harridge suspended Myer, Chapman, and Whitehall for five games and fined them each $100.[32]

Povich, whose account of the affair lingered for a week in his *Washington Post* columns, chided the league for its leniency (he wondered if Harridge was pleased with the fight as a "needed tonic" to remind baseball fans that the "game isn't entirely populated by business-men ballplayers who think only in terms of wages") but explained it as part of the game. Although he acknowledged that Chapman had been out to "get" Myer for a long time, Povich made no mention of Chapman's reputation as an anti-Semite or that anti-Semitism provided him any motivation. Myer, himself, remained publicly silent about what happened.[33]

Thirteen years later, faced with threats to Israel's existence as a new, independent nation and recent revelations about the extent and violence of Nazi atrocities against European Jews, Harold Ribalow interpreted the incident quite differently. In his book *The Jew in American Sports,* published in 1948, Ribalow, as Stanley Frank had attempted in 1936, highlighted the achievements of prominent Jewish-American athletes in order to demonstrate that Jews were no different than other Americans. Examples of courageous Jewish boxers, football players, and baseball players unafraid of "flying spikes," he hoped, would prove that "it is a lie to call Jews cowards." They would also demonstrate an American Jewish tradition of physicality and toughness. Unlike Frank, however, who minimized the importance of professional baseball players, Ribalow, aware of baseball's symbolic importance as America's National Game and the prominence given by the press and radio to the sport, provided more portraits of Jews in baseball than in any other sport. He even included a chapter on Johnny Kling, despite his suspect Jewish origins. Also highlighted was "Buddy" Myer and a full account of his fight with Ben Chapman.

Without any attempt to describe Myer's background or his feelings about being a Jew, Ribalow reincarnated him as a Jewish freedom fighter. Declaring that Chapman was a known anti-Semite, Ribalow surmised that "the fiery Chapman must have been shocked to see the slight Jewish infielder take off against him. Perhaps it made him reconsider his ideas of Jews. Whatever the case may have been, Myer showed that he took dirt from no one. He played his game and did the best he could, but he never let anyone step over him."[34]

Neither Chapman nor Myer publicly offered their interpretations of the fight. Nor do we know much about Myer's religious upbringing, whether his small-town Mississippi childhood provided any sense of ethnic identity, or what his own feelings were about being Jewish. As a prominent athlete identified as a Jew, playing the nation's most publicized game, it hardly mattered to Ribalow or to his Jewish readers.

Goody Rosen, a contemporary of Myer, who remains proud of his baseball career and his Jewish identity, certainly understands his own experiences in these terms. Born and raised in Toronto, George "Goody" Rosen became a Jewish baseball hero to Brooklyn Jews when he played the outfield for the Dodgers in the late 1930s and again, for three years, after the end of World War II.[35] Born in 1912, he recalls his father as a poor, hard-working machinist who struggled hard to put food on the table for his eight children. Although his mother was an orthodox Jew who kept a kosher home, "Goody" remembers that the simple business of surviving took precedence over concern about formal religious training or observance. Between selling newspapers to help make ends meet and playing all sorts of sports in playground leagues and parks, he had little time for religion and was not Bar Mitzvahed. Nevertheless, then and now he retains a strong Jewish sensibility complete with a defiant pride ready to challenge any anti-Semitic threat. Talking about himself in 1984 at the age of 72, he asserted: "I may be old in years but not in mind . . . I have always felt and believed that the Jewish people are far superior in every way to everyone else." Commenting on anti-Semitism he and other Jews experienced on and off the ballfield in the late 1930s, he proudly recalls: "We took care of ourselves, we gave as good as we got and we emerged stronger than ever. I've always," he concluded, "since I was a small kid, walked proudly that I was a Jew, and never took any crap, pardon the word, from anyone."[36]

"Goody" Rosen is not a devout Jew. Yet in his mind, and I suspect in the minds of many who identified with him and other Jewish ballplayers in the 1930s and the 1940s, his lack of religious training did not diminish his sense of Jewishness, one that included a clear physical dimension and a willingness to ward off forcibly any anti-Semitic attacks on his person or his people. Although his playing days began as Goody's ended, Al Rosen, an all-star third baseman for the Cleveland Indians from 1947 through 1956 and currently general manager of the San Fransisco Giants, emphatically endorses these sentiments.

Brought up by his mother and grandmother, Rosen's Miami, Florida, childhood lacked formal religious training but offered plenty of opportunity to defend his faith, one that he has been fiercely proud of since childhood despite the lack of a formal Jewish education.[37] Living in a Gentile neighborhood, Rosen frequently experienced anti-Semitism in its crudest adolescent forms and retaliated in kind. A good boxer who learned the craft at local Miami gyms, Rosen's "Jewish education," as Roger Kahn described it in 1973, "was measured in jabs and hooks." As Al recalls it, although he didn't look for trouble, "when it came to me, I wanted to end it and damn quick."[38]

Rosen's stance as a tough Jew and ballplayer followed him into the major leagues. Described as a ballplayer "who would be at home . . . among the old timers" because of his "fierce disregard for pain and injury . . . and his natural zest for combat," he challenged all comers who in any way questioned his faith or heritage.[39] Newspapers reported such stories and other Jewish base-ballers recall them. Hank Greenberg, who, as general manager of the Cleveland Indians, brought Rosen to the club in 1949, remembered how the city's fans reviled him and unmercifully attacked Rosen as a Jew when he replaced Ken Keltner, a "nice Catholic boy," at third base.[40] Saul Rogovin, who played against Rosen, recalls a game against the Cleveland Indians when one of his teammates called Rosen a "Jew bastard." Rosen, who Rogovin describes as "a tough guy," "walked over to our dugout and said, 'That son of a bitch who called me a Jew bastard, would he care to say that again.'"[41]

Through it all, Rosen made clear his own definition of what it was to be Jewish and his pride in being identified as a Jewish ballplayer. "To me," he insists, "a Jew is a feel. The wanderings and the searchings and the longings are in your background and they make you feel compassion and they drive you to search for something good." Aware that Jewish adolescents saw him as an ethnic hero, Rosen took the job seriously, never played on Yom Kippur, and appeared at numerous charity affairs. While in Cleveland he actively worked for the United Jewish Appeal, the Jewish Welfare Federation, and as a fundraiser for the city's Jewish community center. He even considered changing his name to Rosenthal or Rosenstein so that there would be no mis-taking his roots. As he put it: "When I was up in the majors, I always knew how I wanted it to be about me. . . . Here comes one Jewish kid that every Jew in the world can be proud of."[42]

For Al and Goody Rosen, that image, both personally held and publicly presented, included an assertive pride in being Jewish regardless of the lack of formal Jewish training, an emphasis on strength and physicality, whether protrayed on the ballfield or off, a sense of exclusion and superiority, a com-passion about and sensitivity to human suffering consistent with their own personal struggles to achieve, and a conscious awareness and connection to an historical memory of Jewish suffering and survival that compelled them to challenge any attack on them as Jews. As Roger Kahn put it, describing Al Rosen, "he carries the burden of being a Jew defiantly. Talking to him . . . one suspects that even now, as parent, businessman, and tennis player, he would react to an anti-Semitic remark by shedding his tweed jacket . . . and punching hard to end it fast, the way he used to in Miami . . . so that whoever started this, and whoever was observing would remember, next time, they were inclined to pick on a Jew."[43]

As proud and defiant as he is of his Jewish identity, Al Rosen is also a proud American. Like many major-league ballplayers, Jewish or otherwise, he served in the military during World War II and has enjoyed successful careers as a player and baseball executive. For Rosen, hard work, perseverance, and faith in American values and opportunity has made it all possible. Speaking before the National Conference of Christians and Jews at their annual meet-ing in Washington, D. C., in 1953, for instance, he declared baseball as free of prejudice and an arena where "color and religion don't mean a thing. . . . The only question baseball asks . . . is 'can you produce?'"[44]

IV

Reminiscent of other second-generation Jewish men who made their mark in the world of basketball in the years between the wars, Rosen's loyalty to both Jewish and American connections is neither unusual nor contradictory. But because he and other Jewish major-league ballplayers received far greater public attention than any other group of American athletes, more so than oth-ers they became available heroes and role models for Jew and Gentile alike. Their promotion as national symbols who worked for everyone became part of a conscious effort to rally all Americans in the war against fascism. Although it did not amelioriate all hostility and tension or remove painfully real barriers to full equality for all ethnic and racial groups in the United States, baseball's role as middle ground between minority cultures and an American majority helped create an atmosphere that promised such possibil-ities.

Sportswriters contributed to the effort by downplaying the ethnic identity of Jewish ballplayers. When Harry Danning, Morrie Arnovich, and Phil Weintraub first arrived on the major league scene, stories about them invariably referred to them as "the son of Israel" or the next "Jewish star."[45] By 1940, however, such references were rare. Dan Daniel, writing for the *Sporting News,* explained why. Writing about Harry Danning's emergence as "the best catcher in either league," Daniel noted that in the future his stories about the Giant catcher would deal only with his baseball ability rather than his Jewish background. Despite his own stories over the years that underlined the ethnic attachments of professional athletes, Daniel claimed that to him "it was always . . . senseless to point out that Joe Blotz was the greatest atheist short-stop who ever hit an agnostic pitcher in the clutch because I never heard of a fan who held back his cheer for a homer to see if it was walloped by a member of his church." In the spirit of American consensus and unity in the face of world war, fans, he implied, were concerned with ability and production, not one's religious affiliation.[46]

Efforts to present baseball as a sport open to all where talent and ability, rather than race or religion, were the only requirements for success and accep-tance resurrected a traditional democratic homily about sport in the service of a country gearing for war. Growing anti-German sentiment even allowed exceptional black athletes like Jesse Owens and Joe Louis to become symbols of American democratic dominance over Nazi assertions of Aryan superior-ity.[47] While Nazi atrocities intensified Jewish outrage and a deepened aware-ness of Jewish identity for Jews in the United States, it also encouraged their desire as Americans to join together to defeat Germany. In an effort to unite the country against the Axis powers, they and other ethnic groups were por-trayed first and foremost as part of a larger group—an American force capable of preserving democracy and freedom in the world.

Anyone familiar with the history of these years knows there is another side to the story—internment camps for Japanese-Americans, the celebration of black athletes as heroes of American democracy at a time when American blacks lived in poverty, segregation, and often in fear of their lives, and, for Jews, anti-Semitism of all sorts, from the ragings of a Father Coughlin to the more silent discrimination at corporations, clubs, and colleges throughout the country. Still, despite a clearly mixed record, efforts in and out of the sports-world to mute derogatory ethnic and racial distinctions in the pursuit of the common goal of American victory made it more comfortable for such peoples to feel less self-conscious and hesitant in asserting themselves as Americans.

The Allied victory did not halt the struggle against racism or baseball's role in it. Most significantly, Jackie Robinson's breaking of the color line in 1947 not only desegregated major-league baseball but offered an enduring legacy of symbol and practice to the civil rights movement of the 1950s and 1960s.[48] As portrayed in the press and elsewhere, Jewish major leaguers, while not as prominent, also were put to similar service. Harold Ribalow's 1948 tribute to Jewish athletes, for instance, extolled the world of sport where Jewish base-ball players were given the opportunity to succeed or fail on their merit as representative of a "democratic" and "tolerant" America.[49] Columns and advertisements in the *American Hebrew* emphasized similar concerns for "inter-faith amity" by publicizing a nation-wide "He Can Pitch!" publicity campaign that encouraged Americans not to discriminate against each other. Featured in the paper was a picture of four boys, three whites and one black, preparing to play baseball. One white boy, bat on his shoulder, asserts: "What's his race or religion got to do with it—He can Pitch!" Endorsing the campaign in 1948, the *Hebrew* printed a photograph of Jackie Robinson, "the first Negro to enter the major leagues," and Danny Litwhiler, a Cincinnati Reds player, shaking hands while holding a "He can Pitch!" poster that was to be displayed throughout Cincinnati's transit system.[50] Similar hopes that baseball might become a model of the advantages of an open and tolerant American society were also invoked by Dan Daniel. Reviewing the Brooklyn Dodgers' 1949 lineup, Daniel noted that Branch Rickey, the man most responsible for bringing Robinson into the majors, had done "quite a job building a house of all nations." Referring to the team as an "American melting pot," the columnist declared that "with the Jewish Abrams, the Teutonic Reese, Negroes Robinson and Campanella, Polish Miksis and Hermanski, Slovokian Shuba, Italians Furillo and Ramazotti, Italian-Hungarian Branca, Scandinavian Haugstad and Jorgenson, Celtic Kevin Conners and a delegation representing basic American stocks of English, Scotch-Irish ingredients, there is truly a Yankee appeal to the Brooklyn outfit which may win the pennant."[51]

As any Brooklyn boy knows, the Dodgers won the pennant before losing the World Series in five games to the New York Yankees. While members of Daniel's ethnic and racial lineup all played that year, their contributions to the club's success were not equal. Cal Abrams, the Dodgers' Jewish hope, played in eight games and managed only two hits in 24 at bats. Jackie Robinson, on the other hand, propelled the Dodgers to the pennant with his bat and speed. He led the league in hitting and stolen bases and was second in RBIs and slugging percentage—numbers good enough to earn him the National League's most valuable player award. Jackie managed all this despite constant racist harassment from players and fans.

Robinson faced prejudice and discrimination far greater than any Jewish major leaguer ever experienced. Aware that much more was at stake than the simple success or failure of one man's baseball career, he recalled that when he first came to up to the Dodgers in 1947, one opposing ballplayer in particular encouraged him in his struggle. That year, Hank Greenberg, wearing a Pittsburgh Pirates uniform, was in the last season of a glorious major-league career spent mostly with the Detroit Tigers. Aware of the pressures on the Dodger rookie, the Jewish veteran offered advice and support. The Pirates called Jackie "Coal Mine" and worse, Greenberg remembered. When one pitcher hit Robinson, "he stood beside me on first base with his chin up like a prince. I had a feeling for him because of the way I had been treated. I remember saying to him, 'Don't let them get you down. You're doing fine. Keep it up.'"[52]

Hank Greenberg's own experiences with bigotry on the diamond and the burden he carried as the most prominent Jewish baseball player ever to play the game made him fit teacher for the rookie Robinson. Greenberg remains the greatest American Jewish sports hero of all time. His special importance as advisor, hero, and symbol of all that baseball offered to American Jews demand special attention be paid to the career of this Bronx boy who made good in Detroit.

V

In a September 1935 *Sporting News* story headlined "Oi, Oi, Oh Boy! Hail That Long Sought Hebrew Star," Fred Lieb announced that Hank Greenberg was a good bet to win the American League's most valuable player award. Complete with a caricature of a long-nosed Hasidic Jew bemoaning the fact that the Yankees had let Greenberg "slip away," Lieb's prophetic column also noted that Hank's success and that of other Jewish players, past and present, challenged longstanding explanations for the scarcity of outstanding Jewish talent in the big leagues. Arguments that a lack of opportunity, the small size of Jews, their disinterest in sport, even a supposed cultural unfamiliarity with cooperative efforts nurtured by a centuries-old necessity to rely on individual wit in order to survive had "been knocked into a cocked hat by the big bat of Hefty Hank Greenberg of Detroit. . . ." One year earlier, the Detroit *Jewish Chronicle* reported on a contest in which baseball fans were asked to name the greatest Jewish player of all time. Finishing far ahead of Weintraub, Danning, and Moe Berg and polling twice the vote of runner-up Johnny Kling, Hank Greenberg, only in his second full season in the majors, won easily. If such a poll were held today, only Sandy Koufax would offer a serious challenge.[53]

Greenberg's credentials as baseball star are impeccable. A perennial American League All-Star, "Hammerin Hank" batted a lifetime .313 in a thirteen-year career interrupted by four years of military service during World War II. Four times the right-handed first baseman led the American League in home runs and runs batted in. Four times he led the Detroit Tigers into the World Series. In 1935 he won the league's most valuable player award. Three years later he hit 58 home runs in a furious chase to reach Babe Ruth's record 60. Hank's career totals placed him among the lifetime leaders in batting average (62nd), home runs (41st), slugging average (5th at .605), ratio of home runs to at bats (9th), and the ratio of RBIs to at bats (3rd). In 1956 he became the first Jewish ballplayer to be elected to Baseball's Hall of Fame.

Career statistics and paeans offered by a sportswriter and by fans at the outset of his days as a major-league ballplayer capture a sense of what Hank Greenberg meant to American Jews. His presence and power demolished stereotypes about Jewish physical weakness. As "the long sought Hebrew Star," both second-generation Jews eager for assimilation and acceptance as well as Jews tied more closely to a more traditional European Jewish past took pride in his accomplishments. The belief that a democratic American society had made it all possible by giving this son of an immigrant an ample chance to prove himself offered similar hope to other American Jews struggling through the Great Depression. All this and more are imbedded in Greenberg's story.

Hank was born on Perry Street on New York's Lower East Side in 1911. When he was six, his family moved to the Jewish neighborhood surrounding James Monroe High School in the Bronx. His parents, David and Sarah, were Rumanian immigrants who met and married in America. They kept a kosher home, observed the high holidays, and sent their son to Hebrew school. Hank's father owned a textile shrinking company in Manhattan and worked hard, along wth his wife, to secure a comfortable middle-class life and the possibility of American success for their children. As Hank recalls, his parents, like others of their generation, hoped "their children [would] become doctors, dentists, lawyers, or school teachers."[54]

Regardless of David and Sarah's dreams, Hank remembers a childhood obsessed with sports, especially baseball. Although he played all kinds of sports as a youngster (he was good enough in basketball to lead his high-school team to the city championship), "baseball," he recalls, "was the only sport that really mattered . . . the only game you could find on the sports pages." For Hank and his friends, "a star ballplayer was on a par with Sergeant York or Charles Lindbergh." Eagerly they spent their money in penny arcades, hoping that machines full of baseball cards would yield "a picture of Rogers Hornsby, Christy Mathewson, or some other great star."[55] Ironically, the man who would be known as the "Jewish Babe Ruth" picked the Great Bambino as his idol. He went to Yankee Stadium often, waiting for a chance to see the Babe as he came out of the players' entrance. "I'd watch him with hungry eyes as he walked to a car. When I say that I worshiped Babe Ruth I'm putting into words what every New York kid felt in those days."[56]

Hank's American passion initially disappointed a father's hopes for his son. Interviewed by John Spink of the *Sporting News* in 1940, David Greenberg recalled that "for a time Hank's baseball ambitions had me angry. . . . I wanted him to go to college and become a professional man." Nor did he like family habits upset by Hank's baseball routines. "I had a rule," he told Spink, "that the entire family had to be at the dinner table every evening. Nothing could be served until I came home. Imagine how I felt when we had to wait evening after evening, because Hank was across in the park playing ball."[57]

Hank also recalled that his love of baseball and his decision to make it his career was not warmly greeted by his parent's friends. "It wasn't long ago," he told a reporter for the Detroit *Jewish Chronicle* in 1935, "that the Jewish women on my block . . . would point me out as a good-for-nothing, a loafer, and a bum who always wanted to play baseball rather than go to school. Friends and relatives sympathized with my mother because she was the parent of a big gawk who cared more for baseball . . . than school books. I was Mrs. Greenberg's disgrace."[58] By the time he offered this reminiscence, however, Hank was already a household name and not anyone's disgrace. His success with the Detroit Tigers and public attention over his decision whether to play ball on the Jewish high holidays at the close of the 1934 season made sure of that.

Greenberg's first years with the Tigers were not auspicious. He signed with Detroit at the age of 19, played one game for them in 1930, and spent three years in their farm system before coming up for good in 1933. Harry Glantz, who kept track of Jewish baseballers for his Los Angeles readers, even had trouble remembering his name, often referring to him as Harry. When he corrected himself in a 1931 column, it was only to report Greenberg's demotion to the minors. "S'too bad," moaned Glantz, "as 'Hank' was heralded as one of our greatest prospects."[59]

By the close of the 1933 season, however, Greenberg was being touted by the *American Hebrew* as "the elusive Hebrew star for whose discovery and acquisition John McGraw and Miller Huggins—canny ball club builders of New York—spent fortunes in vain."[60] Such acclaim hinged on Greenberg's rookie-year performance. Playing for a club that finished fifth behind the Washington Senators and batting the same .301 as his boyhood hero, Babe Ruth, Greenberg hit 12 home runs and batted in 87 runs.

Accompanying this praise were different explanations for the failure of the Yankees to sign this Bronx boy as one of their own. According to one tale, once Hank had made up his mind to be a major-league ballplayer, his parents invited scouts from both the Yankees and the Tigers to a Shabbat dinner. When only the Tiger scout showed up to enjoy Sarah's gefilte fish, Hank chose Detroit. Another story had Hank signing with the Tigers because they were willing to allow him to go to college while he played ball.[61] In fact, neither pursuit of an education nor devotion to his mother's Jewish cooking was the key factor in Hank's decision. Although it's true that the Tigers offered to allow him to finish his first year at New York University before coming to Detroit, the opportunity to play determined Hank's choice. A self-described "slugging first baseman," Greenberg felt he had no chance of replacing the Yankee's Lou Gehrig. Setting the record straight midway through the 1934 season, the *American Hebrew* noted that although New York's Jewish baseball fans were still angry at the Yankess for letting Greenberg slip away, "they are all rooting for Hank, hoping that here at last is that Jewish star whom they can all idolize—no matter where his berth may be."[62] Greenberg's actions on and off the field that season fulfilled their dreams.

Hank led the Tigers to the pennant in 1934, batting .339 and driving in 139 runs. The Yankee's Jewish baseball fans no doubt had mixed feelings about accomplishments that helped deprive the Bronx Bombers of still another pennant, but they and other American Jews were less equivocal about Greenberg's decision concerning playing baseball on the Jewish high holidays.

Although not a religious Jew, Greenberg's casual comment that he might spend the Jewish New Year in shul rather than on the field against the Boston Red Sox touched off a flurry of newspaper stories. At issue was whether he should put his religion before the interests of the Tigers, then locked in a close pennant race with the Yankees. The regular Detroit press, after weighing public opinion and even the testimony of rabbis, encouraged Hank to play, arguing that his commitment to the community was more important than his individual religious beliefs. Blurring the complex and inconclusive arguments of one Detroit rabbi, for instance, the *Detroit News* proclaimed, "Talmud Clears

Greenberg for Holiday Play."[63] Although Hank went to synagogue on the day before Rosh Hashonah, on the Jewish New Year he took the field against the Red Sox, announcing his fears that "I'll probably get my brains knocked out by a fly ball." As it turned out, the Tigers won 2–1, thanks to Greenberg's two home runs, including a game-winning blast in the bottom of the ninth.[64] Commenting on Hank's feat, Bud Shaver of the Detroit *Times* suggested something of the conflict that Greenberg experienced in deciding to play. "There was more than the mighty bone and sinew of Hank Greenberg behind those two home runs which went whistling out of Navin Field," he told his readers. "They were propelled by a force born of desperation and pride of a young Jew who turned his back on the ancient ways of his race and creed and helped his teammates." Greenberg, himself, Shaver noted, viewed his home runs as a sign that "the good Lord did not let [him] down."[65] So too did the Detroit *Free Press,* which celebrated the news by wishing Hank "Happy New Year" in Hebrew and by sanctifying both home runs as "strictly kosher." Cleveland's American Jewish newspaper offered similar religious metaphor by announcing that "only one fellow blew the shofar yesterday. . . . He was Hank Greenberg. He blew the shofar twice and the ears of the Boston Red Sox are still ringing."[66]

Ten days later on Yom Kippur, the holiest day on the Jewish calendar, despite a scheduled game with the Yankees, Greenberg chose not to play. Instead, he spent the day at Detroit's Shaarey Zedek synagogue. Whether out of respect for his convictions or because the Tigers had the race seemingly well in hand, the Detroit press praised Greenberg's decision and applauded him as a symbol that made all Jews proud. H. G. Salsinger, sports editor of the *Detroit News,* characterized Hank not only as "the greatest player the Jews have contributed to baseball" but also as "an illustrious torch bearer of his people." Noting that "the public judges peoples by the idols they produce," Salsinger felt Jews fortunate to be represented by a man who was a "fierce competitor" who possessed "a keen eye, a fighting heart . . . set purpose," and "humility." Bud Shaver went even further. "The qualities which make [Greenberg] an appealing figure," he wrote, "are the direct heritage of [his] race and creed. His fine intelligence, independence of thought, courage and his driving ambition have won him the respect and admiration of his teammates, baseball writers, and the fans at large. . . . He feels and acknowledges his responsibility as a representative of the Jews in the field of a great national sport and the Jewish people could have no finer representative."[67]

Greenberg's heroics hardly overcame the increasingly vitriolic anti-Semitism of Detroit's popular "radio priest" Father Coughlin. By 1935, his weekly radio sermons captured an audience of an estimated ten million people, covering every major city in the East and Midwest. He was, according to *Fortune* magazine, "just about the biggest thing that ever happened to radio," and his messages, while offering economic hope to many Americans, implicitly and explicitly placed blame for the country's problems on Jews.[68] Several commentators, however, provided a different image of Jews, by depicting Hank as a hero to all Detroiters, not only because of his baseball skills but because of his conscience. Edgar Guest immortalized these sentiments in verse for the readers of the Detroit *Free Press:*

> The Irish didn't like it when they heard of Greenberg's fame
> For they thought a good first baseman should possess an Irish name;
> And the Murphys and Mulrooneys said they never dreamed they'd see
> A Jewish boy from Bronxville out where Casey used to be. . . .
> In July the Irish wondered where he'd ever learned to play.
> "He makes me think of Casey!" Old Man Murphy dared to say;
> And with fifty-seven doubles and a score of homers made
> The respect they had for Greenberg was being openly displayed.
> But upon the Jewish New Year when Hank Greenberg came to bat
> And made two home runs off Pitcher Rhodes—They cheered like mad
>   for that.
> Come Yom Kippur—holy fast day world wide over to the Jew, And
>   Hank Greenberg
> to his teaching and the old tradition true,
> Spent the day among his people and he didn't come to play.
> Said Murphy to Mulrooney, "we shall lose the game today!
> We shall miss him in the infield and shall miss him at the bat.
> But he's true to his religion—and I honor him for that."[69]

Although it is difficult to know whether such accounts accurately reflected a change in Gentile attitudes about Jews, Milton Bingay of the Detroit *Free Press* felt that Greenberg was "in position to do untold good in breaking down the mean and vicious prejudices against an ancient and honorable people."[70] At least one Detroiter recalls that Hank influenced a Gentile population in ways he never intended. Responding to Greenberg's death in September 1986, an Ypsilanti resident, Lora Dodd, wrote that she had been a fifth-grade Sunday school teacher in a Presbyterian church when Greenberg broke in with the Tigers. Her difficult time getting one student to concentrate on her religious teachings ended one day when she mentioned something about Jesus being a Jew. "You mean like Hank Greenberg," her troublesome pupil blurted out. After that, Dodd recalled, the young boy became more involved in his lessons. "I had an easier time teaching because Hank Greenberg was a Jew."[71]

Jews, with few exceptions, openly embraced Greenberg as their Jewish hero. According to one teammate, Hank did receive some nasty phone calls and letters from fellow Jews after he played on Rosh Hashonah. And a front-page story in the Detroit *Jewish Chronicle* called "Hank's Rosh Hashonah" noted that "many Jews forgot their approach to God—because baseball ruled as king—and that as far as the non-Jewish community was concerned, Greenberg was the only Jew alive." But that same story also acknowledged Greenberg's attendance at synagogue the day before the Jewish New Year and the immense pride and identification the entire congregation, especially the children, took in this man who openly displayed his Jewishness while enjoying tremendous success and praise in his pursuit of the American dream. Referring to Greenberg's Rosh Hashonah exploits against the Red Sox, the *Chronicle* concluded: "It was a great day for Detroiters, who got a thrill out of this one-man game by a Jewish boy . . . and it was a great day for the boys on Chicago Boulevard, Rochester Avenue, Boston Boulevard, and the entire neighborhood bordering on the Shaarey Zedek synagogue. Worshipers on the way to service Tuesday morning heard the word passed around by our boys on those streets: 'Hank will be in shul today.' And Hank was met by a cheering group as he came and left." Even more astonishing for Greenberg was the applause he received from the synagogue's congregation when he attended Yom Kippur services. "I was a hero around town," Greenberg remembers, "particularly among the Jewish people, and I was very proud of it."[72]

Other stories in the next few months underlined Greenberg's powerful draw as a role model for American Jews. In a letter to the Detroit *Jewish Chronicle,* one Herschel Weinstein suggested a plan to institutionalize it. Addressing himself "to all parents of Jewish boys," Weinstein proposed a plan to keep Greenberg in Detroit during the winter so that he could continue to be a "wonderful inspiration . . . to our children." By offering Greenberg the job as the Jewish Center's athletic director, Weinstein argued that "practically all the Jewish boys of Detroit would nag their parents until they were allowed to join." Thus, "the move would benefit both the Jewish Center and the boys, who can do nothing better than to worship a young man like Hank Greenberg, a clean-minded, clean-living and an ideal man for the ledership of boys."[73]

Unfortunately for Detroit's Jewish youth, Greenberg spent the off-season elsewhere, in ways that underlined Weinstein's appreciation of what Hank meant to other Jews. Hank returned home to the Bronx as a local hero—as the *Chronicle* reported, "the boy who made good. The lad who is bringing fame and credit to the Jewish people." Noting the huge homecoming reception offered to Hank by Bronx Jews, the paper added that "every kid in the boro who is able to hold a bat . . . is an embryo Bruggy Greenberg." The story concluded by adding that Hank spent part of the winter months touring the East Coast as baseball advisor to the U.S. Maccabi Association.[74]

The following summer, while in Philadelphia to play the Athletics, Greenberg revealed another measure of his importance to American Jews. As Bud Shaver told his Detroit *Times* readers, Greenberg shared with him a fan letter he had received from a 13-year-old Jewish girl. "To that little girl," Shaver wrote, "Hank is a Jew in shining armor. She had been bitterly disappointed in Jewish boxer Max Baer who had lost the heavyweight championship to Jimmy Braddock [in June 1935] and was banking all on Hank. She begged him not to fail her or his people." Noting that "there were thousands of little boys and girls like her," Shaver described handing the letter back to Greenberg, telling the Tigers' slugger: "You have an immense responsibility." "Hank's face was grave as he tucked the soiled little letter away in his pocket. 'Yes I have,' he said soberly."[75]

Hank Greenberg was not a religious man. By all accounts, as he grew older, he rejected all formal religious practice for himself and for his family. Nevertheless, he also came to acknowledge and appreciate that events of 1934 marked him as a symbol of Jewish pride and accomplishment; an example, as he put it, that if a Jew could make it in the American game of baseball, he could succeed in anything he attempted.[76] In fact, his entire baseball career as player and executive, including its interruption by a stint in the United States Air Force during World War II, enhanced his status as American Jewish hero. Especially important was Hank's stance as a tough, physical player who openly defied anti-Semitic bigots and bench jockeys. Set in the context of the destruction of European Jewry and visible anti-Semitism in the United States, his actions contributed to a definition of American Jewish identity that substituted images of toughness, strength, and defiance for those of the weak victim.

At 6'4" and 210 pounds, "Hammerin Hank" was one of the biggest and strongest players in the majors of his time. Commentators then and at the time of his death in 1986 invariably noted the power of the man, the sheer physicality of his appearance, and the strength and determination with which he played the game. This fact was not lost on his Jewish constituency. Michigan senator Carl Levin's most vivid boyhood memory of his hero is watching "Hank Greenberg doing what he did best. There he is bringing the bat around to his right shoulder and then tightening his muscles and waiting for the pitch and watching it break over the plate and then—and then the ball would sail away from the plate over the fence and into history."[77] Recalling his own Jewish childhood on New York's Lower East Side, actor Walter Matthau remembers that when he "was running around in the jungle of the ghetto . . . you couldn't help but be exhilarated by the sight of one of our own guys looking like Colossus." Greenberg, Matthau insists, "put to rest the stories and the jokes about the only things Jews could wind up doing was working as a presser or a cutter or a salesman. . . . He eliminated all those jokes that started with 'Did you hear the one about the little Jewish gentleman?'"[78] Even more to the point is Ira Berkow, who remembers Hank as a legend in Jewish households like his own—"the first truly great Jewish ballplayer and ironically a power hitter in the 1930s when the position of Jews in the world—especially, of course, in Hitler's Germany—grew weaker."[79]

Greenberg himself understood his importance to American Jews in similar terms. For him, news from Europe after 1938 made "being Jewish carry with it a special responsibility," in both an American and an international context. As he put it:

> After all, I was representing a couple of million Jews among a hundred million gentiles and I was always in the spotlight. . . . I felt a responsibility. I was there every day and if I had a bad day every son of a bitch was calling me names so that I had to make good. . . . As time went by I came to feel that if I, as a Jew, hit a home run I was hitting one against Hitler.[80]

The presence of this powerful, successful Jew in the most publicized and covered of all of American sports allowed Jews to challenge openly, if only vicariously through him, any suggestions of Jewish weakness. The fact that Greenberg was the frequent target of anti-Semitism further magnified his stature among Jews. At times, it didn't even seem to matter if the attacks were real or not. With five games to go in the 1938 season, for instance, Hank had hit 58 home runs, only two short of Babe Ruth's single-season record of 60. Although he played in those five games, Greenberg did not hit another home run. According to Ira Berkow, his uncle and other Jewish fans remained convinced that Hank's futile assault on the Babe's record was undermined by anti-Semitic pitchers who refused to give their hero a decent pitch to hit. Hank gave no credence to this popular claim. Nor was he deterred by the specter of having to consume 61 baseball-shaped gefilte fish promised by his mother if he broke the record. For him, inexperienced rookie pitchers called up from the minors for a look-see by their parent clubs accounted for his problems at the plate.[81]

Greenberg, however, also remembers that his size, religion, and talent subjected him to constant anti-Semitic abuse throughout his career. Fans called him all sorts of names when he took the field, occasionally accompanying their verbal abuse by tossing beer bottles and other objects at him. Players on opposing teams, sometimes as part of the "game," constantly baited him. Even ballplayers on his own team occasionally found it difficult to hide their anti-Jewish feelings. As Hank put it:

> There was added pressure being Jewish. How the hell could you get up to home plate every day and have some son of a bitch call you a Jew bastard and a kike and a sheenie and get on your ass without feeling the pressure. If the ballplayers weren't doing it, the fans were. I used to get frustrated as hell. Sometimes I wanted to go in the stands and beat the shit out of them.[82]

Although he never ventured into the bleachers, Greenberg's response was consistent. Both in his own memory and, more important, in the way in which such incidents were reported in the press, he fought back, even at times with his fists. Typical was Haskell Cohen's coverage of various incidents in Greenberg's career. In a 1947 "Jews Who Make the News" column for the Jewish Telegraphic Agency, syndicated in American Jewish newspapers throughout the United States, Cohen gleefully recounted Greenberg's response to a Pittsburgh Pirate teammate who said to Hank: "For a Jew playing as lousy ball as you are that's certainly a lot of money you are getting." According to Cohen, "Greenie told the player to keep his mouth shut and when the offender continued to spout his bilge, Hank promptly dropped him with a smack to the jaw." Noting that such anti-Semitic incidents were not new, Cohen reported that several years earlier, while still with the Tigers, Hank had been called a "Jew so and so" by a young Detroit outfielder. Greenberg merely picked up a bat, "sidled up to the player in question with a wicked glint in his eye" and warned him that "if you so much as peep once again to me I'll bring this bat across your thick skull." As Cohen concluded, "Needless to say the villian beat a hasty retreat. Hank is plenty big and strong and can take care of these fresh guys trying to get a ride out of him."[83]

Similar sentiments were echoed by Eldon Auker, Tiger pitcher, who remembered Hank's response when a Chicago White Sox player called him a "yellow Jew son of a bitch" during the summer of 1938. According to Auker, when the game ended, Greenberg "took off his spikes and everything" and entered the White Sox clubhouse looking for his tormentor. "That guy who called me a yellow son of a bitch, get on his feet and come here and call it to my face," Hank demanded. "Not a guy moved," Auker recalled. "He was damn lucky, because Hank would have killed him. Hank was a tough guy."[84]

Greenberg's public image as a strong, proud assertive Jew runs counter to Charles Silberman's recent observations about Jewish life in the United States. Silberman argues that in the 1930s and 1940s, many second-generation Jews, striving for middle-class respectability and success, denied their Jewishness and masked their identities in order to succeed in America. "No one was more careful to expunge his or her Jewishness," he concludes, "than Jews who were in the public eye."[85] Yet neither Greenberg nor those Jews who responded to him fit this description. Participating in a sport long hailed as America's game, Hank was marketed as a highly visible Jew and embraced by Jewish baseball fans as an ethnic hero.

Appreciation of class distinction, historical context, and the complexities of assimilation explain this apparent paradox. The aspiring second-generation Jews that Silberman writes about—those who hoped to make it in the corporate board rooms of America and in the professional world outside the boundaries of the Jewish urban communities they came from—found themselves in a dilemma. Anxious for economic gain and social acceptance, many did decide that it was neither safe nor comfortable to acknowledge publicly their Jewishness if they wanted to succeed in business, the professions, or government—areas of prestige and power to which their parents had little access. Professional baseball, too, was business, but one, measured by Greenberg's accomplishments and his public Jewish identity, that did not deny Jews opportunity because of their heritage. Those who denied their Jewishness, dreaming of similar success in their own endeavors, could find only pride and hope in this Jewish hero. For the vast majority of second-generation American Jews living in vibrant ethnic communities, however, being Jewish caused less conflict. For many children of East European working-class immigrants whose Jewishness was as much secular as religious but no less diminished by it, Greenberg's triumphs simply confirmed the possibility that they, too, could find acceptance and success in America without sacrificing their Jewish identity.

For the small number of American Jewish baseball players who followed him into the majors, Greenberg became a special source of pride. Al Rosen, whose own career as an outstanding player for the Cleveland Indians began as Hank's ended, noted that, for Jewish ballplayers, Greenberg "was really a pathfinder," accomplishing much like "what Jackie Robinson did for blacks in baseball." As Rosen saw it, Hank "paved the way for people like me."[86]

Sometimes the path proved rocky in unexpected ways. Just ask Harry Eisenstat. Eisenstat, who was befriended by Greenberg when he was traded to the Tigers in 1938, responded to the question of playing on the Jewish high holidays much the way Hank did. Called up by Brooklyn at the close of the 1935 season, Eisenstat consulted a rabbi about whether or not it was kosher to play on Rosh Hashonah. As luck would have it, on the Jewish New Year, Harry was called in to relieve against the Giants. Confidently he took the mound, having been granted rabbinical permission, like Greenerg, to play, on the grounds that the Jewish New Year was a day of happiness and celebration. Perhaps, but not for Harry. His first pitch in the big leagues was belted for a grand-slam home run.[87]

Despite Eisenstat's misfortune, there is no question that Greenberg's heroics on and off the field in the early 1930s secured his place as Jewish-American hero. The remainder of his public career, including his days as a player, military hero, and successful businessman confirmed this image. Greenberg did more than bolster Jewish ethnic pride and confidence. The adoration he received from Jew and Gentile alike also encouraged better relations between them, suggesting again the promise of sport as a middle ground in the complex process of assimilation.

Nineteen games into the 1941 season, Greenberg received his army draft notice. Thirty years old and close to the age limit for draftees, he was released two days before Pearl Harbor. Within a week after "the day that will live in infamy," however, he reenlisted in the air force. Reporting on his decision in the *Sporting News,* John Spink praised Greenberg by fusing an uncomplicated version of assimilation with American democracy in ways that had appeal for all Americans. According to Spink, as Greenberg pondered whether or not to risk his life, "all the time there lay before [him] a picture. His father and mother had come to this country from Rumania because the way of living there did not correspond to their ideas of going through life. In the United States, the Greenbergs prospered. Their son had an equal opportunity with the sons of other people in this country, and achieved a notable position in a notable profession." Now, Spink concluded, Hank was simply returning the favor for all that American democracy had offered him, and the "fans of America and all baseball salute him for that decision."[88]

Greenberg's anointment as a fully assimilated American who gratefully repaid his debt with patriotism and valor colored his public appearance in the press in the late 1930s and early 1940s. Hank remained in uniform until his release in July 1945. He saw plenty of action as captain of a B-29 bomber squadron in the China-Burma-India theater and returned home an American war hero. When his name did appear in the sports pages, references to him, as with other Jewish major leaguers, continued a trend apparent by the late 1930s—attention to him as Jewish hero diminished as his importance as a symbol for all Americans increased. References to Greenberg as the "Pants Presser," "the youngster with a noodle," and "the greatest Jewish player baseball had seen," common during Hank's early years with Detroit, disappeared by 1938. Neither the *New York Times* nor the *Sporting News,* for example, noticed Greenberg's Jewish connections during his pursuit of Babe Ruth's home-run record in 1938. When both Greenberg and Harry Danning made their league's respective all-star teams in 1940, newspapers did not mention their religion. Tiger consternation over the loss of Greenberg's bat when he joined the air force in 1941 also made headlines, but only in baseball terms.

Even Stanley Frank in a March 1941 article called "Hank Made Greenberg," written for the *Saturday Evening Post*, mentioned Hank's Jewish connection only with a brief reference to the 1934 high holiday affair, choosing instead to emphasize how Greenberg's hard work and determination had made him a great ballplayer.[89]

Whether reporting on his exploits in the 1940 World Series, his attendance at charity dinners for various Jewish agencies, or his brief involvement with a barnstorming professional basketball team appropriately named "Hank Greenberg's All-Stars," the Anglo-Jewish press did not totally ignore Hank's Jewish credentials. But even here, commentary often served larger American ends. When Greenberg and the Tigers visited Boston during the summer of 1938, for instance, a Jewish paper there noted that "we have had pogroms before, we have had wars before, we have had trouble with Arabs before. But never have we had a Jewish home-run king." After explaining what a home run was for readers who might have been unfamiliar with baseball, it added that "the name of Greenberg was hoisted out in Fenway Park last week in eight different languages and twenty-one different dialects," providing that "a genuine fan can't be an anti-semite."[90]

Greenberg's baseball exploits and his willingness to risk his life in order to defend the country he loved made him a popular hero for both Jew and Gentile. The business community certainly recognized this fact. Throughout his playing days, whether selling Grunow radios for a local store in the pages of the Detroit *Jewish Chronicle*, Louisville Sluggers as 1938's "King of Swat," or the Breakfast of Champions ("'A big bowl of Wheaties every morning,' Hank reveals, 'is the Greenberg way to start off a swell day'") in the *Sporting News*, Hank's appeal to American consumers paid dividends for himself and those he represented.[91]

Although Greenberg retired as an active player after the 1947 season, his life off the field did not diminish his appeal. In 1946, Hank married Carol Gimbel, heiress to the Gimbel's department store fortune. Two years later, Bill Veeck, then owner of the Cleveland Indians, hired Hank as an administrative assistant. Unaware that an opportunity for Greenberg to purchase 10 percent of the club had fallen through, the *Sporting News* marveled that an "immigrant's son" had become "the second-ranking stockholder in the Cleveland Club. . . ." In doing so, "baseball's bible," according to a column by Harold Ribalow in the *National Jewish Monthly*, acknowledged "that it is a wonderful thing for American democracy that a Jewish boy had become owner of a great major league team." Like the Pittsburgh Pirates' Barney Dreyfuss and the New York Giants' Andrew Freedman before him and the succession of Jewish entrepreneurs who followed him, eventually Greenberg did become part owner of the club. As general manager he played an important role in producing two Cleveland pennants. Fired by Cleveland at the close of the 1957 season, Hank became part owner of the Chicago White Sox. In 1961, he sold his interest and moved on to new pursuits in investment and finance.[92]

Such a career had something in it for all Jews, regardless of social class, aspirations, or backgrounds. Greenberg's personal lack of religious conviction and his disinterest in raising his children as Jews did not mar for him or for his public his importance as a symbol of Jewish hope and of the promise of assimilation. On and off the field, in marriage and in the board rooms, Hank made it big in ways that appealed to the closet Jews that Charles Silberman describes as well as to the Jews at Dexter and Davidson in Detroit or the Grand Concourse in the Bronx who lustily proclaimed their hero's triumphs. And as Carl Levin, another successful second-generation American Jew, reminded his colleagues in the United States Senate the week his boyhood hero died, Greenberg did more than make other Jews proud of their heritage. He was also a Jewish player that all Americans admired. In language remarkably similar to messages of a bygone era that rallied all Americans in the struggle against Nazi Germany, Levin applauded the "hero worship" of men like Greenberg and Jackie Robinson who showed young boys that "if a player can help the home team win, then the player ought to be admired and accepted for what he can do rather than being rejected because of where he comes from."[93]

Hank Greenberg, Al Rosen, and other second-generation major-league Jewish ballplayers provided comfort, hope, and pride for Jewish-Americans caught up in their own struggle to survive in years of economic depression and world war. By their words and deeds they did so in ways that asserted a physical, defiant sense of Jewishness, that challenged stereotypes about Jewish weakness, and that gave hope to Jews worried about a Jewish future in the United States and the world.

This other and vital side of Jewishness certainly appeared first elsewhere, especially in the exploits of ghetto boxers that gave Jewish immigrants and their children their first ethnic American heroes.[94] But boxing was considered a disreputable activity, participation in which did not serve as the best evidence of acceptance of or comfort with being an American. Baseball, however, was America's National Game, not only because the rhetoric surrounding it extolled its supposed quintessentially American character and virtue, but truly because it was the most popular national sporting activity that people engaged in as particpants and as spectators. The triumphs of Jewish baseball players, however few they were, encouraged Jewish-Americans to be comfortable with a physical and assertive side of their identity. It measured how far the second generation had come from Yekl's pleas to his fellow immigrant tailors at the turn of the century not to be frightened of bullies as they had been in Russia. For Jewish major leaguers and, more important, for the large Jewish audience that followed their exploits, this sense emerged in an environment shaped by world war that heightened anxiety about Jewish survival, muted ethnic distinctions in pursuit of a common victory, and accelerated the assimilation process at the same time that it reaffirmed ethnic belonging. Cutting across the American Jewish landscape, baseball and its Jewish ballplayers both symbolized and contributed to that process.

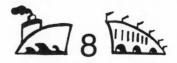

"Oy Such a Fighter!": Boxing and the American Jewish Experience

BENNY Leonard was the lightweight champion of the world between 1917 and 1925, one of the greatest boxers of all time, and folk hero to many East European Jewish immigrants and their children. Early in his carreer he knocked out one Ah Chung during a six-round bout in New York's Chinatown on the Chinese New Year in 1913. Chung, in fact, was a Jewish boxer named Rosenberg. Determined to attract immigrant Chinese fight fans, the bout's promoters convinced him to put on eye makeup and apply yellow body paint to match his billing as a "Peking native" and the "only Chinese boxer in the world." At least one Chinese spectator was not fooled by the hoax. As Rosenberg rested between rounds, a distinguished-looking Chinese gentleman, dressed in a purple and gold mandarin robe, questioned the fighter in rapid-fire Chinese. The fighter, totally ignorant of what the man was saying, perfunctorily nodded "yes." As it turned out, Rosenberg answered correctly. According to one sportswriter, our Chinese patron demanded that the fighter admit he was an imposter. "You no China boy, you fake," he insisted. "China boy got more sense than to stand up and get licking when he can iron shirts and collars."[1]

Laced with its own racist stereotyping of Chinese in the United States common to the early 20th century, this column suggests something of boxing's popularity among immigrants and of the number of Jewish boys who put on gloves. Although this Jew didn't even have a "chinaman's chance," many second-generation young men from East European immigrant working-class families did. Between 1910 and 1940, Jewish boxers more than held their own in the professional ranks. Prior to 1916 most title contenders in the eight weight divisions ranging from heavyweight to flyweight were either Irish, German, or Italian. By 1928, Jewish fighters comprised the largest total. Only

144

two Jews held titles between 1900 and 1909, but then the numbers increased dramatically; four between 1910 and 1919, eight between 1920 and 1929, and ten between 1930 and 1939. Some, like Al Singer, "The Bronx Beauty," lost his lightweight crown after four months. But he was the exception to the reasonably long tenures of Jewish champions. Benny Leonard reigned as lightweight king for eight years. Maxie "Slapsy" Rosenbloom and "Battling" Levinsky each held their light-heavyweight crowns for five years. And Barney Ross topped the welterweight division for five consecutive years and the light-weight division for three—two overlapping with his welterweight crowns in 1934 and 1935.

Ross was the only Jewish champion to hold titles in two divisions at the same time. But Jewish fighters commonly held more than one world title in any given year. The only year between 1910 and 1939 when there was not a single Jewish champion was 1913. In 17 of the remaining 29 years, at least two Jewish boxers were world champions in the same year. In seven years, including 1930, 1932, 1934, and 1935, Jews held three titles simultaneously. In 1933, light-heavyweight Maxie Rosenbloom, middleweight Ben Jeby, welterweight Jackie Fields, and lightweight Barney Ross held four of the eight championship belts. At one time or another, Jews on Chicago's Maxwell Street or in its Lawndale section, on New York's Lower East Side or the Bronx's Pelham Parkway, around Boston's Commonwealth Avenue, or in south Philadelphia could all claim one of their own as contenders or champions. New York, with the largest concentration of East European Jews in the United States, produced 9 of the 16 Jewish titleholders in these years. So prominent were Jewish boxers in certain weight divisions that nine times between 1920 and 1934, Jews fought each other in championship bouts. Three times Benny Leonard successfully defended his lightweight crown against Jewish challengers. "Corporal" Izzy Schwartz won the flyweight belt in 1927 from "Newsboy" Brown. And "Slapsie" Maxie Rosenbloom defended his light-heavyweight title against Abie Bain in 1930, losing it four years later to Bob Olin.[2]

Statistics provide a map of Jewish involvement in boxing, marking out a period between 1910 and 1940 when Jews were a major presence. But they do not explain the significance of this participation, both for those who fought and those who followed the sport. More so than baseball or basketball, boxing combined opportunity for symbolic connection to nationally recognized individuals as well as intimate, community involvement in local sporting activity. Baseball was America's National Game but boxing, with its quest for world championships, permitted its own opportunities for focusing national attention on individual Jewish athletes. Although disdainfully labeled as an activity fit only for society's lower classes, boxing possessed a long history in the United States as local community experience that had served other immigrants well in their quest for stability, place, and identity. Whether appropriated as public symbols or as part of their neighborhood's social world, flamboyant Jewish boxers, more than any other group of athletes, confirmed Jewish toughness and the will to survive, while providing vivid counterpoint to popular anti-Semitic stereotypes. They also served as touchstone for attempts to reconcile traditional, ethnic values with mainstream American culture while making their own special contribution to defining an American Jewish identity in the face of real threats to Jewish existence both at home and abroad.

I

Surrounded by his fellow Jewish immigrant workers in a sweatshop in New York's Lower East Side at the turn of the century, Abraham Cahan's "Yekl" searches for a badge of his new American identity and finds it in boxing. Asked by a presser if John L. Sullivan is still heavyweight champion of the world, he responds as Jake, with all the American enthusiasm he can muster:

> "Oh, no!" . . . Jake responded with what he considered a Yankee jerk of the head. "Why don't you know? Jimmie Corbett *leaked* him, and Jimmy *leaked* Cholly Meetchel, too. You can *betch you' bootsh!* Johnnie could not *leak* Chollie, *becaush* he is a big *bluffer,* Chollie is," he pursued, his clean-shaven florid face beaming with enthusiasm for his subject, and with pride in the diminutive proper nouns he flaunted. "But Jimmie pundished him. *Oh, didn't he knock him out off shight!* He came near making a meat ball of him"—with a chuckle. "He *tzettled* him in three *roynds.*"[3]

Asked what a round is, Jake offers an explanation proudly embroidered with his knowledge of the ring. Not everyone, however, is as taken with his American interest as he is. His newspaper reading interrupted by Jake's reply, Bernstein, described by Cahan as "the rabbinical-looking man" usually addressed by his shopmates as "Mr.," suggests that any "burly Russian peasant . . . would crunch the bones of Corbett himself." Besides, Bernstein adds, "My grandma's last care it is who can fight best." When Jake persists, however, even his shopmate realizes how important boxing is to Jake's emerging American identity. Referring to Jake's passion for boxing and baseball he remarks: "And you Jake, cannot do without 'these things,' can you? I do not see how you manage to live without them."[4]

Jake's choice of the "Great John L." and "Gentleman" Jim Corbett as reference points for his infatuation with boxing and his own identification as an American is not surprising. Sullivan, the "Boston strong boy," won the heavyweight championship of the world in 1882 and held the title until defeated by Corbett ten years later. Both men reached prominence at a time when boxing was considered corrupt, violent, disreputable, and, in many places, illegal sport. Nevertheless, these Irish champions found a special place not only in Jake's heart but especially in the hearts of working-class Irish immigrants desperate for some positive sign of their own American future in a life which offered them little control over their time or destiny. As Eliot Gorn tells us, limited to menial employment, with little prospect for advancement in the workplace, first- and second-generation Irish male immigrants found oppor-

Marty Glickman (left) and Sam Stoller on Board S.S. Manhattan *en route to Berlin in July 1936.* (Courtesy of Marty Glickman)

Jack Dempsey instructs young Jewish boxers at a New York settlement house. (Courtesy of Ellen Uffen)

(left): New York Whirlwinds, 1920–1921. Standing (left to right): Barney Sedran, Ray Kennedy, Harry Riconda, Nat Holman. Seated (left to right): Max Friedman, Chris Leonard. (Courtesy Basketball Hall of Fame)

(right): Dolph Schayes. (Courtesy Basketball Hall of Fame)

Jammy Moskowitz as a Newark Hebrew. (Courtesy of Jammy Moskowitz)

The Dux, 1927–1928. Sammy Kaplan is seated, first on the left. (Courtesy of Sammy Kaplan)

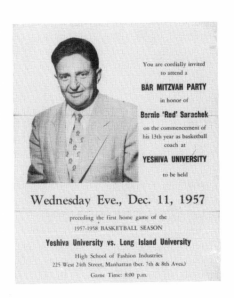

You are cordially invited
to attend a

BAR MITZVAH PARTY

in honor of

Bernie 'Red' Sarachek

on the commencement of
his 13th year as basketball
coach at

YESHIVA UNIVERSITY

to be held

Wednesday Eve., Dec. 11, 1957

preceding the first home game of the
1957-1958 BASKETBALL SEASON

Yeshiva University vs. Long Island University

High School of Fashion Industries
225 West 24th Street, Manhattan (bet. 7th & 8th Aves.)

Game Time: 8:00 p.m.

Red Sarachek at Yeshiva. (Courtesy of Red Sarachek)

Jewish lacrosse players at CCNY, 1929. Sam Levine is standing on the right. (Courtesy of Peter Levine)

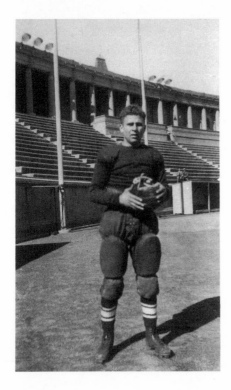

Sam Levine, CCNY football player in Lewisohn Stadium, 1928. (Courtesy of Peter Levine)

Barney Ross at 16. (Courtesy of Ivan Colitz)

Lou Gehrig (left) and Hank Greenberg, 1934. (Courtesy of Richard Bak)

Harry Danning as a New York Giant.
(Courtesy of Harry Danning)

Marshall Goldberg at the University of Pittsburgh. (Courtesy of Marshall Goldberg)

Sandy Koufax as a Los Angeles Dodger. (Courtesy of National Baseball Library, Cooperstown, New York)

Andy Cohen as a New York Giant. (Courtesy of National Baseball Library, Cooperstown, New York)

The Trojans, 1939. Bernie Reisman is wearing the catcher's mitt. His younger brother is next to him, out of uniform. (Courtesy of Bernie Reisman)

Cigarette advertisement, June 1928, California Jewish Voice.

The SPHAs, 1936–1937. (Courtesy of Philadelphia Jewish Archives Center)

Nat Holman and his CCNY basketball team after winning the NCAA championship at Madison Square Garden, 1950. (Courtesy Basketball Hall of Fame)

A Portland, Oregon, JCC basketball team, circa 1935. Harry Glickman is in the front row, second from the right. (Courtesy of Harry Glickman)

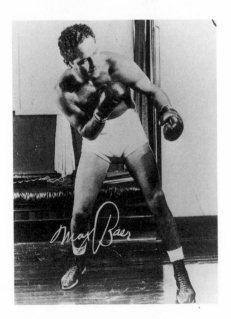

Max Baer. (Courtesy of Hank Kaplan)

Jackie Fields. (Courtesy of Hank Kaplan)

Abe Attell, the Little Hebrew. (Courtesy of
Hank Kaplan)

Barney Ross. (Courtesy of Hank Kaplan)

Benny Leonard. (Courtesy of Hank Kaplan)

Once at the pool, Fields and his friends jockeyed for position on the waiting benches closest to the pool entrance. As Jackie put it, "you start[ed] a fight again . . . we were always fighting for position."

Territorial imperative and anti-Semitism were not the only reasons to learn how to fight. Place and pocketbook also provided incentive. "In that neighborhood," Fields remembers, "you had to be tough. A kid that couldn't take it—you'd call him a sissy. We wouldn't let him with us." Constant challenges and fights among his friends established a pecking order and honed their boxing skills. Occasionally, with towels wrapped around their fists for protection, Jackie and his gang staged fights in the streets, hopeful that people passing by would applaud their efforts by giving up their loose change.[8]

Growing up in a predominantly Irish neighborhood in Philadelphia, Benny Bass, world featherweight champion in 1927 and 1928, also learned to fight in the streets. When he was 14, as one sportswriter told it, his Irish peers demanded that he fight each of them if he wanted to live. "It is a matter of neighborhood record," the reporter noted, "that Bass fought one fight every day for a period of three months. At the end of that time he was wearing a slightly swollen nose, eyes that had a deeper surrounding color than nature bestowed—and also 92 Irish scalps." Confident in his ability, Bass proceeded to enter an amateur tournament and "beat up on Bohemians, Germans, Italians, Greeks, more Irish, a few English and some folks from his own race." Soon after, he became a professional boxer.[9]

Ninety-two Irish scalps! An impressive, if unlikely start, even for a future world champion. Exaggerated though this tale may be, the existence of so many comparable stories confirms its basic truth. Benny Leonard certainly recalls a similar introduction to boxing. The son of Gershon and Minnie Leiner, Russian immigrants who raised eight children on tailor sweatshop wages, Benny grew up in a Jewish neighborhood in New York's East Village near Eighth Street and Second Avenue. As a skinny, frail youngster he remembered being "the butt of Irish 'Micks,' Italian 'Wops' and the hoodlums of a dozen different races." Whether "going to the store or to the public baths," fighting between his Jewish friends and other ethnic groups of adolescents was an everyday experience. As he told it:

> In the winter we fought with snowballs packed tightly around pieces of coal and soaked with water until they were as hard as cannon balls. Then we used baseball bats, stones and loaded canes. These were real brawls. There was many a boy who suffered permanent injury from an encounter with the warriors from the next block.[10]

After one particularly fierce beating at the hands of the "6th Street Boys," Benny's uncle, who clearly was not orthodox, took his nephew to a boxing club on Saturdays to teach him how to protect himself. Within a short time his protégé had become the champion of his block.[11]

Leonard's formal training was a bit unusual for Jewish boys who became professional boxers. Most developed skills initially learned on the streets, in settlement houses, and YMHAs. Jackie Fields's first organized instruction took place at the Henry Booth Settlement in Chicago. Here, as well as in a downtown gym where professional boxers worked out and which he often visited instead of going to school, Fields began learning his trade. Ruby Goldstein, better known as a boxing referee than for his brief career as a middleweight, dedicated his autobiography to New York's "Henry Street Settlement and the Educational Alliance for starting me out on the right foot and paving my way." Describing the Lower East Side's Henry Street in much the same fashion that Jackie Fields remembers Maxwell Street, Goldstein recalls growing up in a poor family whose widowed mother took in sewing and wash and whose grandfather worked in a sweat shop as a finisher of men's clothes. Taken to the settlement house by his older brother, Ruby discovered boxing, feeling too small for baseball or basketball. "With its divisions to suit every size boy, it offered an opportunity for me to advance. Suddenly it had become my favorite sport." Forced to travel uptown, away from his friends, to the annex of the High School of Commerce on West 89th Street and Amsterdam Avenue, Ruby dealt with his loneliness by cutting school and watching Joe Gans, Jack Britton, and other professional boxers train at Grupp's Gym in Harlem. At 14 he quit school, got a job as an office boy for $12 a week, and continued boxing in the evenings at Henry Street. There he met Hymie Cantor, a former boxer who coached kids at the Educational Alliance. Under Cantor's guidance, Goldstein turned to boxing as a profession.[12]

Similar stories belong to boxers as well known as world champions like bantamweight Abie Goldstein and light-heavyweight "Slapsy" Maxie Rosenbloom, who learned their craft respectively at the 92nd Street YMHA and Harlem's Union Settlement House as well as to lesser-known pugilists. New Yorker Sammy Dorfman, a ranking junior lightweight in 1929, took up boxing at Clark House. Lou Bloom, who came to Columbus, Ohio, as a youngster from Minsk in 1908, studied the manly art at the Schoenthal Center, the city's Jewish community center. Known locally as the "Little Heb," he won several amateur state boxing titles before becoming a professional boxer and an Australian national champion. For every Goldstein, Rosenbloom, Dorfman, and Bloom who actually enjoyed success as professional boxers, countless other children of Jewish immigrants learned the sport in similar settings.[13]

At least for one Jewish boxer, the settlement house served a different purpose. Louis Wallach, better known in the boxing world as Leach Cross, used it to keep his father from learning of his passion for the sport. Born in 1886, Louis and his friends on New York's Lower East Side learned to fight in the streets and at the Clark settlement house in order to protect themselves from Irish kids as they walked to school. Wallach attended CCNY, where he became friendly with a boy whose father owned the Long Acre Athletic Club. Here Wallach worked the concessions, all the while nurturing his love of boxing by fighting in preliminary bouts.[14]

The Long Acre was no different from innumerable neighborhood boxing clubs located in New York and other cities. At a time when many states, including New York, prohibited prizefighting, these clubs held "exhibitions" and no-decision bouts for their members and became the chief venues of what passed for professional boxing. Money provided to fighters under the table, lucrative gambling on the outcome of bouts on the side, and "membership" for virtually anyone who wanted to attend kept the sport alive.[15]

Within two years, Wallach advanced to main events and determined to make boxing a career even as he completed his education by obtaining a degree in dentistry from NYU. Knowing that his parents, Chaim and Rosa, would dispprove, Wallach fought professionally under the name of Leach Cross. Questioned at home about his occasional black eyes and bruised face, he covered his tracks by recounting his exploits on the basketball court at Clark House rather than on the canvas at Long Acre.

The ruse eventually caught up with him in 1908 when the young lightweight put away Joe Bernstein in four rounds. Bernstein, billed as "the pride of the ghetto," was at the very end of his long career as one of the great featherweights of the 1890s and early 1900s. Although never a world champion, he contested with the best of his division and emerged as the first Jewish boxer born on the Lower East Side to win the attention of East European Jewish immigrants eager for some recognition of their American existence. As Sam Wallach, one of Louis's brothers tells it, their father learned of his son's triumph one Friday evening when his neighbors stopped him on his way home from work to congratulate him on the news. When the patriarch of the Wallach family came to the Sabbath table in his orthodox Jewish home, he made his feelings on the subject quite clear to his son the boxer:

> So a prize fighter you are. I believe you when you come home with a black
> eye and tell me you got it playing basketball at Clark House. Now I learn you
> are a prize fighter! A loafer! A nebbish![16]

This father's disgust with his son's decision is clear. Like other Jewish immigrant parents who came to the United States in hopes that they, and especially their children, would be able to improve their economic lot, Chaim Wallach could not fathom how his well-educated boy could throw away a worthwhile career to become a boxer. Conflict over economic and social aspiration rather than concern that his son's love of boxing broke with Jewish religious tradition occasioned his ire. Imbedded in the elder Wallach's reaction is the fact that many of his generation had difficulty comprehending that the Golden Medinah offered more than the possibility of a better economic future for their children. It also offered experiences and choices that parents could not control. Obviously, few immigrant children turned to boxing as one of those choices. Nevertheless, this story, like others already told, underlines that much of the conflict engendered between the first and second generation turned on a myriad of daily decisions by children to participate in an American culture on their own terms.

Even boys less prepared than Lewis Wallach to take advantage of what America had to offer met parental disapproval when they devoted themselves to the ring. Abe Attell, the "Little Hebrew" who held the world featherweight crown between 1901 and 1912, remembered an impoverished San Francisco childhood where his Russian immigrant parents struggled to put food on the table for their twelve children. Born on Washington's birthday but named after Abraham Lincoln, he recalled that growing up in a predominantly Irish neighborhood introduced him to fighting at an early age. When he was 13, Abe's father died. His mother sent him to Los Angeles for a year to stay with an uncle. Returning to San Francisco in 1897, Abe sold newspapers in front of the Mechanics' Pavilion on Eighth and Market. He also watched boxing matches there and began fighting in amateur bouts.[17]

Abe's mother was not happy about his interest in pugilism. In August 1900, Attell signed for his first professional fight. Knowing that she would be displeased with his decision, he kept it a secret. But one week before the match, she heard about it from a neighbor. As Attell recalls, "she grabbed me by the neck and laid down the law." Only after Abe promised that this would be his "first and last fight" did she agree to let him in the ring. Attell knocked out his opponent in the second round and earned $15 for his efforts. When he returned home he gave his mother his purse. As he recalled, "she looked at the money, but didn't touch it. Then she looked at my face very carefully. 'You mean the fight is all over and you got this $15.00?' she asked. 'And you don't have no cuts on you at all.' I smiled and nodded my head. . . . She stood up and patted me on the head and in a slow voice asked, 'Abie, when are you going to fight again?'"[18]

Benny Leonard also overcame his parents' opposition to his boxing aspirations. Leonard knew how anxious his mother was that no harm come to him and of her belief that boxing went against Jewish tradition. So, early in his career, Benny lied about how he spent his time. Although his real last name was Leiner, he fought under the name of Leonard in case his mother read news of his bouts in the *Jewish Daily Forward*. Like Leach Cross and Abe Attell, Leonard eventually told his parents the truth. Returning home from a fight with a black eye, he admitted he had been hurt in the ring. He also gave his parents his victory purse of $20. "My mother," Benny recalled, "looked at my black eye and wept. My father, who had to work all week for $20, said, 'All right Benny, keep on fighting. It's worth getting a black eye for $20; I am getting verschwartzt [blackened] for $20 a week.'"[19]

Gershon Leiner's reasoning, developed out of his own sense of exploitation and economic hardship working as a sweatshop tailor, won out over Minnie Leiner's fears. Like Abe Attell's mother, the fruits of his son's labors overrode objections to how it had been earned. By 1916, so successful had their boy become that Benny was able to move his family to a better neighborhood up in Harlem. But he never forgot his mother's concern. In 1925, he retired as undefeated champion of the world, announcing that he had promised his sick mother that he would fight no more. "My love for her," he told a New York *Evening Telegram* reporter, "is greater than my love for the game that has made me independently wealthy, and to which I owe all I now possess."[20] Only the stock market crash in 1929, which wiped out Leonard's fortune earned from boxing, real estate, and vaudeville, forced him back into the ring.

III

Not all Jewish boxers fared as well as Benny Leonard. Nor could they totally escape legitimate protest that their sport often fell prey to criminals and gamblers who rigged fights and threatened fighters with their own brand of violence if they refused to go along. Barely any Jewish fighter avoided such temptation or threat. For instance, Abe Attell's proclivity for the fast buck, which eventually involved him with Arnold Rothstein and the attempt to fix the 1919 World Series, emerged first in his career as a boxer. "The Little Hebrew" was frequently accused of carrying lesser opponents for a few extra rounds and even of throwing fights in order to cover bets or to hustle a bigger-paying rematch. Commenting on his tenure as world featherweight champion, one journalist noted that "during the time Attell held the title he engaged in more crooked bouts than all the champions in the country put together in the last decade. It got so that during the last four or five years no one could tell what was going to happen when Attell stepped into the ring."[21] And though Ruby Goldstein denied he ever gave less than his best in the ring, there's no question that at one time or another, Charlie Rosenhouse and Waxie Gordon, prominent members of New York's Jewish underworld, owned his contract.[22]

Connections to crime and corruption, however, did not diminish the importance of Jewish boxers to their communities. For those looking for quick routes to success, cocky, tough fighters who consorted with well-known gangsters likely provided its own attraction. Either way, Jewish boxers provided a special source of ethnic pride and acceptance. Like Jewish basketball players who came in for their own share of adulation, boxers often lived in the very neighborhoods where they plied their trade. In much the same spirit that basketball games between local teams were transformed into ethnic celebrations, boxing matches became community events. Yet boxers, unlike basketball players, were also part of a larger national sports culture which awarded public attention and praise to those who competed for world championships. Although never as reputable as the few Jewish baseball players who made it into the major leagues, their large numbers, assertive stance, and public presence still made them attractive as symbols of American success and Jewish toughness. Some boxers were popular enough with Americans of all backgrounds that they even received praise for their ability to diffuse ethnic tension. Recollections of childhood heroes, countless newspaper stories regaling the triumphs of Jewish fighters and their loyal followers, and even the fiction of American Jewish writers richly embroider the importance of Jewish boxers as middle ground and the place of boxing in Jewish community life.

Prior to the Great Depression, Benny Leonard personified all that these men meant to their fellow Jews. When "The Great Bennah" died refereeing a fight in 1947, Al Lurie of the Philadelphia *Jewish Exponent* captured a sense of his appeal. Leonard's years as lightweight champion of the world between 1917 and 1925, he wrote, made him "the most famous Jew in America . . . beloved by thin-faced little Jewish boys who, in their poverty, dreamed of themselves as champions of the world." More than inspiration and pride,

Leonard also offered hope of their own acceptance as Americans. As Lurie put it:

> When a people is beaten, persecuted and frustrated, it finds more than mere solace in its champions. Thus, when Benny Leonard reached the heights in boxing, he aided not only himself, but the entire American Jewish community. When Leonard was accepted and admired by the entire fair-minded American community, the Jews of America felt they, themselves, were being accepted and admired. Leonard, therefore, symbolized, all Jewry. And he knew it.[23]

Leonard's contemporaries also recognized that the great champion was both a hero to Jews and a positive force in fostering Jewish acceptance by mainstream America. Commenting on Leonard's recent retirement from the ring in 1925, New York's *New Warheit* provided an interesting measure of his popularity among Jews and Gentiles. Comparing him to Albert Einstein, the paper noted that Benny

> is, perhaps, even greater than Einstein, for when Einstein was in America only thousands knew him but Benny is known by millions. It is said that only twelve people or at the most twelve times twelve the world over understand Einstein, but Benny is being understood by tens of millions in America; and just as we need a country so as to be the equal of other peoples, so we must have a fist to become their peers.[24]

Writing in the midst of sport's so-called "golden age," when even boxing gained respectability and Jack Dempsey reigned supreme along with Babe Ruth as America's greatest heroes, this Jewish journalist recognized the growing importance of sport as part of American popular culture and the place of sports celebrities in it. As he understood it, Leonard's fistic triumphs were more likely to provide Jews in America both ethnic pride and American acceptance than Einstein's genius. At least in this commentary, the importance of Jewish muscle enhanced the possibility of assimilation without diminishing Jewish pride or identity.

In that same year, the *Jewish Morning Journal* carried similar sentiments in a column devoted to Jewish boxers and other Jewish athletes. Confessing both ignorance and a lack of interest in the news of Jewish boxers in the sports pages of the regular press, the paper admitted it was on even shakier grounds when it came to sports such as squash. "It may be a Passover dish of the Reform Jews as far as we are concerned." Nevertheless, news of the triumph of Jewish players over their Gentile opponents, be it in the ring or on the court, filled the paper's reporter with "hope for the Jewish future." "We claim the distinction," he intoned, "of having discovered a Hebrew page in American newspapers."[25]

Over half a century after Leonard's tenure as middleweight champion, novelist Budd Schulberg could still recall in vivid detail the importance of Leonard to Jewish immigrants and their children engaged in their own American struggles. Writing in the boxing magazine *Ring,* Schulberg remembers that when he was a young boy, his hero was "neither the new cowboy star Tom Mix nor the acrobatic Doug Fairbanks. . . . Babe Ruth could hit fifty-four homers that year and I really didn't care." Not even the "legendary Ty Cobb" brought a chill . . . to my skin at the mention of his name. That sensation," Schulberg insists, "was reserved for Benny Leonard." For himself and Jewish boys like him who "tasted the fists and felt the shoe-leather of righteous Irish and Italian Christian children" who accused them of killing Christ while they walked to "shul on the Sabbath . . . The Great Benny Leonard" was their "superhero."[26]

Nor were they alone in their admiration. Before Schulberg was old enough to read, his father, known as B.P., himself only four years older than Leonard, gave him a scrapbook full of pictures and articles about the young Jewish champion. B.P. already was making his mark in motion pictures, splitting his time between New York and Los Angeles. Eventually he moved his family to the West Coast, served as production head for Paramount Pictures, and became one of the Jewish Hollywood moguls who dominated the industry. Although described by one Hollywood historian as a man whose Jewishness consisted of eating delicatessen on Sunday nights, B.P. reveled as a Jew in his admiration of Benny Leonard.[27] As Schulberg put it, "all up-and-coming young Jews in New York," like his father, "knew Benny Leonard personally. They would take time off from their lunch hour . . . to watch him train. They bet hundreds of thousands of dollars on him" and relished his boast that no matter how hard the battle no one ever "mussed" his thick black hair "plastered down and combed back in the approved style of the day." As Schulberg recalls, when Leonard's "hand was raised in victory, he would run his hand over his sleek black hair, and my father, and Al Kaufman, and Al Lichtman, and the rest of the Jewish rooting section would roar in delight." Much like the thousands of Jewish followers who crowded the Harlem street where Benny lived with his mother the night he first won the lightweight crown and cheered him by waving American flags and shouting his name, for B.P. and his friends, "The Great Bennah" symbolized the possibility of their own American success. As Schulberg reminds us, he also allowed them "to shake in his invincibility" and to retaliate against all those who had demeaned them and their children because they were Jews. In Schulberg's words:

> To see him climb in the ring sporting the six-pointed Jewish star on his fighting trunks was to anticipate sweet revenge for all the bloody noses, split lips, and mocking laughter at pale little Jewish boys who had run the neighborhood gauntlet.

In 1921, Schulberg almost got a chance to see and feel such things for himself. As he recalls it, approaching his seventh birthday, he had two ambitions in life: to become a world champion like his hero and "to see the Great Benny in action." While the first possibility remained remote, news that his father would take him to a championship bout between Leonard and the Irish contender, Richie Mitchell, filled him with great anticipation. Nor was he alone. According to one sportswriter, the fight, staged in Madison Square Garden on January 14, 1921, less than a year after the New York State legislature legalized boxing, would help the sport's reputation. The fact that the Garden's promoter, Tex Rickard, planned to stage it as a benefit to help raise money for a war-torn France and that governors, philanthropists, and members of high society were all expected to attend, figured in his assessment. Arnold Rothstein, still embroiled in the Black Sox scandal, also was excited about the bout. According to one story, his friend Benny Leonard had told him he would knock Mitchell out in the first round. Accordingly, Rothstein bet $25,000 on Benny and an additional $2,500 on behalf of the champion. Rumor had it that Leonard himself wagered his own $10,000 on the fight.

Schulberg never made it to ringside. When he and his father arrived at the Garden on East 23rd Street, ticket takers informed them that no one under the age of 16 would be allowed into the arena. Heartbroken, the young Schulberg was rushed home by his father in a taxi. B.P. then hurried back downtown while his young son wallowed in miserable realization that by the time he turned 16 his hero would long since have retired from the ring.

Although he missed the fight, his father recreated every detail for him. Mitchell's surprising knockdown of Leonard in the third round that made "thousands of young Jews" in attendance will their champion up off the canvas received less attention than B.P.'s vivid description of the bloody sixth round. In it Benny unmercifully bloodied and shredded Mitchell's face until the Irishman's corner threw in the towel.

As it turned out, little more than a decade later, Schulberg did get to see his hero fight. Despite earning lots of money through boxing, real estate investments, and an occasional turn on the vaudeville circuit, Leonard lost it all in the Depression and came out of retirement in 1931. After a series of unimpressive victories against run-of-the-mill opponents, he signed to fight Jimmy McClarnin, a promising Irish welterweight contender who boasted a string of victories against Jewish boxers. Schulberg, then a freshman at Dartmouth, drove to New York to witness the bout.

Benny's return to the ring once again evoked Jewish admiration and pride. "There is scarcely a Jew whose blood runs red," as one sportswriter for Los Angeles' *B'nai B'rith Messenger* put it on the eve of the bout, "who is not vitally interested in the outcome of the long-looked-forward-to Benny Leonard-Jimmy McClarnin set-to. . . ." Admitting that Leonard was a decided underdog, he recognized that, as a "sportswriter," Benny didn't have a chance. But, he inisted, as "the JEWISH man on the streets, I give this fight to Benny Leonard. Tomorrow morning," he continued, "I will know just how wrong I really am. But at least I will know that no matter how wrong I was, I was still right in believing that Benny Leonard would win—FOR win, loss, or draw, this compatriot of mine will have shown the world that he was a true fighting man."[28]

The fight was a mismatch. As Schulberg recalls, McClarnin toyed with his balding, overweight hero before knocking him out in "six of the saddest rounds I ever saw." When it was over, he didn't have the heart to call his father back in Los Angeles who awaited news of the outcome. Instead, then, and in later life, Schulberg preferred to think of that famous "Round Six" that he had only heard about in order to recreate the memory of Leonard's importance and place among his Jewish constitutents.

Irving Rudd's memories of Benny Leonard and of Jewish involvement in boxing evoke similar responses. Although at different times in his career he worked as publicity director for the Brooklyn Dodgers and for Yonkers Raceway, he began his trade promoting local fight cards in Queens and Brooklyn. Today, in his seventies, Rudd does the same job for Top Rank Boxing. Growing up in the Brownsville section of Brooklyn in the 1920s, Irving recalls that in his neighborhood, Leonard was a "deity." If his memory is correct, even McLarnin's knockout could not tarnish Benny's image. Given the chance to interview the great champion for his school newspaper, Irving remembers going backstage at a New York vaudeville theater to talk to him. There he also received Benny's photograph, on which Leonard wrote: "To My Friend Irving Rudd. If anyone wants to hit you, just send for me. Your friend, Benny Leonard." Needless to say, the next day at the local candy store, Irving was the envy of all his friends.[29]

For Rudd and countless other Jewish boys and men, Leonard was the greatest but hardly the only Jewish boxer in these years who evoked their passion, loyalty, and pride. In New York, Detroit, Boston, Chicago, or Los Angeles, every Jewish neighborhood boasted its own heroes whose names frequently appeared on posters in neighborhood store windows, on the marquees of local boxing clubs, or in newspaper stories describing their fights. Examples are endless. Jewish boys in Providence, Rhode Island, kept track of the exploits of their local hero, Maurice Billingkoff, a Russian immigrant who moved from Montreal to Providence at the age of seven in 1904 and who fought as a bantamweight. A newspaper cartoon of his knockout of one Kid Moran in March 1916 must have delighted local Jewish followers with its caption: "Oy! Such a fighter!" Chicago papers kept careful track of "ghetto boy" Morrie Bloom, as he fought his way through the Midwest and West Coast in the decade before World War I. Reporting on the whereabouts of this middleweight in 1929, the Chicago *Jewish Chronicle* noted that "one of the greatest Jewish fighters ever turned out in the midwest" now trained businessmen and their sons in the manly art. Announcing world featherweight champion's Louis "Kid" Kaplan's upcoming Chicago fight with Frankie Schaeffer in June 1925, the Chicago *Tribune* also informed "Jewish followers of the boxing racket" of the chance to see one King Solomon fight Gene Tunney in July. Pages of the *New York Times* throughout the 1920s catalogued the accomplishments of Jewish boxers on almost a daily basis. In similar fashion the Los Angeles *B'nai B'rith Messenger* kept its readers in touch with the exploits of local Jewish favorites such as welterweight Mushy Callahan. Jackie Fields, who spent part of his childhood in Chicago but who lived in Los Angeles as an adult, found himself claimed by Jewish fans in both cities as their local hero. Newspaper advertisements in Yiddish featuring boxers engaged in combat praising the virtues of Old Gold cigarettes confirms the popularity of the sport among Jews. Even the *American Hebrew* kept its more sophisticated German-Jewish audience aware of the "many Jews in professional pugilism."[30]

In fact, as Irving Rudd recalls, in crowded urban Jewish neighborhoods like his own, it was impossible not to be aware of the presence of Jewish boxers and the feelings they evoked. Memories of his childhood friendship with Bernie Friedkin, who, like Budd Schulberg, dreamed of becoming a Jewish boxing champion, poignantly capture this sense.[31] Friedkin actually fought with moderate success as a lightweight in the late 1930s and early 1940s, at times promoted by Rudd himself. But as an adolescent, Bernie's dream jarred with images of the future held out to Rudd by his hard-working immigrant parents who hoped that "their designated genius," as Irving put it, would become "chief surgeon at Mount Sinai hospital" or at worst an orthodox rabbi. As adults, Rudd served as his friend's promoter. As boys, Irving filled in as a punching bag. Friedkin, whose basement was set up as a boxing ring and who learned to read by consuming *Ring,* once took Rudd on a tour of his East New York neighborhood. There, Irving remembers, "in the windows of the kosher butcher, the candy store, the hardware store . . . [were] big cardboard posters advertising professional boxing bouts at local clubs—the Broadway Arena and Ridgewood Grove. I [saw] names that [were] neither Irish, Polack, or German: "Pal" Silvers, Lou Feldman, Georgie Goldberg, and Marty Fox." Anxious to impress him with his knowledge of Jewish fighters, Friedkin revel[ed] him with stories of Ruby Goldstein, declaring that when the "Jewel of the Ghetto" loses a fight, the whole Jewish community "sits shiva."

Although he never claimed that all Jews mourned his defeats, Ruby Goldstein also remembered how important he was to his loyal Lower East Side Jewish fans. "In that crowded neighborhood," he wrote, "I walked in a crowd of my own. . . . My social club was still Steinberg's candy store. Placards announcing my fights were hung in the windows of the store. Pictures were on the walls. Tickets for my fights were sold there. After every fight, it was jammed with 'members' waiting to see me." Even more impressive to the New York lightweight was the nickname sportswriters gave him. Known as the "Jewel of the Ghetto," Goldstein recalled that the handle evoked memories of Joe Bernstein, the "Pride of the Ghetto." In Ruby's words, Bernstein remained "a figure in our folklore" and a name that even "bearded patriarchs who had never seen a fight . . . and who couldn't have named the name of another fighter, still spoke of." The fact that his own nickname might evoke similar responses from the same people filled him with immense pride.[32]

Goldstein's hope that even Old World Jewish patriarchs might identify with his success should not obscure the fact that for every one of them who came to the United States between 1881 and 1924, far more Yekls made the trip. Clearly many East European Jewish immigrants and their children were avid followers of the ring. Like Irish, Italians, and blacks, they came out to cheer on their landsmen, wager on the outcome, and enjoy a sense of independence and freedom in a separate male world that combined fierce ethnic loyalties in praise of athletes that personified both ethnic pride and, however crudely and starkly, the importance of individual effort, hard work, discipline, and competition as keys to succeeding as Americans.

Fight promoters were not conscious of their own role in providing entertainment that implicitly educated immigrants in American ways, but they were keenly aware of the ethnic and neighborhood loyalties of their faithful patrons. Bouts arranged by astute entrepreneurs that emphasized ethnic conflict brought out working-class Jewish fans anxious to prove their superiority over their Irish and Italian neighbors who also filled local arenas. Leach Cross, for example, who fought over 150 times between 1908 and 1918, recalled that many of his fights in neighborhood boxing clubs like the Manhattan Casino and the Empire Athletic Club pitted him against Irish fighters. "The Irish used to come to see me get licked," he noted, and "the Jewish fans came to see me win."[33] So strong was his following among New York's East European Jewish community that after defeating Frankie Madden on St. Patrick's Day in 1908, the *Jewish Daily Forward* devoted part of its front page to a description of the fight and to a picture of the triumphant Jewish boxer. Five years later, when Cross traveled to New Orleans to take on Joe Mandot, "The Louisiana Wildcat," a special telegraph line was set up in front of the Western Union office on Rivington Street so that his loyal Jewish fans could follow the fight. Nat Fleischer, a childhood friend of Cross's and later founder and editor of *Ring,* suggests that "through Leachie, 1000s of New Yorkers who might never have followed boxing, became ardent fans."[34] Some 20 years later, matches between Chicago's lightweight Davey Day and his cross-town Italian rivals Frankie Siglio and Nick Castiglione regularly packed Chicago Stadium with 13,000 Jews and Italians eager for each other's throats. As one reporter noted, fans "cared more about a boxer's national or religious persuasion than his weight."[35]

While such match-ups appeared to inflame ethnic hatred, some commentators suggested that they allowed Jewish boxers to act as a middle ground in the service of assimilation and ethnic harmony. Just as Abraham Cahan realized that Irish champions could also be Jewish heroes, several columnists argued that champions like Benny Leonard were popular with all people. Ted Carroll, for instance, told his *Ring* audience that Benny's "immense following was drawn from every segment and strata of society." And Arthur Brisbane, writing for the Hearst newspapers, noted that Leonard's reputation as a tough boxer as well as his participation in exhibition bouts to raise money for Catholic charities did "more to conquer anti-Semitism than 1,000 textbooks." Benny, as Brisbane put it, has "done more to evoke the respect of the non-Jew for the Jew than all the brilliant Jewish writers combined."[36]

Boxing promoters were also aware of the potential in pitting Jewish boxers against each other. Leach Cross's victory over Joe Bernstein that so enraged his father was only one of many such bouts that brought together neighborhood rivals as the unofficial standard bearers of different Jewish neighborhoods. Benny Leonard's two fights with Lou Tendler, the son of a sweatshop tailor who came out of Philadelphia's Market Street Jewish ghetto to challenge the great lightweight champion, stand out here. The first bout, billed as

the Jewish lightweight championship of the world, took place at Boyles Thirty
Acres in Jersey City on July 27, 1922. In a savage display that left both boxers
bloodied at the end, Leonard held on to his title in a no-decision bout before
a crowd of some 60,000 fans, many of whom were Jewish. One year later, the
two met again, this time in Yankee Stadium before some 58,000 spectators
who paid $452,648, then a record for a lightweight bout. Anticipating the bat-
tle for its fight fans, the *Jewish Daily Forward* commented that "while only one
of the two combatants will exit the arena a champion, neither will leave the
place unmarked." According to Heywood Broun, who covered the fight for
the New York *World,* Leonard won a decisive victory. His description vividly
captures the sport's visceral appeal to Jewish fight fans from Philadelphia and
New York who came to cheer on their favorite. As Broun put it:

> The wonder is that Tendler still had a head. Rights and lefts, hooks and jabs
> rocked him from the beginning. Water cascaded from the top of the Phila-
> delphian's pompadour as if he had been Old Faithful, the Geyser. Now his
> head went back. Next it sagged, but mostly was doubled from side to side as
> Leonard landed first with one hand and then with the other. . . . Distinctly
> this was highbrow entertainment, for it was boxing developed to its most
> lofty phase as a fine art. The only trouble was that it was not a contest between
> two masters. The participants were professor and pupil.[37]

Whether fighting against each other or against other ethnic foes, Jewish
boxers occasionally showed their appreciation of Jewish support by sacrificing their own profits for Jewish causes. Much like Jewish basketball players
who played ball in the spirit of the Jewish tradition of tzedakah, Ruby Goldstein, Charlie Phil Rosenberg, Art Lasky, and Maxie Rosenbloom fought exhibitions to raise money for the Palestine Relief Fund or for local Jewish charities. In July 1925, for instance, Rosenberg, then world bantamweight
champion, "K.O." Phil Kaplan, and Abie Goldstein appeared before 13,000
fans on a card at New York's Velodrome that raised over $63,000 for the
Hunt's Point Jewish hospital.[38]

Participation in such events endeared Jewish boxers to their Jewish fans.
Name-changing also played a part here. Although Benny Leonard, Leach
Cross, Mushy Callahan, and a number of other Jewish fighters anglicized their
Jewish names either to disguise their occupation from disapproving parents
or because they thought it would promote their careers, others emphasized
Jewish monikers in hopes of attracting ethnic audiences. Charley Phil Rosenberg's given name, for instance, was Charles Green. Born on the Lower East
Side in 1902, he grew up in Harlem where his mother struggled to survive as
a pushcart peddler. One of his friends, Phil Rosenberg, made a few extra dollars as a boxer. One day Rosenberg became ill and unable to make a scheduled
fight. Green took his license, convinced the promoter that he was Phil Rosenberg, and earned $15 for his effort. Green kept his newfound professional
name and went on to become world bantamweight champion in 1925.[39]

Even more telling is Barney Lebrowitz's story. Born in Philadelphia in
1891, Lebrowitz began his boxing career in 1906 under the name of Barney

Williams. After seven mediocre years in New York clubs as a light-heavy-weight, he became the property of "Dumb" Dan Morgan. More astute than his nickname implied, Morgan immediately arranged a fight for him with Dan "Porky" Flynn at New York's St. Nicholas arena. Aware that bouts between Jews and Irish were moneymakers, he persuaded the arena's promoter to advertise his fighter as Battling Levinsky, the Jewish boxer ready to take on any Irishman in the country. Levinsky handled Flynn and quickly became a favorite with Jewish fight fans, not only for his name but for his successes in the ring. During a career that spanned three decades, he reigned as light-heavyweight champion between 1916 and 1920, fought in 272 bouts, and took on all comers, including Georges Carpentier, Jack Dempsey, and Gene Tunney. Along with Leach Cross, Benny Leonard, Davey Day, and a host of other Jewish boxers, Levinsky wore a Star of David on his trunks in case Jewish fight fans forgot his Jewish name.[40]

Name-changing one way or another did not always guarantee boxers their desired results. The Leiners and the Wallachs knew who Benny Leonard and Leach Cross were just as Los Angeles Jewish fight fans recognized that Mushy Callahan was their beloved Vincent Morris Schneer. So too did the faithful in Chicago and Los Angeles who claimed Jackie Fields as their own. Fields's birthname was Jacob Finkelstein. When he began his career as an amateur boxer in Los Angeles, he changed it because promoters thought his Jewish name would present the wrong image for him. As he told it, "a Jew wasn't supposed to be a tough fighter. A Jew is supposed to be a guy for the books." Searching for a "high-class name," Finkelstein remembered his Chicago roots and picked Fields, the last name of Chicago businessman and philanthropist Marshall Fields who owned the department store of the same name. Jackie, "just American for Jacob," Fields remembered, took less thought.[41]

That's how most Americans who took any interest in boxing first came to know the young Jewish boxer. At a time when the Olympic games hardly captured the public's attention as they do today, Fields traveled to Paris in 1924 as part of the American Olympic team. After a series of elimination bouts he won the welterweight championship from one of his own teammates, becoming, at sixteen, the youngest boxer ever to win an Olympic gold medal. In its brief coverage of the boxing competition, the *New York Times* identified Fields either as an "American" or as a "Californian," making no mention of his Jewish immigrant roots. Regardless of his name, by the time he concluded his professional career in 1933, this colorful welterweight who won 73 of 87 bouts and who reigned as world champion in 1929 and 1930 and again between 1932 and 1933 was better known as a tough Jewish fighter and a popular favorite of Jewish fight fans.[42]

IV

Two stories about Jewish fighters and their names suggest another reason why Jewish fighters were so important to Jews growing up in America in the first part of the 20th century. One, handed down by Irving Rudd, tells of a match in a western coal-mining town between Benny Leonard and one "Irish" Eddie Finnegan. Unfortunately for Eddie, cries from spectators urging him to "kill the kike" or "murder the Yid" enraged Benny. In Rudd's telling, Leonard attacked his opponent with a furious flurry of jabs, stabs, and moves, busting up Finnegan's eyes and lips. Holding on for dear life, "Irish" Eddie grabbed Leonard in a clinch and pled for mercy, gasping in Yiddish that his real name was Seymour Rosenbaum.[43] The other story appeared in Elias Lieberman's "Melting Pot" column for the *American Hebrew* in June 1919. Titled "Irony," it told the saga of "slugger Kid Cohen's" fight with a boxer named Kid Paul. As Lieberman presented it, depressed over news of pogroms in his Polish homeland, Izzy Cohen fought listlessly against a much lesser opponent "who would have failed miserably were it not for the Jew's obvious lack of interest." Between rounds Cohen told his handlers that the news made him wonder "if I'm any earthly use to either my people or myself." A Jewish voice from the crowd shook Izzy out of his lethargy, urging him to destroy Kid Paul because he is a "Polack." With "childhood memories of Kiev flamed before his eyes" and "boyhood tales of Kishineff . . . in his ears," Cohen proceeded to clobber his opponent, symbolically offering retribution for the punishment Polish Jews endured from their own countrymen. "Praise God, thundered the avenger, in purest Hebrew, as he flung aloft his mittened hands." And "from his feet came the same cry in weaker tones: Praise God, Oh, Israel!"[44]

In both stories, Jewish fighters disguise their identities only to incur the wrath of superior Jewish fighters who use their fists to challenge anti-Semitism directed at themselves and against other Jews. Even respectable organs of Jewish public opinion like the *American Hebrew,* which at other times disapproved of boxing as proper sport for assimilating Jews, could appreciate the positive effect of such stories in demonstrating that Jews were fit to be Americans and in developing an American Jewish identity that embraced physicality and toughness as necessary for Jewish survival. Although Jewish advocates of sport and Jewish baseball players like Hank Greenberg made their own contributions to these connected strands of American Jewish history, Jewish dominance in a sport defined by physical violence, strength, and toughness brought them together in special ways. Despite its reputation as a disreputable sport, no other activity provided such a clear way to refute stereotypes of the weak, cowardly Jew that anti-Semites employed to deny Jewish immigrants and their children full access to American opportunities. Nor did any other sport that Jews engaged in provide better connection to an historical tradition of Jewish physical strength and power employed in behalf of Jewish protection and survival in a hostile world.

Boxing's role in challenging anti-Semitic stereotypes and in shaping a Jewish-American identity emerged most fully in the years between the wars. We know, however, that some Jewish spokesmen at the turn of the century, in the spirit of Max Nordau's European cries for "muscular Jews," urged East European Jewish immigrants to participate in all sport for similar reasons. Even earlier, at least one Jewish writer anticipated boxing's special potential in this respect. Writing at a time when East European Jewish immigrants first began coming to America, Isadore Choynski used the pages of the *American*

Israelite to inform his German-Jewish readers of his son's ring triumphs. In 1885, when Joe Choynski, the first great Jewish-American boxer was only 17, Isadore boasted that his boy was "able to knock Sullivan out . . . in a single round."[45] Just in case this assertion failed to impress the great John L., the elder Choynski provided additional evidence after Joe won the California amateur heavyweight crown two years later. With references to a Union Civil War marching song that identified his American attachments, his own father's orthodox Jewish disdain for physical violence, and a distinguished boxing heritage of European Jews, Isadore announced his son's victory to his readers:

> We are coming Father Abraham! The boys of the Jewish persuasion are getting heavy on muscle. Many of them are training to knock out J. L. and it may come to pass. It is almost an everyday occurrence to read in our papers that a disciple of Mendoza . . . has knocked out the best of sluggers. . . . This week a youngster who calls himself J. B. Choynski, 19 years old, native of this city, weighing 160 pounds, fought for the championship and gold medal with one named Connelly, and the lad with the Polish name knocked out the well-knitted Irish lad of much experience in three rounds, and carried off the medal and the applause triumphantly. . . . I knew that boy's grandfather quite well. He is dead several years but if the pious, learned grandfather could lift his head from the grave and look upon the arena where mostly the scum of society congregate and behold his grandson slugging and sparring, fighting and dodging . . . he would hang his head and exclaim, "What is this horrible show for?"[46]

In one brief paragraph Choynski captured contradictory themes about Jewish physicality that became increasingly relevant to future generations of East European Jews and their children. Recognition of a heritage of Jewish boxing ability dating back to England's Daniel Mendoza, disdain for involvement in questionable activity even by standards of American respectability coupled with traditional Jewish disgust with such behavior, and yet pride in this display of Jewish physicality that helped Jewish boys establish their American place anticipated the range of responses that accompanied later Jewish involvement in the ring.

Several months later, when Joe successfully defended his title by knocking out an Irish blacksmith named William Keneally, Choynski connected his son's victory to a tradition of tough Jews willing and able to risk their lives in behalf of Jewish survival. As he reported:

> The Choynski boy fairly wiped the floor with the Irish gentleman, and finished him in four hard contested rounds. The Jews, who take little stock in slugging, are glad that there is one Maccabee among them, and that the Irish will no longer boast that there is not a Jew who can stand up to the racket and receive punishment according to the rules of Queensberry.[47]

Sportswriters, sportsmen, Jewish boxers, and their fans continually drew the same lessons about the importance of Jewish boxers in the 1920s and 1930s. Some even made direct connections to other Jewish heroes who risked their lives defending their own people. Reporting on the victories of Cleveland boxers Henry Goldberg, George Levine, and Sammy Aaronson one reporter for Cleveland's *Jewish Independent* in 1926 scoffed at those people who express surprise in "the prowess of the Jew in athletics." "A perusal of the ancient records," he noted, "will prove beyond question that even in antiquity, athletics and physical development were qualities that were sought and encouraged among Jewish men." Any doubters only needed to remember that "Sampson the Strong is still the ideal of the strong men of the world."[48]

Several years later, Bill Miller, a sportswriter and boxing publicist, added another voice to a growing chorus that underlined the critical role Jewish boxers played in refuting charges of Jewish inferiority and weakness. Looking back on his childhood, Miller reminded his Los Angeles *B'nai B'rith Messenger* readers of a story that always brought "a belly laugh" when Jewish comics told it on the vaudeville circuit. "Vell, vun time," the comic began, "me und mine brodder, und mine oncle, und nine uff mine relations, ve nerly licked a Irishman vunce!" Now, however, thanks to the glorious achievements of Jewish boxers which Miller briefly recounted, charges of Jewish impotence were "inane and pointless." Never again, he insisted, will be there a recurrence of the "excruciating jest" about a bunch of weak Jews and an Irishman that so pained him as a child. Now, he concluded, "it's pretty nearly the other way around."[49]

H. P. Hollander, an English welterweight and member of the British Maccabi Association, presented a similar if more measured account of the same theme for readers of the Detroit *Jewish Chronicle.* In an article entitled "Why Jews Make Good Boxers," Hollander noted that throughout their history Jews found "few opportunities for play" in their "desperate struggle for existence." With time only for infrequent recreation at night, their "amusements were more intellectual than physical, more of the brain than of the body." Emphasizing popular theories of human development and the environment, he continued that such practice, coupled with living conditions that were often unhealthy, not suprisingly failed to develop a people with "recognized athletic slender build," but rather built ones who are "generally short, muscular, and broad." Even with these handicaps, however, Jews "spread thinly all over the face of the world," and although "outnumbered and downtrodden," also inherited from their ancient ancestors "pride of birth and virile instincts." Resentful of "slurs" and "sneers" about "their small stature and lack of skills in manly sports," the result of circumstances that prohibited opportunity for participation, the individual Jewish boxer, Hollander suggested, vindicated what had been denied his people. "Once he could get into the ring, The Jew could show the world that he could fight—and fight with brain and with strength and with courage. Then no one could deny him that he was a man amongst men, for few sports appeal to the general imagination than boxing." Jewish history, the Englishman concluded, "has made him a boxer of purpose and determination."[50]

The praise of Jewish toughness and physical strength appeared in a Jewish newspaper that in the same year reported news of the Nuremberg Laws,

Father Coughlin, and the plight of the Palestinian homeland movement. Although Hollander did not explicitly connect his appreciation of the physically tough Jewish boxer to everyday concern about Jewish survival, others did. Bill Kadison, a sportswriter for the Los Angeles *B'nai B'rith Messenger,* offered his own contribution by recounting a string of triumphs of American Jewish boxers over German opponents in the early 1930s. "Ever since Herr Hitler inaugurated his 'rid Germany of the Jew' campaign," Kadison wrote in 1933, "his boys have suffered defeat every time they stepped out against ring warriors of the 'faith.'"[51]

Benny Leonard echoed similar views even before Adolph Hitler's rise to power. Interviewed by David Barzell, a reporter for the *Jewish Tribune* at the height of his career, "The Great Bennah" reviewed Jewish history and concluded that "the Jew has always been a fighter when he has a fair chance." Talking about his own sport and his own times, Leonard insisted that of all nationalities represented in the ring, the Jew was the "most fightingest of them all." Leonard, Barzell concluded, believed that the Jewish people are judged "as a whole" by the actions of individual prominent Jews. As one of those people, Benny took "his responsibility for the rest of Jewry" seriously. "A Jew has no right to be mean or puny," Barzell noted, "and Leonard seeks to live up to this ideal."[52]

Three years later Leonard extended his commitment to Jewish strength and survival in a most explicit way by associating himself with Camp Hakoah, a summer athletic camp designed to prepare Jews for potential combat with their enemies. Situated on Sackett Lake near Monticello, New York, in an area fast becoming the vacation grounds for New York City's large Jewish population, the camp, as advertised in the *American Hebrew,* was named after "the mighty and heroic Hakoah Soccer Team, which is the standard bearer of Jewish strength." There, Benny Leonard, "our own national hero," whose picture appeared in the advertisement, would head the physical training department. Developing Jewish "children to the highest degree of physical perfection," the camp hoped to "produce Jewish men of brawn who will form the vanguard of the Jewish people with a view of protecting them against attacks." Added inducement for signing up included the prospect of receiving periodic recommendations throughout the year about diet and exercise from Benny and the chance to write him about individual needs.[53]

There is no record of how much Leonard earned for his participation in this venture or whether it involved any more than brief, symbolic appearances by the athlete as celebrity so common to sports camps today. Moreover, even at the advertised reduced rate of $175 (marked down from $300), this summer experience was well beyond the reach of most of New York's East European Jewish population. Still, the stated purpose of the camp undeniably emphasizes the constancy with which the success of Jewish boxers remained tied to concerns about the need for physical, tough Jews able and willing to resist all threats to Jewish existence.

Certainly not everyone embraced Jewish involvement in boxing as a positive contribution to either Jewish survival or Jewish assimilation. But even here, writers did not dispute a tradition of Jewish strength. Chicago's Yiddish-language *Daily Jewish Courier,* for instance, in 1923 took issue with a local "gentile newspaperman" who argued that "the number of Jewish pugilists in the front ranks of this country's fighting fraternity" demonstrates the false-ness of "the theory that Jews are physical cowards." While voicing approval of Jewish participation in sport, the *Courier's* correspondent doubted that it was "proof of the physical courage . . . let alone the spiritual courage of that people." "The Jews," he proclaimed, "have never been lacking in either." As for Jewish boxers, the writer's disgust both for their sport and for their claims as Jews was clear:

> as for our highly honored members of the fighting fraternity, we may say that if the Jewish people has anything to contribute to the common civilization and culture of the race, such contributions are rather to be sought in the realm of their intellects than in their fists. . . . As a matter of fact none of these pugilists may be said to be Jews except in the accident of their birth. We should certainly encourage clean athletics but we need not bother about the pugilists. Let them take care of themselves. They believe they can very well do so.[54]

The *Courier's* criticism recognized the importance of a Jewish tradition of physical courage, but only when tied intimately to Jewish spirituality and intellect. As John Hoberman argues, even physical-culture enthusiasts like Max Nordau praised and encouraged Jewish muscularity only when managed by what he considered to be a superior Jewish intellect.[55] Characterizing all Jewish boxers as unconnected to a Jewish tradition where mind ruled over muscle, the *Courier* excluded them as part of an important and heroic heritage of Jewish physicality. Implicit in its remarks is a disdain for these men and their backgrounds—"Jews by accident of birth" who came primarily from immigrant working-class families where the daily struggle for existence and the personal aspirations of many left little room for intellectual concerns or formal religious practice.

Within this framework it's also reasonable to assume that the *Courier's* editorialist would not have been swayed by stories of Jewish boxing triumphs that linked victory not only to their physical strength but also to their intellect. Accounts of Benny Leonard's triumphs, for instance, invariably commented on "his brains" as being as important to his success as his strength. Nat Fleischer described him as a man "with a pair of dark brown eyes that sparkled intelligence" who "combined the boxing ingenuity of Young Griffo; the masterful technique of James J. Corbett; the clout of Jack Dempsey; the alertness of Gene Tunney; and the speed of Mike Gibbons." Above all, he noted, "Leonard had a hair-trigger brain. As he shifts about the ring, the fans could almost read his thoughts as he mapped out his plan of attack." Leonard, himself, dubbed the "king of scientific fighters" by one reporter, argued that "it was the Jewish fighters who put the science in the game." Even more emphatic about the intelligence of the Jewish boxer was Johnny Ray, the manager of the great Irish heavyweight Billy Conn. Commenting on his fighter's defeat by knockout at the hands of the immortal Joe Louis in a championship fight

young protagonist, Billy Bathgate, feels about himself and his own neighborhood when he returns for the first time as an acknowledged member of the
Schultz mob. Wearing a new satin jacket of a sports team known as the Shadows and his new sneakers, Billy realizes:

> I represented another kind of arithmetic to everyone on the block, not just
> the kids but the grown-ups too, and it was peculiar because I wanted everyone
> to know what they figured out easily enough, that it was just not given to a
> punk to find easy money except one way, but at the same time I didn't want
> them to know. I didn't want to be changed from what I was, which was a boy
> alive in the suspension of the judgment of childhood, that I was the wild kid
> of a well-known crazy woman, but there was something in me that might
> grow into the lineaments of honor, so that a discerning teacher or some other
> act of God, might turn up the voltage of this one brain to a power of future
> life that everyone in the Bronx could be proud of. I mean that to the more
> discerning adult, the man I didn't know and didn't know ever noticed me who
> might be living in the building or see me in the candy store, or in the school-
> yard. I would be one of the possibilities of redemption, that there was some
> wit in the way I moved, some lovely intelligence in an unconscious gesture
> of the game, that would give him this objective sense of hope for a moment,
> quite unattached to any loyalty of his own, that there was a chance, bad as
> things were, America was a big juggling act and that we could all be kept up
> in the air somehow, and go around not from hand to hand, but from light to
> dark, from night to day, in the universe of God after all.[60]

Billy Bathgate could well be Jewish; Doctorow doesn't tell us. Dutch Schultz,
born Arthur Flegenheimer, certainly was. Neither Billy nor Dutch were boxers. Nor did careers as boxers or gangsters signify Jewish arrival within the
American economic or social mainstream. Boxing was at best considered a
marginal sport and the life of crime, by definition, unacceptable. But as the
fictional Bathgate suggests, in dire times the escapades and accomplishments
of even boxers and criminals offered hope of an American future and confirmation that the decision involved in leaving old ways behind, however ambiv-
alent, might still be worth it. Even without this special atraction, however,
Jewish boxers challenged stereotypes of the weak Jew and helped define an
American Jewish identity that included physical toughness as an acceptable
trait. Both as symbols of possibility and as part of Jewish community experience, they offered their own contributions to how immigrants became Americans.

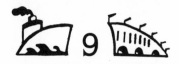

"Fighting for All My People": Jewish Champions and American Heroes

JOE Bonaparte and Billy Bathgate may seem too far removed from the everyday reality of the life of Jewish boxers and the world they inhabited to be credible witnesses of that experience. Not so Barney Ross and Maxie Baer. Ross, without question the greatest Jewish boxer of the 1930s, struggled more openly than most Jewish fighters with the "world of his father" to emerge as Jewish champion and American war hero. Baer, a legitimate heavy-weight contender in these same years, appeared to many as a man of questionable Jewish connections who wore his ethnic identity only as a matter of convenience. Both men found their own careers intimately connected with those of other ethnic heroes—be they the Irish-American Jimmy McLarnin, Nazi Germany's Max Schmeling, or the great black American champion, Joe Louis—in ways that personified the symbolic importance of boxing in the struggle for Jewish survival and American victory in the midst of world war. Their stories, in different ways, encapsulate the rich themes that define Jewish involvement with the manly art during the first half of the twentieth century.

I

On September 12, 1933, before 34,000 spectators in New York's Polo Grounds, Barney Ross successfully defended his combined lightweight and junior welterweight titles against Tony Canzoneri, who had lost the titles to him earlier in June. Reporting the fight for the *American Hebrew*, Henry Levy noted that Ross so dominated the fight that many of the "assembled experts" already recognized in him the second coming of "The Great Bennah." According to Levy, one pundit even declared Ross as "the best lightweight I've seen in twenty years. I won't say he is a Gans . . . but I do think he could have whipped Benny Leonard, and Benny can put that in his old calabash and smoke it!" Other ringside observers agreed, that, once again, "the lightweight class ruled over so long by Benny Leonard, once more ha[d] a Jewish boy as 'head man.'" Less than a year later, in May 1934, Ross added the welterweight crown by defeating Jimmy McLarnin, lost it back to him in September, and then regained the crown the following May. He retained that title until the great Henry Armstrong defeated him three years later. Ross also kept his light-weight belt until 1935, when he could no longer make the lower weight. During an eight-year professional career, he compiled a record of 74 wins, four losses, three draws, and one no-decision. Although boxing experts might debate whether his boxing credentials matched or surpassed Leonard's, there is no question that Barney took on Benny's mantle as American Jewish folk hero.[1]

Boxing, however, was not what his parents anticipated for their son, born Barnet David Rasofsky, on New York's Lower East Side on December 23, 1909. Isidore and Sarah Rasofsky met and married in Brest Litovsk. Confronted by anti-Semitism, pogroms, and difficult economic circumstances, the Rasofskys, like many other East European Jews, resolved to try their luck in America. Isidore came by himself in 1903 and eventually saved enough money to send for Sarah. Two years after Barney was born, the family moved to the Jewish immigrant neighborhood surrounding Chicago's Maxwell Street where his parents opened a small grocery and dairy store. Here the Rasofskys kept a strictly orthodox home and dreamed of their son's future as the Talmudic student and Hebrew teacher that had eluded Isidore.[2]

Most Jewish immigrants harbored more secular dreams for their children. Aware of Jewish religious tradition and custom, they adapted or discarded it in a variety of different ways as they struggled with the perils and opportunities of American life. Some, like Isidore and Sara Rasofsky, did their best to maintain religious orthodoxy in their home even as they sought to survive and prosper. Barney Ross's memories of his Chicago childhood richly recreate that world in ways that evoke the Jewish urban American ghetto life common to other youngsters of his generation, whether they lived on Maxwell Street, Commonwealth Avenue, or Hester Street.

Barney grew up in a home in which his father's authority was absolute and in which the family "followed every custom and edict of the Orthodox Jewish law." Keeping kosher was only a small part of the Rasofskys' traditional Jewish ways. As Ross put it, in his at times over-sentimentalized autobiography, *No Man Stands Alone:*

> we went around wearing yarmulkes and tzitziths, we washed our hands and said a blessing every time we ate even a piece of bread, we went to Rabbi Stein's cheder every evening, we did not write, ride, carry money, play ball, put on light, play the Victrola, or tear paper on Saturday. . . . We followed the rule against doing any work on Saturday so strictly that we wore handkerchiefs bound around our wrists, instead of carrying them in our back pockets

as we did all week. We tore a wad of toilet paper into strips every Friday so that there would be no necessity to tear in the toilet on Saturday.[3]

Even the task of earning a living did not disrupt his father's traditional ways. Each morning Isidore would get up at five, put on tefillin and say the morning prayers before opening "Rasofsky's Dairy." When time came for afternoon and evening prayers, no matter who was in the store or how busy it was, he would abruptly move to the back, "close his eyes and daven from memory."[4]

Close living quarters made it easy for Barney to observe his father's actions. Isidore and Sarah, along with their five children, occupied two small rooms at the back of the tiny dairy store that occupied the street front. Barney slept in one bed with two of his brothers, his father and oldest brother slept in another, his mother and sister shared a mattress placed on the kitchen floor, while his youngest brother had his own small mattress. Only on Saturday afternoons, when his parents took an after-dinner Sabbath nap, did he recall his parents sleeping together.

Aside from work, the Sabbath dominated the Rasofskys' family life. Along with assisting in the store, Barney's mother spent Thursday and Friday preparing for the Sabbath. In loving detail Barney describes the rituals that so engrossed her and other Jewish women each week:

> On Thursdays, Ma would start making the flour for the Sabbath bread or chal-
> lah. She would begin cleaning our dingy flat and wash the windows and
> floors. She'd polish the brass sticks that proudly held the candles for our Fri-
> day night dinner, wash and iron a big white tablecloth and press the blue suits
> that we would wear to synagogue. On Thursday nights she would mix the
> flour together with two or three yeast cakes, salt, eggs and water, until it
> formed a great mound of dough. Then she would knead the dough and set it
> in a pan on the back of our little stove to rise. On Fridays, she would light the
> stove again, shape the dough into twisted loaves and heat it till she was ready
> to say her blessings over the candles and set the table. On Thursdays too, Ma
> would peel six pounds of potatoes, then leave them in cold water overnight
> to prepare it for the cholent, a Sabbath delicacy that by tradition among the
> Jews of Eastern Europe descent is served to the menfolk when they come
> home from synagogue. . . . Ma and the other women on our block would
> blend and season their cholent Friday then take it to the bakery . . . and let it
> cook all night on a low fire in the baker's stove.[5]

Sabbath preparation also included weekly baths for the children in a kitchen washtub, and the family's attendance at Saturday services at the Pola Zedek shul, "a small dark synagogue on Maxwell and Roosevelt Streets." "Pa would look elegant in his derby hat, his frock coat, a stiff celluoid collar and his good shabbas suit," Ross recalls. "Ma would have on her one good dress and her shabbas hat. We kids wore hand-me-down clothes but Ma would have them pressed and patched for Saturday and our hair under our yarmulkes would be slicked with Vaseline."[6] After a morning service that lasted over three hours, the Rasofskys went home, ate their cholent, rested, and then returned to shul in the late afternoon for services, food, and shmoozing that often included debates between Isidore and the rabbi over the Talmud.

In Barney's childhood world there was little toleration for deviating from his father's interpretation of how to be Jewish, whether it involved putting the milk container too close to the meat in the icebox—an error that once produced a whipping with his father's cat of nine tails—or a young boy's involvement in street gangs or fighting. Like Benny Bass, Jackie Fields, Benny Leonard, and countless immigrant children, Barney lived in a neighborhood where adolescent, ethnic gangs did combat in the streets and school yards. Even with their own kind, fistfights and petty thievery from the pushcarts that dominated Maxwell Street were part of the price for group acceptance that Barney and his friends all paid.

Fighting, Ross remembered, particularly galled his father. In his mind it went against Jewish religious tradition and the place the Torah established for himself and his children as descendants of the "cohains," the rabbis who studied, interpreted, and administered Talmudic law. To Isidore, "anybody who got into a fist fight on the street was a tramp and a bum." Even Benny Leonard was no exception. "Once," Barney recalled, "when somebody told him about the great Jewish boxing champ, Benny Leonard, Pa's face turned blood red. 'What shame this Leonard has brought on his father and mother!,'" Isidore exclaimed.[7]

Aware of his father's beliefs, Barney claimed he never started fights but only defended himself. More than once, however, he learned from his father's words and from his whip that self-defense did not guarantee absolution. "Always Pa impressed on me that the beatings were nothing he liked," he recalled, "but that he had to do it for my own good. Unless you are punished so that you know you must not break God's laws, how will you be able to follow the right path, and earn God's blessings."[8]

Isidore never lived to see his son become a world champion and a man revered by other Jews. Barney, however, had no doubts that if his father had been around, he never would have approved of his son's career. As he put it:

> even if I'd been built like the Hollywood version of a champion prize fighter, it would have been the most terrible blasphemy for me to even start a discussion about boxing in my house. If Pa had lived, I think he would have killed me before he ever would have permitted me to put on a pair of gloves and climb into a ring.[9]

Ironically the violent death of this religious, stern, but caring man propelled Ross away from his religious upbringing and ultimately to a career as a boxer. As he tells it, arriving at the store on a December day in 1924 to pick up a sandwich before he left for high school, Barney found his father lying in his own blood, the victim of a senseless shooting by two would-be robbers.

According to Jewish custom, Isidore's body remained in the family's apartment until the day of his burial. Sitting with him, Barney vividly reflected on the man he loved and the ethnic world that had been his life:

I kept seeing Pa in the few happy moments of his life crammed with poverty
and misery. I saw him in the Turkish baths, laughing as Morrie [one of Barney's brothers] and I gasped in the rolling waves of steam; I saw him ramrod-
straight and handsome in his Shabbas suit, waiting to take Ma to the annual
benefit show of the Ladies Auxiliary of the synagogue. I saw him at my bar
mitzvah, standing proudly next to me as I faced the Torah, and repeating
every word silently to himself as I chanted the service. I saw him later at my
bar mitzvah party, accepting mazel tovs with a broad smile, passing favorable
comments on my bar mitzvah speech, and eagerly sampling the gefilte fish.[10]

The reality of death quickly intruded on these fond memories. Barney's
mother suffered a nervous breakdown and was taken to Connecticut to recu-
perate with relatives. He and his brother moved in with a cousin; the younger
Rasofsky children were sent to a Jewish orphanage, and the dairy was sold to
pay expenses. Although only 14, Barney resolved to bring his family back
together. This "special obligation" he imposed on himself fueled his interest
in the ring.[11]

The failure of the police to hold two murder suspects because an eyewit-
ness became too frightened to testify also affected Ross. His strong religious
upbringing already tested by his father's tragic death, Barney totally rejected
all that his father had taught him. Although he continued to say Kaddish for
his father, he gave up his daily prayers, stopped wearing tzithith and tefillin,
and discontinued observing the Sabbath. "I wanted to be as bad as bad can be.
I felt as if I wanted to knock over anybody who walked in front of me. . . .
Suddenly I changed from being the retiring little kid who believed all the
things about good and evil that he'd been taught."[12]

Ross became a troublemaker in school, earning the nicknames of "Beryl
the Terrible" and "One Punch Rasofsky" by regularly thrashing his school-
mates. He left high school after two years, held a series of odd jobs, and sup-
plemented his income by running crap games. For a time he even worked as
a messenger boy for Al Capone, a contact that was to mature after Ross established himself as a boxer. More steady work at Sears, Roebuck as a stockboy
followed, but its $12 a week salary hardly bankrolled into the kind of money
he needed to bring his family back together. Boxing provided the ticket.

Encouraged by friends who knew his ability first hand, Barney entered
amateur bouts, often fighting several times a week as a bantamweight to win
the gold watches and medals victory brought. Frequent trips to local pawn-
shops where he traded in his spoils for cash propelled him toward a professional career. So too did the occasional mentions he received in local boxing
columns that described his victories and proclaimed his possibilities as "the
West Side Jewish kid" who "has all it takes to become a top-notcher."[13]

Barney's friends were excited about his success, but he met a different
reception at home. Although he began fighting under his given name, Barnet
Rasofsky quickly became Barney Ross in order to keep his mother, now back
in Chicago, from finding out what he was doing. Inevitably, however, as with
Abe Attell, Benny Leonard, and other Jewish boys who entered the ring, Mrs.
Rasofsky learned the truth and responded in predictable fashion. Calling up

the memory of his father, she reminded her son that he had already dishonored him by turning away from God. "Now you want to be a fighter," she shrieked. "Never, never. . . . I forbid it!" Only Ross's assurances that he would quit the ring as soon as he earned enough money to bring the family back together won her approval.[14] It took Barney longer than he thought. By the time he reunited his mother with her children in 1933, he had become the professional lightweight and junior welterweight world champion and Benny Leonard's successor as Jewish-American hero.

Ross's promising start as an amateur culminated in 1929 when he won the national Golden Gloves featherweight championship. That year, with the encouragement of Jackie Fields, then welterweight champion of the world, he turned professional and joined the fighting stable of Sam Pian and Al Winch, an Italian-Jewish manager-trainer team that handled Chicago's best Jewish and Italian prospects in the 1930s. Although he won his first professional bouts, Ross did not train seriously and spent a good deal of time with his unemployed childhood friends drinking and organizing crap games for Marshall High School students. Only after his managers threatened to drop him did Barney devote himself to boxing. Matched against popular Irish and Italian fighters to bring out the crowds, Ross soon became a local favorite. Within four years he earned a shot at the top—a title fight in Chicago on June 23, 1933, with Tony Canzoneri for both the lightweight and junior welterweight championships. Before 13,000 fans at Chicago Stadium Ross won by decision and confirmed his status among Chicago's Jewish population.

Al Capone and his mob also enjoyed the victory. Although Ross was never accused of participating in any rigged bouts, there is no question that Capone and his friends frequented his matches, bet on their outcome, and occasionally offered Ross their company. This kind of connection between boxer and gangster, evident as well in the careers of Benny Leonard, Abe Attell, and Ruby Goldstein, clearly did not enhance boxing's respectability however it might have titillated the imaginations of second-generation Jewish adolescents who admired courage and audacity, be it in their athletic or even their criminal heroes.

Even before topping Canzoneri and without Capone, Ross's hometown ring triumphs elevated him to Jewish hero. Ben Goldberg, better known as Ben Bentley, presently supervisor of Chicago's city parks and at one time a prominent ring announcer, recalls that when Ross fought on Friday night in Chicago, the entire working-class Jewish community paid attention. Jewish people walking down Roosevelt Road on the way to the baths before attending synagogue, he remembers, would talk about the fight. Later in the evening, restaurants on the street turned up loudspeakers that blared news reports of the contest. As Bentley told me, "Barney Ross was a symbol of the Jewish people in those days in that if he can do it then we can do it."[15]

Out of pride and fear, Barney's mother also became caught up in the adulation her son received. Anxious about his safety, she sewed a Star of David to the inside of his boxing trunks while he was still an amateur so that he would "have protection from God."[16] Whenever Barney fought, she demanded that one of her other sons call her as soon as it was over to let her know that "Barnele" was all right. Often, however, she passed out before the phone rang. When Ross learned of his mother's dilemma, he encouraged her to attend his Chicago fights. Her first experience alleviated her anxiety so well that she decided to make it a habit. The only problem was that many of her son's matches were on Friday nights. Refusing to compromise totally her Sabbath observance which prohibited driving to Chicago Stadium or the various local clubs where Barney boxed, she resolved the problem by walking to and from the arenas, often accompanied by neighborhood children who idolized her son. Ross remembers:

> Ma followed this strange custom. First, she went to synagogue to pray for me. Then she put on her most comfortable shoes, said goodbye to the neighbors and started walking. Morrie kept her company but he always complained his feet were killing him! And after a while Ma got more company. The young kids in the Roosevelt Road section, who also regarded me as some kind of a hero, began to accompany Ma to the fights and back in a big group. . . . It got to be one of the strangest weekly marches that Chicago has even seen.[17]

Indeed on the night that Ross defeated Canzoneri, Barney accompanied his mother on the five-mile walk back to her apartment to a family recently reunited thanks to his ring accomplishments. "Beryl," he remembers his mother telling him, "there are no more orphans in this family. Pa is looking down on you and he is very proud of you."[18]

Ironically, Ross's emergence as an American Jewish hero in an activity abhorred by his Russian immigrant father hastened Barney's reconciliation with the Jewish upbringing he had deserted. It also allowed him to put his image as a tough Jew in the service of an American Jewish identity that included avenging Jewish oppression and anti-Semitism. Again, Ross provides the heart of the story. As he recalled it, his mother's words of praise after the Canzoneri fight rang hollow. How could his father be proud of him when he had rejected his religion and teachings? Determined to resolve this painful question, Ross took along his father's library of religious books to his training camp in Loretta, Wisconsin, where he went to train for his scheduled September 1933 rematch with Canzoneri. In between workouts and in the evening he reread the ancient texts and their messages about morality, justice, love, and family and wrestled with his father's death and how it had affected his own life. Finally, Barney concluded:

> the Lord had given me and my family compensation [for his death]. Ma was over her worst sickness, the family was together again and though I was in a trade I would never have touched if Pa had lived, it was allowing me to give Ma and the rest of the family comforts and luxuries they'd never had before. It was also bringing them a lot of honor and pride.[19]

That night Barney dreamed of his Pa up in the clouds, smiling down on him. Taking this as a sign from God that his approving father was in heaven, Barney put on his tefillin for the first time in several years, and said his morning prayers before taking off for his road work.

Even more dramatic was the final act in this reconciliation. Ross retained his titles in a hard-fought rematch against Canzoneri in New York, a match, as one reporter for the Los Angeles *B'nai B'rith Messenger* put it, that "saved the lightweight championship for the Jewish people."[20] After the bout, Ross returned to Chicago and visited his father's shul on Maxwell Street. Recognized and welcomed by some of the old men he had known since childhood, nevertheless he worried whether Rabbi Stein, his mentor and father's friend, would accept his presence. In prose comparable to the scenes from the original version of "The Jazz Singer" which Ross may well have seen, he describes what happened when the rabbi turned to his congregation to call one of its members to the Torah to recite the first aliyah—an honor for any devout Jew:

> Rabbi Stein threw a glance at the congregation and suddenly saw me. I couldn't be sure but it seemed to me as if his eyes lit up. Then he called out, "Yahamoad Dov Ber David ben Yitzchak hacohain. Stand up Barnet David, son of Isidore of the priestly sect." He was calling me to the Torah. He was giving me the honor of reciting the first aliyah. Like a sleepwalker I moved forward. Every eye in the synagogue was on me. I placed my talis against the Torah and then kissed it. With a loud voice, I recited the blessing from memory. I didn't miss a word—everything came back to me in a rush. When I finished, Rabbi Stein shouted, "Amen," and stretched out his hand. There were tears in his eyes. We clasped hands and then he threw his arms around me. "Gott zei dank," he said. "You've come back."[21]

Reconciliation did not mean a return to any form of traditional life familiar to his father. Ross continued to fight and spent a good deal of his time betting huge amounts of money at race tracks all over the country. By one estimate, over the course of his boxing career, he lost most of the $500,000 he earned in the ring through gambling.[22] Nevertheless, for Barney and his followers, his symbolic importance as a tough Jew whose victories challenged notions of Nazi supremacy more than made up for any distance between his own American life and that of his father.

Critical here were a series of three fights with Jimmy McLarnin in 1934 and 1935. Moving up in weight class, Ross fought the popular Irish welterweight champion of the world in New York in May 1934. Money certainly motivated Ross, who owed bookies all over the place. The fact that the Irish-Jewish angle would bring out the crowds was not lost on him, especially since McLarnin, as boxing columnists made clear, had earned the reputation as the "Jew beater" because of his consecutive victories over Sid Terris, Ruby Goldstein, Al Singer, Louis Kid Kaplan, and Benny Leonard.[23]

Even more important, however, was Barney's role as a Jewish champion who would refute Nazi claims of Jewish weakness. Reminding him that he was one of the best-known Jews in America, his rabbi and his mother urged him to set a good example for Jews all over the world by challenging the "horrible lies Hitler is telling." Ross's own reading of press reports of the mistreatment of Jews in Nazi Germany coupled with speculation that he would be the next in the long line of Jews that would fall to McLarnin because he lacked a "fighting spirit" also spurred him. As he told one friend, "I had never been so keyed up and so tense before a fight. The news from Germany made me feel I was . . . fighting for all of my people."[24]

That's how many Jews viewed his hard-fought 15-round victory over McLarnin at New York's Long Island Bowl before 45,000 fans on May 24, 1934. In what some commentators called one of boxing's most exciting bouts, Barney came off the canvas in the ninth round where McLarnin had put him for the first time in his career, returned the favor, and hung on for a split decision to become the first boxer ever to hold three world titles simultaneously. Listening to the fight on her radio in Chicago, Mrs. Rasofsky told her grandson that "Barney is fighting for the good name of our people." When she learned that it was broadcast internationally, she nodded approvingly and added that "Hilter will know about it then. Maybe he'll learn something from it about our people. He should know that he can kill millions of us but he can never defeat us." Ross recalled similar responses, not only from Jews but from people of all backgrounds. In Chicago, he recalls, even weeks after his victory, "in the ghetto, every delicatessen, every grocery, every tailor shop carried a big picture of me underneath the words, 'Our Barney.'" Jewish neighborhood pride was matched by Jewish and civic groups throughout the city who demanded Ross's appearance at celebrations of his victory.[25]

Ross went on to fight McLarnin two more times. Four months after their first bout, the Irish contender regained his title by decision, one that some Jewish fight patrons viewed skeptically. Noting that "ten of the fifteen ring experts at ringside" believed Barney deserved the victory, the Detroit *Jewish Chronicle* claimed their man had been robbed of his title. Several weeks later, in a column titled "Three Cheers for Barney Ross," Morris Weiner, a *Chronicle* reporter, charged that fight referee Arthur Donovan had voted for McLarnin because they were both Irish. Donovan, Weiner assured, "is being burned in effigy on all the sidewalks of [New York] which the Irish don't claim for their own."[26] Presumably, Jewish arsonists rested easy in May 1935 when Ross won the welterweight crown back in another 15-round decision, this time in New York's Polo Grounds. Forced to give up his lightweight crown because he could no longer make weight, he successfully defended his welterweight belt a number of times over the next few years before being badly beaten by Henry Armstrong in his last fight in May 1938. Through it all, he continued to be heralded as the great Jewish champion, an identification he nurtured with generous contributions to a host of Jewish charities.

Although retirement from the ring removed Ross from center stage, he remained for many a symbol of the tough Jew willing and able to put himself on the line for the Jewish people and for his country. Appropriately, his first public venture after boxing was a small part in a production of Clifford Odets's *Golden Boy*. Far more important, however, was his decision to volunteer for the Marine Corps after the Japanese attack on Peark Harbor. As Barney put it, someone had to represent his family in the struggle against fascism and he was the only one available.

Film buffs familiar with *Body and Soul* (1948) and *Monkey on My Back* (1957), both loosely based on Barney Ross's life, know the rest of the story. Fighting at Guadalcanal, Barney was seriously wounded trying to help a scout patrol trapped in a foxhole by a Japanese machine-gun nest. Back home, news of his heroism, which earned him a Silver Star and the Distinguished Service Cross, transformed this Jewish champion into an American hero. Both the *American Hebrew* and the New York *Sun* reported that "today" the three-time former champion "holds the greatest title he ever possessed. He was called a 'damned good Marine' by his captain." When the Boxing Writers Association of New York heard the news of his deeds, they considered no other names in unanimously voting Barney as "fistiana's Man of the Year." A young Jewish sports announcer named Marty Glickman understood that his childhood hero served both a Jewish and an American purpose when he witnessed a five-minute standing ovation Ross received at ringside before a championship match in New York's Madison Square Garden soon after he returned from the Pacific.[27]

Ross's triumphal homecoming was not without problems. It took Barney quite a while to recover from his injuries. Recuperation included additional horrors: an addiction to morphine that almost cost him his marriage and his life. Ross eventually overcame his habit and publicly spoke out against drugs. Like other men of his generation, he measured his commitment to Jewish causes by helping to raise money for Jewish charities and by becoming a fierce supporter in behalf of the movement to establish an independent Jewish nation in Israel. Although no longer able to put his body on the line in real or symbolic defense of Jewish survival, he participated in schemes to smuggle guns into Israel to help defend the country after it became an independent nation in 1948.[28]

Eddie Cantor, the legendary vaudevillian who wrote the dedication to Barney's autobiography, recognized the varied purpose of his friend's life and the meaning it had for others. Ross, Cantor wrote, was a "Champion who is entitled to the largest capital letter any printer can set." "Barney Ross has always been a giver. He gave of himself for his family, for his country; he wanted to give again as a leader of a volunteer army to help the young democracy of Israel in its darkest hour. . . ." Sometime in the early 1950s, an up and coming young Jewish boxer named Milt Aron captured Ross's importance more succinctly. Spying a poster for one of his own fights in a Philadelphia gym that billed him as "the greatest Jewish fighter in twenty years," Aron, as one sportswriter described, "stopped. His jaw sagged, as it wouldn't under a terrific wallop. 'Didn't they ever hear of Barney Ross?' he ejaculated."[29]

Milt's astonishment may well have been what some shrewd fight promoter who designed the poster had in mind. Boxing aficionados in the 1930s and 1940s rightly recognized Ross as one of the great boxers of all time. Jewish fight fans and even Jews less taken by such sport especially appreciated his climb to success. Both in terms of his actual experiences and for what he came to symbolize, in one way or another, his well-publicized life likely included some aspect of their own coming of age as the children of immigrants between the wars. The child of poor orthodox Jewish Russian immigrants, Barney learned to defend himself in order to survive on Chicago's streets. Not without struggle, he reconciled the traditional world of his parents with the opportunity that America offered him as a boxer. As a flamboyant, tough, proud Jew who became world champion in the midst of the Depression and the age of Hitler, his very presence put the lie to anti-Semitic stereotypes and offered hope of survival and success to other Jews. Above all, however melodramatic and unusual his particular life story, Ross emerged as a man fiercely proud of both his Jewish and his American identities, meshed together in ways that brought him honor and attention both as an American patriot and as a standard-bearer of Jewish strength and survival.

II

In January 1934, the California *Jewish Voice* reported Adolf Hitler's "pleasure" that the manager of the German heavyweight contender Max Schmeling was Joe Jacobs, an American Jew. What better proof, Hitler claimed, that "Germany is not anti-Jewish." The *Voice,* of course, would have none of it. "After all that has happened to the Jews in Germany," it noted, "Hitler . . . [is] still trying to pull the wool over the eyes of gullible people by denying everything that is happening to the Jews." The paper also informed its readers that Hitler had ordered Schmeling to withdraw from his scheduled match against Kingfish Levinsky, set for Chicago in mid-February. The Kingfish, a Maxwell Street native born Hershel Krakow, was not happy about the Führer's decision. "I hate to miss this Schmeling fight more than any in my career," he told one reporter. "If Hitler will let Schmeling fight me, I'll agree to meet him at Soldier's Field to a free gate, and I'll take on Hitler the same night after I've brushed Schmeling out of the ring." Too bad, the *Voice* concluded, that Levinsky would not get his wish. Not only the Kingfish, but "quite a few Jewish fighters (and many who aren't fighters) . . . would like to knock some of the teeth out of Schmeling's mouth and tear his tonsils out; wrap all of these into one little package to be specially sent to Hitler to show him what we think of him and his fighters."[30]

Although the Kingfish never got his chance, the *Voice*'s violent message of revenge suggests something of the appeal and purpose images of tough, strong Jews served even at the outset of German persecution of the Jews. Barney Ross's triumph over Jimmy McLarnin and Hank Greenberg's emergence as Jewish hero in America's National Game in 1934 encouraged acceptance of the fierce, physical Jew unafraid to meet his enemies. In its own way, so too did the controversial career to Maxie Baer, a boxer of questionable Jewish credentials who reigned briefly as heavyweight champion of the world.

Six months after Levinsky's disappointment, on June 14, 1934, in New York's Long Island Bowl, Baer, a 6'4", 220 lb. heavyweight wearing boxing trunks emblazoned with the Star of David, crushed Primo Carnera in eleven rounds and captured the world heavyweight championship. Today, caretakers of the achievements of Jewish athletes deny him a place in their record books on the grounds that Baer was not Jewish. They point out that Maxie, born

Maximillian Adelbert Baer in Omaha, Nebraska, in 1909, was the son of a Scotch-Irish mother and a father only nominally Jewish. Baer's marriage to a Catholic and the lack of any evidence of a Jewish upbringing provide further argument that Baer's public display of Jewish identity was simply a clever ploy to increase his value as a box-office attraction. Much of this criticism is correct. Even in the mid-1930s, similar charges were made by people close to Baer, including a former trainer who claimed that Maxie only sewed the Mogen David on his trunks to bring out Jewish fans. Ray Arcel, the legendary Jewish fight trainer who handled 21 professional world champions and who shared many shower rooms with the fighter, even attests to the absence of one of the boxer's more essential Jewish credentials.[31] Ultimately, however, what make's Baer's story interesting is not how "Jewish" he was but the way in which he encouraged and was appropriated by others as a symbol of the tough Jew whose very presence challenged anti-Semitic stereotypes be they American-bred or Nazi-made. For a short time, his persona as a powerful, strong Jew who became heavyweight champion of the world by defeating alleged symbols of fascist Europe caught the imagination of some commentators who understood that many American Jews were rightfully anxious for any sign of successful resistance to Jewish destruction.

Certainly that's how Baer and some members of the Jewish press played up his victory over Schmeling in 1933; one that set the stage for his title fight with Carnera. Schmeling had won the heavyweight title by disqualification in a controversial fight with Jack Sharkey in 1930. He lost it back to the American in 1932 but was a prohibitive favorite to take care of Baer when they met at Yankee Stadium on June 16. Much to everyone's surprise, Baer scored a technical knockout in the tenth round. According to the *American Hebrew*'s Henry Levy, many American newspaper stories and editorials about the contest saw Baer's victory as a "huge joke at the expense of 'Herr Hitler'" whose "Nazi theory of Nordic superiority" had been "made to look . . . ridiculous." Germans, Levy noted, were not amused that their champion had been defeated by a Jew. Baer, who wore the Star of David for the first time in this bout, pushed the same argument in disputing charges that he was not Jewish. Hitler, he insisted, certainly believed he was. How else to explain the Chancellor's reaction to the defeat of his German boxer whom he had offered to the world as proof of Aryan supremacy? As Maxie told it, so upset were the Nazis with his victory that they blamed it on a Jewish conspiracy of "reds" and "international bankers."[32]

Similar attempts to depict Baer as a Jewish champion met mixed results when he won the title from Primo Carnera the following year. Complicating matters was the status of his "fascist" opponent. Carnera certainly was Italian. He also was a huge specimen of a man—at 6'7" and 275 lbs. the largest ever to hold the heavyweight crown. Although popular with young Italian-Americans who, like their Jewish counterparts, took pride in the sportive accomplishments of their own kind, his connections to Mussolini were as questionable as his ability as a boxer. Unskilled and clumsy, Carnera's American boxing career began in 1930 after a brief stint as "The Terrible Giovanni," a wrestler in a Spanish circus. Handled by men who worked for mobsters Owney Madden and Dutch Schultz, most of his fights were fixed. So bad was his reputation that the California Boxing Association took away his license to fight in the state. Even his title fight with Jack Sharkey, held in New York in June 1933, was dominated by gangsters. According to sportswriter Paul Gallico, "the training camps of both gladiators were simply festering with mobsters and tough guys," including members of the infamous Jewish "Purple Gang" from Detroit. Moreover, unlike Hitler's early embrace of Schmeling as Aryan champion, nothing in the press suggests that either Primo or Mussolini made any claims on each other. Perhaps the Italian leader took to heart the opinion of one member of the New York State Athletic Commission who held rather low opinions of both Carnera and Baer. Commenting on Maxie's victory, he said, "He's still a bum. He won because he was in there with a bigger bum."[33]

Nevertheless, other quarters acknowledged Baer as "the first Jewish heavyweight champion of the world." Recognizing the importance of the heavyweight title as the ultimate symbol of manliness and strength, one commentator noted that "for many years it has been taken for granted in boxing circles that while Jews make good lightweights, welterweights, and even middleweights, it was simply not in the cards for them to develop a ring husky good enough to win the heavyweight crown. . . . Now Maxie has broken the jinx." The California *Jewish Voice,* in an ironic choice of words, reported that the most satisfying part of the "Baer-Carnera holocaust" was "the Mogen David worn by Baer on his trunks. He's a great champ." When Maxie lost the crown the following year to James Braddock, the Detroit *Jewish Chronicle* noted that the defeat of the "first Jew in modern times" to hold the heavyweight crown "overshadowed everything else in boxing during the past year."[34]

Baer, who was known as much for his antics as playboy and erstwhile movie actor, offered his own version of his significance to Jews in a published interview with Haskell Cohen. Titled "Jacob's Irish Max," Maxie began by declaring that he was "an actual Abie's Irish Rose," with the exception that his father's name was Jacob. Detailing his family's lineage, which, he claimed, included a Jewish father and grandmother, he insisted: "I am Jewish if I am anything at all." Baer did admit that his father was not at all religious (his "outstanding Jewish characteristic" was his pinochle game). Still he claimed to be "the first bona fide heavyweight champion of the Hebrew race" who had proudly brought the title back to "America and to the Jewish people."[35]

Baer was far less successful than Barney Ross or Hank Greenberg in challenging stereotypes of the weak Jew or in portraying Jews as loyal Americans who stood ready and able to resist their oppressors. Still, attention to such concerns in his boxing promotions suggest the powerful appeal such images had for Jews in these years. Ironically, Joe Louis, a black fighter from Detroit, did more to put the lie to notions of Aryan supremacy and to rally all Americans to resist German aggression than Maxie Baer ever accomplished. Critical here were his two fights with Max Schmeling in 1936 and 1938. Engineered by managers and promoters who were American Jews, the battles between perhaps the greatest heavyweight champion of all time and the fighter from Nazi Germany took place in highly charged times when evidence of Nazi discrimination and aggression was more commonplace than it had been only a few years earlier. Here, Jewish concerns merged with a broader American interest in a symbolic conflict between "democracy" and "fascism" replete with curious twists for both Jews and blacks and their struggles for American acceptance.

III

Maxie Baer's tenure as heavyweight champion was short-lived. On June 13, 1935, one day less than a year after he won the title, James Braddock took it from him. A more significant moment in boxing history, however, occurred a few months earlier when Mike Jacobs convinced John Roxborough, the black manager of a promising young black boxer named Joe Louis, that he could make his fighter the next heavyweight champion of the world.

Jacobs, then in his early fifties, was the child of East European Jewish immigrants. Born and raised on New York's Lower East Side, he had been involved in fight promotion since 1915, learning the trade by assisting Tex Rickard, preeminent sports promoter in the 1920s and 1930s. In 1934, he broke with his mentor, organized the Twentieth Century Sporting Club, and over the next two decades became boxing's dominant figure. Anyone who fought in a major bout in the United States went through "Uncle Mike." Before illness forced his retirement in 1949, Jacobs staged 61 championship fights and 320 boxing cards at Madison Square Garden alone. By one count, in 1942 he promoted 250 boxing shows with a total gate of $12.5 million. Although not known for his charm or grace, he so monopolized his sport that boxers, managers, and trainers who sought his services at his offices on New York's West 48th Street near Madison Square Garden renamed the street "Jacob's Alley."[36]

The key to Jacobs's success was Joe Louis. Aware of the young heavyweight's potential and of the problems facing a black fighter determined to win the heavyweight crown in a segregated America, Jacobs assured Roxborough that he could match Louis in important bouts and provide the kind of national exposure that would lead to a title shot. Roxborough had no doubts about his fighter's ability. He also remembered the vehement reaction of racist white Americans to the last black heavyweight champion of the world, Jack Johnson, who won the title in 1908. Johnson's ring dominance, his flamboyant life-style, and his publicized affairs with white women which flaunted white standards of how blacks should behave, stood as an arrogant threat to white supremacy and white racism and as a symbol of black hope and revenge. Anyone familiar with the history of boxing or of American race relations knows that Johnson paid dearly for the risks he took to live life on his own terms in an openly racist society. Determined to destory him as a symbol of

black resistance and pride and to make a buck in the process, boxing promoters sought a white fighter to wrest the title from "Papa Jack." After Johnson
pulverized Jim Jeffries, "The Great White Hope," in 1910, government officials joined the battle. They confronted Johnson with an array of charges,
including sexual misconduct under violation of the Mann Act, which allowed
any man to be prosecuted for crossing a state line to have sex with a woman
other than his wife. Convicted unanimously by an all-white jury in 1913 and
sentenced to one year in prison and a $1000 fine, Johnson fled the country.
He spent the next few years fighting exhibitions and performing vaudeville in
Canada and Europe. Finally, in 1915, he agreed to defend his title against a
white American giant named Jess Willard in Havana. Willard knocked Johnson out in the 26th round, part of the deal Johnson said he made with the FBI
for the right to return to the United States. Whether or not Johnson's claim
was true, he was no longer heavyweight champion of the world. Boxing's
establishment also determined that a black boxer would never again fight for
the sport's most important crown. As a black manager who understood history, Roxborough knew that on their own, Louis's opportunity to make it to
the top was problematic.[37] In 1934 they took a chance and signed on with
Mike Jacobs and the Twentieth Century Sporting Club.

Jacobs realized that Louis's talent as a boxer would not be enough to
secure a title shot. Somehow he had to make Louis acceptable to white Americans. Like Roxborough, he agreed that it was important for the fighter to present himself as a polite, well-intentioned man who dressed conservatively,
stayed away from white women, and generally comported himself in an inof-
fensive matter. Just as important were his efforts to present Joe as an American hero in democracy's fight against fascism.

Jacob's first promotion for his new fighter, the Brown Bomber's match
against former champion Primo Carnera at Yankee Stadium on June 25, 1933,
illustrates this intent. Apparently he was more successful than Maxie Baer.
Drawing parallels to Italy's sweep into Ethiopia, some Northern sportswriters
depicted the bout in racial and international terms—suggesting that the black
American would do to the Italian fighter what Haile Selassie, Ethiopia's
emperor, could not prevent. According to one account, after Louis knocked
out Carnera in six rounds, black youth in Harlem, either as a sign of American
democratic patriotism or pan-African sensibilities, shouted "Let's get Mussolini next!"[38]

Jacobs was overjoyed. Confident of Louis's enormous power and new reputation as a fighter in the service of American democracy, he proceeded to
make Joe boxing's top attraction. Even Maxie Baer figured here. After he lost
his title to Braddock, Baer signed on with Jacobs. Now, with Louis's popularity
established, Jacobs pitted his two boxers together for a September 1935 bout.
Maxie did his part in promoting the fight, offering colorful copy to the press
and his own newspaper accounts of his "Life and Loves." Unlike the hype for
his earlier fights with Carnera and Schmeling, however, not once did he mention anything about his supposed Jewishness. Perhaps Baer thought that his
color rather than his ethnic or religious background would be a more pow-

erful draw. Conjuring up memories connected to a far more controversial black champion, at least one sportswriter noted Maxie's new standing as the "lone White Hope" who would defend "Nordic supremacy" by thwarting Louis's rush to the title.[39] Although there is no way of knowing if such promotion influenced the turnout or if Jacobs encouraged it, some 80,000 fans jammed into Yankee Stadium to witness the fight while an NBC radio audience listened to a live, blow-by-blow broadcast. The bout provided the first million-dollar gate since the immortal 1927 Dempsey-Tunney fight. Unfortunately for Max and any white supremacists in the audience, however, he was knocked out by Louis in the fourth round.

Even more ironic than Baer's shift from Jewish savior to Great White Hope were Jacobs's continuing efforts to present Louis as an American hero. Without question, the most important steps in that process were his two fights with Max Schmeling, the first of which took place on June 22, 1936. From a practical standpoint, Louis needed the victory. Schmeling was the only other legitimate contender for the heaveyweight crown, then held by James Braddock. Moreover a fight with the German boxer provided a striking opportunity to make Louis acceptable to white Americans by promoting him as a champion of American democracy against Nazi Germany incarnate. Louis's defeat of Schmeling in a fight where nationalism and political ideology were more important than race would guarantee him a championship fight.

So Jacobs hoped. In fact, however, he had his work cut out for him. Numerous Jewish organizations already engaged in promoting an American boycott of the 1936 Olympic games, scheduled that summer for Berlin, demanded that Jacobs cancel the bout. They also urged Joe Jacobs, Schmeling's Jewish manager, to discontinue his relationship with the fighter. Americans, especially Jewish-Americans, they argued, needed to disengage from all sportive contact with Nazi Germany as matters of conscience and protest.[40] The fact that, ever since his loss to Maxie Baer, the German government had disowned Schmeling as their Aryan hero, further complicated the promoter's scheme. As Westbrook Pegler derisively put it, as far as Hitler was concerned, Max "was absolutely on his own, because there seemed an excellent chance that having already been knocked out by a Jew, he would now be stretched in the resin at the feet of a cotton-field Negro."[41]

Schmeling, however, proved ready to the task. After battering Louis for the entire fight before 45,000 fans at Yankee Stadium, he knocked him out in the 12th round, accomplishing in one moment what Jacobs had hoped to create. Overnight Schmeling became the hero of Nazi Germany. Declaring to American reporters that he owed his success to "Hitler's inspiration," Max found himself embraced by a Nazi establishment that had previously ignored him. According to Pegler, Hitler cabled Schmeling on "his splendid victory," Goebbels embraced it as a "splendid patriotic achievement," and the German press pronounced his triumph "as a great example of the new Youth and . . . a victory for Hitlerism."[42]

Henry Levy spelled out the ominous consequences of such connections for Jews around the world as well as for other American minorities. Recalling a conversation he had with a friend at the fight's conclusion, Levy told his *American Hebrew* readers that the German's triumphs "will be used by Goebbels' propaganda machine" to keep Hitler in power by bolstering German morale. More immediately, American anti-Semites, "the Pelleys, the Edmondsons and their ilk," will use the victory to similar ends to "illustrate Nordic supremacy over the Negro, the Jew and all others they want to propagandize against." Levy then referred specifically to William Dudley Pelley, publisher of *Pelley's Weekly* and organizer of the "Silver Shirt" brigades in California and North Carolina, modeled after Hitler's infamous SS corps. News of Louis's defeat, he insisted, would be used to persuade Pelley's anti-Semitic followers, whom Levy numbered in the hundreds of thousands, that "the Negro Louis was yellow, as are all Negroes, or that Germans and Nordics are the physical superiors of Jews, Catholics and others." Although Levy didn't mention it, things might only get worse, for Schmeling's victory put him next in line for a title shot with Braddock.[43]

American public opinion and the machinations of Jewish fight promoters, however, robbed Max of that opportunity. Determined, as one writer put it, to prevent Schmeling from "tak[ing] the title back to Germany and present[ing] it to Adolf Hitler for the German Museum," the Non-Sectarian Anti-Nazi League, led by New York's mayor Fiorello La Guardia, threatened to mount a boycott of a proposed championship fight between Braddock and Schmeling. The group, which barely missed achieving a U.S. boycott of the Nazi Olympics, definitely influenced Joe Gould, Braddock's Jewish manager who, according to most accounts, worried more about the loss of a big gate than the political implications of Schmeling's ascendancy to the heavyweight crown.

Certain that Braddock would be no match for either Schmeling or Louis, Gould, with the help of Mike Jacobs, took advantage of the political controversy surrounding the German. Claiming concern over the boycott and the possibility of an Aryan world champion, he reneged on his contract with Schmeling and Joe Jacobs. Once again, as he had in 1930, when he thought his fighter had been knocked down by a low blow in his championship fight with Jack Sharkey, Joe Jacobs cried foul. Then his protest gave Max the title by disqualification. This time it was to no avail. Guaranteed $500,000 by Mike Jacobs, as well as 10 percent of the net profits of all Louis heavyweight title fights for ten years should Louis defeat Braddock, Gould signed his fighter to a title defense against the Brown Bomber.[44] On June 22, 1937, Louis destroyed Braddock and became the first black heavyweight world champion since Jack Johnson. His victory launched his reign as one of boxing's greatest champions and secured his place as hero of an oppressed American black population. It also set the scene for one more battle with Max Schmeling that enhanced Louis's status as a hero for all Americans.

The Louis-Schmeling rematch, scheduled for Yankee Stadium on June 22, 1938, was billed everywhere as a struggle between American democracy and Nazi fascism. When Schmeling arrived in New York he was met by hundreds of pickets on the docks of New York, who mocked him with Nazi salutes and demanded his return to Germany. Again, the Anti-Nazi League, the American Jewish Congress, and other groups demanded that Mike and Joe Jacobs cancel the fight. Even "Uncle" Mike's offer to donate 10 percent of the gate to help Jewish refugees failed to mollify his critics. No more persuasive was his argument that Louis, by destroying Schmeling, would damage the Nazi cause. Louis himself promised that he was "backing up America against Germany, so you know I am going to town."[45]

Whether or not Jacobs protestations were sincere, they certainly didn't hurt what boxing promoters fondly referred to as the "steam-up." Writing in the New York *World-Telegram,* Joe Williams remarked that the political controversy surrounding the fight would enhance its gate attraction. "Those who view in Schmeling a political symbol will be desperately hopeful for his downfall. If they have the cash they'll come, because you can do your wishful thinking a lot better when you're on the scene."[46] And come they did. Over 70,000 people paid over $1,000,000 to watch Louis annihilate Schmeling with a devastating first-round knockout.

Louis's "blitzkrieg" of the German hero established him as democracy's champion. As one newspaper put it, "the Aryan idol, the unconquerable one had been beaten, the bright, shining symbol of race glory has been thumped in the dust. That noise you hear is Goebbels making for the storm cellar."[47] Ironically, the architect of the victory was a black man whose own people still were subject to lynchings, discrimination, and oppression in an American society dominated by whites. While this victory and his years as heavyweight champion made Louis an important symbol of hope and strength for American blacks, it did little to lessen either racism or the lack of opportunity they faced. One southern paper put his victory in more realistic perspective. Although it applauded Schmeling's defeat as proof that the Germans were "stupor men" rather than "supermen," it reminded Louis that he was still a "colored boy."[48]

Louis's victory hardly presaged black assimilation into the American mainstream, yet it did contribute in minor key to a growing American consensus to resist Nazi Germany. Obviously, more important events prior to the fight, from the Nuremberg laws to the Anchluss, as well as Munich, "Kristallnacht," and Germany's invasion of Poland that followed soon after, were far more influential in shaping American public opinion and government action. Still Joe Louis made his own contribution by beating Max Schmeling. Recalling its importance to his own childhood, Art Buchwald remembers that he and his friends were sure of three things: "Franklin Roosevelt was going to save the economy . . . Joe Dimaggio was going to beat Babe Ruth's record [and] Joe Louis was going to save us from the Germans."[49]

Poets and historians have rightly captured the importance of Joe Louis to American blacks in the 1930s and 1940s. By standing up to and defeating "the man" in the midst of a society dominated by whites, Louis became black people's most celebrated symbol of equality and opportunity.[50] Other Americans also had reason to respect and honor this black hero. Paul Gould, a correspondent for the *American Hebrew*, unintentionally explained why in a 1946 story that praised Mike Jacobs's essential role in giving Louis a chance to become heavyweight champion of the world. Challenging those who "wanted a white man to maintain the legend of white supremacy," Jacobs provided Louis with the chance to deliver "a terrific blow to the theory of race supremacy." American Jews who battled anti-Semitism at home and suffered the death of six million European Jews at the hands of the Nazis could well appreciate the importance of Gould's message.[51]

Joe Louis, in a sense, reminded Jews of their own Barney Ross or Benny Leonard—a public figure who visibly symbolized resistance to enemies who threatened both Jewish and American existence. In its Jewish-American configuration, as represented by Jewish fighters, it combined reconciliation of Old World tradition and new American ways with a fierce determination to fight for Jewish survival. This version of the Jewish-American clearly resulted from a particular world historical context. Embodied in especially visible ways in the careers of Jewish boxers who dominated their sport in the 1920s and 1930s, neither it nor Jewish involvement in the ring is as obvious today. Although an occasional Jewish fighter rose to prominence after Barney Ross, Jewish participation in the fight game since World War II remains limited to involvement as managers and promoters.[52] Despite their symbolic importance to many Jewish-Americans, even in the 1920s and 1930s, Jewish boxers were a distinct minority among their brethren who grew up in the same urban neighborhoods. However much men like B. P. Schulberg revered their Jewish boxing heroes, most second-generation Jewish men opted for the more conventional avenues of education, business, and the professions as their ticket to American success. Some, like Mike Jacobs and Nat Fleischer, were able to combine their passion for boxing with their entrepreneurial skills, a tradition carried on today by the likes of Bob Arum and other Jewish boxing promoters. But the wide range of economic opportunities increasingly available to second-generation Jews and especially their children after World War II, compelled them to build their own versions of the American Dream far removed from any vision that a Barney Ross might have had.

American Jews today, living in a society quite tolerant of their own ethnicity, one in which the sounds, accents, and customs of their East European grandparents and their children are becoming increasingly muted by death and the passage of time, appear to have little need for symbols like Benny Leonard or Barney Ross. Although aware of the Holocaust, the immediacy of those days and the tenuous quality of Jewish existence it engendered remain elusive to most contemporary American Jews who now generally enjoy the kind of success and acceptance for which their parents and grandparents struggled. Their images of tough Jews, when they do appear, are more likely to be Israeli commandos and soldiers rather than boxers or baseball players—new physical heroes tied to concern with Israel's survival and its connection to American Jewish identity.[53]

Philip Roth, a child who came of age in the shadows of World War II when memories of Jewish boxers as defenders of the faith still lingered, anticipates in his recollections of those days what seems commonplace today. "For a while during my adolescence," he tells us:

> I studiously followed prizefighting, could recite the names and weights of all the champions and contenders, and even subscribed briefly to *Ring*, Nat Fleischer's colorful boxing magazine; as kids my brother and I had been taken by our father to the local boxing arena, where invariably we all had a good time; from my father and his friends I heard about the prowess of Benny Leonard, Max Baer, and the clownishly Slapsie Maxie Rosenbloom—yet Jewish boxers and boxing aficionados remained, like boxing itself, "sport" in the bizarre sense, a strange deviation from the norm and interesting largely for that reason. In the world whose values first formed me, unrestrained physical aggression was considered contemptible everywhere else. I could no more smash a nose with a fist than fire a pistol into someone's heart. And what imposed this restraint, if not on Slapsie Maxie Rosenbloom, then on me, was my being Jewish. In my scheme of things, Slapsie Maxie was a more miraculous Jewish phenomena by far than Dr. Albert Einstein.[54]

Echoed here is the high esteem for and pride in Jewish boxers held by Roth's second-generation father and yet the unfamiliarity of the aggression of the sport for a young Jewish boy presumably brought up with a sense of Jewish religious tradition that questioned the necessity of unbridled physical strength. Growing up in a time when the horrible possibilities of "unrestrained physical aggression" had become the realities of Auschwitz, had decimated Europe, and had burned out Hiroshima and Nagasaki may also have informed Roth's perspective.

What may have been astonishing for Roth, however, hardly was the case only a few decades earlier, when, if the *New Warheit* was correct, Benny Leonard was better-known among American Jews than Albert Einstein and Barney Ross ruled the boxing world. For B. P. Schulberg, Philip Roth's father, and countless other Jewish men and boys, Jewish boxers proclaimed American Jews as a strong people capable of defending themselves against anti-Semites and doing what was necessary to protect their own country and the Jewish people. Today, this particular image of the tough Jew seems distant. Yet it remains part of a Jewish-American historical memory that, as we will see, can help American Jews today as they struggle with the question of Jewish survival in an American world far different than the one that gave us Benny Leonard and Barney Ross.

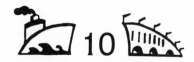

"Der Yiddisher Vildkat" and the "Hebrew Hillbilly": College Life and College Sport Between the Wars

ON April 5, 1929, the *American Hebrew* highlighted the unusual career of Sidney Frumkin. Born in Brooklyn, New York, in 1905, the son of East European Jewish immigrants, a Columbia College graduate and some-time artist, this young man, known to the world as Sidney Franklin, was the only non-Latin bullfighter in Mexico. According to Samuel Tenenbaum, who interviewed Franklin in Brooklyn at his parents' home, the matador had been raised in a "fine Jewish home" where he had "received a good Jewish upbringing." As the reporter's eyes "wandered" to framed pictures of "men with beards and women with sheitels, undoubtedly European kinsmen of the family," that lined the parlor's walls, he mused "what a strange and glorious people Jews are. In 1492, the Jews were driven from Spain. In that same year Columbus discovered America. Now, several hundred years later, this America sends forth its native son to excel in Spain's national sport—and this American happens to be a Jew!"

Franklin's story always merits special mention in encyclopedias of Jewish athletic accomplishment. So too do the achievements of first- and second-generation Jewish athletes such as Myer Prinstein, Abel Kiviat, Lillian Copeland, Irving Jaffee, Jackie Fields, and others who confirmed their status as Americans by representing their country in the Olympic games.

Very few Americans, Jewish or otherwise, became bullfighters or competed in the Olympics. But for Jewish immigrants and their children who enjoyed basketball, baseball, boxing, and other sports, often within the confines of Jewish community, their participation, both as athletes and as spectators significantly contributed to their development as Americans and Jews.

Be it Sidney Franklin's tale, a discussion of American Jewish Olympians, more detailed analysis of Jewish sports entrepreneurs or sportswriters, or discussion of the way in which elite German-American Jews used sport to separate themselves from their East European cousins while striving for full acceptance by a Christian American majority, a variety of other choices exist for enhancing what we already know about the place of sport in the experiences of first- and second-generation Jewish-Americans.

Embellishing themes already established, this chapter and the one that follows engage two such possibilities: an account of the Jewish collegiate athletic experience prior to World War II and the saga of Marty Glickman, a young American Olympian whose dreams of Olympic gold were shattered at the 1936 Nazi Olympics. Both in terms of actual experience and as a symbol, they highlight sport's role as a critical middle ground for understanding how Jews became Americans. In different ways, they also contribute to our understanding of the development of an American Jewish identity, relevant to the reality of the second-generation experience and important as legacy to succeeding generations of American Jews.

I

Rehearsing the achievements of Jews in the United States at the close of 1931, the *American Hebrew* highlighted Jewish success in the world of intercollegiate athletics. In a featured article replete with pictures of Jewish lads hitting baseballs, football players in three-point stances, hoopsters shooting free throws, and boxers throwing punches, Henry Levy began his survey with the following declaration:

> Year after year, it becomes more difficult to comprehensively survey the Jewish intercol ·giate sports scene. No longer is it necessary editorially to overplay the few isolated athletes that come to one's attention. Rather, today the problem is one of selection, the stars must be separated from the near stars and the near stars must be kept apart from those who were not "just quite good enough" to earn their letters, but were retained by their coaches as members of the squad. It all bespeaks a healthy condition in the colleges, a condition in which the Jewish student is recognized on the basis of his own ability and personality, rather than as in the not so very distant past, in the mass aggregate when he was casually dismissed as "a Jew." So far as we know, no Jewish boy has been kept off an athletic team because of his religion. . . . Truly no limitation was placed upon the boys and girls of the faith; they achieved whatever heights their ability and their popularity warranted.[1]

For writers like Levy, eager for the full acceptance of immigrant Jews into mainstream American society, the abundance of Jewish college athletes, the absence of discrimination, and celebration of the American ethos of success based on ability and merit all evidenced increased toleration, acceptance, and opportunity for Jewish-Americans.

Not every observer of the American Jewish scene in 1930 was as optimistic as Levy about the situation of American Jews in college or elsewhere. All could agree, however, that obtaining a college degree and participating fully in the college experience were critical steppingstones for rapid rise out of the immigrant ghetto into the land of American economic and social opportunity. Assessments and perceptions of college life, including anti-Semitic discrimination and Jewish involvement in college sport, became one of the many litmus tests for gauging how well Jews were proceeding in their struggle for American acceptance. The actual experiences of Jewish collegiate athletes and the way in which they were showcased for public consumption also provided another highly visible demonstration of sport's contribution to American Jewish identity.

II

The influx of East European Jewish immigrants to America between 1880 and 1920 coincided with the rise of the modern university and the beginnings of mass higher education. Those responsible for the development of the modern university at the turn of the century heralded college as a critical experience for all youth interested in participating in a new America. Emerging out of social and economic circumstances of the last half of the 19th century, the university no longer served as the training ground for elite gentlemen schooled in a limited curriculum revolving around the classics, mathematics, and natural philosophy. Instead it became the place to obtain the necessary, practical education that would produce the professionals, managers, and technicians capable of running a modern, urban, industrial society.[2]

Numbers indicate that more and more young people took advantage of a college education as a means of reaching these goals. Between 1900 and 1930 attendance at American colleges and universities increased 300 percent, with the most dramatic rise coming in the 1920s. By 1930, almost 20 percent of all college-age youth attended some kind of school; a statistic anticipating a future when college attendance would become the birthright of virtually all American adolescents.[3]

No group participated more fully in this increase than the children of Jewish immigrants, who flocked to both private and public colleges in numbers far exceeding their proportion of the general population. According to one account, by 1920 both Hunter College and the City College of New York (CCNY) had enrollments that were over 80 percent Jewish. Prior to World War I Columbia's Jewish enrollment reached 40 percent; New York University's (NYU) was somewhere in the same vicinity; and Harvard's approached 20 percent.[4]

While the *Jewish Daily Forward* might take pride in these obvious signs of Jewish "love for education," a 1923 editorial in the *Nation* acknowledged these impressive enrollment figures in less complimentary fashion. The Jew, the magazine reported, "sends his children to college a generation or two sooner than older stocks, and as a result there are in fact more dirty Jews and tactless Jews in college than dirty and tactless Italians, Armenians, or Slovaks."[5] Even more direct was a popular collegiate song from a decade earlier that captured the concern some felt about the increasing presence of Jews on college campuses:

> Oh, Harvard's run by millionaires
> And Yale is run by booze,
> Cornell is run by farmers' sons,
> And Columbia's run by Jews.
> So give a cheer for Baxter Street,
> And another one for Pell,
> And when the little sheenies die,
> Their souls will go to hell.[6]

Implicit in the *Nation's* attack and in this verse was an understanding of the college experience between the wars that directly affected the situation of Jewish college youth. Ironically, the development of the American university—with its goal to prepare students for life and work in a new modern world, its emphasis on professionalization, the expansion of faculty and disciplines, and the removal of limited curriculum choices that had so dominated 19th-century elite colleges—also encouraged attitudes of freedom and choice that, at least in the short run, backfired. By all accounts, at both public and private institutions, many students rejected scholastic achievement as the goal of college life. Be it the fraternity, extracurricular activities, and increasingly college athletics, inclusion in a peer world of conformity that emphasized social success became the popular measure of what college was all about.[7]

Genteel behavior, proper dress, the right friends, membership in the right organizations, and "gentleman's C's," however, did not characterize the goals of most Jewish college students, especially those from East European backgrounds. Stereotypes of Jewish students as "people of the book" dedicated only to intellect and learning do not accurately depict the actual experience of Jewish college students. Yet no group pursued academic success more vigorously than they did. Time and again, Jewish students outdid their Gentile peers in the classroom. Determined to use their college experience as an escape from their immigrant working-class roots, they were both a challenge and anathema to wealthy and middle-class students who viewed college life in far different terms.[8]

It is this context that gives significance to the athletic and social experiences of Jewish college youth prior to World War II. Although describing general tendencies rather than absolutes, this contrast between two models of college life, set against the larger pattern of anti-Semitism in America between the wars, guaranteed conflict and discrimination for Jewish youth in college campuses. Depending upon time and circumstance, many confronted discriminatory policies and quota systems that limited both their opportunity for admission into certain universities as well as their participation in extra-curricular activities. Denied full access to activities often depicted at the heart of college life, they were then ridiculed by those who labeled them as unfit and different—arguments in turn that became the basis for further discrimination.

III

The reality of discrimination experienced by Jewish college students both off and on the athletic field between the wars is well documented. The same year that Henry Levy offered his optimistic appraisal of Jewish collegiate athletic success, two journalists, Heywood Broun and George Britt, wrote a book called *Christians Only.* Based on extensive interviews with both Jews and Gentiles, it dramatically detailed the persistence of anti-Semitism that limited opportunities for Jews both in the workplace and in the university. Nowhere was this more obvious than in the development of college admissions policies that dramatically reduced opportunities for Jewish youth to attend private institutions, especially in the Northeast where the Jewish population was largest. Instead of admission based solely on academic performance, new measures including character and psychological tests, recommendations from high-school teachers and principals, interviews, and the submission of photographs became part of the admissions process in the 1920s and 1930s. Aimed at identifying Jewish applicants and reducing the numbers accepted, they augmented novel attempts to admit students from diverse geographic backgrounds. Claiming the desirability of a diverse student body drawn from all parts of the country, admissions officers consciously set quotas by state and region, consequently reducing the number of students from cities and towns closest to them with large Jewish populations in favor of attracting students from new areas.[9]

None of these measures would come as any surprise to high-school students today applying to elite private institutions in any part of the United States. Questions of a student's character and personality as well as the attraction of a cultural and geographic mix among students are universally accepted as part and parcel of the admissions process. Indeed, today, when protest is raised, it most frequently comes from a white majority concerned that such processes stack the deck unfairly in favor of a black or Asian minority. Nor is it possible to deny the very real pressures colleges felt to reduce enrollments because their facilities and faculty were simply not sufficient to keep up with the explosion of young people seeking admissions.

It is indisputable, however, that many colleges seized on this very real problem to devise admission procedures with the distinct objective of limiting Jewish enrollment. In 1922, for instance, Yale University, at the urging of Robert Corwin Nelson, chairman of the Yale Corporation and former Yale football captain and athletic director, initiated a study of their Jewish students aimed at establishing a quota system. Nelson's request was well met by administrators and professors who characterized the school's Jewish population as full of "personally and socially unacceptable" boys who "contribute very little to class life." Taking special note of the large number of New Haven East European Jewish students who lived at home and who made up the large proportion of the school's Jewish students, the college's dean, Frederick Jones, even held them responsible for real damage to the overall academic performance of other Yale students. Although he acknowledged that "many of these Hebrew boys are fine students," Jones argued that their "general effect on the scholastic standing is bad." Other Yale men refused to do their best at their studies for fear of becoming identified with Jews who were known only for their scholarly achievements. As evidence for this assertion, he pointed to a recent poll among Yale students which showed that they admired the winning of a varsity sports letter more so than admission to Phi Beta Kappa—an attitude which he attributed "in part to the feeling that the Jew is properly the 'greasy grind' and that other students may hesitate to join the group." According to Daniel Oren's account of Jews at Yale, by 1924 the college instituted a new admissions policy that successfully limited Jewish admissions. Designed and approved by men openly prejudiced against Jews, it assured "discrimination against Jews" as "a cornerstone of Yale undergraduate admissions for the next four decades."[10]

At Yale and elsewhere, these policies were instituted quietly by administrators eager to avoid the negative publicity full disclosure of their intentions might bring. All too fresh in their minds was what had happened at Harvard only one year before Yale began serious but secret consideration of limitations on Jewish students. Between 1900 and 1922 the proportion of Jewish undergraduates at Harvard grew from 7 to 21 percent. Alarmed by this increase, President A. Lawrence Lowell, former vice president of the Immigration Restriction League, secretly pushed for character and psychologcial testing as a way of weeding out Jewish applicants. Undeterred when news of his efforts became public, Lowell and other Harvard men defended their actions by arguing that too many Jewish students denied others the true Harvard experience. As one supporter of restrictive Jewish admissions argued, the presence of too many Jews polluted the spirit of the institution—that "peculiar flavor of unique value" that "men send their sons there to attain, rather than any mere form of scholarly equipment." Certain that this "flavor" was most easily acquired by "men of the old New England stock," he insisted that others achieve it only if they are present in small numbers so that they can become "well immersed in social groupings of the original character. . . . Better one true Jewish Harvard man," he concluded, "than ten mere Jewish scholars."

Confronted by these open declarations of anti-Jewish feeling, Jewish spokesmen, joined by a variety of other voices, including the American Federation of Labor and the governor of Massachusetts, denounced Harvard's proposals. As a result, Lowell publicly retracted his plan for a quota system and the Harvard Board of Overseers unanimously came out against racially based, discriminatory admissions policies. Although the *American Hebrew* applauded these decisions as victories for democracy and opportunity, the Harvard case made clear to college administrators at Yale and elsewhere the need to proceed quietly and carefully in order to implement restrictive admissions policies.[11]

And proceed they did. At Columbia, Yale, Syracuse, and other eastern schools, Jewish enrollment figures dropped markedly as new admissions requirements came into effect. Denied full access to elite private schools, Jewish boys and girls enrolled elsewhere in greater numbers, rebuffed but not deterred from seeking a college education. Depending upon where they went, anti-Semitism and discrimination remained part of their college experience.[12]

A survey of Jewish college students at 66 institutions undertaken by Jewish students in the late 1920s suggests that prejudice varied in proportion to the number of Jews in attendance. Not surprisingly, eastern schools where Jewish students were in the majority, such as CCNY, Cooper Union, Hunter College, and Philadelphia Textile, revealed no anti-Semitism at all. Several southern schools, including the University of Alabama, also made the list as did the University of Utah and the University of Vermont—none of which had more than a handful of Jewish students. The category labeled as "slightly anti-Jewish feeling" included the major campuses of state universities in California, Colorado, Nebraska, Missouri, Georgia, Purdue, and Wisconsin; three private Boston schools; and Pennsylvania and Syracuse. Sixteen schools located in the Midwest and East showed "moderate" degrees of anti-Semitism. Included here were Harvard, the University of Chicago, Michigan, Rutgers, and NYU. Finally, the survey grouped 18 schools known for "pronounced" anti-Jewish feelings. Along with the major campuses of state universities in Virginia, Ohio, Minnesota, Kansas, Texas, and Pennsylvania, private institutions located in areas with large Jewish populations also made the list. These included Adelphi, Northwestern, Columbia, Yale, and Johns Hopkins. Cornell University also was part of this group.[13]

Commenting on this survey, the authors of *Christians Only* concluded that anti-Semitism was scarcely a problem where Jewish students were either very few in number or made up the overwhelming majority. Prejudice was more apparent in schools that featured a large minority of Jewish students and that were situated in cities with a high density of Jewish residents. Problems were also more likely in private institutions than in public universities.[14]

Exactly what those problems might be were also summarized in the report. "Manifestations of anti-Jewish feeling" that accounted for the categorization of schools by degrees of anti-Semitism included "slurring remarks, social aloofness, exclusion from honorary fraternities, glee clubs, managership of social organizations; difficulty of election to honorary fraternities, discrimination in campus politics, exclusion of Jewish fraternities from inter-fraternity boards; offensive jokes in student publications and student dramatics, general unfriendliness." Balancing both this litany of discrimination and the classification of schools by anti-Semitism, the report noted that only one-quarter of all of the schools included in its survey reported "any serious cases of anti-Jewish feeling at all." Even on these occasions, it concluded, often only a few students offered testimony of discrimination.[15]

The report's equivocation on the extent of anti-Semitism matched the recommendations Jewish college students offered their own kind for coping with
prejudice and restrictions. Admitting that "to a certain extent anti-Jewish
feeling will always exist in college," it advised them to "bravely face [this]
fact." In doing so, it suggested that the degree and intensity of anti-Semitism
varied in "direct proportion to the outward manifestations of their Jewish
characteristics; in other words to the visible difference between the Jewish
and the non-Jewish students." Consequently, it concluded Jewish students
should strive for two things in order to alleviate discrimination. First, they
should make every effort to "eradicate the merely apparent and fortuitous
traits and characteristics which set the Jew apart and which have no real basis
in the Jewish character and teachings." Having done so, they should then,
"cultivate real Jewish characteristics" so that their struggle with anti-Semitic
students might be based on "realities," thus yielding "results which may be
of benefit to both sides."[16]

What a curious document! What exactly were "fortuitous traits and characteristics"? Did the report accept the notion that Jews were outsiders who
cared little for public virtue? Did its authors believe that Jews were too
intense, too pushy, and too interested in scholarship to be involved in athletic
or social activities—all supposed "Jewish characteristics" that became part of
the argument for restricting Jewish access to universities? And what were
"real Jewish characteristics"? Exactly what combination of religious, moral,
political, or social beliefs did its authors have in mind that distinguished Jews
from Gentiles? None of this is clear in a document that provided suggestions
for reducing discrimination and fostering greater opportunities for Jewish students. Combining an assertion of the existence of anti-Semitism as well as an
apology for "Jewish" behavior, its lack of consistency and clarity provides its
own measure of the difficulties inherent in balancing the desire to become
successful Americans while maintaining Jewish ethnic and religious ties.

Although Heywood Broun and George Britt did not comment on these recommendations, their own evidence of discrimination against Jews on college
campuses remained consistent with the survey's presentation and with news
of college life as reported in the Jewish press. Exclusion from fraternities that
denied Jews access to other student positions, difficulty in participating in
campus political life, failure to be considered for inclusion in secret societies
and informal snubbing by other students appear most frequently in these
accounts. As one student at Maine's Bowdoin College put it after he "learned"
that it was considered inappropriate for him to attend his school's dances,
Jewish students were "treated as intellectual equals and social inferiors."[17]

Jewish students at Yale understood first-hand patterns of exclusion, a product, Daniel Oren argues, of both anti-Semitism and their own disinclination
to defy it. Prior to World War I, the fact that most Jewish students at Yale lived
at home limited their opportunity to participate fully in undergraduate life. In
the 1920s and 1930s, consistent with the imposition of new admissions policies and national restrictive immigration laws, overt restrictions against Jews

at Yale increased. Although Jewish students still could join the orchestra and the debating teams, whether in eating clubs or secret societies, discrimination and segregation became a "routine part of undergraduate life" that Jewish students rarely challenged. Perceiving anti-Semitism at Yale to be part of a universal problem, they believed that their situation there and in the United States was preferable to what they might be experiencing elsewhere in the world. As Oren concludes, "where Jews were welcome, they entered. Where they were unwanted, they stayed out."[18]

Even in situations where possibilities were more open, there were limits placed on Jewish involvement in campus life. Consider the case of Mannie Levy, a fictional creation of Broun and Britt, whose story summarizes much of what Jewish students actually experienced. Determined to attend Columbia, this young New York City Jewish boy fills out the school's eight-page application, provides information on his religious and family background, sends in his picture, asks his high-school principal to complete a confidential appraisal of his character and personality, takes an intelligence test designed to measure his suitability, undergoes a physical examination to verify his fitness, and travels to the Upper West Side Manhattan campus for a personal interview. All to no avail. Columbia rejects Manny, making no mention of whether his identity as a Jew had anything to do with its decision. Dismayed but determined to seek out an Ivy League education, Manny hears that the University of Pennsylvania admits a high proportion of Jews and even maintains a kosher dining hall for its Jewish students. And so our "average Jewish boy" enrolls there.

Befriended by other Jewish students, Manny quickly learns about the opportunities and restrictions available to Jews at Penn. According to "campus opinion," he may:

> go out profitably for the baseball and basketball teams. There have been Jewish captains in basketball, wrestling and tennis. He may try for *Junto* or *Red and Blue,* the literary magazines. He may become editor of the *Quarterly* or of *Punch Bowl,* the humorous monthly. If he is very good he may become a member of the Dramatic Club. That organization was strongly Jewish a few years ago, and lost status thereby; so the Jewish members themselves adopted a strongly anti-Semitic policy in electing successors and restored the club to favor. Debating is his big chance, here as in many other colleges. On the other hand . . . there are some activities on which it is not worth while to waste effort. Unless he is superlatively good, they advise him not to go out for football. . . . It is hardly worth while to try for the *Pennsylvanian,* the daily newspaper. . . . He'll never make Mask and Wig, the exclusive club which produces the musical show. . . . He shouldn't set his heart on Phi Kappa Beta—the junior honorary society, nor Phi Beta Kappa—or Friars or Sphinx, the senior societies. And he can't be elected president of the senior class or a member of the undergraduate council.[19]

At schools where prejudice existed, virtually every aspect of this imaginative recreation reflected reality. Although he took issue with his school's

Semitic claims that Jews were too intellectual and too debilitated physically to become fully assimilated Americans. The large numbers involved, their displays of physical prowess and excellence in a variety of sports, and their election as team captains all became evidence for arguments that Jewish college students and, by implication, Jews in general, if given a chance, were as eager and capable as Gentiles to participate in all that college and American life offered. News of their athletic triumphs in ever-increasing numbers also provided comfort that these goals were obtainable and that the world was not always as hostile as it sometimes appeared.

Not surprisingly, local papers tended to concentrate on the success of their own people or of Jewish athletes attending college in their town in making such points. Benny Friedman's exploits as Michigan's All-American quarterback in the mid-1920s, for example, consistently made the pages of both his hometown's Cleveland *Jewish Independent* as well as the Detroit *Jewish Chronicle*. Nor did the *Independent* forget the achievements of other local youth making their athletic mark at Ohio State. A 1926 article titled "Cleveland Jewish Students Prominent in O.S.U. Activities" made sure of that. The Los Angeles *B'nai B'rith Messenger* provided similar coverage of West Coast tennis players, swimmers, cagers, and football players for its readers. In 1930, for instance, the paper highlighted the fact that Jay Cohn, a local boy from Santa Monica, was the number one singles player for the University of Nebraska's tennis team. One year later, commenting on the exploits of Morris Markowitz, Chuck Grodinsky, and a host of other Jewish players who dominated the football and basketball teams of Los Angeles' California Christian College, the *Messenger*'s Harry Glantz concluded, "Jewish athletes everywhere . . . and begorra, it's proud I be of them."[22]

Occasionally, newspapers and magazines like the *Messenger,* the *Independent,* and the *American Hebrew* also carried athletic news that went beyond local interest. We already know that Jewish domination of eastern collegiate basketball, evidenced by the exploits of the NYU Violets, St. John's Wonder Five, and the succession of fine teams turned out by Nat Holman at CCNY, caught the attention of the Jewish press from coast to coast. The fact that three "Jewish lads" from Dorchester, Massachusetts, Brooklyn, New York, and Des Moines, Iowa, all were members of the University of Iowa freshman swimming team in 1929 also impressed Harry Glantz. Struck by this disproportionate number of Jews on a collegiate team, he provided coverage of the backgrounds and swimming specialities of athletes participating in a sport that rarely received any attention in the press. In 1926, the Cleveland *Independent* moved sports to its front page, erroneously reporting on July 16 that for the first time a Jewish student had been named to captain a major sport, football, at Harvard, the nation's most prestigious university. The honor, the paper reported, fell to Isadore Zarakov, "the son of a Cambridge tailor," an "immensely popular" figure on campus who also starred in hockey and who was "voted as the best all-around baseball player of the Harvard team." The paper also mentioned that Arnold Horween, a former Harvard All-American fullback who had returned from World War I to lead the Crimson to a victory in the Rose Bowl on New Year's Day, 1920, and who in fact had been the first Jewish captain of a Harvard eleven, had recently been named to coach the squad.[23]

On this occasion, the *Jewish Independent* did not bother to spell out the obvious import of such news. Here were American Jewish boys and men, the children of East European immigrants, one a student, the other an adult who had already put his life on the line for his country, succeeding in a game characterized as manly American sport at America's elite university. Henry Ford and Madison Grant to the contrary, what better proof was there that Jews enjoyed the full range of college activities, that their success in sport broke down barriers of discrimination, and that full assimilation and access to the promise of American life were open to all. Preceding his weekly litany of Jewish athletic achievement in colleges and elsewhere in 1931, Harry Glantz explicitly captured these sentiments in a commentary on an article about Jewish athletes that appeared in the Los Angeles *Daily News.* According to Glantz, the column, which apparently praised Jewish athletic accomplishment, "was a wonderful expression of good will toward our people." "Jewish athletes," he concluded, "have endeavored to give of their best at all times. They climb to great heights because success means glory to their race. Their good, clean sportsmanship wins the friendship of their neighbors. What matters more?"[24]

Even more pointed in supporting Jewish participation in collegiate sport, the Yiddish-language Chicago *Daily Jewish Courier* vigorously argued its effectiveness in combating anti-Semitism and restrictive admissions policies. In 1923, the *Courier* published "Jewish Sport and American Intellect," an article written by a Dr. A. Margolin, that concerned attempts to establish a quota on Jewish admissions at Syracuse University.[25] As Margolin told it, those behind the quota argued that supposed Jewish disinterest in sports made them undesirable "students at American universities." When Jewish students there challenged this accusation as false, the "New York Jewish press" chastised them for not realizing that even if they were "superior athletes, they would be persecuted for other reasons." Coming at a time when a number of colleges and universities established restrictive admission policies for Jews, Margolin did not deny that the issue of sport may have been convenient to anti-Semites. He insisted, however, that Jewish participation in American sport should not be ignored.

Writing in the midst of the so-called "Golden Age of American Sports" when American passion for both spectator and participant sport reached new heights, Margolin emphasized the importance of sport as part of American culture and the emergence of superior athletes as "national heroes." "Ornaments of American society" and part of the "national pride and wealth of the country," American athletes, he insisted, earn far greater respect than American scientists. "A citizen who is not interested in sports," he asserted, "is not considered a full-fledged citizen. . . . If the Jewish students at the University of Syracuse were known to be good athletes, no one would dare hound them and demand restrictions upon their educational opportunities."

Margolin's understanding of the growing importance of sport in American culture was correct, even if his assessment of the situation at Syracuse was not entirely accurate. At the very time that the university instituted restrictive admissions policies against Jews, its athletic teams sported a number of Jewish athletes. According to the *American Hebrew*, which highlighted Jewish achievement at Syracuse in a December 1924 issue, while the "occasional appearances of superb" Jewish athletes no longer required "extraordinary press comment," the large number of Jewish athletes playing ball for the Orangemen did. By the magazine's count, nine Jewish lads, led by Mordecai Starobin, played football for Syracuse that season. They joined other Jewish athletes who played basketball, soccer, hockey, and water polo, and ran track. Jewish participation in extracurricular activities was not confined to sport. Be it in school journalism, dramatic clubs, or musical organizations, Jewish boys and girls found equal opportunity to show their talents. "Last but not least," the *Hebrew* also acknowledged "the admitted excellency of Jewish scholarship," most notably marked by the election of two Jewish women to Phi Beta Kappa. "Thus," it surmised, "it is easily perceivable that the Jew, where given an equal opportunity, has shown himself to advantage."[26]

Sport as middle ground between Jew and Gentile, as a source of Jewish pride, and as evidence of Jewish normalcy and the promise of acceptance remained a consistent part of the *American Hebrew*'s coverage of collegiate sports news in the 1920s and the 1930s. Always anxious to promote the full assimilation of Jews into American life, the *American Hebrew* proudly announced in November 1925 that its own informal check of the nation's sports pages indicates "what we have always contended: that in American colleges there is no discrimination on the athletic field against those Jewish young men who possess a strong body, a keen mind and a courageous heart to make good in athletics." Noting the accomplishments of Jewish boys playing for college teams all over America, it concluded that "no coach who has regard for the university he serves and for his own reputation will discriminate against a candidate for a team on any ground other than inability to make good for his alma mater."[27]

Even more emphatic was its review of the 1928–29 year, which began with a list of Jewish college footballers participating all over the United States and recognized nationally for their excellent play. According to Henry Levy, he could just as easily have begun the piece with similar exploits of Jewish swimmers, baseball, hockey, basketball, tennis players, or tracksters—"for there are Jewish lads shining as stars of no small magnitude in each of these sports." Even more impressive were the legions of lesser-known Jewish boys in all sports who had won varsity letters and achieved "local or sectional fame." Over 500 Jewish youths alone had played football for their colleges during the past season. As for other sports, Levy refused to guess how many had earned varsity letters during the year. "Even if he did nothing else the year round, to completely cover the country in quest of Jewish athletes" would be an impossible task, so great were their numbers. This multitude of Jewish collegiate athletes, he concluded, was "a healthy sign":

It indicates that an athlete who is a Jew is not looked upon or exploited as a freak. He is just another of the candidates, or letter winners, or stars of his team. No particular significance is attached to his achieving or failing to achieve stardom; the press does not refer to him as the Jewish star as against the Protestant star, the Catholic star, or the Baptist star. It is, more than anything else, an indication of equality, of assimilation, of tolerance.[28]

Both as part of these annual surveys and occasionally as separate articles on particular athletes, the *Hebrew* offered capsule summaries of the individual exploits of both men and women, emphasizing, whenever possible, other accomplishments as further proof of their abilities and normalcy. Special attention was always given to individuals who captained their teams. Acknowledgment of Jewish leadership capabilities clearly helped challenge claims that Jews did not fit or find acceptance among their Gentile peers. While individual achievements in major male sports such as basketball, baseball, and especially football received the most space, success in minor sports was not ignored. Elevating collegiate boxing to undeserved status, a 1932 article praised featherweight Bobby Goldstein for becoming the first Jew at the University of Virginia to captain a "major sports team." A fine student and fraternity boy, the *Hebrew* also acknowledged that this "balanced and rational young man realizes that college is more than boxing and has . . . led a complete and well-rounded collegiate life." Touting Irving Weinstein as the best Jewish tennis player in the United States in 1928, the paper described him as "a splendid type of the modern American young man." "Aside from his ability in athletics," the *Hebrew* continued, "he was an able student at the University of California . . . a member of the Winged Foot Helmet Honor Society" as well as the school's premier courtsman. Although women athletes rarely received much attention in the *Hebrew* or other Jewish periodicals, a month later the paper offered similar praise of Clara Greenspan, whose triumph in the Women's New York State doubles tennis championship offered further proof that "the Jewish athlete in America . . . competes on terms of perfect equality with his Gentile brother." A fine student at Hunter College, Clara was preparing herself for a career as a Latin teacher while serving as captain, coach, and manager of the school's women's tennis team. It also seems she shared a passion for baseball, or at least for its most prominent Jewish player of that year. Her one great ambition, the story concluded, is neither to beat Helen Wills, the reigning women's tennis champion, or "even to be a great Latin scholar, though her marks indicate the possibility of such a happening. . . . More than anything else in the world, Clara Greenspan wants to meet Andy Cohen."[29]

Even the country's economic collapse failed to halt these healthy signs of Jewish eagerness for assimilation and of American openness. In his 1932 year-end "roundup" of the college sports scene in which he focused on the exploits of Jewish college football captains and stars such as Harry Newman of Michigan, Abe Eliowitz of Michigan State, Aaron Rosenberg of the University of Southern California, Sid Gilman of Ohio State, and Abe Itzkowitz of NYU, Henry Levy noted that, despite the country's economic plight, "there has been no depression in Jewish athletes" as the "amazing number of sports participants" makes clear. An editorial in the same issue noted that such evidence demonstrated that prejudice against Jews was on the wane. Jewish youth, it insisted, succeeded or failed on the basis of ability and not because of discrimination. In response to letters it received every year from "disappointed college students . . . charging that so and so could not make the football team because of his Jewishness or was thrown off the basketball squad for the same reason, or was denied a Phi Beta Kappa key on the same ground," the *Hebrew* offered the impressive accomplishments of Jewish students in rebuttal. Arguing that unsuccessful Jewish students often failed because of their own shortcomings, it admitted that "in some instances, the Jewish student may have to be a little more on his toes than his non-Jewish competitor" and that "some athletic coaches are not yet thoroughly convinced that a Jewish lad may be an athlete on par with a non-Jewish lad." Nevertheless, the very success of Jewish youth both on and off the athletic field was slowly helping to remove prejudice as an obstacle to Jewish achievement. Nor, the editorial concluded, should Jews ignore the "very serious failings of Jewish students on campuses which cause attitudes in certain quarters of which we complain."[30]

The *Hebrew*'s admission that Jewish malcontents might encourage anti-Semitism on college campuses, coupled with its firm belief that discrimination was clearly declining, is quite remarkable, given contrary evidence amassed by others less sanguine about the decline of prejudice there or in the larger society. Eager for Jewish acceptance, the magazine downplayed incidents of discrimination, content to point out situations of Jewish success as proof of Jewish potential for assimilation. Clearly, Jewish athletic success on college campuses provided hope that other aspects of campus life, be it admissions or social activities, or, for that matter, other areas of American life, would also open up in the face of incontrovertible proof that the children of Jewish immigrants were just as normal and capable of fitting into the American mainstream as its native sons and daughters.

Gentiles could make their own use of Jewish intercollegiate athletic success. Particularly after the Harvard admissions fiasco in 1922, college officials anxious to avoid accusations that they engaged in discriminatory admissions policies or tolerated prejudical treatment of Jewish students could point to this positive, visible Jewish presence in campus life as evidence to the contrary. The basketball situation at Yale University in the late teens and early 1920s provides one example of such possibilities.[31] At a time when eastern basketball on all levels was the "Jewish game," Yale was no exception. Drawing heavily from its New Haven Jewish students, many of them first-generation Americans who had honed their skills as members of New Haven's all-Jewish Atlas Club, Yale's basketball team between 1914 and 1921 had its fair share of Jewish ballplayers, including Joseph Weiner, the first Jew to play for the Eli and a member of its 1914–15 Intercollegiate Basketball League championship team. In 1922, however, coincident with its institution of restrictive admissions policies which limited Jewish enrollment, the basketball squad, without any Jewish members, fell to last place in the conference. Equally embarrassing was its exhibition loss to the Atlas Club by a score of 42–22. The game, ironically a benefit for the Jewish relief fund, attracted 3000 spectators—at that time the largest home crowd ever for Yale basketball.

Upset with the team's performance and with the general state of Yale athletics, an alumni committee containing no Jewish members investigated the Yale athletic program. Its report severely criticized what it found to be inept management and called for a complete overhaul of its operation. One of its specific charges that drew the attention of the national press was the claim that Yale coaches consciously excluded Jews from their teams. Nowhere was this more blatant and damaging than on the basketball team. Rejecting the athletic department's explanation that a lack of good players accounted for the squad's poor performance, the committee reported that it "has learned that capable men were cut off the squad without handling the ball. Jewish candidates," it went on, "say that they were discriminated against. No Jew made the squad."

While the New Haven *Evening Register* dismissed the report, Elias Lieberman of the *American Hebrew* offered his own version of its significance. Denying charges that "Jewish boys" at Yale were "humiliated in a land that proclaims human equality and equal opportunity and at a college whose seal bears a Hebrew symbol," nevertheless he applauded the fact that "a group of alumni, non-Jewish in character," had taken a public stand in favor of "fair play" and "against any kind of discrimination in the selection of athletes for intercollegiate athletics." For Lieberman, the committee's actions underlined that anti-Semitism was on the decline and that Jews must continue to have as their slogan: "Hope in the future, Faith in God and in the ultimate justice of Americans and American institutions, and the greatest of these—Charity for the wanton slanderers who attack us."[32]

Lieberman must have been gratified by Yale's response to the alumni investigation. Although James Angell, Yale's president, rejected their report because it was not initiated by the university, within a year the school reorganized the athletic department. Among other things, Yale appointed a new basketball coach, Joseph Fogarty. The Eli mentor publicly declared that he would choose boys regardless of whether they were "black or white, Jew or Gentile, so long as [they could] play basketball." Unlike today, in 1923 the operative word for success on the court was "Jew" and Fogarty promptly recruited Jewish talent. Led by Pete Gitlitz, Eddie Suisman, and Sam Rite, Yale climbed from the cellar to the championship in one season. The following year, captain Rite and his teammates captured the Eastern Collegiate League title; successes attributed, as the *Evening Register* put it, to Fogarty's "guts" in "pick[ing] the best players at Yale." "Yale," the paper concluded, "has obviously found the Jewish undergraduate a credit both as an athlete and a scholar." Such publicity could only have pleased a Yale administration involved in instituting restrictive admissions policies yet anxious to counter any charges that it discriminated against Jews.

Although there is no evidence that University of Wisconsin officials awarded its Kenneth Sterling Day Award to Louie Behr in 1928 to achieve similar ends, the action certainly did no harm to its image as a great state university open to all. The Day award went annually to a Wisconsin senior of "reasonable intellectual and athletic ability" considered by a faculty selection committee to be the best example of "Christian character" on campus. Behr, chosen from among 15 finalists, was the first Jew to win the award. Captain of the basketball team that had closely contended for the Western conference crown, an economics major with an 89.5 average—the highest average among all conference athletes—and a member of the National Honorary Economics Society, Behr also won election to his school's junior and senior honor societies as well as to Pi Kappa Phi, the national honorary scholarship and activities society. During his stay at Wisconsin, he also held every major office of the Phi Sigma Delta fraternity and served as president of Wisconsin's B'nai B'rith Hillel Foundation. Explaining how it could bestow an award for "Christian character" on a Jewish boy from Rockford, Illinois, the chair of the selection committee told the school paper that "Christian" designated "possession of certain qualities" regardless of denominational affiliation.

News of the award did not escape reporters. Local Madison papers, with headlines such as "Christians Honor Jew," told the story, as did the national press. The New York *World* included Behr's own modest reaction, one in which he emphasized the role of his parents, his orthodox religious beliefs, and his professors in developing his "sound moral character." And in a full-page story titled "Jewish Lad Honored for Essential Christian Worth," the *American Hebrew* lauded Behr for bringing honor to the Christian community of the University, the Jewish community, himself, and, most important, to his parents.[33]

Source of Jewish pride and catalyst for Gentile acceptance of Jews eager and ready for assimilation, public perceptions of Behr's honor demonstrate once again the variety of meaning imbedded in the success of collegiate Jewish athletes. Nowhere was this more apparent than in treatments of Jewish athletes competing in football, by far the most popular of all college sport.

V

Some of the potential for Jewish interest in college football emerges in a tongue-in-cheek fictional account called "A Litvak's Monologue: The Football Game," that appeared in the California *Jewish Voice* in 1937. Written by a B. Kovner, it describes the football experience of a "hundred and twenty, sixty-two years [*sic*] old . . . Litvak," recently arrived from the old country, who now lives with his "poor" son and daughter-in-law somewhere in the Bronx. Despite his son's poverty, the Litvak tells us that his boy is "as interested in American games as a pious Jew is in the Talmud." Ignorant of American pastimes himself, our narrator, one Saturday afternoon, curiously follows a large crowd of people. "Coming to a place where they did not let anyone in without a ticket . . . [he] plunked down a dollar and they let [him] in, or rather [he] was pushed in." There he observed:

> I saw a big place with wooden benches around a vacant circle. Thousands of people were sitting there, so I sat down too. All of a sudden two doors flew open and a gang of burly, healthy fellows dressed as clowns, ran into the circle. The crowd started yelling at the top of their voices: "Syracuse! Colgate! Syracuse! Colgate!" . . . Thinking that everyone must yell I joined them: "Syracuse! Colgate! Syracuse! Colgate!" Those sitting nearby started to laugh. "You must not cheer for both teams at the same time," they said to me. "Cheer either for one or the other." I replied: "It is none of your business for whom I cheer. I paid a dollar, hard-earned money for a ticket, so I have a right to cheer for whomever I want. This is America and no one can tell me what to do!"[34]

The spoof continues, complete with malapropisms and uninformed descriptions of the contest. "If you'll ask me what I saw," our Litvak concludes, "I cannot answer you. One thing I know! I lost a hard-earned dollar. Had I bought something with my money, I would have enjoyed it better."

In fact, however, our Litvak had purchased something—passport to the heart of what life in America promised—the freedom and opportunity to make choices. Be it his decision to participate in an event he understood to be "American" or his decision about which team he chose to support, this immigrant's football experience helped acclimate him to American ways while underlining the lure America offered to immigrants.

College football, especially when played by Jewish boys, offered even more to this Litvak and especially to his son. Despite Jewish prominence and success in college basketball, Benny Friedman, Marshall Goldberg, Harry Newman, and Sid Luckman, along with a host of lesser-known gridsters, consistently received the most attention of all Jewish college athletes. There is no great mystery here. Since the turn of the century college football was heralded as one American institution capable of producing "muscular Christians"—strong-willed, moral, physical men who would lead the nation to greatness. Searching for a sense of national identity in the midst of what many critics perceived to be a time of social crisis in the 1890s, college football, along with baseball, received attention as quintessential American experiences. Praised as a crucible for forging American men of character and toughness and as a critical factor in attracting alumni financial support, the game became a major commercial venture at the center of intercollegiate extracurricular activity. Well into the 1940s, it remained far more popular than the game's professional version. More than in any other college sport, Jewish success on the gridiron provided opportunity to challenge stereotypes of the weak Jew and to demonstrate that Jews deserved acceptance as Americans.[35]

Certainly that was the perception of those reporters who catalogued Jewish accomplishments on the gridiron for Jewish newspapers. In its 1927 year-end review of Jewish college athletes, headlined "Brilliant in the Firmament of College Sports," the *American Hebrew* recognized the role of college athletics in encouraging "college spirit" and loyalty. Crucial here was football, "the major college sport . . . that holds first place in the hearts of the students, alumni and the general public." Having established the importance of the game to Americans and to university life, the *Hebrew* proceeded to revel in the accomplishments of Jewish boys who had made good on the gridiron. One year later, writing about the 1928 football season, another report correctly noted that "in recording the athletic exploits of Jewish collegians the accounting usually begins and ends with the gridiron. Although it may be taboo, the fact remains that it is the pigskin our sons love to touch." Complete with a page of photos of Jewish football captains at the University of Chicago, Brown, CCNY, St. John's, Delaware, and Rutgers, it went on to describe the achievements of individual stars and to emphasize the increasing "numbers of Jewish lads on . . . teams . . . in all sections of the country," including a special note on Sammy Behr of Wisconsin, "brother of the famous Louis, who proved himself to be the best 'Christian' on the Wisconsin campus."[36]

Similar stories regularly appeared in Jewish newspapers throughout the country. Los Angeles, Pittsburgh, and Detroit readers were all kept well informed of the success of their own kind in the rough and tumble world of college football. Commenting on the chances of the University of California at Los Angeles, for instance, Paul Freed assured readers of the California *Jewish Voice* that the Bruins would be "almost taken over bodily by . . . husky Mogen David Youths" during the 1937 campaign. So tedious and familiar did reportage of Jewish success on the gridiron become that, at times, reporters provided special twists to catch their readers' attention. Surveying Jewish talent in 1930, Harry Glantz observed that although "the Notre Dame football team may be known as the Fighting Irish . . . that doesn't alter the fact that three Jewish boys are playing more than a passing note on the Rockne squad. Kaplan, Schwartz, and Brill are the representatives of our faith, and blimy, what a trio."[37]

The proliferation of Jewish boys playing college football produced annual selections of Jewish all-star teams that carried their own message of Jewish ability. In 1934, for example, Morris Weiner, sports editor for the Jewish Telegraphic Agency, with help from Jack Weinberg, sports editor of the *American Jewish World,* and G. M. Cohen of the Louisville *Spokesman,* selected a team that in their minds would "stand up against the All-American pick of grid experts anywhere." The following two seasons, Irv Kupcinet, a sportswriter for the Chicago *Times* and for the Seven Arts Feature Syndicate, and himself a former All-American fullback at the University of North Dakota, chose All-American squads that appeared in the Detroit *Jewish Chronicle.* Featuring "Mad" Marshall Goldberg from Pittsburgh and Sid Luckman from Columbia, consensus All-Americans on anybody's team, Kupcinet's picks, at least in 1935, caused some disagreement among his readers who felt that he had slighted other worthy candidates.[38] Henry Levy's picks for the *American Hebrew* in 1937 might well have generated similar protest, so difficult did he find it to choose the eleven best players from the large numbers of Jewish boys playing college football throughout the country. Along with a squad headed again by Goldberg and Luckman, Levy also chose Benny Friedman, then coaching at CCNY, as head coach. "Benny," Levy remarked, "has been doing a swell job . . . with poor material. . . . Give Benny the above team, as I should like to, and you'd have a Rose Bowl winner."[39]

Not all Jewish sports columnists looked favorably on the naming of such teams. Writing for Pittsburgh's *American Jewish Outlook* in 1937, Haskell Cohen deplored them as "farce." For him, how Jewish players matched up against their non-Jewish peers was the more important test of their competence. As he told it, the fact that several Jewish players named to Jewish all-star teams had also received praise from the Associated Press and from college football coaches was better proof of Jewish ability.[40] More typical, however, were the remarks of George Joel, who underscored the significance of his selections of a 1927 Jewish All-American football team in a syndicated article written for the Jewish Telegraphic Agency. Noting the "injustice" that would be done "to the host of other Jewish boys that starred on the gridiron this past season" if he picked only eleven players, Joel offered his readers three teams representing schools scattered throughout the country. "Give these 33 men to any football coach in the country," Joel exclaimed, "and watch his face light up. There isn't a team playing the game that could beat this bunch by more than two touchdowns."[41]

Although not the most fulsome of compliments, Joel went on to explain the significance of this fine group of Jewish boys playing the game of American manhood. "In spite of the old kick that our boys are weaker and smaller than their Gentile brothers," he emphasized that "most of the great Jewish players have been linemen." Having challenged the mythology of Jewish weakness, he then moved on to questions of normalcy and acceptance. "Football as a Jewish sport," he began, "has come to stay and each year sees a greater number of our boys out on the gridiron ready to break a leg or arm for the glory of a new stadium and the endowment fund." Such contributions to the good of the university itself, coupled with the eagerness with which Jewish boys took up football, warranted acknowledgment that they had earned the right to full participation in whatever college or American life had to offer. As Joel cautioned, however, "in spite of the great number of Jewish athletes in both football and other sports there still persists echoes of the myth that the Jew is unpopular in college because he does not take part in college athletics. . . . What will . . . Jewish boys have to do," he implored, "to completely dispel this myth, or is it perhaps that our prejudice seeking friends wish the idea to live?"[42]

Whatever else they did to overcome "echoes" of prejudice, certainly their football prowess did not hurt their cause. Claims of Jewish greatness were neither extravagant nor distorted versions of reality. Even more so than in the years before World War I, when the exploits of players like Albert Loeb, "der Yiddisher Vild-kat" from Georgia Tech, Joe Alexander, a Syracuse guard named to Walter Camp's All-American teams in 1919 and 1920, or Harvard's

Arnold Horween highlighted Jewish gridiron accomplishment, it is clear that in the 1920s and 1930s increasing numbers of Jewish boys enthusiastically played the sport. Their success in a game that emphasized strength and toughness not only challenged anti-Semitic claims of Jewish debility and weakness but also occasionally encouraged such traits as part of an American Jewish identity suited to a world in which Jewish survival was hardly secure. Nowhere was this more apparent than in the stories of Benny Friedman and Marshall Goldberg, who, along with Sid Luckman, were the best-known Jewish college players between the wars.

Born in 1905, Benny Friedman grew up in a Jewish neighborhood on Cleveland's East Side. His father, who worked as a tailor, and his mother, who took care of a household of six children, both were Russian immigrants. Although he went to cheder, he recalls his experiences there with strong distaste—uncomfortable with being forced to learn words that had no meaning to him taught by "a dirty old man" who disciplined his students by hitting them with his umbrella. The fact that it kept him from "play[ing] ball" did not encourage his interest.[43]

Benny's Jewish education was cut short before he was Bar Mitzvahed when his parents removed him from the school after he received a beating. Despite the lack of a formal Jewish education, Friedman, like many of his generation, understood his Jewish identity as a given, tied more to family and community connections that included a kosher home, lighting candles on Friday night, the smell of fresh-baked challah emanating from his mother's kitchen, and her Saturday ritual of putting aside 18 cents, symbolic of the Hebrew word chai which, she told her son, meant "life," to help needy Jews. Equally important, at least as Friedman describes it, his youth was defined by his devotion to sport, an interest tolerated by his father and encouraged by his mother, who took pride in her son's accomplishments.

A high-school standout in his senior year, Benny attracted the attention of several colleges, and in the end chose the University of Michigan. Playing at a time when players went both ways, Friedman starred at quarterback, safety, and placekicker, while leading Michigan to consecutive Big Ten championships in 1925 and 1926. Each season, he earned selection to several All-American squads. Although never explicitly connected to his Jewish background, praise of his talents frequently focused on Benny's intelligence. Previewing the 1926 Michigan eleven, the Chicago *Tribune* noted that Benny, "one of the brainiest quarterbacks in the country," had been named as the Wolverine's captain. His coach, Fielding "Hurry Up" Yost, called him "the quarterback who never made a mistake." Grantland Rice, the famed sportswriter, even compared him favorably with his immortal contemporary, Illinois's "Galloping Ghost," Red Grange. The Michigan star, Rice insisted, was "a great quarterback, a marvelous passer . . . and a brilliant field director who deserves equal rank with Grange."[44]

Friedman enjoyed his years at Michigan both on and off the field, not only because of his gridiron success but because of the attention accorded him as a Jew. A member of Sigma Alpha Mu, a Jewish fraternity, he marveled at this public recognition. After being named captain of the 1926 squad, Benny received congratulatory telegrams from Jewish people all over the country. The *Jewish Daily Forward* even sent out a reporter to interview him who, as Friedman recalled, barely spoke English and knew nothing about the sport.

In short, regardless of his limited religious training or commitment, Friedman, identified as Jewish by birth and background, became a symbol of group pride and of the possibilities of assimilation. Certainly that's how the *American Hebrew* understood his accomplishments. Recognizing Benny "as the best quarterback in the Western Conference" at the close of the 1925 season, the magazine reiterated its claim that no coach would discriminate against Jews "on any ground other than inability." Two weeks later, after he had been named as Michigan's captain, it featured him in an article titled "Benny Friedman—Gridiron Hero." Praising him as a "Jewish progidy of America's greatest sport" and his reputation among coaches and sportswriters as a "football brain," the *Hebrew* emphasized that his selection as captain "crystallized in one act a new sentiment which appears to be prevalent in many American colleges and universities." The "new sentiment" of "widespread tolerance," based "on recognition of character, intrinsic merit, and pleasing deportment," only underlined the message that Jews who sought and deserved it would find acceptance into mainstream American society and its opportunities. Friedman, who played professional football for several teams including the New York Giants and the Brooklyn Dodgers and who coached at Yale, CCNY, and Brandeis, concurred. Only once in his entire football career could he recall even a brush with anti-Semitism. As he told one interviewer in 1940, "we are not a people apart. Physically and in general mental attitudes, there is nothing that distinguishes the Jewish athlete from any other. In the locker room, everyone is stripped clean of all sham and pretense. You're either a man or you're not."[45]

Although he played college football a decade after Friedman and came from a much different world than Cleveland's East Side, Marshall Goldberg shared similar experiences with the Michigan star. Goldberg's father, Saul, emigrated from Uman, Rumania, to Cumberland, Maryland, where he met and married the woman who would be Marshall's mother. The couple settled in the small mountain community of Elkins, West Virginia, some 170 miles from Pittsburgh, set up a ladies' clothing store, and welcomed Marshall into the world in 1917. Eventually his father became the owner of the local movie theater and the family prospered.[46]

Goldberg has fond memories of Elkins; 60 years later he still goes back occasionally to participate in the local Mountain State Forest Festival and to underwrite a scholarship program for local high-school kids. Not surprisingly, however, what he remembers has little to do with any sense of Jewish community or training. A star athlete who captained his high school's football, basketball, and track teams in his senior year, he was a popular student who dated the prettiest cheerleader, even serving as her escort when she was elected princess of the very first festival. Except for four other families, including his uncle's, there were no other Jews in a town of some 7500. The nearest synagogue, as best as he can remember, was in Morgantown. Although he vaguely recalls some celebration of the high holidays in his home, Marshall's first introduction to any formal Judaism awaited his college days at the University of Pittsburgh. Instead, in a town dominated by Methodists and Presbyterians and featuring a Presbyterian college, Davis-Elkins, Goldberg regularly attended a Methodist church where his football coach doubled as a Sunday school teacher. His two brothers, who went on to play football for Davis-Elkins, split their church time between a Presbyterian and a Baptist church.

An all-purpose running and defensive back in high school, Marshall was heavily recruited by a number of colleges, including Notre Dame. "Biggie" or, as he was sometimes called, "Mad Marshall" ended up at Pittsburgh to play for Jock Sutherland, after his father, Saul, who consulted with the school's recruiters, made the decision for him. Although it is not clear whether his father chose Pitt because they promised him a seat on the bench, Saul, always an avid supporter of Marshall's promising career, enjoyed being part of the attention and success. Indeed Marshall recalls that prior to the Panthers' 1937 Rose Bowl game with the University of Washington, Jock Sutherland read a telegram from his father to the entire squad which encouraged the team "to bring home the bacon, and you know how I hate pork." Whether it helped or not, Pitt won the game 21–0, one of the highlights of Goldberg's three varsity seasons in which he led the Panthers to a 24–3–2 record over the 1936–38 seasons, including a national championship in 1937.

A consensus All-American in his last two seasons and twice runner-up for college football's highest individual award, the Heisman Trophy, Goldberg received plaudits in the regular press not only for his football ability but for his clean living. According to one account, this modest fraternity boy's only "dissipation" was "ice cream at the corner drug store." In similar fashion, Jock Sutherland, after praising Marshall's gridiron talent, told one season-ending banquet crowd that if he had a son "I would want my boy to have all the fine traits of Marshall Goldberg."[47]

Although one football magazine described "college football's No. 1 Star" in 1938 as a "studious clean-living Jewish boy" who was the "son of a Russian immigrant," rarely did laudatory news of his accomplishments in the regular press refer to his ethnic background. As Goldberg recalls, however, Jewish newspapers and organizations were a different story. Both in college and later, during his ten-year career as a professional player with the Chicago Cardinals, the "Jewish" or "Hebrew Hillbilly," as the Jewish press labeled him, was the subject of newspaper and magazine articles that emphasized his athletic successes as a Jewish man. These accounts often linked Marshall with one of his Jewish contemporaries: Sid Luckman, the famed Columbia quarterback who went on to lead the professional Chicago Bears to four National Football League championships between 1940 and 1946. Here and in public appearances before Jewish organizations, the focus was football. Unspoken was the obvious—the success of a man identified as a Jew in an American game who might be an inspiration to others with their own American dreams.[48]

The very nature of football as a physically violent game that demanded toughness and courage from its participants gave Goldberg's success and that of other Jewish football players additional meaning. Hitler's treatment of European Jews, he insists, conditioned public response to his football exploits. Much like the attention paid to Hank Greenberg and a host of Jewish boxers, Jewish people followed his career avidly, Marshall argues, because "here's a guy named Goldberg who's a football player, and Jews aren't supposed to be football players and Jews aren't supposed to be strong."

How influential such coverage was in encouraging Jews to embrace physical toughness proudly as part of their identity or to believe that full assimilation was possible without abandoning Jewish connections is not easy to assess. For Goldberg and others of his generation, however, such goals were not incompatible. Remembrances of Nazi Germany, a knowledge of Jewish history, and attachment to Israel as a symbol of Jewish survival define his sense of Jewishness. Never a religious man nor personally exposed to prejudice despite his public identity as an American Jew, he remains proud of his accomplishments as a Jew and as an American. For him, they include successful careers in football and in business, his work as a member of his alma mater's Board of Trustees, and his contributions of time and money to Jewish charities, including a position as Illinois state chairman of the U.S. Maccabi Committee. As he put it:

> I know the history of Passover and I think it was a wonderful thing, but I also know the history of Valley Forge and I think that was a wonderful thing and I think I'm part of both and I respect both of them for it. I don't go into mourning for the people who were destroyed on Masada and I don't go into mourning for the people Washington lost in the crossing of the Delaware. I think that I've led a good life and I think I can say that as a Jew . . . I think that my life has probably been exemplary in the manner in which I have lived it. . . .
> I have lived within the laws of the United States, I have been a fairly good contributor to Jewish causes and Jewish charities, I have been identified with the Jewish people and I observe all . . . the moral laws and rules of Judaism.[49]

Goldberg's self-assessment consciously embraces American patriotism and pride in a Jewish past that permits him personal acceptance of his credentials as both an American and a Jew. It is a theme, as we have seen, not uncommon to other second-generation Jewish-Americans who came of age between the wars. Clearly many Jewish sportswriters believed that Jewish fans who followed the exploits of Goldberg and other Jewish college football players absorbed some of the same possibilities. In its survey of the accomplishments of Jewish athletes for 1936 that featured pictures of Goldberg and Luckman, for example, the *American Hebrew* left no doubt that in the "number one sports loving country" in the world, "millions of Jews" are among the "most devoted followers" of sport. "No better indication of the Americanization of the Jew," it reported, "is to be noted."[50]

Reports of thousands of New York Jewish fans packing Yankee Stadium to see Goldberg's Pittsburgh team battle the Fordham Rams or similar accounts of Jewish fanatics who followed the professional football careers of Goldberg and Sid Luckman when they both played in Chicago provide additional testimony. So too does Justin Kestenbaum, my colleague at Michigan State, who fondly remembers reading about both men when they played for the Columbia Lions and the Pittsburgh Panthers. Born in New York City, Kestenbaum spent a good deal of his childhood at the Pleasantville Cottage School, a home for some 300 Jewish boys and girls whose parents were unable to support them during the Depression. With obvious warmth and detail, he recalls that in 1938, the year of his Bar Mitzvah, the Pleasantville boys were invited to a Jewish temple in nearby White Plains, New York, to hear Sid Luckman, then a junior at Columbia, talk about sportsmanship, the importance of a college education, football, and his pride in being a Jew.[51]

Kestenbaum was not a football player. But, like countless other Jewish boys and girls, he did secure an education that guaranteed him a better economic future than his parents or grandparents ever imagined for themselves. With the exception of Jewish youth who attended colleges like CCNY—schools predominantly Jewish and situated in the very neighborhoods and communities where Jews lived and worked—those who attended college between the wars clearly experienced various forms of discrimination, depending upon their choice of school and their particular extracurricular interests.[52] Rarely, however, were they denied the opportunity for a college education on the basis of their religious or ethnic identity. And the educational choices they made there fueled the economic success and assimilation of second- and third-generation American Jews in post–World War II America.

Jewish college students able to participate in intercollegiate athletics played a special role in this college experience by serving a spectrum of contradictory interest. College administrators concerned abut denying legitimate charges of discrimination and restriction eagerly praised their success. Sometimes apologetically, Jewish assimilationists searching for evidence that opportunity and full acceptance awaited able Jews provided even more vigorous praise. More important, at a time of increasing crisis for Jews around the world, everyday Jewish people sensed in their achievements what these athletes often recognized for themselves—in this country it was possible to achieve real success without abandoning or denying ethnic attachments.

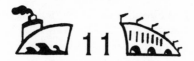

"My Father and I, We Didn't Get Our Medals": Marty Glickman's American Jewish Odyssey

IN 1984, Los Angeles hosted the summer Olympic games. As part of the festivities, the Southern California Jewish Historical Society mounted an exhibit celebrating the exploits of Jewish athletes in Olympic competition. Inviting people to come and "celebrate 88 years of Olympic gold," it declared that "since the first modern Olympics in 1896, Jews have been counted among the world's fastest, strongest, nimblest sports competitors in the world." Jewish Olympians, it proclaimed, "have brought honor to themselves and to their country" and "are a great source of pride to Jews everywhere."[1]

A poster announcing the exhibit detailed these Jewish achievements for each Olympic games. Some of the entries noted more than athletic triumph. Even casual observers of Olympic history, looking at this poster in 1984, likely recalled the events depicted in its description of the 1972 games—both the seven gold medals of American swimmer Mark Spitz as well as the tragic murder of eleven members of the Israeli Olympic team by Palestinian terrorists. Many, no doubt, were less familiar with the entry for the 1936 games, the so-called Nazi Olympics. The text beside a picture of the United States gold medal basketball team, which included both a Jewish player and a coach, reminded viewers of Jewish attempts to boycott the games as a protest against Nazi Germany. It also recorded that some Jewish team members from several countries, including the United States, were not allowed to compete. Not mentioned were two American Jewish runners who were denied the opportunity to participate and the fact that an American track coach, not Adolf Hitler, was responsible for the decision.

One of these athletes, Marty Glickman, went on to enjoy great success as a collegiate track star and football player before beginning a prominent career in sports broadcasting. For any boy growing up in the Northeast in the 1950s and 1960s, his radio accounts of football's New York Giants and basketball's New York Knickerbockers were familiar music. A pioneer of basketball broadcasting and still active in the business in his seventies, Glickman, as he has been told many times by middle-aged New Yorkers who stop him on the street to shake his hand, is "an experience and a voice out of their youth" that conjures up not only memories of "Sweet Water" Clifton, Harry "the Horse" Gallatin, and Charlie Conerly but also of childhood and family. Glickman's significance, however, is hardly limited to his contributions to sports broadcasting or his ability to rekindle the past. As a prominent Jewish athlete embroiled in anti-Semitic controversy in the 1936 Olympics and as a second-generation American Jew who found success in one of the more visible expressions of the American way, his life story illuminates both the passage to assimilation for many Jews of his generation and the meaning of Jewish identity in America today.[2]

I

Marty Glickman was born in 1917 in the East Bronx in an area today called Fort Apache. His parents, Harry and Molly, knew each other in Rumania, met again in New York's Lower East Side as teenagers, and married in their early twenties. Although born in the Bronx, Glickman and his family moved to Brooklyn when he was five, living first in an apartment house owned by his grandfather next to Thomas Jefferson High School. His family, however, which he described as lower-middle-class, moved every few years, from Flatbush to Bensonhurst and back again, taking advantage of the rent concessions offered by builders who were flooding Brooklyn with new apartment houses for Jewish immigrants and their children who had done well enough to leave the Lower East Side.

Although Marty lived in an extended family in which Yiddish was the everyday language of grandparents, aunts, and uncles, he remembers that his father refused to speak Yiddish or Rumanian. "He wanted to be an American, and so we spoke only English in the house." Choosing to "be an American," however, did not mean discarding religious belief or practice. The family celebrated the Jewish holidays and occasionally attended shul at the Ocean Parkway Jewish Center. Glickman also went to Hebrew school and prepared for his Bar Mitzvah. The ceremony took place in a small synagogue in Glen Wild, New York, near Monticello, while he was at a summer camp.

Marty's religious training, however, was hardly pleasant. Nor did it leave him with a deep love for Jewish observance. As he recalls it:

> I went to Hebrew school starting at the age of ten. I also had individual
> Hebrew instructors come into my house. I remember one old rabbi with a

huge beard who smelled. He had a terrible body odor and he would sit along-side me and go over my maftir and Haftorah. It was just an ordeal for me to sit there alongside of him. I was far more interested in getting out, in getting through with the lesson and playing ball and running and doing what every-one else was doing than studying. I realize now how ridiculous those lessons were and even Hebrew School was because I was taught to speak Hebrew without knowing what the words meant.

Such experiences help explain Glickman's lack of religious observance today despite a very strong sense of his own Jewish identity.

Growing up at a time when Jewish immigrant parents and their children often experienced great conflict about how children should live, the language they should speak, and even their participation in sports, Glickman remem-bers nothing but encouragement and love for his early involvement and suc-cess in athletics. Describing "one of the great moments in my life," Marty recalled the "enormous support" his mother offered him. In search of a new pair of sneakers, mother and son walked the two miles from Coney Island Ave-nue to Flatbush Avenue to a sporting-goods store. As he remembers:

Sneakers in those days might cost a $1.25 or a $1.50, maybe even a $1.75. They would be an unusual pair of sneakers. I looked at the sneakers on the shelf and I saw a pair of black sneakers. In those days there were white sneak-ers only, and they were ankle high sneakers. I saw a black pair. They were called "Black Flash." I kept trying on sneakers and I kept looking at the black ones, fondling them. But I didn't ask for them. My mother said to me: "You really want that pair of sneakers, don't you?" I said, "But Mom, it's $5.00. It's more than double what we pay for sneakers." She thought about it and I felt around and we looked at the other sneakers and tried them on and all that. Then she said, "Moey, Moey, try on those sneakers." I tried on the "Black Flash" and she bought me $5.00 sneakers. That was one of the great joys of my life . . . to have my mother support me that way.

Although Glickman's relationship with his father was more troubling, he also remembers the man's avid interest in his athletic ability. Harry Glick-man's career as a cotton-goods salesman foundered in the Depression. An attempt to start his own company led to bankruptcy. Although the details are vague, Marty recalls that a year after his Bar Mitzvah his father was sent to debtor's prison for one year when the court decided that he had withheld funds with which he could have paid his creditors. The family moved back into his grandfather's house and Marty's mother took up the slack, working as a seamstress.

Calling his father's stay in jail "one of the shocks of my life," Marty remembers visiting him there and the turmoil his incarceration created for the family. Described by his son as a "poor and beaten man" during the '30s, Harry worked occasionally as a laundry deliveryman when he came out of jail. His penchant for playing the horses, however, caused even more conflict when Marty's mother learned that her husband had convinced their son to give him his Bar Mitzvah money to cover his bets.[3]

Saddened by his father's plight and confused by the troubles at home, Marty entered James Madison High School, where Jammy Moskowitz and Nat Krinsky taught gym and coached the basketball and track teams. A successful athlete in junior high school, Glickman quickly became a star in high-school track and football. He played on a high-school football team that won the city championship in his senior year in 1934, one in which he was named the most valuable player in New York despite the presence of another young Jewish football star from Erasmus High School named Sid Luckman. By his senior year Marty was fast enough in track to establish himself as the national schoolboy sprint champion. Athletic success provided self-esteem and brought him closer to his father. Often unemployed, Harry went to all of his son's football games and track meets. He even attended team practices and occasionally spent half-times in the locker room with Madison's Highwaymen. As Marty put it, in his household there was "never the Jewish antipathy towards sports that I'm told other Jewish athletes experienced."

Glickman's success as a high-school athlete and his Jewish background gave him the opportunity to go to college. Recruited by a number of schools as an athlete, Marty decided on Syracuse University. Several Jewish Syracuse alumni who were anxious to increase Jewish enrollments there convinced him to become an Orangeman. Although the university did not offer him a scholarship, they paid Glickman's way through his freshman year. After a successful year on the track, Marty received an athletic scholarship from the university. At a time when colleges and universities did not hide their established quotas for Jews, Glickman wonders whether the university initially failed to offer financial aid because he was Jewish. In any case, occasional calls to his Jewish patrons in New York for money whenever the bursar demanded tuition payments allowed him to go to college and to pursue his athletic interests at a time when family circumstances did not permit it. Much to his surprise, he also got the chance to represent the United States in the Nazi Olympics.

II

When the International Olympic Committee (IOC) awarded the 1936 Olympic games to Germany at its meeting in Barcelona, Spain, in May 1931, Adolf Hitler was not in power and National Socialism did not dominant German life and politics. Those who thought at all about the significance of the decision saw it as nothing more than another sign of the growing acceptance of Germany as part of the international community after the end of World War I. By the time Marty Glickman tried out for the American track and field team in July 1936, however, things had changed dramatically.

As early as 1933, Jewish groups like the American Jewish Congress (AJC) began to question whether a fascist country with professed racist policies that included open hatred and overt discrimination of Jews and other "non-Aryan" people could be trusted with conducting the games in the spirit of Olympic ideals emphasizing fair and open competition. Charles Sherill, an American member of the IOC, and Avery Brundage, then president of the

American Olympic Committee (AOC), who both had traveled to Germany in 1934 and 1935 to investigate conditions, guaranteed that the German government would allow German Jews to participate in German Olympic tryouts. Nevertheless, a variety of voices rightly questioned Nazi intentions. Emanuel Celler, a Jewish congressman from Brooklyn, accused Brundage of making up his mind about Germany before he left the United States. Heywood Broun, responding to Brundage's claims that he found no evidence that the German government had denied any Jew the opportunity to compete for the German Olympic team, sarcastically questioned whether tryouts had been "held in all the concentration camps." Samuel Untermyer of the Anti-Defamation League announced a list of instances of Nazi persecution of German Jewish athletes and called for a boycott of the games by the United States.[4]

Untermyer's appeal resonated with broader efforts encouraging American Jews to protest news of Nazi anti-Semitism by boycotting all goods made in Germany. Various segments of the American Jewish community, including the AJC, the Jewish Welfare Board, and the newly formed Jewish Labor Committee (a coalition of Jewish labor unions and the Workmen's Circle) spearheaded the drive for an American boycott of the 1936 games. Prominent Jewish sports personalities such as Nat Holman also joined the cause. Continued news of German repression and atrocity, from the passage of the Nuremberg Laws that denied German Jews their citizenship to an account of the death of a Polish Jewish soccer player at the hands of a mob of anti-Semitic German fans, encouraged American Jewish newspapers to press for an American boycott of the Olympic games. Throughout 1934 and 1935, the Detroit *Jewish Chronicle,* the Los Angeles *B'nai B'rith Messenger,* and especially the *American Hebrew* bombarded its readers with stories and editorials on the subject. Along with the obvious concerns about the oppression of Jews, these papers also called for a boycott as protest against Hitler's discrimination against Catholics and as a means of denying the Third Reich its stated objective of using the games as a means of showcasing Nazi accomplishment and power.[5]

A shared sense of outrage at Nazi policies, concern for the plight of German and Polish Catholics, and internal struggles for control over the American amateur athletic community encouraged other individuals and groups to join the boycott movement. Jeremiah Mahoney, president of the Amateur Athletic Union (AAU), and Fiorello La Guardia, the mayor of New York, played prominent roles in the battle. State governors and United States congressmen added their voices in protest. Resolutions from city governments and labor unions, including the American Federation of Labor, came out against American participation. According to the *American Hebrew,* which compiled a survey of "American public opinion against the Berlin Olympics" in November 1935, organizations throughout the country, from the Catholic War Veterans to the Fraternal Order of the Beavers, spoke out in favor of the boycott. They were joined by literally hundreds of newspapers and magazines as nationally prominent as *Commonweal* and as local as Augusta, Maine's *Kennebec Journal.*[6]

Avery Brundage, who led the pro-Olympic forces, proved a worthy opponent. Whether manipulating votes among AAU members to gain its support for sending an American team or purging the AOC of its most vociferous boy-cott spokesman, Brundage kept up relentless pressure to insure victory. A major part of his strategy included spreading the idea that Communists and Jews had joined together in a conspiracy to keep American athletes at home. This thinly veiled anti-Semitic attack, officially sanctioned by the AOC, was made public in October 1935 when Brundage published and distributed a pamphlet called *Fair Play for American Athletes* to members of the AOC, the AAU, editors of some 650 newspapers, and college and high school coaches throughout the nation. In the end Brundage won, and the United States, along with 52 other nations, sent its athletes to Berlin. Among those who went along was Marty Glickman, dreaming of glory and Olympic gold.[7]

III

Marty Glickman was not the only American Jewish athlete faced with the decision about whether or not to participate in the Nazi Olympics. In March 1936, New York's 92nd Street Y informed Dan Ferris, secretary-treasurer of the AAU, that it would not send any representatives to the organization's 50,000-meter walk race, the competition designated as the Olympic trial for the Berlin games. Although this action denied Y athletes likely places on the United States Olympic team, Jack Nadel, the Y's executive director, urged other Jewish organizations to take similar action as a protest against Nazi Ger-many. Herman Neugass, a New Orleans Jew of German descent, also declined an invitation from the AOC to be considered for the United States track team because he would not participate as an athlete in a country "in which the fun-damental principle of religious liberty is violated as flagrantly and as inhu-manely as it has been in Germany."[8]

Jewish newspapers encouraged Jewish athletes to boycott the games. The California *Jewish Voice* paid special attention to Sam Balter, the great UCLA basketball star who had been chosen to play for the United States. Claiming that Balter admitted that he might be guided by public opinion in making his decision, the paper invited its readers to express their views. Despite the fact that "approximately 80 percent of the letters urged and begged Balter not to go," Sammy chose to play. Reporting on the news, the *Voice* deplored the deci-sion, noting that "in troubled times like these, we sorely need captains who will represent us as a proud and justice-loving race. Sam had the opportunity to act as a spokesman for his brother Jews, but the attitude he took banishes all such high office." In similar tones, Henry Levy of the *American Hebrew* reported the "disheartening" news that Balter, along with Harold Isaccson, an equestrian, and Norman Armitage, a fencer, had joined the U.S. Olympic team. "These three," Levy added, "comprise, I hope, the entire Jewish rep-resentation on the 1936 American Olympic team. Three are enough black sheep."[9]

As it turned out, Levy's count was off in more ways than one. Six Jewish athletes became members of the 1936 U.S. Olympic team. Joining Glickman and Balter were Sam Stoller, a sprinter, Morris Doob, a member of the pistol team; David Mayor, a weightlifter; and Herman Goldberg, a baseball player. Recently interviewed about his experiences in Germany, Goldberg recalls that he and some of his Jewish teammates did talk about the boycott but decided not to participate in it unless the whole team stayed home. "We were really American athletes of Jewish religion . . . not Jewish ballplayers" or "Jewish sprinters," he explains, who were "selected . . . to represent our country."[10]

Glickman offered other reasons for his decision. Excited about his track successes during his freshman year at Syracuse, Marty realized that he had a chance to make the Olympic team. Although well aware of the boycott movement, he chose to ignore it. Glickman's desire to compete won out over political considerations. As he tells it, "for purely selfish reasons I chose to participate . . . in the Olympic games. . . . I wanted to be on the Olympic team. . . . it was my ambition. Any athlete wants to be at the top and make the Olympic team. Holy Gee! It was my goal." As he tells it "I qualified my desire . . . and my actual drive to be on the Olympic team in Nazi Germany by rationalizing that if a Jew could make the Olympic team and run in Germany and win, then he would help disprove this myth of Nazi Aryan supremacy." Glickman never seriously considered boycotting the Olympics. Nor was he ever approached by anyone involved in the boycott movement to drop out of the Olympic trials or the games or to participate in the World Athletic Labor Carnival, an alternative protest competition organized by Jewish labor groups and held in New York in August 1936.[11]

Although Marty appreciated that anti-Semitism existed in Germany he had a naïve sense of its dimensions. Germany, he believed,

> a few years before Kristallnacht, a few years before the war, was like America in terms of anti-Semitism, with its quotas for medical schools, with its difficulty in getting into some schools, with its restriction of country clubs, with all the bigotry that existed in America at that time towards Jews. . . . that was the feeling I had. There was bigotry and anti-Semitism all over in Germany. You live with it.

Although it is unfair to expect from an 18-year-old college freshman what governments throughout the world failed to acknowledge, Glickman was wrong. Almost a year before the summer games opened in Berlin, the Nazis had enacted the Nuremberg Laws, which deemancipated Jews, barring them from citizenship, with all its rights and protections. Already the forerunners of Treblinka and Auschwitz existed. If Marty had been more aware of Nazi reality, what happened to him in Berlin would not have shocked him. As it was, his experience in making the United States Olympic team served as appropriate prelude to his August in the Third Reich.

Long before Coca-Cola and other corporate sponsors began underwriting American Olympians, the AOC arranged tryouts for the team in ways to raise money to send its athletes to Berlin. Hoping to come up with the estimated $38,500 to send the men's track and field squad, its selection committee arranged for a graduated series of competitions culminating in the final trials to be held in New York in late July 1935. Glickman participated in this process, qualifying for one of three regional semi-final trails held on June 26 and 27 at Harvard Stadium in Cambridge, Massachusetts. There, representing New York's Grand Street Boys Club, Glickman won the 100-meter race in a time of 10.5 seconds, turning back Ben Johnson, Columbia University's great black sprinter, and two other competitors.[12]

The final trials were held in early July, in New York's sweltering summer heat, under the shadows of the Triborough Bridge at the city's newly constructed Randall's Island Stadium before some 10,000 people. Marty finished third in his preliminary heat behind the incomparable Jesse Owens. Along with six other runners, he qualified for the final of the 100-meter run. His competition included Jesse Owens, the world's fastest man, from Ohio State; Ralph Metcalfe of Marquette, a silver medalist in the 1932 Olympic games; California's Mack Robinson, Jackie Robinson's older brother and another veteran from the 1932 Olympic games; Frank Wykoff, who had appeared in three previous Olympics, and Foy Draper, both from the University of Southern California; and Sam Stoller, an outstanding Jewish runner from the University of Michigan. All seven were guaranteed spots on the U.S. Olympic track team. Supposedly, the top three finishers in the 100-meter final would run the same race in Berlin, and the others would make up the 400-meter relay team.[13]

In an era before starting blocks and tartan tracks, Marty Glickman recalls the race:

> With my little garden trowel I started to dig my starting holes and looked to see who was on either side of me. To my right in lane 6 was . . . Metcalfe. To my left was Jesse Owens. . . . I trembled as I scraped at the cinders to firm up my holes and my legs quivered as I backed in and crouched down in the sprinter's start position to test the holes. The seven of us now stood in front of our places waiting for Johnny McHugh to call us to our marks. He had started many of my schoolboy races and all of the Madison Square Garden indoor sprints. "To your marks," he barked, and I started to place my left foot against the back wall of my front hole. With the weight on my right leg my left knee began shaking so badly I could not put it in place. I stood there shaking, bent half way over. The others were now in position. Frightened, I looked up to my right at McHugh, who was staring at me. His face softened and he called, "Everybody up." . . . McHugh called me over. "Take your time, Marty, be easy, calm down . . . jog up and back a bit." I thanked him with my eyes. Moments later he called us to the mark again. This time I could get into my holes. I was conscious of the two dark, muscular bodies alongside. "Get set!" I leaned up and forward, most of my weight now on my finger tips, all of me straining for the sound of the gun. It must have gone off because I was driving down the straightaway between Owens and Metcalfe. We were even at 10 yards, then 20 yards as we gradually rose to full sprinting form. I was not aware of running; I was moving along between them, with them. At 40 yards, they began to edge away from me. I was aware of digging harder, trying to stay with them. At 60 yards I saw the others. Owens and Metcalfe were out of reach, the rest were somewhere alongside. The tape was coming up and I leaned towards it, yearning for it. Then it was over and I looked right and

looked left. On my right Stoller and Robinson were in back of me. To my left, Wykoff . . . was with me and Draper was behind. "I'm third," I thought, "I'm third"—but I couldn't be sure. . . . I knew Owens and Metcalfe were one, two and I knew I wasn't last.

Ted Husing, the well-known sportscaster covering the trials for his radio audience, concurred with Glickman's initial judgment and called "the kid from Brooklyn" over to interview him as the third-place finisher. As Glickman recalls, however, Husing stopped in mid-sentence when he realized that the judges had moved Wykoff into third. After interviewing the California runner, Husing introduced Glickman as the fourth-place finisher but again changed his call when the judges placed Draper ahead of Glickman and moved him down to fifth position.

Viewing films of the event years later, Glickman has no doubt that he finished at least a yard ahead of Draper and in a virtual dead heat with Wykoff. He blames the decision to drop him to fifth on the unfair pressure that Dean Cromwell, the head track coach at USC as well as the assistant coach of the 1936 American Olympic track team, put on the judges to place his California runners ahead of him.

IV

Similar explanations have been offered to explain why Marty Glickman and Sam Stoller, both Jews, were denied the opportunity at the last minute to compete for the United States in the 400-meter relay race in Berlin. Although aware of them, Marty Glickman rejects them all. For him, anti-Semitism and international sports politics, not favoritism, combined to deny him his place in Olympic history.

Confused about what happened at Randalls Island but with little time to think about it, Glickman still anticipated travelling to Europe and competing on the 400-meter relay team in Berlin. Only three days after the conclusion of the trials, on July 15, with Marty and the U.S. Olympic team aboard, the S.S. *Manhattan* set out across the Atlantic for Bremerhaven. Arriving at the Bonn Hotel after a train ride from Hamburg to Berlin, the American squad, the men wearing blue blazers and straw hats, were met by a huge welcoming committee and the press. In the crowd, a man whose name he no longer remembers tapped him on the shoulder and asked him if he was Marty Glickman and if he was Jewish. Within a few moments Glickman learned that the man, also an American Jew, had come to Germany to attend medical school after having been denied admission to American schools. Marty remembers asking him about anti-Semitism in Germany and was told that although "everyone is on his best behavior" because of the Olympics, "in normal times, in the small communities, it can be difficult for the Jews. In the big cities, you don't see much." Although not accurate about what was really going on in Germany, the response only confirmed Glickman's belief that the situation of Jews in the United States and in Germany was similar.

Over the next two weeks, while American sprinters, led by Jesse Owens, dominated the 100-, 200-, 400-, and 800-meter runs, Marty practiced passing the baton with Draper, Wykoff, and Stoller in preparation for the 400-meter relay scheduled for August 8. According to the *New York Times,* although Owens had hoped to run a leg in the 400-meter, Lawson Robertson, the track coach at the University of Pennsylvania and head coach of the U.S. Olympic track squad, felt that Owens had done his share. As the *Times* reported it, Glickman, Stoller, and Draper were "certainties" to run, with Wykoff the likely addition.[14]

That's certainly how Marty felt. "For the ten days or so we were there before the race, we practiced passing the baton every day. Sam and I along with Foy Draper and Frank Wykoff. . . . Sam was the fastest starter, I had power down the straightaway, Foy could run the turn the best, and Frank was the seasoned veteran of three Olympic games. That is the way we practiced and were coached."

On the morning of August 8, the day qualifying trials for the 400-meter relay were set, the track squad met for a team meeting. Glickman expected a strategy session and final pep talk before the biggest athletic moment in his young life but instead learned that he and Stoller would be replaced on the relay team by Jesse Owens and Ralph Metcalfe. In disbelief he listened to Robertson's explanation for the change: rumors had it that the Germans had been hiding their best sprinters for the 400 meter in order to upset the heavily favored American team and he was taking no chances. Metcalfe and Owens had finished one-two in the 100-meter run and would be added to the squad to guarantee victory.[15]

Interviewed years later about the episode, Jesse Owens believed that Stoller and Glickman deserved the opportunity to compete. Recalling the team meeting, Owens recalls speaking out and urging the coaches to replace him with Sam Stoller. Both Frank Wykoff and Ralph Metcalfe remember things differently, insisting that Owens privately lobbied the coaches for the chance to compete for a fourth gold medal. Nor do they recall him openly questioning the decision to drop Stoller and Glickman. Here, their own memories diverge. Metcalfe, who went on to become a Democratic congressman from Illinois, recalls that although he deserved a spot on the relay team because he had the fastest finish, he openly protested the decision to exclude Stoller and Glickman at the team meeting. Wykoff recalls that the 400-meter relay team originally contained himself, Metcalfe, Stoller, and Glickman. Convinced that they could have set a world's record because they had practiced baton-passing, he remembers feeling "very bad" about the last-minute changes. As he put it, "down in my heart, I think it was done the way it was because of the Jewish thing. I'm sorry but I believe that."[16]

The two Jewish runners, the only members of the U.S. Olympic track and field team who did not get a chance to compete in Berlin, offered their own versions of events. Stoller, who received the disappointing news on his 21st birthday, declared that he would never run again. Although the Michigan senior reneged on his vow and went on to win the NCAA 100-meter championship, there is no doubt that his experience in Berlin was devastating.

Excerpts from a diary that he kept there show Stoller, buoyed by the assurances of Lawton Robertson, confident of his place on the relay squad. Four days before the team meeting on August 8, Robertson told him that he was in and Foy Draper was out. According to the diary, Draper, anxious to keep his place on the team, recognized what was going on and proposed that the white members of the squad "protest against running the relay with Negroes," an idea which Stoller rejected.[17]

Although Stoller's account does not offer any explicit interpretation of subsequent events, his diary entries suggest he believed that anti-Semitism had nothing to do with the decision. As he observed at the time, Draper urged Cromwell, his college coach, to intercede with Robertson and replace Stoller with the California runner. Cromwell himself, according to Stoller, called this interpretation into question on board ship as the U.S. Olympic team returned home. Seeking out Stoller, Cromwell assured him that he had "warned Robertson that if I didn't run there would be hell to pay in the U.S. He also said that he wanted an all-white relay team. He put the blame entirely on Robertson for my not running." Stoller doubted Cromwell's explanation. In his last diary entry about the incident, he added that Robertson admitted to him that he had "made a terrible mistake not letting me run—in place of Metcalfe!"[18]

Stoller's private explanation matched his public pronouncements. Two days after the race, in a story headlined "Stoller Declares He Will Quit Track," the New York Times noted that the Michigan senior was so upset by the way Robertson and Cromwell handled matters that he planned to give up running. Denying that "there was the slightest question of prejudice involved," Stoller underlined "the shock" it was "to get the bad news after being assured on Saturday morning that I was certain to compete." Claiming that he, Glickman, Draper, and Wykoff "were certain to win regardless of the opposition," he expressed dismay and confusion over the unfair treatment he had received.[19]

Several weeks later, on board the S.S. Roosevelt bound for the United States, Stoller expanded his version of the events in an interview with Bernard Postal for a story that appeared in the Detroit Jewish Chronicle. Asked if he felt that he was kept off the relay team because he was Jewish, Stoller rejected the argument. "I was given a raw deal," he countered. "The real reason why Glickman and I were dropped was the influence of other coaches who wanted their pupils to run."[20]

Although the Chronicle did suggest the possibility that "anti-Semitic prejudice" may have contributed to the exclusion of Glickman and Stoller, it accepted the Michigan runner's conclusions, noting in passing that Stoller, the son of a Cincinnati real estate man, "had little contact with Jews" and grew up in a home with a German Protestant stepmother. The paper also reported that Glickman subscribed to the same explanation, specifically that Cromwell had played favorites and given his Southern California runners the chance to run because they were his boys.[21]

I asked Marty Glickman if the Chronicle's account accurately reflects what he felt in 1936. Although he doesn't deny the possibility of favoritism, he believes today, as he did then, that anti-Semitism—Brundage's, Cromwell's, and Hitler's—was at the heart of the decision to deny him and Stoller the chance for Olympic glory. With a little bit of hindsight, Glickman correctly notes that both Cromwell and Brundage were pro-Nazi sympathizers and members of the America First committee. Brundage especially was outspoken throughout the '30s in support of the Nazi cause and accepted Nazi theories about Jews. As Glickman asserts, in games organized and promoted by the Nazis to demonstrate their superiority to the world,

> American black athletes were making shambles of the claim of Nazi Aryan supremacy. Owens had won the 100 and 200, Archie Williams the 400, John Woodruff the 800, Cornelius Johnson the high jump, Jesse the long jump—and all of them blacks. . . . Avery Brundage and Dean Cromwell and others who I took to be American Nazi sympathizers did not wish to further embarass their Nazi friends by having Jewish athletes stand on the winning podium to be cheered by 120,000 Germans in the Olympic stadium and further millions see and hear this through motion picture newsreels and radio broadcasts around the world.

Even today it is easy for Marty to recall the anger and disappointment he experienced 50 years ago and his firm belief that anti-Semitism was its cause. Astonished by Robertson's announcement at the team meeting and remembering himself as "a brash eighteen-year-old," he reminded Robertson that the best German sprinter, Erich Borchmeyer, had finished a poor fifth in the 100-meter final and that any of the seven American runners could beat him. "Coach," he added, "you get to be a world class sprinter by running in world class competition. You can't hide world class sprinters. . . . We'll win by fifteen yards, no matter who runs." After Robertson rejected his arguments, Glickman recalls, Jesse Owens spoke up and questioned the coach's decision. "Coach, let Marty and Sam run," Owens countered. "I've already won three gold medals. I've had it. I'm tired. They deserve to run. Let them run." Dean Cromwell, however, whose own college runners remained on the 400-meter relay squad, pointed his finger at Owens and told him to do as he was told. Vividly recalling the end of the meeting, Glickman recounts: "Jesse looked at him and was quiet. I said, 'Coach, you know that Sam and I are the only two Jews on the track team. If we don't run there's bound to be a lot of criticism back home.' Cromwell said, 'We'll take our chances.' We walked out of the room in silence. The Americans won as I watched the race from the stands."

Led by Owens and Metcalfe, the American squad swept their heat in world record time of 40 seconds and then captured the final with a time of 39.8. As Glickman predicted, the German team finished a distant fourth, 15 yards behind the Americans. Marty watched the race along with 120,000 other spectators in the magnificent stadium the Germans had built to celebrate Aryan supremacy. Surrounded by huge black swastikas jutting out from the walls and with Hitler and Goebbels no more than 100 feet away, he remembers feeling relief from not having to worry about dropping the baton or running out of a lane, a sense of enormous loss ("something terrible had happened and I wasn't even sure what the hell it was"), and anger at having been denied the opportunity to compete. "Those liars, Cromwell and Robertson . . . those fucking liars"—those were the words that the young Jewish athlete mouthed as he saw the Germans fall far behind the field. Watching his American teammates mount the victory stand and listening to the playing of the "Star Spangled Banner" as they received the accolades of the crowd, he thought, "I ought to be out there, I should be out there . . . and I'm not."

The decision to remove Glickman and Stoller from the race caused some discussion at home. John Kieran, a reporter who covered the games, noted the world record time set by the American team, applauded Cromwell's decision, and dismissed the possibility of anti-Semitism as a motive for dropping the Jewish runners. As he put it, the substitution of two blacks for two Jews was "a transfer that would not have sent Herr Hitler off into raptures of delight, even if he had paid any attention to it."[22] Commenting on the removal of Stoller and Glickman on the day of the trials, the *New York Times* made no mention of the Jewish issue but predicted criticism from "those Americans who feel that as many of the boys as possible should get a chance to compete."[23] Although the day after the race Lawson Robertson privately apologized to Glickman and admitted he had made a mistake by removing him, publicly he and Cromwell defended their decision and denied that anti-Semitism influenced it. Robertson told one *Times* reporter that although he hoped "to let everyone run . . . we're here to win all the events possible . . . my job is to put the best possible team in the race." Although he did not mention either Stoller or Glickman by name, Avery Brundage, in his final report for the American Olympic Committee, concurred with the track coach. Labelling as "absurd . . . an erroneous report . . . that two athletes had been dropped from the American relay team because of their religion," Brundage argued that the two had been taken to the Olympics as substitutes, having come in fifth and sixth in the Olympic trials. The winning relay team, he noted, included the top four finishers in the trials. The fact that they broke the world record in Berlin, Brundage concluded, only "proved the wisdom of adhering to the rules."[24]

The American Jewish press offered mixed reactions to the affair. Summarizing American Jewish accomplishment in the world of sport in December 1936, the *American Hebrew* simply reported that the decision to bar Stoller and Glickman from the race, despite their "magnificent records . . . as outstanding sprinters . . . resulted in much controversy and hard feeling." Paul Freed of the California *Jewish Voice* was less kind to "our staunch advocates of Judaism." Although he agreed that they had been unjustly deprived of their right to run, he insisted that those "two 'kikes'" had no right to their outrage or pain; "petty" indeed compared with the great wrongs dealt their fellow-coreligionists by a barbarous group of brutes." As Freed put it, "they had a chance to show their protest, by not taking the trip to Germany. By sacrificing their honor for a free boat ride, they have sacrificed all right to sympathy."[25]

Historians who have written about the 1936 games, while avoiding any judgments about Glickman and Stoller, have been no more conclusive than any of the participants in the controversy about why the two athletes were not allowed to race. Rejecting both anti-Semitism and claims of favoritism, Richard Mandell suggests that the "badly timed" substitutions indicate an intense desire for victory and new records on the part of the American coaches that "overwhelmed customary standards of sportsmanship, international morality, and the feelings of individuals." William O. Johnson, Jr., who offers the most detailed description of the events and the views of those involved, refuses to give his own interpretation. Most recently, William Baker, in his fine biography of Jesse Owens, argues that while Marty Glickman's assertions about Brundage and Cromwell are quite plausible, they are difficult to prove. More likely, he suggests, Cromwell's desire to take care of his own athletes coupled with pervasive anti-Semitism both in the United States and among the Olympic establishment made it possible to exclude the Jewish runners with little fear of public outcry.[26]

No doubt a variety of considerations contributed to the final outcome. Whether or not Avery Brundage had anything to do with the decision, there is no question that he was an ardent friend of Germany and often openly anti-Semitic. There is also reason to take Cromwell and Robertson at their word. Coaches of the largest track and field squad ever assembled by the United States and participating in games openly portrayed as a struggle between democracy and fascism, their paramount concern was American victory. Thus, it is understandable, if not praiseworthy, that they chose to go with proven Olympic winners in the 400-meter race. Nor is it possible to discount Cromwell's desire to make sure his Southern California runners maximized their opportunities for Olympic gold. For our purposes, however, the real question is not why things happened but what Marty Glickman believed to be true, how that perception impacted his life, and what his story offers about the shaping of an American Jewish identity.

V

The story of the 400-meter relay controversy made American sports pages for a few days. It lingered a bit longer in the Jewish press. But it hardly warranted sustained attention even there in the face of stories about relief efforts for European Jews, criticism of the Nuremberg Laws, and concern for Palestinian Jews that dramatized more poignantly and tragically the precarious nature of Jewish survival. Except for a brief moment, it had little immediate effect on Glickman's own future.

Marty returned home after competing successfully in a series of European track meets. He went back to Syracuse, played football in the fall, and returned home for Christmas vacation to prepare for an appearance in the Sugar Bowl track meet scheduled for January 1, 1937. After one too many sessions on the snow and ice of Coney Island's boardwalk, a track friend suggested that he practice with him at the indoor track of the New York Athletic Club in Manhattan. Glickman eagerly accepted the offer but never got past the lobby. As he recalls it, Paul Pilgrim, the club's athletic director who knew Marty, refused to allow him to use the facilities because he was Jewish. Shocked and enraged at this injustice Glickman has refused to this day to participate in any activity of the club, despite many subsequent offers and assurances that the club is no longer restrictive.[27]

Aside from this reminder of his summer in Berlin, the anger and turmoil Marty experienced there soon disappeared. Studies, track, football, and the chance to start a career in sports broadcasting filled his time. Capitalizing on his celebrity status as college football player and not as spurned Jewish Olympian, Glickman became involved in radio in the middle of his junior year. After a spectacular game at tailback against Cornell in which he returned a punt for a touchdown, intercepted two passes, and made a couple of touchdown-saving tackles, a local haberdasher, eager to cash in on his fame, asked him to do a 15-minute radio sports program that he sponsored. "You don't want me," Marty replied, "I'm nervous, I stutter and stammer, I've never been on the air before." He said, "I'll pay you fifteen dollars a broadcast." Marty said, "I'll take it."[28]

At a time when football players went both ways and the NCAA did not care about how athletes spent their spare time, Glickman continued his apprenticeship in broadcasting and his athletic career at Syracuse. He graduated in 1939, and except for service as a lieutenant in the Marines during World War II, has been involved in sports broadcasting ever since.

Initially Marty continued both careers simultaneously, playing semi-professional basketball in Syracuse and football for the Jersey City Giants, the American Association farm team of the New York NFL franchise, while working as a part-time salesman at Gimbel's department store and as an unpaid gopher for Bert Lee and Dick Fishell at WHN in New York. There, for two free box-seat tickets to Yankee games on Sunday, Marty ran errands and helped prepare dramatized 15-minute recreations of the Yankees' games for their nightly sports shows.

Although Glickman eventually got on the air with his own late-night sports summary program—he was paid $50 a week—and as commentator on broadcasts of Madison Square Garden's indoor track events, his big breakthrough and first major contribution to sports broadcasting occurred on his return from World War II in 1945. Glickman notes that "in those days broadcasters came to prominence by doing certain sports. Red Barber and Mel Allen were baseball announcers. Clem McCarthy was the race track announcer, Don Dumphy was the boxing announcer and Bill Stern and Ted Husing did football. Nobody did basketball, and I was determined to do it." Still in Marine uniform awaiting discharge, Glickman did the first broadcasts of college basketball doubleheaders from Madison Square Garden in 1945–46 and the following year became the voice of the New York Knickerbockers. His association with the Knicks lasted for 20 years, during which time he honed his skills and perfected a style that made him one of America's premier sports announcers.

Two years after he began doing Knickerbocker games, Glickman started broadcasting football games for the NFL's New York Giants. From a perch in the Polo Grounds scoreboard accessible only by crawling on a catwalk on his hands and knees to his days at Yankee Stadium Marty has covered the Giants and the NFL from a time when games barely attracted 15,000 spectators to the celebrated sudden-death 1958 NFL championship game between the New York Giants and the Baltimore Colts and on to the present, when the Super Bowl has become the major sporting event of the year.

Based in New York and not interested in national network affiliation, Glickman also found time to broadcast a wide range of events. Aside from doing New York City high-school basketball and football games, Marty put in a 17-year stint as the track announcer at Yonkers Raceway. He also has covered the New York City marble-shooting championships, six-day bicycle races, and professional wrestling. By his own account, describing the Ringling Brothers and Barnum and Bailey Circus to an audience of blind people was his toughest show.

Although Marty still does an occasional Rose Bowl or New York Jets football game, his involvement in sports broadcasting since the early 1970s has focused on two different concerns that underline his presence and significance in the history of the profession: cable television and teaching the art of sportscasting.

Today as a consultant, and originally as its first sports director, Marty developed sports programming and broadcasting for HBO, the first major cable network. He was the first person seen and heard on HBO when, in November 1972, he covered a hockey game from Madison Square Garden to all of its 365 subscribers in Wilkes-Barre, Pennsylvania. In addition to doing the play-by-play of basketball games and covering rodeos for the network, he traveled throughout the United States talking to sports entrepreneurs and testifying before the FCC as part of a successful effort to make sports an integral part of cable television.

Glickman has also served an important role as a teacher of his craft. Marv Albert, NBC's up-and-coming star of a new generation of broadcasters, recalls that as a teenager he began learning his trade by paying rapt attention to this master's voice as he listened to Knickerbocker and Giant broadcasts. Involved informally throughout his career in helping ex-athletes become sportcasters, since 1982 Marty has served as coach and critic of NBC television's cast of professional football commentators. Concerned that sportscasters "talk too much," he tells them to "speak up, keep it simple, study the game, and listen to your partner." He also helped prepare Mary Lou Retton for her work as NBC's gymnastics analyst at the 1988 Olympic games.

Although this behind-the-scenes work rarely receives notice, Marty's recent tutelage of Gayle Sierens, a news anchor in Tampa, Florida, who became the first woman to give play-by-play commentary on an NFL telecast, made *TV Guide* and newspapers throughout the country, underlining his continuing presence as a significant figure in the history of sports broadcasting.

Even today, he continues to experience success and satisfaction in ways that fulfill his father's hopes for his son.

Marty Glickman, the child of Rumanian immigrants, made his mark as an American in the world of sports. He did so first as a young track and football star at a time when participation in sport was actively promoted as one means of transforming the children of immigrants into productive American citizens and in a family setting that offered support and opportunity, as his father put it, "to be an American." Glickman clearly shares his father's vision. He childhood hero was the quintessential American muscular Christian, the fictional Frank Merriwell. He is proud of his achievements in athletics and in sports broadcasting and still revels in his father's recognition of his success. When he began his career in broadcasting he rejected the advice of Bill Stern, one of the best-known voices of the airwaves, who suggested that he change his last name to Mann or Manning as Stern had changed his own from Sterngold and as Mel Allen had changed his from Israel. Marty rejected the idea, not only because he was proud of being Jewish but, as he tells it, because "my father was very proud of me . . . and there was no way I wanted him to say, 'Hey, did you hear that fellow on the air, Marty Manning. That's my son.'" For him, his own success story links him as an American to a father whose own accomplishments were clearly mixed.

But there is another link as well, forged unexpectedly through remembrances and experiences in the realm of sport that is crucial to Glickman's own sense of Jewishness. In August 1985, Marty Glickman, successful sportscaster, well-known personality, a man seemingly very comfortable with his life, returned to the Olympic Stadium in Berlin. A friend of Jesse Owens since their days there 50 years earlier and the only white Olympic teammate at Owens's funeral in 1980, the Jewish runner from Brooklyn had come back as a member of the Jesse Owens Foundation to plan a track meet that would honor the memory of his friend's Olympic achievements and raise money to help send needy children to college. The experience, much to his surprise, vividly brought back the emotions of his youth:

> As I walked into the stadium, I began to get so angry. I began to get so mad. It shocked the hell out of me that this thing of forty-nine years ago could still evoke this anger. I mean I was fucking mad. I was cussing. I was with people, colleagues of mine, and I was cussing. I was really amazed at myself, at this feeling of anger. Not about the German Nazis. . . . That's a given. But anger at Avery Brundage and Dean Cromwell for not allowing an eighteen-year old kid to compete in the Olympic games just because he was Jewish.

Memory of that day in 1936 also evokes for him other connections that link him both to his father and to his grandchildren, from first-generation immigrant to fourth-generation assimilated American Jews. Talking about his father in an unpublished account of his life, Glickman introduces his version of the Berlin affair with a story that his father liked to tell about his own childhood. By his own account, Marty's father was the fastest runner in his school back in Iasi, Rumania. One day, at the urging of his friends, he beat the mayor's son in a foot race at a school picnic. "In telling the story," Glickman adds, "my father, a short, husky, balding man would smile ruefully, chuckle and then say, 'I won the race, but the medal they gave to the Mayor's son. Me, they gave two pennies.' My father and I," Glickman concludes, "we didn't get our medals." Concluding his account of his experiences at the Nazi Olympics, Glickman observes that "sometimes I . . . feel disappointed that I can't show an Olympic gold medal to my grandchildren. Almost always, however, "I immediately feel guilty for placing value on a medal denied me by Nazi sympathizers who cooperated with those who helped create the Holocaust."[29]

An incident that happened to Marty Glickman's father at a schoolboy race in Eastern Europe calls up images of anti-Semitism, pogroms, and flight for survival that are linked to his own experience as a young American runner barred from Olympic competition. It is this Marty remembers when he thinks of his disappointment in not being able to show his grandchildren an Olympic medal. As he tells it, the tinge of guilt he expresses reminds him how trivial his own disappointments are when compared with the need to keep the memory of the Holocaust alive for them, a part of which he experienced in minor key in 1936 and that was rekindled on his return to Berlin in 1985. A man as Jewish as he is American and proud of both, Glickman's Jewish identity, like many of his generation, is bound to an historical memory of struggle and oppression that connects his own life to that of a people who have survived defiantly over the centuries.

These experiences define Marty's involvement as a Jew today. Although not an observant Jew, he is proud of the fact that he never works on the Jewish high holidays and that his two sons were Bar Mitzvahed. Glickman is a strong supporter of Israel, a symbol for him of Jewish peoplehood and survival, and he gives generously of his time and money on its behalf. When he talks before B'nai B'rith fundraisers or American Jewish Committee meetings he speaks of what he knows best—his own Olympic experience and the importance of recognizing the accomplishments of Jewish athletes as acknowledgment of their ability and of their struggle to maintain themselves both as Americans and as Jews.

This message, forged out of Glickman's own past, informs the situation of American Jews today. Jews of Marty Glickman's generation experienced much more immediately than their children or grandchildren the fragility of Jewish survival and the conflict over retaining a sense of Jewishness while proving themselves as Americans. Especially in the 1930s and 1940s these children of immigrants dealt with not only atrocities abroad but also anti-Semitism of all sorts at home.

American Jews today are far more a part of American culture and society than they were when Marty Glickman was growing up. As avenues of economic and social opportunity have become more open, the role of sport, both as a limited arena of mobility for a few individuals and as a vehicle by which a larger Jewish population could forge a strong identification with their own kind who were making it in America, has virtually disappeared. Some fore-casters of American Jewish doom have noted that accompanying these changes has been an increase in intermarriage and a sharp decrease in the number of Jews attending synagogue, observing ritual, and providing a for-mal Jewish education for their children. For them, in the face of worldwide threats to the existence of Judaism and Israel just half a century after the Holo-caust, this image of the culturally assimilated Jew who claims Jewish identity without connection to traditional religious custom and teaching is simply not sufficient to insure Jewish survival.[30]

Marty Glickman's story suggests another possibility that reverberates with the ideas of a number of Jewish scholars who remain optimistic about the future of American Jewry even in the face of this relentless process of Amer-icanization. Herbert Feingold, for one, argues that a corporate historical mem-ory of the struggle to survive gives American Jews "a cultural identity not rooted in territorial space . . . a residual feeling of belonging to the Jewish people" despite their assimilation as Americans, a duality that makes them simultaneously part of and separate from the American scene. For Feingold, this identity and the vitality of American Jewry is not measured solely by the number of Jews attending synagogue or marrying within the faith. Just as important is this connection to a larger historical past, most obviously dis-played by concern for Soviet Jews, by a growing interest in keeping alive memories of the Holocaust, or by support of Israel—the symbol of Jewish sep-arateness, peoplehood, and survival.[31]

Marty Glickman is no more a Jewish scholar than Sammy Kaplan, Hank Greenberg, Benny Leonard, members of the Basketball Fraternity, Al Rosen, Barney Ross, Benny Friedman, or Marshall Goldberg. None of these men con-sciously developed or articulated a philosophy of how to be Jewish as part of their life's work. But memories of their own everyday experiences growing up as second-generation American Jews reinforced their connection with this larger global historical memory. More by example than by design, their actions and deeds as visible Jews in the world of sport have had an important impact on the shaping of an American Jewish consciousness that combines American pride with a fierce, even physical commitment to the survival of all Jewish people.

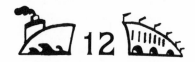

"Where Have You Gone, Hank Greenberg?": Sport and the American Jewish Experience Since World War II

IN December 1957, Andy Cohen became manager of the New York Yankees' Denver farm team, taking over for Ralph Houk, who had been called up to coach in New York. Reporting on the news for the *New York Times,* John Drebinger informed his readers that in 1928 Cohen had replaced the great Rogers Hornsby as the New York Giants' second baseman. Nowhere in the story did Drebinger mention that Cohen was Jewish or the tumultuous response he received from New York's Jewish population at the time. Instead the story line focused on Cohen's new assignment, one "scarcely . . . less formidable" than replacing Hornsby—taking over for "Major Houk."[1]

Drebinger's sense of history is at once both wrong and telling. Managing a Yankee farm team in Denver was not more challenging than taking over for a baseball legend still at the peak of his game. Especially so when Cohen's identification as a Jew by the press and by New Yorkers in 1928 was as much an issue as his baseball prowess. Thirty years later, at least as Drebinger understood his audience, no one really cared that Cohen was Jewish. Baseball, plain and simple, was the bottom line.

Over a decade later, a different twist on the same tale appeared in another *New York Times* column. Writing in 1972, David Anderson reminded his readers of the irony of another Jewish ballplayer's success. Talking about Ron Blomberg, he noted that for decades "the Yankees have been searching for a Jewish star . . . and now that they have one they're scheduled to move into Shea Stadium for the next two seasons while Yankee Stadium is being refurbished." Even more to the point, as Anderson told Blomberg, much of that Bronx Jewish audience once sought after by the Yankees had vacated the borough for the suburbs. The young slugger's boast that he "would bring them back" hardly was fulfilled by any Jewish gentrification of the South Bronx.[2]

A year before Anderson's column appeared, Haskell Cohen, publicist for the National Basketball Association (NBA) and columnist for the Jewish Telegraphic Agency, chose his annual collegiate Jewish All-America basketball team. Remarking on how difficult it was to make selections 30 years earlier when there were so many fine Jewish ballplayers, he bemoaned the fact that it was still problematic, but for an entirely different reason. As Cohen told his readers, "let's face it folks, there just aren't many good Jewish basketball players around anymore." Desperate for Jewish talent, Cohen even called the coach of a Texas school on the suspicion that a player's name on its roster sounded Jewish. The boy turned out to be a cooperative Catholic who told his coach that "if it will help any" he had no objection to being included on the squad.[3]

Cohen's explanation for the decline of Jewish basketball talent was straightforward. He observed that the decay began when second- and third-generation Jewish families began the trek from the city to the suburbs. Expanding on this analysis, one sportswriter explained why, by the 1970s, there were so few professional Jewish athletes. "In most Jewish families," R. D. Rosen suggested, "being a pro athlete ranks low on the scale of Significant Things, somewhere between the priesthood and polo. When they communicate their career preferences to their children, Jewish mothers and fathers are seldom heard to say, 'Sonny, your mother and I feel you should spend a little less time with the science club and a little more time working on your reverse dribble.'"[4]

Jewish youngsters and their parents, including those who fled the Bronx and other cities for the suburbs and who hoped to become doctors, lawyers, or corporate executives, did not abandon all interest in sport after World War II. The burgeoning sports programs of today's Jewish community centers testify to a continued Jewish involvement. So too does a 1980 American Council of Education survey of college freshmen which shows that 42 percent of Jewish students rate themselves above average in athletic ability. This figure, 2 percent higher than for non-Jewish students was up over 50 percent among Jewish students surveyed in 1970. Although too old to participate in this survey, my own memories confirm these statistics. Growing up in Brooklyn I played every sport imaginable with my cousin Jeffrey Goldberg, Richie Steinberg, Kenny Birnbaum, Burtie Whiteman, and my other Jewish friends in playgrounds and streets filled with Jewish youngsters whose passion was sport. Some of us even won a junior high school letter at P.S. 234 for being members of the only class ever to win school championships in touch football, basketball, softball, and punchball in a single year. Thanksgiving football classics known as "Bierman Bowls," pitting my cousin and myself against my older brother and his friend Steve Bierman, remained annual events on my athletic calendar until cancelled by my brother when Jeffrey and myself proved too much to handle. For readers more convinced by rich description than by statistics or nostalgia, Philip Roth's depiction of one fictional surburban New Jersey Jewish household from his novella *Goodbye Columbus* should suffice. The Patimkins not only produced an Ohio State basketball player whose wet jockstraps decorate the family's bathroom. They lived in a virtual gymnasium. Their backyard, as described by one character, contained its own basketball court and twin oak trees that might better be called "sporting-goods trees. Beneath their branches, like fruit dropping from their limbs, were two irons, a golf ball, a tennis can, a baseball bat, basketball, a first-baseman's glove, and what was apparently a riding crop."[5]

These vignettes capture the major tendencies of the Jewish experience in American sport since the close of World War II. More so with every passing decade and in virtually every measurable way, the number of Jews participating in organized intercollegiate or professional athletics, especially team sports, declined dramatically. With few exceptions, those who have competed rarely received either the amount or the kind of attention accorded Jewish athletes who made their mark during the first half of the 20th century. Increasingly, Jewish-Americans have engaged in a wide range of recreational sport, expending far more time and money than their parents or grandparents on such diversions. Often, this activity takes place at modern Jewish community centers which rely on their sports programs to attract new members. There are even occasional instances where Jews who honed their tennis and golf skills at country clubs and Jewish community centers have made their mark at center court at the U.S. Open or on the Ladies' or Men's Professional Golf Association's tours. For the most part, however, accounts of these accomplishments rarely mention any Jewish connection.

Both as actual experience and as symbol, sport's role as middle ground in the experience of American Jews after World War II no longer carries the same meaning it did for earlier generations. As both Haskell Cohen and R. D. Rosen suggest and as sociologists and economists will attest, the incredible degree to which second-generation American Jews successfully participated in the wide range of opportunities offered by post–world war economic development and education played a significant role in this transformation. As Jewish economic and social mobility surpassed even their wildest expectations, increasing numbers of Jews built their own versions of the American Dream that included abandonment of the urban, ethnic communities of their youth. Equally important, they have come of age in a society seemingly more tolerant of ethnic diversity; one in which everyday attachments to their own ethnicity increasingly diminished with the simple passage of time and the death of grandparents and parents. In such a setting, they have had less need to seek out ethnic heroes like a Hank Greenberg or a Barney Ross to prove to themselves that they too might succeed or to defend themselves against charges that Jews were too different and exotic to become full-fledged Americans. Their very success as Americans has also provided them with the means to define their Jewish connections in new ways—through support of Israel and by identifying with new physical heroes who prove their mettle on Middle Eastern battlefields in defense of Israel rather than on the gridiron, the baseball diamond, or in the ring. Exploring the meaning of these changing pat-

terns of Jewish involvement in sport over the last 40 years reaffirms its importance for understanding the American Jewish experience.

I

Hank Greenberg's sons both went to Yale. Glen, the oldest, played football
there. Steven played soccer and captained the baseball team. In 1970, his
senior year, the *Sporting News* reported that Steven hoped to follow "in his
father's footsteps" by becoming a major-league baseball player. Although he
didn't make it as a player, today Greenberg serves as major-league baseball's
deputy commissioner. Then and now, baseball's "bible" did not mention that
Steve was Jewish nor his father's critical role as American Jewish hero in the
1930s and 1940s. Several years earlier, preparing to do a story on Glen, a New
Haven reporter discovered that the young man had designated his religious
preference on Yale's athletic department biographical file as "Congregationalist." Confused, the reporter asked, "You're Hank Greenberg's son. You're
Jewish, aren't you?" To which Glen replied, "I don't know." The young
Greenberg went on to explain that his family did not practice any formal religion and that he had not been Bar Mitzvahed. "Dad never told me I was a Jew.
The closest he came to that was when I reached thirteen years of age and he
gave me a ring. He said, 'This is the ring my father gave to me when I was
thirteen. In the Jewish religion when you turn thirteen you are said to be a
man. And now I pass this ring on to you.'" High school requirements at Ando-
ver demanded that Glen attend chapel and read the New Testament. The
school was Congregationalist and thus his choice when it came time to fill out
publicity forms.[6]

If Hank Greenberg served as a symbol of Jewish pride, accomplishment,
and strength for many second-generation Jews, these stories about his sons
represent something of the distance third-generation American Jews traveled
from the world of their fathers. Diminishing Jewish participation in Hank
Greenberg's game, both as actual experience and as cultural symbol—illustrates the degree to which Jewish-Americans have become more comfortable
with their status as accepted individuals capable of enjoying the full opportunities of American life.

Jewish decline in major-league professional baseball is clearly apparent by
the numbers. During Hank Greenberg's heyday it was not uncommon to find
as many as ten Jewish ballplayers in the majors in any single year. Although
this figure was attained several times during the 1960s, the decades since
World War II generally evidence a gradual decrease. During the 1950s and
1970s no more than six appeared in major-league uniforms in any single season. Through the 1980s the total diminished to two players a year.[7]

Although Jewish boys never flocked to professional baseball in great numbers, differences in background and economic circumstance help explain what
happened following World War II. For the most part, Jewish major leaguers

who played ball between the wars were born between 1900 and 1925. They came from predominantly lower-middle-class or working-class Depression families living in urban Jewish neighborhoods. Those who made it to the majors in more recent times most frequently grew up in suburban middle-class families in a society that offered a wider range of opportunities for education and economic success than existed for earlier generations. Although hardly definitive, incomplete evidence on the education of Jewish professional major leaguers suggests something of their different backgrounds. Of the 54 ball-players born between 1900 and 1925, 19, or 35 percent, attended at least one year of college as compared with 23 of the 30, some 77 percent of those born after 1925.[8]

Broader social and demographic patterns also affected Jewish participation in baseball. Prior to 1945, when Jackie Robinson signed with the Brooklyn Dodgers organization, white ballplayers, Jewish or otherwise, did not have to compete with black or Hispanic talent for the few spots available on major-league teams. And baseball magnates still consciously sought Jewish ballplay-ers as potential drawing-cards for local Jewish audiences. Over time, increased competition from minority ballplayers and the gradual disappearance of Jew-ish neighborhoods diminished the opportunities for Jews to make it in base-ball. Although first-generation immigrant resistance to the athletic interests of their children clearly existed, second-generation young men from working-class backgrounds who grew up in the midst of economic depression and in a society that placed clear restrictions on career opportunities for Jews may have met less resistance in pursuing careers as professional athletes than their more comfortable third-generation peers raised by parents who clearly expected their children to take full advantage of the economic possibilities open to them.

That's how Mike Epstein remembers his struggle to become a major-league baseball player.[9] Born in the Bronx in 1943 in a Jewish neighborhood where his grandparents lived, his family, which he described as upper middle-class, moved to Long Island when he was five. When Mike turned 13, his father, Jack, a manufacturing representative for a women's accessories com-pany, relocated the family to Los Angeles for business reasons. Passionate about his love for sport and competition, Epstein recalls disappointment grow-ing up in the city's Jewish Fairfax section where the aspirations of most of his peers were set on different sights.[10] As he put it, "they didn't have the same desires that I had to excel in sports. They did wind up excelling in a lot of other things, business, medical professions, you know they were professional peo-ple. Me, I wanted to be a ballplayer."

Jack Epstein did not share his son's dream. Mike went to the University of California at Berkeley where he played both football and baseball, majored in social psychology, and graduated in 1964. During his junior year, Tommy LaSorda, now manager of the Los Angeles Dodgers, and then a scout for the team, offered Epstein, who was still a minor, a contract. Mike's father refused to sign it. "He wanted me to be a lawyer," Epstein recalls, "rather than a bum like the rest of the ballplayers." At the least, Mr. Epstein demanded that his son first complete his bachelor's degree so that he would have "something to fall back on."

Mike eventually signed with the Baltimore Orioles, who sent him to their minor-league training facilities in Thomasville, Georgia. Although a large man at 6'3" and 230 pounds, Epstein confronted competition that he had never experienced before—"black kids" bigger than he was "who could throw balls through a wall and could hit them over buildings . . . I mean physical specimens from North Carolina, Tennessee, and Alabama" who, he concluded, had more ability than he did. In fact, Epstein went on to a successful nine-year major league career that included two pennants and one World Series victory with the Oakland Athletics in the early 1970s. Today a successful Colorado cattle rancher, ironically, Epstein believes that his "Jewish side"—a tenacity and perserverance that comes from a people who survive, enabled him to overcome his doubts and make it in the big leagues.

Reminiscent of generational conflict between fathers and sons supposedly more common to an earlier time, Epstein's story, like those of other Jewish ballplayers of his generation, is set in a much different historical context than the one that produced a Hank Greenberg or an Al Rosen. At best, only echoes of past themes reverberate in the lives of these successful third- and fourth-generation American Jews. Whether in the regular or Jewish press, stories about their lives do not touch on accounts of boys turning to the game to escape the working-class poverty of their families, recognition that in some significant way their identity as Jews marked them as ethnic standard bearers or as challengers to racist stereotypes, or appreciation that their success demonstrated the possibilities of assimilation in an open and democratic America. Rarely are the religious affiliations of Jewish ballplayers the concern of sportswriters. Even columns that include these references do not embrace them with the meaning and symbolism common to discussions of Jewish ballplayers a generation earlier. Instead of serving as proof of Jewish normalcy, Jewish desire for assimilation and the openness of American democratic society, or, as in the pages of the Chicago Yiddish press, a call for the development of strong, tough Jews able to insure Jewish survival, most often they simply celebrate expected assimilation and success.

Jackie Robinson's breaking of the color line and the influx of black and Hispanic ballplayers into the major leagues over the next few decades also contributed to the decreasing symbolic importance of Jewish major leaguers. In the midst of the triumphs and tragedies of the civil rights movement, the experience of black ballplayers dominated commentary concerning connections between baseball and the promise of American life for minority groups. Most emphatically, however, the continual economic and social progress of Jewish-Americans in all fields of endeavor made focus on the success of Jewish baseball players, limited as it was, symbolically insignificant.

Signs of these tendencies are apparent as early as the late 1940s and 1950s, when men such as Al Rosen, Cal Abrams, and Sid Gordon still served as Jewish heroes. Offering its opinion on the role of sport in American society, the *Amer-*

ican Hebrew, for instance, in February 1948 suggested to its readers that the history of American sport demonstrates how "America's unrealized ideal of equality is becoming a reality in the sports world." Although it did mention the success of Hank Greenberg as proof of its contention, the column focused primarily on the recent achievements of black athletes—from Jackie Robinson to Levi Jackson, Yale's first "Negro" football captain—for the bulk of its case. Hopefully, it concluded, "millions of sports-lovers" will carry this same spirit into other areas of American life, thus "inspiring further progress towards realization of the American promise: Freedom and equality of opportunity for all."[11] Several months later, in the *Hebrew's* regular column on "Jews and Sports," Paul Gould went one step further. Commenting on the Brooklyn Dodgers' chances to repeat as pennant winners, he noted that a key role would be played by Jake Pitler, who served the "Bums" as first-base coach. "Though Jake is Jewish," Gould noted, "hardly an eyelash will be flickered in his direction. He has become part of the Flatbush scene as much as Ebbets Field itself." In case his point was not well understood, Gould went on to describe Jewish involvement in sport, be it in horse-racing, track and field, football, baseball, or basketball, as "accepted as part and parcel of the American scene." Although not without struggle against "prejudice and bigotry . . . Jews, indeed, have come of age in the sports world . . . pervad[ing] all aspects of competitive pastimes." Their presence, Gould implied, was no longer cause for surprise or special comment.[12]

By the time Mike Epstein and Ron Blomberg arrived on the scene these sentiments were commonplace. Sportswriters did remind readers of past attempts by New York clubs to find a great Jewish ballplayer when Blomberg came to the Yankees in 1971. Little else, however, was said about the Jewish connections of this Atlanta, Georgia, native. Nor did Blomberg do much to attract what remained of an urban Jewish audience. As he told one reporter, "I'm a Southern person . . . I don't think I could live forever in New York; I'd like to have a house someday where I could see trees and grass . . . What I am," he concluded, "is just a kid from a typical middle-class Jewish family in Atlanta."[13]

When the Yankees first acquired Blomberg in the annual free-agent draft in December 1967, sportswriters "promptly tabbed him as 'the new Mike Epstein.'"[14] Significantly, no mention was made of Hank Greenberg as the appropriate touchstone. That literal giant of a former era who came to symbolize Jewish strength and toughness as well as the promise of assimilation scarcely seemed relevant to Blomberg's Jewish-American world of the late 1960s. Rather, the connection was with another large man who lamented the fact that Jewish audiences in cities where he played rarely paid attention to him as a role model or hero.

Part of the problem may have been Epstein's light-hearted public image as "SuperJew," one that he encouraged and appreciated. Tagged with the nickname by a minor-league coach in 1966 who admired the slugger's power, according to one account, Mike "was so enchanted by the sobriquet that he wrote it on his cap and shower shoes." At least for this reporter, Epstein's ability at the plate, which accounted for 30 home runs and a league-leading .338 batting average for Stockton in the California League that year, was not the only reason he deserved his title. Amusingly playing with references that for an earlier generation might have invoked invidious sterotypes of weak, decrepit Jewish men tied to Talmudic study, he noted that equally impressive was his "intellectual bent." "Quoting freely from Socrates and Emerson," Mike "quickly proved to be a scholar with muscles everywhere except his ears." Epstein was not offended by such references. When asked whether "SuperJew" was spelled as one or two words, he answered, "Well, you spell Superman with one word."[15]

Epstein has fond memories of such stories and the press attention he received as "SuperJew." "I thought it was very complimentary, I really did," he insisted. And except for one incident involving Billy Martin, when the former player and now and again Yankee manager headed the Detroit Tigers, does he recall experiencing any anti-Semitism during his baseball career. At the same time, he also remembers that Jewish organizations in the towns that he played in paid almost no attention to him. Never did he have a "night" at the ballpark so common even for journeymen Jewish ballplayers a generation earlier. In 1972 when the Oakland Athletics won the World Series with the help of Epstein's bat and Ken Holtzman's Jewish arm, he recalls that there was no response at all from the local Oakland Jewish community.

Even more telling about the distance between generations marked by the baseball experiences of a Hank Greenberg and a Mike Epstein are Epstein's own connections between what he sees as his Jewish identity and his life. By his own account, Epstein's Jewishness is grounded more in feelings rather than practice. Although his family does celebrate the Jewish high holy days, they rarely go to synagogue or maintain formal religious ritual. One of Mike's daughters went to religious school and was Bat Mitzvahed but his young son, who has his own aspirations to be a great baseball player, chose not to go because it conflicted with scheduled baseball games. Yet Epstein, who gave his son the opportunity to make that decision, is proud to be a Jew. For him, it comes from memories of growing up in a home where Jewish tradition was alive and, most importantly, from seeing himself as a survivor among a people of survivors. Moved by recent popular recreations of the Holocaust, he believes that it could happen again to himself and to his family and stands ready to "fight you for who I am."

Despite his lack of interest in formal religion, Hank Greenberg became important as a symbol of Jewish strength and survival at a time when such images served the needs of American Jews. Epstein, who feels strongly his Jewish identity and who clearly relishes his own physicality and determination, expresses disappointment that succeeding generations of American Jews have had little need for such athletic role models. To be sure, Epstein's willingness to play with his image as "SuperJew" suggests his own awareness that tough Jewish athletes no longer carry much weight. Nor did his credentials ever match Hank Greenberg's. But even if they had, it is unlikely that he would have served the same purpose to his generation as "Hammerin Hank" did for his own. Greenberg himself remains no more than a distant memory to Jewish boys who came of age in the affluence of post–World War II America. As Epstein himself put it, when he was growing up "there weren't any Jewish ballplayers. . . . The last real Jewish idol that I can remember was Hank Greenberg. And that was before my time."

II

Steve Stone, whose 25–7 record with the 1980 Baltimore Orioles earned him the American League's Cy Young award as the league's best pitcher, first came up with the San Francisco Giants in 1971. When one newspaper reporter reminded him that he had now joined "an illustrious list of Jewish ballplayers who had played for the Giants," Stone admitted that he didn't remember Sid Gordon, Andy Cohen, Harry Danning, or Phil Weintraub. When it came to Jewish ballplayers, "a guy my age," he volunteered, "can only identify with Sandy Koufax."[16]

You don't have to be a Steve Stone to recognize Koufax as the only Jewish major leaguer in recent times to approach the kind of status Hank Greenberg enjoyed among Jews in the 1930s and 1940s. Second-generation adolescents like Larry King, today one of this country's best-known talk-show hosts and Koufax's friend since high school, and myself, a Brooklyn-born third-generation historian whose father taught Sandy American history, proudly remember his triumphs on the diamond—his major-league records for shutouts and strikeouts in the same season, the number of seasons in which he struck out 300 or more batters, and his Cy Young and National League Most Valuable Player awards. Jews certainly took pride in Koufax's accomplishments. But time and circumstance guaranteed that his symbolic importance as Jewish hero was of a much different order than what Hank Greenberg experienced a generation earlier.

Born in Brooklyn in 1935, Sandy spent his early childhood in a Long Island suburb but returned to Brooklyn's Bensonhurst section by the time he was old enough to attend Lafayette High School. Although the migration to the suburbs (and interminable debates within families like my own about whether to move to Long Island or New Jersey) certainly was under way, Bensonhurst, like other urban ethnic neighborhoods then in transition, still contained a healthy mixture of middle-class second-generation Jewish and Italian families. Then known as Larry Zeiger, Larry King recalls that both groups were very proud of their ethnic heritage and lived peacefully with each other. Although Koufax offers nothing about his own Jewish upbringing, King insists that while his circle was not religious, parents and children went to synagogue on the high holidays, kept kosher, and emphasized what he calls "Jewish values" of family, loyalty, and assisting the less fortunate. As young boys passionately involved in sport, King also recalls that opportunities to follow the exploits of local and national Jewish athletes like New York University basketball star Sid Tannenbaum or Sid Luckman, a Brooklyn boy then making his mark as quarterback for the National Football League's Chicago Bears, fostered a sense of Jewish pride among his friends.[17]

Koufax also recalls an adolescence engulfed by sports. Although various versions of baseball involving broom handles, brownstone stoops, and "spaldeens" dominate their reminiscences, "basketball," King insists, "was the theme of the neighborhood." Sandy excelled at the game, in school-yard games in Bensonhurst and Brighton Beach, as captain of his neighborhood's Jewish Community House team which won the National Jewish Welfare Board championship in 1952, and at Lafayette where his court play earned him an athletic scholarship to the University of Cincinnati in 1953. There baseball intervened, shortening Koufax's stay in college and pointing him in the direction of Cooperstown.

Prospects of a team trip to New Orleans convinced Sandy to go out for the school's baseball squad in the spring of his freshman year. Good success on the mound earned him tryouts with several major-league clubs that summer. When his home-town Dodgers offered a $6,000 starting salary and a $14,000 bonus for signing—enough money, as Sandy remembers, to guarantee him the opportunity to go back to college if baseball didn't work out—he accepted their offer.

Koufax's first years with the Dodgers were disappointing. League rules demanded that players who signed as "bonus babies" stay with the major-league club rather than report to the minors. Sandy spent his first three seasons in Brooklyn where his brief appearances on the mound were at best inconsistent. I remember spending many a Saturday and Sunday afternoon in the Ebbets Field bleachers futilely trying to catch the attention of my father's star high-school pupil while he shagged balls in the outfield during pre-game warm-ups. For the most part, however, Koufax did not receive much notice from the public or the press either for his baseball ability or his Jewish background. Predictably, when Sandy first signed with Brooklyn, Dan Daniel compared Dodgers' owner Walter O'Malley's action to John McGraw's incessant search for Jewish talent 30 years earlier. He also noted the magnate's concern to repair relations with Brooklyn's Jewish fans for allowing Brooklyn-born Sid Gordon to sign with the Giants. Even so, O'Malley understood that 1954 was not 1934. As he told Daniel, although Brooklyn's Jewish fans were not "adverse to seeing a Hank Greenberg or an Al Rosen in Flatbush . . . they wanted a winner without regard to race, creed, or color."[19]

Ironically, by the time Koufax became one of the game's preeminent hurlers, the Dodgers were long gone from Brooklyn. In fact, during his first six seasons with the club, the fast-balling left-hander known for his wildness compiled only a modest 36–40 won-lost record. Between 1961 and 1966, however, Sandy found his game. Along with Don Drysdale, he led the Los Angeles Dodgers to three National League pennants and two World Series victories. During these years he won 129 games and lost only 47. His best single season was 1963, one in which he went 25–5, struck out 306 batters, threw 11 shutouts, pitched 311 innings, and compiled an ERA of 1.88. Koufax retired with a sore arm at the end of the 1966 season. In 1972, at the age of

37, he became the youngest player ever to be elected to the Baseball Hall of Fame.

Koufax's success resulted in considerable attention. Feature stories about his career appeared in virtually every national magazine including *Look* and *Time.* Jewish newspapers and the regular press dutifully reported his diamond triumphs. Focused primarily on his baseball career, however, rarely did these stories make much of Sandy's religion or probe deeply into his personality. Typical was a 1962 feature in the *Saturday Evening Post* that described him as "baffling as an athlete" and "enigmatic as a person . . . who lives by himself in the tasteful ranch house he owns in a lonely section of the San Fernando Valley" where he "reads Thomas Wolfe, George Santayana . . . and other writers of substance . . . takes solitary drives in the country, and collects symphonic albums."[19]

Mordecai Richler, reviewing such stories and Koufax's autobiography in 1966, detected an implicit anti-Semitism in coverage that depicted Koufax as a moody, isolated intellectual whose tastes ran to classical music and deep thinkers; a man who remained aloof from teammates and a reluctant athlete who did not enthusiastically rave about his life as a baseball player. On the other hand, he also suggests that Sandy's own denial of all such description in his life story appear as "a sad effort at self-vindication, a forced attempt to prove once and for all that he is the same as everybody else."[20]

Richler's comments about some of the accounts of Koufax's career are reasonable. Also plausible are his observations about Sandy's autobiography. He might have added that unlike Larry King's reminiscences of an adolescence full of connections to Jewish neighborhood and family life, Koufax makes no mention of his participation in that same world. Like the many newspaper and magazine stories about him, the only direct reference in *Koufax* to his religion concerns his consistent refusal to pitch on Rosh Hashonah or Yom Kippur because he was Jewish.[21]

For some commentators, this would be enough evidence to indict Koufax, as others of his generation have been, as self-hating Jews, unsure of their status and uncomfortable with their Jewish identity especially as they found success in the larger society. Whatever such speculations might suggest about Koufax's own self-image, public perceptions of his actions reveal far more about the changing situation of American Jews in post–World War II America. In this respect, different responses to decisions about playing baseball on the Jewish high holidays 30 years apart are illuminating.

Historical context explains public reaction to the way in which Hank Greenberg and Sandy Koufax confronted the same issue. Greenberg's choice appeared as critical dilemma—how to balance loyalty to parents, religion, and tradition with commitment to his American profession and his desire to fully participate in his American life. Equally important, he made it at a time when American Jews still did daily battle with stereotypes about their weakness in a world full of real threats to Jewish existence. By the time Koufax chose not to play, Greenberg's dilemma no longer existed for most American Jews. While they proudly acknowledged Sandy's decision, it hardly signaled hope for their own American ambitions or symbolically challenged insistent anti-Semitic claims of Jewish inferiority. Their own remarkable success in the decades since World War II and the appearance of a new breed of Jewish hero far more capable of countering such charges than any baseball player both figured in their response.

Two tales, both involving the 1965 World Series between the Dodgers and the Minnesota Twins, underline the difference between the way in which Greenberg's and Koufax's personal decisions were perceived by others at two very different times in the history of Jewish-American assimilation. The first game of the 1965 series coincided with Yom Kippur. Walt Alston, the Dodgers' manager, knew that Koufax would not pitch and scheduled Don Drysdale to open the series against the Twins in Minneapolis. While Koufax spent the day in synagogue, the Dodgers lost 8–2. Drysdale was knocked out in the third inning after giving up six runs. When Alston came to the mound to take him out, he handed his manager the ball and said, "I bet right now you wish I was Jewish too."[22] Even in jest, the notion that being Jewish carried positive meaning reflected the real progress Jews had made toward full assimilation by 1965. Increased toleration and acceptance since World War II included a lessening of discrimination throughout American society, an appreciation of individual accomplishment for its own sake rather than in terms qualified by ethnic or religious connotation, and a growing confidence among Jews in asserting their status as successful Americans.

While the Twins chased Drysdale from the mound, Koufax prayed. But not in a small conservative Minneapolis synagogue where a teenage girl listened to her learned father, a Holocaust survivor, preach to his congregation. At the beginning of his sermon, he noted with approval Koufax's decision not to play on Yom Kippur. Much to his daughter's mortification, however, so out of touch was he with American culture that he referred to Sandy as a football player. Luckily, as she recalls, her father's gaffe passed over the heads of many of the congregation who were busily whispering details of the Twins' victory passed on by those worshipers who took a break from day-long services by listening to the game on their transistor radios. Although they doubtless approved of Koufax's decision, the success of their ball club against all comers, Jewish or not, was far more important than the symbolism of his act. By the time the series was over, they could only have wished that Yom Kippur came more often. Koufax shut out the Twins twice as the Dodgers became world champions.[23]

Twenty years later, the issue of baseball and Yom Kippur briefly made news again when several hundred Jewish New Yorkers protested the decision to schedule two National League playoff games involving the New York Mets on the Sunday evening and Monday afternoon of the holiday. League officials and baseball's commissioner admitted that they had tried to work around the conflict but were forced to go ahead in order to avoid scheduling the games in direct television competition with the American League play-off game and with ABC's Monday Night Football. Although one protester found the decision "appalling, offensive," and "discriminatory," Rabbi Marc Gellman of Temple Beth Torah in Dix Hills, New York, put the controversy in its proper perspective. As a high school student in 1965, he recalled Koufax's decision not to pitch on Yom Kippur "as a powerful experience of Jewish pride." No one at the time, he remembered, "even thought of asking the game to be canceled. The notion that Jews would ever tell the commissioner of baseball—in our imagination a man just under the President of the United States—that the schedule should be changed would have been an outrageous act of chutzpah." Not so in 1986, Gellman concluded, when "Jews are more confident today about their place in American society."[24]

While part of the explanation for that confidence lay in the phenomenal economic and social success experienced by American Jews, events outside of the United States also contributed to making sports figures like Koufax less important as American Jewish heroes. Specifically, the founding of Israel as an independent nation in 1948 and subsequent successful attempts to defend its integrity, most especially the June 1967 Six-Day War, gave American Jews a new breed of tough Jewish heroes to idolize and support far more relevant to their Jewishness than anything Koufax offered. Although they do not agree on whether or not such identification bodes well for the future of American Jewry, political commentators, historians, and other observers of American Jewish life recognize the flowering of the image of the successful tough Jew, embodied in the exploits of Israeli soldiers, as a critical component of how American Jews today increasingly define their own Jewish identity. With the Six-Day War, as one writer put it, Israel and its survival became for many American Jews "the most important thing, perhaps not in their life, but certainly in their Jewishness."[25]

Be it through their generous financial support in behalf of Israel's survival; the popularity of a genre of American and Jewish fiction, from Leon Uris's *Exodus* to a host of more recent novels depicting the exploits of bronzed, hardened Israeli freedom fighters; the reputation of the precision, courage, and toughness of Israeli commandos garnered through such exploits as the raid on Entebbe in 1976 to free Israeli and American hostages held in Uganda; or survey research data that tells us it is so, Jewish strength and toughness successfully employed to guarantee Israeli survival has become an important part of American Jewish identity. Fully assimilated American Jews no longer need to be reminded, as Hank Greenberg did for an earlier generation, that anti-Semites and bigots could be challenged or that it is possible to enjoy economic prosperity and social success. Instead, their very success, so often combined with increasing distance from the ethnic and religious culture of parents and grandparents, has compelled a search for new anchors of Jewish identity, including adulation of tough Jews able and willing to successfully guarantee Israel's survival.[26] However tough and strong a pitcher Koufax was, he clearly was no match for Moishe Dayan and his legions of commandos when it came time to search for heroes and deeds symbolic of the contemporary Jewish experience.

III

Even as the importance of Jewish involvement in America's National Game diminished, increasing numbers of American Jews found themselves attracted to a variety of individual sports. Sports like golf and tennis hardly remained the exclusive domain of Gentiles prior to World War II. As early as the 1920s wealthy German Jews, denied access to restricted country clubs, built their own. And an occasional Jewish youngster from less auspicious backgrounds, like New York's Clara Greenspan, excelled on public tennis courts and links.[27] It was not until the late 1950s and 1960s, however, that participation in both sports became widespread for Jew and Gentile alike. The impact of television, the ability of creative sports entrepreneurs to capitalize on its commercial potential, and the rise of professional stars who encouraged amateur hackers and whackers to pick up clubs and rackets combined to make both tennis and golf popular sports in a consumer-oriented society increasingly intent on promoting fitness and health. Second- and third-generation Jews and their children, on the move to new homes and better jobs in suburbia, flocked to them as eagerly as other groups. Their very participation in these sports of rising economic expectations provides still another sign of progress toward full assimilation.

In ways somewhat different than indicated by changing public perceptions of major-league Jewish baseball players, so too does the coverage of those exceptional Jewish athletes in individual sports who competed successfully in national and international competition. Increasingly over time, when they have been singled out, it is because their stories identify them not as Jewish heroes but as representative American athletes whose experiences underline larger issues concerning the sportsworld or American society.

In 1951 Dick Savitt was the talk of the tennis world. A New Jersey native born in Bayonne in 1927, he first learned the game at the predominately Jewish Berkeley Tennis Club in Orange, New Jersey, one that he described as consisting of "six courts and a broken down clubhouse."[28] Dick's mother became ill a year later and the family moved to El Paso, Texas, the same town that had produced Andy Cohen. Here Savitt's game flourished. After a stint in the Navy, Dick enrolled at Cornell University, hurt his knee playing varsity basketball, and turned his attention to tennis. Within two years he was ranked as the 26th best male player in the United States. Savitt graduated in 1950. By the end of that summer, after reaching the semi-finals of the U.S. National championships at Forest Hills, his ranking jumped to sixth. The following year, after first capturing the Australian Open in January, Savitt repeated his triumph at prestigious Wimbledon, becoming the first Jewish player ever to win the men's singles title. Along the way he defeated another American Jewish player, Herb Flam, in the semi-finals.

The Jewish press certainly took note of this accomplishment. No matter that, by his own account, Savitt was Jewish only by birth rather than by practice or interest. As one columnist for Philadelphia's *Jewish Exponent* put it, Savitt's victory at Wimbledon was a "remarkable feat" that deservedly added a "new name . . . in the hall of fame of Jewish athletes." Noting that "tennis has long been a country club affair that makes it tough for a Jewish player to crack the barrier of anti-Semitism," it concluded that Savitt's accomplishment "is a tribute to his skill."[29]

Emphasis on Dick's talent and his special place in tennis history as much as his Jewish birth resonated with more popular depictions of his victory. *Time's* cover story on him that summer focused on his tenacious play and on his opportunity to become only the third man to ever capture the Australian Open, Wimbledon, and the U.S.Open in the same year. Only once, in the midst of detailing Savitt's remarkable success and his world of elite amateur tennis, did it make any direct reference to his Jewish background. Asked if he experienced any "trouble in Germany" while playing there, Savitt responded by noting the "enthusiasm" of the Berlin crowds. When he realized that the reporter was alluding to the fact that he was Jewish, he replied, "No, I never had any trouble that way. I know some clubs are prejudiced because they don't have any Jewish members . . . I don't think much about it." Describing his comfortable upbringing in "New Jersey's middle-income suburbia" where he enjoyed "a happy-go-lucky youth," the magazine asserted that "Dick has never had much reason to think about it."[30]

Both Savitt and *Time* dismissed the possibility of anti-Semitism for a young Jew who clearly had arrived in the American mainstream. That theme also dominated discussion of events later that year when Savitt, who along with Herb Flam had been named as the first Jews ever to play for the United States Davis Cup team, was kept out of final-round competition against the Australians. Although Savitt made clear his outrage and disappointment, neither he nor the Jewish press attributed the decision of team captain Frank Shields to anti-Semitism. Reporting on the controversy in January 1952, the Boston *Jewish Advocate* did not even consider the possibility that Savitt had been excluded because he was Jewish. Instead it noted that Savitt's own status as the world's best player faltered somewhat after his Wimbledon triumph and that tennis experts disagreed about whether his style was best suited to compete against the Australian team. Savitt himself, who had no qualms about playing in amateur tournaments sponsored by country clubs that prohibited Jewish members, consistently denied any personal experiences with anti-Semitism. In this instance, he argued that Shields's decision was based on his personal friendship with Ted Schroeder, the man who took Savitt's place, rather than any animosity he might have had toward Jews. At the same time, Savitt insisted that both he and the Australians recognized who was better. As Savitt pointed out, certain that he would play the final round, the Australians had replaced Ken McGregor, the man he had defeated in both the Australian and Wimbledon finals, with a different player.[31]

In past times, for other American Jewish athletes, similar decisions evoked vehement cries of discrimination and protest. Not so in 1951. Instead, both the acclaim and controversy surrounding Savitt's accomplishments and disappointments centered on his court triumphs and on the quality of his play. The debate over whether he should play against Australia, as he was the first to admit, focused on typical sports questions of judgment and ability, not on his ethnic identity.

In more recent times, other American Jewish tennis players have gone on to far more lucrative and well-known careers than were possible for the best of Savitt's generation. Harold Solomon, in the 1970s, and, most recently, Aaron Krickstein, Brad Gilbert, and Jay Berger have all made their marks and earned millions by dint of their backhands and volleys. But only an occasional column in the American Jewish press ever makes mention of the fact that they are Jewish. Although Solomon earned the sobriquet as one of the "Bagel Twins," it had nothing to do with any passion for this once ethnic bread that is now served even by McDonald's with sausage as an option. Rather it was because he played doubles with Eddie Dibbs, who earned the name the "Bagel Kid" because he often lost sets by 6–0 scores.[31] When Jay Berger and Aaron Krickstein, a doctor's son from the wealthy Detroit suburb of Grosse Point, played each other in the 1989 quarter-finals at the U.S. Open, not the *New York Times*, the wire services, nor national television commentators ever mentioned that both players were Jewish. They were just tennis players, millionaires all, able and lucky enough to make it in the material world of commercialized sport in the 1970s and 1980s.[32]

Only slightly different are the experiences of Amy Alcott, one of the more consistent winners on the Ladies' Professional Golf Association's Tour in the last decade. Born in Kansas City, Alcott, a dentist's daughter, honed her skills in a homemade driving net, putting lawn, and sand trap that he built for her. An outstanding amateur player, she turned professional in 1975 at the age of 19 with the backing of several members of a California country club, including Dean Martin. Selected rookie of the year, Alcott has gone on to capture a number of major tournament victories and remains a popular player with the growing legion of fans that have made women's professional golf big business. Few of them, however, would know that she is Jewish. Even those who might learn about it in an occasional item in the Jewish press are not encouraged to see any particular significance in the fact. Typical was a 1976 Jewish Telegraphic Agency news release about Amy's victory in the Trenton Diocese Ladies' Professional Golf Association Tournament. After accepting her prize, Alcott, the story went, remarked to the priests and nuns in attendance: "I don't know if you people know it, but I'm Jewish. To win a tournament run by the Catholic Diocese is really a thrill. I came out to show you all how to do it."[33] In fact, for Alcott and other Jewish women athletes like Olympic basketball player Nancy Lieberman who made their mark in professional sports in the 1960s, 1970s, and 1980s, the fact that they were pioneers in breaking down the barriers of a male-dominated American sports structure was far more worthy of press attention than their religious beliefs or ethnic backgrounds.[34]

The sexual revolution has clearly influenced the place and shape of American sport since World War II. So too has the expansion of the American marketplace and the explosive growth of a consumer-oriented society. Since the Civil War, there have always been sports entrepreneurs, a fair share of whom

Jewish, who understood sport as business, and athletes who recognized their value as commodities. Thanks primarily to television, however, the possibilities have expanded far beyond A. G. Spalding's or Babe Ruth's wildest dreams. The story of one Jewish athlete dramatizes this transformation in ways that demonstrate in still another way Jewish absorption into the American mainstream.[35]

For a brief moment in 1972, Mark Spitz was the world's most celebrated athlete. Thirty-six years after the 1936 Berlin games, the Olympics returned to Germany—this time to the West German city of Munich. Here the young Californian Jewish swimmer emerged as its greatest champion. Already established as one of the world's renowned swimmers and winner of the 1971 James E. Sullivan award as the United States outstanding amateur athlete, Spitz astonished the sporting world by capturing seven gold medals in eight days. In every event, he set a world record, winning four individual and four relay medals.[36]

Although reporters covering the games occasionally mentioned that Spitz was Jewish, for the most part, they reveled in his remarkable achievements as an athlete and as a representative American. In a brief biography of the swimmer, the *New York Times* included only one comment about religion. When his swimming interfered with Hebrew lessons, his father, according to the account, who intensely encouraged his son's interest, explained to the rabbi, "Even God likes a winner."[37] After he had won his fifth gold medal, the *Times* added that "in a sport that generally attracts conservative, polite, middle class Anglo-Saxon teenagers with the shortest haircuts in their schools, Spitz . . . is the first Jewish athlete to make it big in the sport and his bushy moustache and his outspokenness don't fit the swimmer's 'image.'" According to the paper and confirmed by his private coach, other American swimmers in the past had made Spitz aware of his difference, taunting him with anti-Semitic remarks during the 1968 Mexico City games when he boasted unsuccessfully about how he would sweep the competition.[38] Far more typical, however, in both the American Jewish and the regular press, were glowing reports of Spitz's triumphs over East German swimmers, often coated with the patina of nationalism so typical of coverage of this quadrennial athletic exercise in Cold War politics. Along with reports of huge crowds of teenage girls panting after this new demi-god who "looks like Omar Sharif" and pictures of jubilant teammates carrying Spitz on their shoulders after he captured his seventh gold medal, they clearly overshadowed any Olympic storyline that focused on Jewish concerns. When such stories did return, Mark Spitz was hardly the center of attention.[39]

On September 5, members of the Arab terrorist group Black September, in an attempt to force Israel to release 200 Arab commandos, held hostage and eventually murdered 11 members of the Israeli Olympic team. News of this horrible tragedy, the subsequent killing of four terrorists, memorial services held at the Olympic Stadium, and the decision to continue the games after a brief postponement dominated both press and television coverage.[40] Concerned about the possibility that Mark Spitz might also be a target of the terrorists, Olympic officials placed him under armed guard and flew him to London shortly after the hostages were seized. Expressing both shock and sadness "as a human being and as a Jew" about the events, Spitz, who had planned all along to leave Berlin immediately after his competition was over to attend dental school, announced his decision to retire from competitive swimming and flew back to the United States.[41]

Already an American Olympic hero, within the next year Spitz became both an American cold warrior and an American commodity. Ten days after the tragedy, Mark made the *New York Times* again, this time in an editorial titled "Seven for Spitz." Talking about sports heroes and world records as if the tragedy of Munich was already distant memory, the paper asserted that "nothing has happened in Munich this summer [that] can compare with the awesome feats of Mark Spitz, swimmer extraordinary." After reminding its readers of his record grab bag, the editorial concluded: "Mark Spitz, like Bobby Fischer, provides a useful reminder that old fogies inclined to denigrate Americans under thirty need to take a better look at this new and very promising younger generation."[42]

In this brief note, remarkable for its insensitivity to the real significance of the Munich games as much as for its veiled commentary about young American war protestors who were actively resisting American participation in Vietnam, the *Times* linked two young men as proof that the American future was in good hands. The swimmer and chess genius established themselves as the best in the world by defeating East German swimmers and Russian grandmasters at a time when Cold War rhetoric still blew hot. Most remarkably, the editorial failed to mention that both Spitz and Fischer were Jewish—instead they were just good American boys drawn into political battle in defense of democracy and capitalism.

Although an unwitting cold warrior, Spitz actively pursued his love of capitalism to the point of self-commodified caricature. Postponing plans to attend dental school, he signed on with the William Morris Agency, intent to cash in on his Olympic success. Within a few months, his picture appeared on billboards and in television commercials hawking the benefits of milk and the virtues of the Flexamatic 400 Schick razor. Pubescent teenagers unconcerned about healthy teeth and bones and too young to shave could still identify with their heartthrob and hero by purchasing any number of posters featuring Mark in his Olympic swimsuit, his bare chest adorned by Olympic gold. Guest appearances with every major celebrity on television from Bob Hope to Sonny and Cher only enhanced his value. In these attempts to cash in on his athletic triumphs, Spitz, whose endorsement contracts had an estimated potential value of $5 million, unabashedly declared himself "a commodity, an endorser."[43]

Not everyone applauded Mark's game plan. One *Sports Illustrated* piece, aptly titled "On Your Mark, Get Set, Sell," detailed Spitz's ever-expanding commercial interests while lightly criticizing his attachment to material things. Far more direct was a *New York Times Magazine* piece by Susan Lydon in which she decried Spitz's crass efforts to cash in on his triumphs as unpatriotic acts designed to dupe an adoring public. Emphasizing his arrogance as much as his determination to succeed, she quoted teammates who described him as tactless and difficult. As example, Lydon offered his response to one sportswriter who asked him if he thought it ironic to play "the conquering Jew in Munich." Supposedly Spitz replied, "I always liked this country . . . even though this lampshade is probably made out of one of my aunts." Equally offensive to Lydon was his gold-medal poster which, in her opinion, "c[a]me off looking like the most blatant exploitation of the human body since Marilyn Monroe's celebrated nude calendar." In the end, suggesting that even his marriage has been arranged for maximum career benefit, Lydon warned her readers to beware that Spitz is "a carefully packaged product," offered for sale to Americans as cover boy and potential entertainer by his managers. Noting Spitz's picture, along with Bobby Fischer, as champions of 1972 in *Life's* year-end issue, as well as their joint appearance on the television show of "America's most patriotic entertainer," Bob Hope, she concluded that these "national heroes" had devoted so much of their lives to athletic and intellectual excellence that it "almost precluded any development of any other facets of education, character, social personality." Not surprisingly, to Lydon, both were determined "to convert those skills into as much cash as the market would allow."[44]

Similar stories about public personalities who happened to be Jewish half a century earlier would have provided classic opportunities for anti-Semitic harangue and ethnic ridicule. In the early 1970s, however, Spitz and Fischer appeared solely as "ugly Americans," hardly complimentary but in its own way another indication of Jewish acceptance and assimilation.

Spitz himself found no fault with his actions. Today, when even journeymen baseball players sign annual million-dollar contracts and superstars like a Michael Jordan make five times that amount for endorsing basketball shoes, Spitz views himself as a pioneering sports capitalist. Although his history is a bit off, he believes that he "was really the first one to take advantage of what's out there. I realize today that if someone had come up to me just before a race and offered me a $100,000 a year for five years if I stepped down off the platform right then and there and retired, I would have done it. Right then."[45]

In a consumer-oriented society whose values emphasized material success and a win-at-all costs philosophy—be it in Vietnam or the halls of corporate America—Mark's actions, not surprisingly, also received support. Letters to the *New York Times Magazine* in response to Lydon's article chastized her for painting an unfair, vindictive portrait that failed to give Spitz credit for "the determination and dedication" that produced his victories. Most telling was the response of one reader who took issue with Lydon's warning about the manufacturing of Spitz as an American hero. "Miss Lydon," she began, "we don't buy—or have—heroes anymore. We ought to know by now that when we demand, and get champions, we are apt to get single-minded, sometimes lop-sided winners. We don't send them to Munich to be models of tact, compassion or amiability. We send them to win. Mark Spitz," she concluded, "is a winner."[46]

Legitimate hero or not, both critics and supporters seemed to agree on one essential point. For better or worse, Spitz's determination to succeed in the swim and to capitalize on it marked him first and foremost as a representative American, 1970s style. In the years that followed, Spitz did take time from his busy career in business and real estate to help raise money to support the United States Maccabiah team, one that he had swam for in his youth. Publicly, however, in an American society disturbingly short on historical memory, he remains, when noticed at all, as American Olympic hero. Interviewed about his plans to train for a place on the 1992 U.S. Olympic swim team at the age of 40 on a nationally televised sports program in November 1989, Spitz called it a "challenge of a lifetime," one that would cost him some "real estate development prospects" but that fit into his life philosophy that it was never to late to try anything. Although the commentator identified the youthful-looking Spitz as the winner of seven Olympic gold medals, it made no mention of his religion nor of the tragedy that indelibly marked the Munich games.[47]

IV

In 1950, a Brooklyn Jewish weekly newspaper reported that both the Pitkin Avenue Merchants Association and the Kings Highway Merchants Association, organizations embedded in changing ethnic neighborhoods still populated with first- and second-generation American Jews, had given achievement awards to the great Jewish boxer Barney Ross. Ross, the paper added, had just presided over an awards ceremony in which he handed out medals and trophies to the Police Athletic League (PAL) baseball team sponsored by the 61st Precinct in Brooklyn. Alongside this story, in a regular feature titled "I Remember," Nat Krinsky, physical education teacher and track coach at Brooklyn's James Madison High School and former member of the famed Brooklyn Invincibles and Nat Holman's first CCNY basketball team, deplored the decline in participation of the borough's Jewish youth in organized Jewish athletics. Recalling a time when the Jewish Welfare Board (JWB) actively sponsored athletics through YMHAs and community centers, Krinsky remembered its development of "a most active athletic program that kept the names of our Jewish players in the limelight." Now, however, "the program among our Jewish institutions has dwindled into nothingness. Here in the greatest Jewish community in the world, nothing to speak of is being done to develop and encourage Jewish youngsters' interest in sport. Pretty soon," he surmised, "we shall be extinct in the field." "Let us awaken the spirit of rivalry and activity," Krinsky concluded, "so that in years to come the Jewish youngsters of today will have something to remember."[48]

On the surface, Nat's concerns seem overstated. Even if he was right that Jewish organizations were not sponsoring athletic programs to the degree they had in the years prior to World War II, boys from ethnic Jewish neighborhoods still had opportunities offered by schools and by organizations like PAL to participate in athletics. Judging by the success that spring of the City

College Beavers who, thanks to the sterling play of Irwin Dambrot and Eddie Roman, captured both the NIT and NCAA basketball championships, quality Jewish athletes existed. Even great Jewish athletes of a previous time such as Barney Ross still rang a bell among youthful Jewish audiences.

In a larger sense, however, Krinsky's comments were accurate. Although Jewish boys and, increasingly, girls continued to participate in athletics, the context and the settings in which such participation unfolded were far different from what Nat himself experienced. For third- and fourth-generation Jewish youngsters in the 1950s and 1960s, living in families fully assimilated and far removed from the tightly knit ethnic urban worlds of their grandparents, sport was neither the middle ground nor the critical assimilating experience it had been for men like Krinsky, Sammy Kaplan, Jammy Moskowitz, or Nat Holman. Nor were basketball games or boxing matches involving local Jewish athletes any longer important community events that encouraged ethnic celebration and pride.

Nowhere is this more obvious or the explanation more apparent than in Jewish participation in basketball, a sport so dominated by Jews in the years before World War II that some called it the "Jewish" game. Much of this story we have already told. The lack of attention paid to Jewish involvement in the basketball fixing scandal of 1951 presaged what was to follow. Professional basketball's transformation from local, part-time minor sport to national entertainment spectacle, the continual erosion of the ethnic communal world that had spawned Jewish community basketball teams like the Brooklyn Dux and the Philadelphia SPHAs, significant and continual decline in the number of Jewish men playing college and professional basketball, and the abundant success of the children of the second generation in an American society more open to them than to their parents or grandparents all contributed to the disappearance of basketball as a significant ethnic community experience. Although Sandy Koufax led his Bensonhurst Jewish Community Center senior basketball team to a national JWB championship in 1953, there is no evidence to suggest its importance as an ethnic community event so familiar to the Nonpariels and the Dux of an earlier era. Whatever the victory may have done for Sandy's ego or sense of manhood, there is no reason to believe that such an experience held the same meaning it did for Jewish boys of a different generation who found in basketball significant opportunities within an ethnic, Jewish setting for learning what it was to be an American.

Scattered accounts of Jewish ballplayers who had successful college careers in post-World War II America confirm this assessment. Although Haskell Cohen's lament about the continual decline in the number and ability of Jewish ballplayers was accurate, Jewish boys did not totally give up the game. Down through the 1970s, Jewish names still predominated on City College rosters. Even All-American teams occasionally included a Jewish name. For instance, Art Heyman, Larry Brown, and Lenny Rosenbluth—New York boys from suburban Long Island, Brooklyn, and the Bronx respectively—all had outstanding college careers in the late 1950s and 1960s for Duke and North Carolina. Heyman, whose father had played for NYU, became the first player ever named to the Atlantic Coast Conference All-Star team for three consecutive years. A two-time All-America, in 1963 as team captain he was named the most valuable player in the NCAA tournament and the college basketball player of the year by the Associated Press, United Press International, and *The Sporting News*.[49] Brown and Rosenbluth both had fine college careers at the University of North Carolina, some five years apart. A tough, small back-court star, Larry captained his team in 1963 and was named to the conference's all-star team. Subsequently, in 1964, he helped the United States Olympic men's basketball team capture the gold medal. Today, head basketball coach of the NBA's San Antonio Spurs, Brown has enjoyed a well-traveled but successful career as a professional and college coach. Seven years before Brown put on the Carolina blue, Rosenbluth captained and led the Tar Heels to the national championship in 1957 against Wilt Chamberlain's Kansas team, earning individual honors as an All-American and as the most valuable player in the NCAA tournament.[50]

Stories about these and other Jewish basketball players did appear in Jewish newspapers and in Jewish encyclopedias but without the didactic comments about assimilation and symbol so common to discussion of prominent Jewish athletes in the 1920s, 1930s, and 1940s. Other public commentary generally paid even less attention to the players' ethnic or religious identity. The 1958 National College Basketball Blue Book did note that a "Jewish boy named Lenny Rosenbluth" had led North Carolina to the national championship.[51] And Frank McGuire, his college coach, felt that Lenny exhibited real courage by never "show[ing] a sign of weakness" in the face of anti-Semitic taunts from opposing fans. As McGuire put it, "he did a lot for his religion in the South." Speaking in terms of both basketball and interfaith harmony, McGuire concluded that "the more Rosenbluths we get down here the better."[52] But such references, either to Jewish identity or to the role of Jewish athletes in combating anti-Semitism, were the exception. By 1988, in all the national attention Larry Brown received coaching the Kansas Jayhawks to a national title no mention was ever made of his Jewish connection. Nor was his religion part of any of the stories in mid-June of that year that reported his decision to leave Kansas for a five-year, $3.5 million contract to become the head coach of the San Antonio Spurs.[53]

Ironically, the major exception to this general disinterest in Jewish basketball players involved Yeshiva University, a school designed by its founders in the 1920s to incorporate opportunities for secular higher education with continued orthodox Jewish religious training. By 1956, as the orthodox Jewish family base that had accounted for most Yeshiva students diminished in the face of suburbanization and assimilation, the university took steps to attract less orthodox Jews, predominately from New York's suburbs, by introducing its Jewish Studies Program (JSP). Aimed at preparing students lacking in sufficient Jewish education for eventual integration into the more typical advanced Jewish training offered at Yeshiva, the JSP instituted its own admission policies that required far less preparation in Jewish education than normally required for admission into the school's regular course of studies. Its introduction sparked continued debate within the Yeshiva community that ultimately involved the status of the school's basketball program and the reputation of the school's coach and athletic director, Red Sarachek.[54]

Basketball had been played by Yeshiva boys since the 1930s, but not without controversy. Those who supported it, as Jeffrey Gurock explains, appreciated the opportunity basketball provided for orthodox Jewish boys "with sporting inclinations to participate in this most all-American activity in a Jewish environment" without violating observance of Jewish law. Victories on the court, they argued, especially against Gentile clubs, only encouraged ethnic pride among Yeshiva students. On the other hand, more traditional members of Yeshiva's community questioned the time such games took away from religious study and objected to the undignified appearance of Yeshiva athletes and fans as "ill-fitting the men of Torah."[55]

Matters took a more serious turn with the introduction of JSP. Gurock, who played for Red in the 1960s, and who is now a history professor and sometimes assistant basketball coach at the university, remembers that those who were against JSP often referred to it as the Jewish Sports Program and its students as "guys who come to shoot baskets, take the college courses, and go home." Members of Sarachek's basketball teams were often ridiculed as Jews of little faith with no interest in Jewish studies who ended up at Yeshiva because their basketball talents were not good enough to attract scholarships from schools with better basketball programs. These charges were especially strong during JSP's first years of operation, when Red's recruits, most with no formal religious training beyond what was required to prepare for Bar Mitzvah, enrolled in the program.[56]

During the first years of JSP, when Sarachek actively recruited student athletes with minimal religious background but good basketball skills, Yeshiva did well against local college competition. By the mid-1960s, however, as the pool of Jewish public-school athletes continued to decline, Red ended up recruiting less-skilled players from the Metropolitan Jewish High School League. Victories decreased but so too did criticism that his players diluted the meaning of a Yeshiva education.[57]

V

Larry Brown's decision to become head coach of the San Antonio Spurs produced an interesting situation. As the 1988 NBA season opened, the league contained more Jewish coaches and owners and as many commissioners as it did basketball players. The player was Danny Schayes, whose father, Dolph, unquestionably was the greatest Jewish basketball player to play professionally in the years following World War II. A diminishing cast of Jewish ballplayers, in both talent and number, put in their minutes in NBA uniforms between the time Dolph starred for the Syracuse Nationals and Danny's more recent moments with the Denver Nuggets and Milwaukee Bucks. But it is the story of this father and son that best illustrates the changing role of sport in the American Jewish experience and its connection to American Jewish identity.

Dolph Schayes, like others of his generation, grew up the son of first-generation immigrants to America, in an urban, ethnic Jewish world. Born in 1928 to Rumanian immigrants who came to the United States in 1920, he lived in a Bronx lower-middle-class Jewish neighborhood bounded by 183rd Street, Davidson and Burnside avenues and Fordham Road.[58] His parents, who were not practicing Jews, did not send their son to Hebrew school. Dolph was not Bar Mitzvahed nor did he attend a synagogue until he was an adult. Yet in a neighborhood where all his friends were Jewish, where he dated only Jewish girls, where his parents ate only kosher meat because only kosher butchers had stores there, and where his childhood heroes included Hank Greenberg, Sid Luckman, and Marshall Goldberg, he recalls that a "Jewish presence" pervaded all aspects of his life, even his avid interest in athletics.

In the same spirit as Sammy Kaplan's Dux, Dolph and ten of his Jewish friends formed a social and sport club, first known as the Trylons and then the Amerks. By the time he was in junior high school, the Amerks, short for Americans, had developed into one of the best basketball teams in the Bronx and played a full schedule of games against all comers, including teams fielded by Jewish community centers. Hardly limited to hoops, the club also fielded football and baseball teams but spent more time with basketball for the simple reason that school-yard baskets at P.S. 91 were far more accessible than traveling to Van Cortlandt Park to find a baseball diamond or football field.

The Amerks' preference for roundball suited Dolph. Almost 6'7" by the time he began playing for Dewitt Clinton High School, Schayes was recruited by Purdue, St. John's, and Columbia but chose to enroll at NYU on an athletic scholarship. As he recalls his decision, "we were city kids, and NYU to a middle-class family was a fine school to go . . . and I could live at home."

Dolph's father was too busy driving a truck for Consolidated Laundry to watch his son play basketball in school yards and high-school gyms. Yet his father, who once had his own dreams of becoming a professional prizefighter, avidly followed sports, especially baseball and boxing. Once Schayes began playing for NYU, his father regularly attended his games. Although he traveled less frequently to watch his son play professionally, Dolph recalls that his father "was a well-known fixture at the games. . . . Coming from the old country, it made him feel very proud to have a son in the limelight."

Dolph's childhood world of a tightly knit Bronx working-class community dominated by Jewish sights, smells, and sounds was far different from the one experienced by his son. Born in 1959, Danny Schayes spent most of his youth in a suburb of Syracuse, New York, while his father finished his career as a ballplayer for the Syracuse Nationals and began a successful construction business. Although there were other Jewish families in his upper-middle-class neighborhood, Danny describes it as a mixed community where everyone was friendly toward each other—as he put it, "like growing up on Richie Cunningham's street."[59] Danny's reference point is television's quintessential WASP teenager of television's "Happy Days," far removed from the ethnic world of his father's childhood, but scarcely surprising for an American sub-urban adolescent experience quite common for third-generation American Jews whose parents, be they basketball players, building contractors, lawyers, or professionals, were enjoying productive careers in the 1960s and 1970s.

While Dolph's immigrant father relished the attention his son received as a college and professional player because it marked his own progress in becoming an American, such reasons were not factors in the support Dan enjoyed from his own parents. Because of his father's connection to basket-ball—as player, then professional coach and owner of a summer sports camp—Dan was always around the sport. His family belonged to the local Jewish community center in order to take advantage of its handball courts and gymnasium floors. Although his father did not push his son into the game, sports were so much a part of his family's life that it would have been more unusual if he had not received encouragement.

Just like his father, Dan was heavily recruited by colleges and chose to play for his hometown university. Dolph's scholarship, however, was more critical to his ability to afford NYU than the one his son received to attend Syracuse. Taller than his father by a good four inches, the 6'11" center enjoyed a solid but unspectacular college basketball career. Always a good student, Dan majored in organic chemistry, with little thought of playing professional bas-ketball. Somewhat to his surprise, he was picked by the NBA's Utah Jazz. His decision to try professional basketball received the enthusiastic backing of his parents.

Throughout his professional career, whether for Utah, the Denver Nug-gets, who traded for him in 1983, or more recently with the Milwaukee Bucks, Danny has been a solid role player either as power forward or occasionally at center. Over a six-year period between 1981 and 1987, he played almost 20 minutes a game, averaging 8 points and 6 rebounds a contest. These numbers are no threat to his father's incredible statistics. Dolph signed first with the Syracuse Nationals of the National Basketball League and stayed with the team when it became a member of the NBA, playing for that franchise from 1949 through 1963. He finished out his playing career with the Philadelphia 76ers in 1964 and then took a brief turn at coaching in the professional ranks. Although in 1966 he was named NBA coach of the year for leading the 76er's to an Eastern Division title, it was as a player that Schayes earned his election to the Basketball Hall of Fame. Voted to 12 consecutive NBA all-star teams, Dolph concluded his 16-year professional career with a total of 19,249 points, at the time far ahead of anyone else. From February 17, 1952, until December 27, 1961, he played in 764 consecutive games, another NBA record that lasted well after his retirement. Indeed at one time or another, the "Patriarch of the Pros" held league records for most games played, most consecutive games, most points, most field goals, most free throws, and most rebounds. Known as a tough, hustling player who could drive the lane as well as shoot from the outside, Schayes led the Syracuse Nationals to one NBA title in 1955 while establishing himself as one of the best-known and durable players ever to play professional ball.[60]

For all of his labors, Schayes's total career salary as a professional basketball player barely approached half of what his son earns in one season. Dolph's highest annual salary with the Nationals was $21,000. In 1988, when Danny renewed his contract with the Denver Nuggets, he signed a six-year contract worth $9 million— a 250 percent yearly increase over the mere $425,000 he earned during the 1987-88 season.[61]

Much more similar have been public perceptions of their careers. As with coverage of the declining number of major-league Jewish baseball players after World War II, both the frequency and meaning of reference to the Jewish identity of father and son have been far different than Jewish hoopsters who played before them. Although references to Dolph's Jewish background appear in official league promotional material and in an occasional newspaper column, for the most part the regular press focused on game descriptions, box scores, and on his ability, toughness, and discipline as one of the game's premier players. Jewish publications more often took note of Schayes' ethnic background, but even here, as in a 1958 Boston *Jewish Advocate* story, they simply described his status as a "major star on the American sporting scene."[62]

The lack of public attention to Dolph's religious preference is evidence itself of the gradual movement toward Jewish acceptance and normalcy that distinguishes the years since World War II. By the time Danny started playing professional basketball such coverage was all but absent. As far as he can remember, he has never seen any reference to his religion in the regular press although Jewish periodicals occasionally mention it.

Despite clear differences in upbringing and opportunity, father and son also share similar feelings about their Jewishness. When I interviewed Danny in 1988, he was a resident of a Denver, Colorado, suburb and a guest member of a local reformed congregation that he occasionally helped in its fund-raising activities. Rarely, however, did he attend services, either at home or when he was on the road. At the same time, although no public notice has ever been given it it, he refuses to play basketball on Yom Kippur—a personal decision that for other ballplayers in other times was cause for public controversy. It comes as no surprise to Danny that the public no longer pays any attention to such matters. For him, it is another sign of "the maturing of American culture" in his lifetime and the absence of "hate and bigotry" in his own experiences as an American.

Although some contemporary critics of American Jewry would take issue with him, Schayes sees no inconsistency between his lack of formal observance and his very clear sense of being Jewish. As he put it, going to temple is not a measure of his emotional involvement as a Jew. "I was never one who really got involved or felt that the only way was to be traditionally religious as far as the ceremony of it. I always felt that what you felt in your head or your heart was the important thing and not whether you were always on time for synagogue." And what is in his heart is a strong sense of identification with Israel, nurtured by this trips there in 1977 and again in 1981, as a member of United States Maccabiah games basketball teams. Aware of the notion of Israel as the Jewish homeland long before he went, Danny's visits gave real meaning to what he sees as the extreme circumstances under which Israel exists and the role of Jews in the Diaspora to help and support its survival while still retaining the right to be critical of its policies.

No doubt his father's example was influential here. A member of Jewish sports halls of fames in both the United States and Israel, Dolph actively participates in Jewish fund-raising activities for Israel and for other Jewish causes. Although not an observant or "temple Jew," as he calls it, he has played an especially active role in raising money for the Maccabiah games. In 1977, he even coached the American basketball entry, one that included his own son and that won the championship medal with an upset victory over a more seasoned Israeli team. As he tells it, participation in the Maccabiah games has increased his own Jewishness—one that he defines as "faith in the strength and elasticity of the staying power of Jews." Coaching and raising money for the games also allows him to help young Jews from the United States and elsewhere to stay in touch with this heritage of survival and strength that otherwise may be completely forgotten.

Clearly, what these men have to say about their Jewish beliefs may be viewed with despair or with optimism in terms of any assessment of the future of American Jewry. Naysayers obviously will lament their lack of formal religious interest and training and question whether American Judaism can survive, despite their good intentions and concern about Israel. Optimists, on the other hand, less concerned about the decline in formal attention to traditional Jewish teaching and orthodoxy, will applaud the confidence of these Jewish-Americans and their commitment to Israeli survival as testimony to the strength of American Judaism. Another perspective on the same evidence is also worth considering—one grounded firmly in the historical experience of American Jews.

It is difficult not to marvel at the incredible change and progress American Jews have experienced since the mass migration of East European Jewry to this country 100 years ago. In a way, Dolph and Danny Schayes represent something of that experience. Proud of their physicality and their Jewishness as they define it, the Schayes define a progression from a time when anti-Semites labeled Jews as unacceptable and un-American in part because of their supposed debility and weakness to a new era of self-assertion and confidence accompanied by a decline in anti-Semitism, increased Jewish acceptance into the American mainstream, and continued connection to Jewish concerns.

Obviously the ability of a father and a son to find success as professional athletes is not the typical experience for any American family—Jewish or otherwise. Yet, in the context of our story of assimilation and its connection to the American sporting experience it does illuminate the broader experience of Jewish-Americans in the last 40 years. Taking advantage of choices and opportunities increasingly open to them, each succeeding generation has been able to enjoy fully the promise of American life that first lured their ancestors to this country. Along the way, as Jews have historically done, those choices have included the ability to adapt religious custom and belief to new circumstances facing them both at home and abroad.

While it would be foolish to assert that the vitality of American Judaism does not require attention to the continuation of formal Jewish education and teaching, it would be just as dangerous to dismiss as unimportant or as frivolous the sense of Jewish identity exhibited by Dolph and Danny Schayes, itself part of a rich tradition of Jewish toughness and viscerality rooted in the experiences of the children of East European immigrants. Growing up in a relatively tolerant society which increasingly became more open for Jews, they are more comfortable with their sense of confidence and pride in their physical ability than an earlier generation of Jewish men who found in sport an opportunity to challenge anti-Semitism while at the same time shaping themselves as Americans. Able to be more critical of both their own society and of Israeli policy than an earlier generation whose sense of American patriotism and blind faith in Israel is rooted in memories of world war and the Holocaust, they are no less concerned about Jewish survival and no less willing to support it. Images of the tough, fighting Jew now focus on Israeli soldiers and not on visible American Jewish boxers, football players, or baseball players, yet this tradition of Jewish strength and toughness committed to Jewish survival remains a vital part of American Jewish history.

VI

Attempts to keep alive this tradition are as much a part of the contemporary American Jewish world as is the decline of prominent Jewish athletes. Sometimes it takes the form of nostalgic recitation of past achievement—coffeetable books on great Jewish athletes or articles reprinted in the *Jewish Digest* that recreate "all-time, all-Jewish" professional baseball teams or depict the careers of individual greats. Jewish baseball enthusiasts have gone a step further, specializing in the collection of baseball cards that feature Jewish players and joining together in collaborative efforts to gather as much biographical information as possible on Jewish major-league ballplayers.[63]

More visible and meaningful expressions of this same impulse are the activities of Jewish sports lodges and halls of fame scattered throughout the country. Initiated primarily by second-generation men who grew up idolizing heroes like Hank Greenberg and Barney Ross, they regularly canonize both local Jewish heroes and nationally known Jewish athletic saints. These celebrations keep alive rich memories of their youth and also help new generations appreciate their American heritage of Jewish strength. They also provide a focus for philanthropy designed to foster Jewish survival both in the United States and in Israel.

Sports lodges of the B'nai B'rith located in New York and Chicago share these features. Altered in 1975 to include the name of Max Kase, longtime sports editor of the New York *Journal-American* who helped organize it, the New York branch originated in 1950 as part of the efforts of the B'nai B'rith's Anti-Defamation League (ADL) to combat anti-Semitism and foster religious tolerance. Guided by well-known second-generation Jewish sports personalities such as Mel Allen, Haskell Cohen, Marty Glickman, Ruby Goldstein, Irving Rudd, and Al Schacht, early in its history the lodge decided to hold an annual Sports Award Dinner as a means of raising money for various causes. In 1950, they included the establishment of the Benny Leonard Boxing Club in Tel Aviv and the funding of trips for American Jewish athletes to visit hospitalized American soldiers wounded in the Korean War. More recently, they involve support of three B'nai B'rith organizations: Hillel foundations on American college campuses, the B'nai B'rith Youth Organization, which provides sport and social programs for teenagers in a Jewish setting, and a career and counseling service for young people. Similarly, the Chicago branch, which holds monthly meetings, utilizes contributions garnered from awards banquets and other festive events to buy Israeli bonds, support the work of the ADL, and provide college scholarships for Jewish athletes in metropolitan Chicago.[64]

Jewish sports halls of fame located in Chicago, Pittsburgh, Providence, St. Paul, Hartford, and Detroit provide similar opportunities to honor Jewish athletes and to raise money for Jewish causes. Typically, the core of these groups are also second-generation men with strong memories of their own participation in sport. Their meetings, celebrations, and charities, as the men who founded Michigan's Jewish Sports Hall of Fame told me, is a way of remembering sport's role in their own assimilation while using it as a way of attracting others to Jewish causes. The Michigan hall's annual banquet honors Jewish athletes past and present but also recognizes the athletic excellence and good works of others. Organized in 1985, it gives an annual award for contributions to sports in Michigan that has gone to prominent non-Jewish personalities such as Detroit Tiger broadcaster Ernie Harwell. But its Hall of Fame roster includes only Jewish athletes who made their mark in Michigan. Not surprisingly, the first four entrants included three second-generation greats: Benny Friedman and Harry Newman, both quarterbacks of University of Michigan fame in the 1920s and 1930s, and the incomparable Hank Greenberg. Other inductees include William Davidson, the current owner of the Detroit Pistons, and local Detroit athletes like Myron "Susie" Schechter, who, along with other immigrant Jewish basketball players, learned the game at the Hannah Schloss Jewish Center before leading Detroit's City College (now Wayne State) to a championship season in 1926.[65]

Detroit's present-day Jewish population of some 80,000 are not all invited to the Hall's annual dinner. Those 500 who do attend know that their contributions are part of fund-raising activities that support a variety of Jewish causes, including sponsoring American Jewish athletic participation in the Maccabiah games as well as an annual athletic festival for Detroit's Jewish developmentally disabled. Most recently, the group inaugurated the Hank Greenberg invitational golf and tennis tournament as a way of honoring their boyhood hero and supporting cancer research. Whether they participate in the tournament or attend the organization's annual banquet, Detroit's Jews can learn about its tributes by visiting the impressive Detroit Jewish Community Center located in suburban West Bloomfield. Here, in an immense facility that houses a Holocaust Memorial museum and that provides athletic, recreational, and social services to a large suburban Jewish population, the Hall remembers its inductees with plaques designed to keep alive for others an historical memory of Jewish athletic pride and strength. Certainly this is the expressed purpose of Chicago's Jewish Sports Hall of Fame. Welcoming guests to the group's inaugural dinner in 1982, Harry Heller, its executive director, proclaimed the thrill he received in honoring both inductees and nominees to the Hall while announcing its goal of "inspiring pride in our Jewish athletes in our youth. . . . This is a night we shall long remember," he told his audience, "but the dedication to our Jewish legends must not end with this tribute. We expect to carry on this spirit of Jewish pride in sport in succeeding years. Today we honor our athletes of yesterday and today," he concluded, but "we look forward to honoring our stars of tomorrow."[66]

One way Jewish sports halls of fame keep alive a proud tradition of Jewish athleticism and strength is by supporting the Maccabiah games. The so-called "Jewish Olympics" has its roots in late-19th-century efforts of European Jewish intellectuals and Zionists to mobilize the physical prowess of middle-class Jewish youth in the face of increased oppression and violence throughout Eastern Europe. No one spoke more vigorously in behalf of these efforts to engage Jews in physical and athletic activity as a means of survival than Max Nordau, who called for "a generation of muscular Jews" to secure a Jewish future. Hopeful that Jewish physical revitalization would provide group pride in the face of anti-Semitic attacks and foster interest in the creation of a Jewish homeland in Israel, Jewish athletic clubs bearing the names of ancient Jewish warriors like Maccabi and Bar Kochba as well as Hakoah and Hagibor, the Hebrew words for strength and strong man, formed throughout Europe.

Despite resistance from orthodox Jews who insisted that attention to the physical went against Jewish religious teachings, over 100 Maccabi clubs operated in Europe by World War I. Most of them were formally associated with the World Zionist Congress and its plans to create an independent Jewish homeland in Israel. In 1921, club delegates agreed to form a Maccabi World Union. Eight years later, Yosef Yekutieli, a Russian-born Jew and Palestine's only representative to the Union, proposed that Jewish athletes throughout the Diaspora meet in Palestine to engage in athletic competition as a way of confirming common Jewish ties and building a new Jewish state. The event, held during the first two weeks in April 1932, marked the first Maccabiah games.[67]

American Jews, preoccupied like other citizens with surviving the Great Depression, showed limited interest in this inaugural event. Nevertheless, with the help of the JWB, which sponsored tryouts for the team, and the newly formed United States Maccabi Association, which raised money to send them, 13 athletes—11 men and two women—were chosen to represent the United States. Sent off by New York City's mayor Jimmy Walker, who told the athletes at a City Hall ceremony, "You bring home the bacon and I'll eat it," the contingent won its share of medals in track and field and swimming. Three years later, as readers of American Jewish newspapers like the Detroit *Jewish Chronicle* well knew, another small group of American Jewish athletes led by

Lillian Copeland, who more than matched her 1932 Olympic feats by winning six gold medals in track and field, fared even better.[68]

Although World War II interrupted Maccabiah competition until 1950, the spirit of the Maccabee movement did not entirely disappear. Commenting on the arrival of the Palestine Maccabee soccer team in Detroit for an exhibition match against the University of Michigan in October 1936, the Detroit *Jewish Chronicle* urged its readers to turn out in force and in unity with their Jewish brethren. Calling the soccer players "Jewish pioneers," the *Chronicle* recognized them as "symbols of the new life in the Jewish Homeland . . . standard bearers of the efforts for the strengthening of the Jewish back and the injection of a new life and spirit in our people." "The work of these athletic groups provides proof," the paper concluded, "that the Jewish pioneers are not weaklings and that they gain strength and courage which is placing them on a par with athletes throughout the world."[69]

Continuation of such spirit in the hopes of preserving a Jewish future both in Israel and in the United States has certainly been behind the efforts of the United States Committee Sports for Israel (USCSI), which has been the chief agency responsible for organizing the American Maccabiah team since 1950. In its own words, it aims at "fostering physical strength and athletic prowess among Jewish youth" and "instill[ing] a sense of pride in their heritage which links them forever to Eretz Israel." Coordinating the fund-raising efforts of a variety of Jewish organizations including sports halls of fames and Jewish community centers, it raises money to send American athletes to Israel, picks those who will participate, and promotes adolescent interest in athletics by sponsoring regional and national competition for American Jewish youth. Be it sending American coaches to train Israeli athletes, helping to develop the Orde Wingate Institute for Physical Education as the training ground for Israeli physical educators, or raising money for an Israeli national tennis center, the committee also works to develop athletics in Israel.[70]

Not surprisingly, although the committee's operation today rests in the hands of a younger generation of men and women, many of its earliest supporters and organizers were the children of immigrants who recognized the importance of sport in determining their own American and Jewish identities. This link between their own experiences and the purpose of the Maccabiah games is reinforced by the international Jewish Sports Hall of Fame, located at Wingate and initiated by the USCSI in 1978. Although it includes prominent Jewish athletes from all over the world, theirs is a decidedly American emphasis—most especially in its first group of inductees, all of whom were American. The group did choose Mark Spitz and Sandy Koufax, but second-generation American Jews including Red Auerbach, Jackie Fields, Benny Friedman, Barney Ross, Benny Leonard, Hank Greenberg, Dolph Schayes, and Sid Luckman predominated. For those involved in the Maccabiah movement, commemoration of their achievements here and elsewhere confirms Jewish involvement in sport as metaphor for Jewish struggle and survival. Celebration of Jewish athletic strength simply reinforces these ideas as a critical part of Jewish historical memory and as a critical factor in a Jewish future.[71]

At times, however, even American Jews intimately involved in the Maccabiah movement wonder if the serious purpose behind its inception has been replaced by nothing more than grand athletic exercise. Certainly the increase in the size and the success of American teams rather than concern about the spiritual meaning of the experience takes up most of the space in the newsletters and programs of the USCSI. At the 12th Maccabiah held in 1985, for example, 500 American athletes collected 246 medals, more than any nation ever has won at the games and 32 more than the second-place Israelis, a fact proudly detailed in such publications. Even Haskell Cohen, one-time president of the Committee and active in its affairs since 1950, questions whether the games "accomplish anything aside from a joy ride for Jewish jocks."[72] For him, however, and for others who engage in support of American participation in the games in the sincere hope that participation does contribute to developing an American Jewish identity tied to concern for Israel, the response of athletes themselves is enough to sustain their belief that the experience is worthwhile. Making this point in his regular sports column for newspapers serviced by the Jewish Telegraphic Agency in 1977, Cohen offered the comments of one American diver who competed in the 10th Maccabiad. Expressing his appreciation for the opportunity to compete, he noted that the games not only gave him the chance to experience international athletic competition but "most importantly . . . opened my eyes religiously. I feel that every Jew should do his best to see and visit Israel. Upon my return," he concluded, "several friends even noticed change in me. Suddenly I have become much more outspoken about my Jewish heritage and the Jewish cause in Israel."[73]

VII

Annual hall of fame dinners and American involvement in the Maccabiah games provide occasional opportunities to remember an American Jewish tradition of strength and athleticism in ways that emphasize a continuing commitment to Jewish survival. They do so by creating momentary immersion in Jewish athletic experiences that serves as a reminder of the Jewish world of the second generation. There is, in these efforts, a certain irony. Settlement house workers and social reformers hoped sport would break down the ethnic walls of Jewish bounded space and encourage immigrant children to become Americans. Offered opportunities, more often than not these children participated on their own terms in ways that established sport as a middle ground instrumental in determining their own American and Jewish sensibilities. Over half a century later, fully assimilated American Jews with only dim memories of extended family and ethnic community commemorate this Jewish athletic tradition in new ways that enhance and reaffirm their own Jewish identity.

The transformation of sport from an agency of assimilation to a source of Jewish renewal is even more apparent in the changing role of Jewish community centers. Early-20th-century YMHAs, settlement houses, and educational alliances provided a variety of social, educational, and recreational programs designed to encourage the Americanization of East European Jewish immigrants. Today, Jewish community centers, employing sport as a central part of their activities, consciously serve as the key agency for maintaining and encouraging Jewish identity in a contemporary world bereft of ethnic urban neighborhoods and extended Jewish family life.

This alteration in the role of centers and Ys has been gradual, ongoing, and responsive to the changing situation of American Jewry. As early as 1925, Jewish social workers raised the possibility that they had been too successful in their endeavor to acculturate East European immigrants. Special concern that second-generation youth were losing touch with the Jewish world of their working-class parents defined one activist's suggestions for strengthening programs of Jewish activities at community centers. Writing in a new publication, *The Jewish Center,* in 1925, Dr. Mordecai Soltes bemoaned the failure of YMHAs and educational alliances "in strengthening the Jewish consciousness of our youth" and in providing "for their adequate Jewish education, the very life-blood upon which the existence and future preservation of our people depend." Certain that Jewish community centers were "destined to play a leading role" in that process, he urged Jewish centers to use their "informal, extra-curricular activities for the purpose of intensifying the Jewish consciousness of our growing youth."[74]

Not surprisingly, Soltes's exhortation appeared in a publication sponsored by the JWB, an organization first established during World War I to coordinate efforts aimed at caring for the needs of American Jewish soldiers and war veterans. By 1925, the JWB had reorganized itself for peacetime, reconstituting itself as an umbrella organization for an assortment of Jewish organizations, including YMHAs, YWHAs, educational alliances, and the new phenomena of Jewish centers. Staffed primarily by professional social workers, its stated goals were to assist member organizations in selecting its personnel and designing their programs in ways that gave Jewish meaning to the recreational and educational leisure-time activities provided for their members.[75]

The JWB's new mission recognized the changing nature of American Jewry. Today known as the Jewish Community Centers Association it has continually reevaluated its programs and the role of Jewish centers in the spirit of developing appealing programs that encourage Jewish sensibilities. In that spirit, increasingly since World War II in response to ongoing Jewish assimilation and success, Jewish centers consciously offer themselves as substitutes for Jewish bounded space formerly defined by ethnic community life. The expansion of Jewish community center facilities throughout the United States since the late 1940s and the effort to make them the focus of Jewish community life reflect the fact that the disappearance of ethnic urban neighborhoods denied younger, more prosperous, scattered suburban Jews the daily confirmation of their ethnic identity so readily available to their parents and grandparents during the first half of the 20th century. In all these efforts to make Jewish community centers the key agency in maintaining and encouraging Jewish identity, interest in sport and athletics in the broadest sense has remained an important element.[76]

Just as settlement houses and YMHAs used sport as a lure to attract immigrant children, so too have centers. David Sorkin, who in the late 1980s served as chief consultant for the JWB on matters of Health, Physical Education, and Recreation, acknowledges that while the major goals of the Jewish center movement are Jewish education and identification, fully 85 percent of all members join because of athletics or wellness programs centers provide.[77] Focused largely on recreational rather than competitive sport, an array of offerings in aerobics, swimming, and individual sports complement programs on nutrition and stress reduction. Opportunities for team competition in sports like basketball still exist, but gone are the likes of Sammy Kaplan's Dux or the 92nd Street Y hoopsters who made basketball an intergal part of a rich second-generation Jewish community life.

In the modern Jewish community center, sport no longer serves as a vehicle of Americanization but rather, as Sorkin insists, as a mechanism for attracting Jews into an artifically constructed Jewish space that substitutes for that forgotten everyday ethnic world. Part of that process involves developing programs that encourage an appreciation of Jewish background and cultural heritage through sport—be it center participation in the North American Maccabi Youth Games, center sponsorship of Jewish summer camps that combine sport and Jewish living as a daily experience, or the recruitment of center athletes into other center activities involving Jewish culture, philanthropy, and education.

The philosophy and operation of Detroit's Jewish Community Center amply illustrates the changing role of such organizations and the place of sport in them. Its 1989 annual report explicitly declares that its efforts to "strengthen Jewish identification, family life and group survival" depend upon its ability to counter "the breakdown of old Jewish neighborhoods, the increasing isolation and geographic distance between individual Jewish members, and the disappearance of extended families as vehicles for transmitting Jewish values." Mort Plotnick, its current director who has worked there since 1963, confirms the center's place as "an overt manifest representation" of a Jewish world that used to be. He also appreciates the importance of sports programs in attracting members. Plotnick estimates that some 60 percent of the 2,500 people who came to the center daily do so to participate in athletics. Much of the center's 250,000 square feet situated on 132 suburban acres provides facilities for these activites—be it indoor and outdoor tennis courts, swimming pools and running tracks, racquetball and squash courts, gymnasiums for basketball and aerobics, soccer fields, cross-country ski trails, weight rooms, and a health club.[78]

Athletic facilities may attract people to the center and take up a substantial part of its annual $6 million budget, but they are only part of a full program of activities designed to encourage members to experience their Jewishness. A wide variety of educational and cultural programs including lecture series,

a book fair, the Michigan Jewish Sports Hall of Fame, theater, even travel—
all in a Jewish context—provide Detroit's Jewish population, regardless of
background or religious devotion, a common ground for maintaining and
enriching their Jewishness. For Plotnick, Sorkin, and other center activists,
the ability of Jewish community centers to adapt their social, educational, and
recreational programs to the needs of their constituents will continue to play
a major role in the strength and survival of American Jewry.

Not everyone concerned with the American Jewish future shares such
optimism. Consider the plight of Sidney Plitnick. As described by Haskell
Cohen in his syndicated sports column for American Jewish newspapers in
1974, Plitnick, an orthodox Jew and a Yeshiva University graduate, was also
president of the Long Island Jewish Basketball League. Each of the 24 Long
Island temples in this confederation fielded youth basketball teams, including
one representing the orthodox synagogue to which Sidney belonged. Rather
than serving as a model for the connection between sport and Jewishness that
Jewish community center leaders might expect, the basketball league, at least
in Plitnick's mind, had become a Jewish nightmare. Eager for victory, several
teams, as Cohen reported, began recruiting non-Jewish ballplayers to
strengthen their rosters. Gentiles not only replaced Jews on the court but also
in the courtship of Jewish girls who attended games. Plitnick and other parents concerned about such interfaith dating expressed real fear that "sooner
or later we are going to have a flock of inter-faith marriages resulting from
meetings which develop in temples and possibly in synagogues, the shrines of
Judaism." Dismayed at "this new way of encouraging and endorsing assimilation, all in the name of religio-social activity emanating from our temples,"
Cohen urged Plitnick to call a meeting of rabbis and directors to resolve the
problem, noting that the situation was hardly unique and deserved "considerable attention."[79]

While certainly worth attention, it is still too early to accept the judgment that
American Judaism is doomed, destroyed by intermarriage, the lack of attention to traditional orthodoxy, or by the promise of material American life.
Similar doubts were once raised about the beliefs of earlier generations of
Jewish youth who played basketball, boxed, ran races, scored touchdowns,
and rounded the bases in ways hardly controlled or always condoned by their
Jewish elders. Nevertheless, they contributed to a vital Jewish and American
world relevant and important for their own times. Sport no longer serves the
same purpose today as it once did. Accounts of Sandy Koufax and Israeli soldiers or Mark Spitz and American capitalism make that clear. But these and
other stories of Jewish involvement in sport illuminate the significant
changes that have taken place in contemporary American Jewish life. Be it
Dolph and Danny Schayes, Jewish sports halls of fame, or the ability of Jewish
community centers to adapt to the needs of their constituencies, they help us
appreciate the ability of American Jews to maintain important Jewish connections in an ever-changing world.

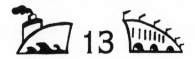 13

Conclusion

SHORTLY before his death in 1988, Dick Shawn, the well-known Jewish comedian and actor, appearing on Johnny Carson's show, joked that he had recently read a book on great Jews in American sport. Not surprisingly, he noted, it was very short. Relying on his audience's familiarity with long-standing stereotypes that depict Jews as physically inept and uninterested in sport, Shawn was funny, if not entirely correct. Funny or not, remarks about the scarcity of outstanding American Jewish athletes belie the significant connections between sport and the American Jewish experience that this somewhat larger book is all about. In trying to understand them and what they tell us about assimilation, the formation and meaning of Jewish and American identities, everyday people's role in determining their own lives, and the legacy of it all, my overriding purpose has not been to idealize and mourn worlds lost, but to marvel and appreciate new worlds created. This, after all, is what the Jewish experience, in America and elsewhere, has always been about.

I

East European Jewish immigrants grappled with their new American lives in a society that accepted sport as legitimate leisure-time activity fast becoming an important part of American popular culture. Both for many immigrants and their children as well as for American social reformers, immigrant involvement in sport became one of the many litmus tests of their American experience. A source of both conflict and reconciliation, their participation in it provides a window into the rich story of how Jewish immigrants and their children became American Jews.

While it hardly eliminated conflict between parents and children, coming to terms with America took place within a familiar, ethnic world of Jewish bounded space. Today, such a world no longer exists, doomed by the simple passage of time, the death of the first generation, and the determination of many of their children to enjoy the benefits of American life. If the proscriptions of turn-of-the-century social reformers and the notions of historians and sociologists who subscribe to theories of "straight-line assimilation" are correct, immigrants were transformed as they responded predictably to the instructions of the majority culture. Their ethnic communities were merely temporary way-stations, places where American agencies, be they the American capitalist workplace or the admonitions of settlement-house workers, encouraged them to pick up the skills and values necessary to move upward and onward as Americans.[1]

If the Jewish experience in sport is any indication, however, something quite different unfolded in these communities in the first half of the 20th century. Although Americanization undeniably took place, it did not mean the abandonment of Jewish identity but rather, in typically Jewish fashion, its redefinition. Throughout these years, but especially noticeable in the decades between the two world wars when second-generation children grew up and became adults, both this redefinition and the emergence of their own sense of what it was to be an American took place within the culture of a rich ethnic community and family life that everyday people actively determined. Be it Sammy Kaplan and the Dux, Benny Leonard and Ruby Goldstein, or other less well-known children of immigrants who, as adolescents and young adults boxed in the gyms of the Educational Alliance, played on basketball teams sponsored by public schools or YMHAs, or who merely played in the streets, they did so on their terms. In their love of American sport and play, by dint of their own enthusiasm and inventiveness, those who participated learned about American values, American capitalism, and even the possibilities for economic success often elusive to their first-generation parents. Sport, directly for them and vicariously for family and friends, was one area of their life over which they could exert real control, one that encouraged assimilation, freedom, and choice.

Jewish involvement in sport helped mitigate the shock of assimilation while furthering the enterprise. Cutting across differences in the size and location of Jewish communities, both as actual experience and in very visible, symbolic ways it did so as a middle ground, both between the Jewish community and the majority culture, between Jews and other ethnic groups, and between Jewish immigrants and their children. Time and again, American games and sporting opportunities became transformed in the hands of Jewish athletes and spectators into ethnic experiences that served Jewish community ends while inadvertently encouraging integration into the American mainstream that so many desired. When local Jewish audiences came out to cheer Benny Leonard, Andy Cohen, Nat Holman, and far less well-known Jewish youngsters who participated in a wide range of organized American sporting activities, they turned such moments into community social celebrations of ethnic life. On special occasions—be they boxing matches or basketball games to raise money for Jewish refugees or to purchase Passover matzoh for the

Jewish poor—they even served very specific Jewish ends. Yet the very decision to attend such an event marked a kind of freedom unfamiliar to Jews in Eastern Europe. Accepting their right to enjoy the many leisure opportunities offered in the United States, even in the worst of economic times, was itself a transforming American experience.

Becoming American did not mean the abandonment of some idealized version of first-generation immigrant Jewish life. The choice, recounted time and again in these pages, was rarely between remaining attached to an orthodox Jewish shtetl culture totally cut off from the American landscape or discarding all remnants of past attachment as passport to full acceptance into an American Gentile world. The former never existed and the latter was never possible. What was available, however, was the opportunity to determine actively what it was to be American and what it was to be Jewish. Although not without conflict both within Jewish communities and between Jews and the larger culture, this opportunity to participate in the process critically set off the second generation from their immigrant parents who came from a world where such freedom simply did not exist.

The visible success of Jewish athletes also served important symbolic purpose. Jewish physicality became a badge of being comfortable as an American. Triumphs in the ring, on the basketball court, baseball diamond, or football gridiron diminished stereotypes about Jewish weakness and countered anti-Semitic charges that Jews were unfit to be full Americans. They also invigorated Jews with a sense of pride in their physical abilities that contributed to a positive sense of Jewish identity. This theme became most apparent in the 1920s, 1930s, and 1940s, when economic depression, American anti-Semitism, and worldwide threats to Jewish existence contributed to a definition of Jewishness that included a visceral, physical dimension committed to the struggle for Jewish survival. Emerging far less from formal religious training than from a particular community and family context and a specific set of historical circumstances, it became an integral part of working-class and lower-middle-class second-generation communities. Symbolized by the exploits of Hank Greenberg, Barney Ross, Marshall Goldberg, and other prominent Jewish athletes and experienced first-hand by countless thousands of Jewish adolescents and young adults in playgrounds, YMHA, or in neighborhood streets, the image of the physically tough Jew, proud of his ethnicity, capable of defending himself against anti-Semitic attacks, and ready and willing to fight for Jewish survival became a critical part of a meaningful Jewish identity in the years between the wars. Recalling a childhood filled with enthusiasm and love of sport, Jewish writer Meyer Liben insists that Jewish athletes "were champions for us in a world which we had far from made our own. . . . Our sports heroes . . . represented us against the world, which, we were coming to know, was filled with enemies, threatening us for obscure reasons. These heroes were fighting for us—each hook, pass, basket was a kind of blow against oppression."[2]

Jewish sports heroes also mitigated conflict between Gentile and Jew. As the United States drew closer to its own involvement with Nazi Germany, men like Hank Greenberg became American heroes for Jew and Gentile alike, helping to soften racial and ethnic tensions at a time when all Americans were urged to unite in common struggle against fascist agression. Not every instance of Jewish involvement in sport provided the same opportunity for symbolic meaning as Greenberg's career. Nor did those appropriated as symbols avow, by their private lives, that they were models of Jewish orthodoxy or belief. Nevertheless, both the majority and minority cultures fashioned their own interpretations of such individuals and in the end became more familiar and comfortable with each other.

Both as experience and as symbol, sport also served as a middle ground between generations of Jews. For first-generation parents and their American children in conflict about what it meant to be Jewish and American, participation in sport certainly served as one of many battlegrounds. Moe Berg, Red Auerbach, and Phil Weintraub offer eloquent testimony to this fact. Yet there is also abundant contrary evidence: Philip Roth's remembrances of how he and his father followed Jewish boxers, Ira Berkow's recollection that he learned about being both an American and a proud Jew by listening to his uncle and father reminisce about Hank Greenberg, and the stories of Harry and Saul Danning, Harold and Morris Judenfriend, or Marty and Harry Glickman—first-generation fathers and second-generation sons bound together by their love of athletics in ways that mitigated conflict and encouraged common appreciation and acceptance of American culture. In short, sport—watching it, playing it, or following it in the newspapers or on the radio—permitted shared experiences identified as distinctly American that allowed opportunities for reconciliation and companionship between parents and children of different generations not always available in the day-to-day struggle to put food on the table that so often served as definitions of parental responsibility.

Jewish participation in sport unfolds a story of assimilation within an ethnic environment, one of community and family, full of conflict and reconciliation shaped by individual choices, class, geography, and historical circumstance, one that had the potential to alter the meaning of American sportive experiences into ethnic events and that confirmed both meaningful Jewish identity and American status. Time and again, depicted in the stories of Jammy Moskowitz, Marshall Goldberg, Barney Ross, Al Rosen, Marty Glickman, Sammy Kaplan, and countless others, are men uncompromisingly proud of their American and Jewish identities—identities shaped more by personal experience and historical context than by formal education or ritual practice. Fiercely patriotic Americans who proudly fought the war against fascism, they offer a strong faith in American capitalism and an American political system that gave them the opportunity their immigrant parents never had known in their native lands. These men are equally proud of the secular version of Jewishness they helped create. Although not especially connected to orthodox religious observance, it emphasizes the importance of ethnic community and family ties, a passion for freedom and opportunity, traditional Jewish concern for the oppressed, and acceptance of Jewish toughness committed to

Jewish survival. Never, in their minds, was this strong sense of Jewishness incompatible with their proud identities as Americans.

Sammy Kaplan, celebrating the 65th anniversary of his Brooklyn Dux basketball club, provides one final example of this powerful ability to retain Jewish connections tied to memories of an ethnic, communal world while proudly announcing American accomplishment. Calling old teammates, their wives, widows, and friends once again to "Kaplan's Kamelot" for an afternoon of friendship and remembrance, he urges them "at sixty-five, not to retire!" "When boat people throughout the world are risking their lives to pass through the 'GOLDEN DOOR' to breathe free, we the representatives of 'THE AMERICAN DREAM,' should be there, figuratively speaking, to greet them." Evoking memories of Brownsville streets and public-school playgrounds, he tells his friends that their annual meetings demonstrate that "the American Dream is a reality" and that "the sacrifices our immigrant parents made were not in vain." "So come," he concludes, "come you examples of the American Dream to celebrate an outstanding 20th century American Achievement—65 years of 'THE BROOKLYN DUX CLUB.'"[3]

The Dux, indeed, were both "an American achievement" and a product of a vibrant ethnic Jewish world. Although surviving members still meet every year, their numbers inevitaby decrease and their festivities more frequently are punctuated by tributes to those no longer alive. Major economic and social changes under way since the 1950s and the simple passage of time have virtually extinguished the second-generation American Jewish world of which the Dux were so vital a part. If this book helps us remember their world of rich experience, one critically defined and shaped by the choices and actions of everyday people, it has been successful. The pace and push of contemporary American life encourages actions and thoughts tied only to the moment, with too little regard for the consequences of such behavior for future generations. There is something to be said for appreciating, even savoring the past as a means of reminding ourselves that we are all part of a larger history.[4]

II

Recreating the world of sport and Jewish community that was also my father's helped me understand more of where he came from than I ever obtained from talking to him. Talking to men of his generation, I learned about their hopes and fears, their American and Jewish sensibilities, and about other Jewish fathers and sons. Conversations I never had with my father gave me the chance to better understand what was missing in our own relationship and what he and his generation had to offer about being Jewish and about life itself. Evoking both love and anger for a man who did not live long enough to be interviewed for this book or to tell me what he thought of it, writing it has helped me better understand who I am and how I feel about him. In a way it has been a chance for my father and myself to "talk" in ways we never did when he was alive and for me to appreciate and accept what we had and didn't have together.

I hope this story of the Jewish experience in American sport also has meaning for Jews today who debate whether or not Jewish life is still possible in the United States. Pick up any publication devoted to Jewish affairs—be it temple bulletins or national magazines—and you can be sure to find an article assessing the prospects of the American Jewish future. Leading Jewish scholars writing for both popular and academic audiences devote whole books to the debate.

Those most pessimistic about the future hardly agree on the degree of religious orthodoxy or the quality of Jewish life among first-generation immigrants. Some argue that original emigrants from the Pale were devout Jews committed to religious orthodoxy and Jewish teaching as a way of life. Others see them as poor, uneducated people who abandoned religious orthodoxy when they left Eastern Europe in order to take advantage of American opportunity. Regardless, they depict the ongoing erosion of American Jewish life. Whether emphasizing increasing rates of intermarriage, breakdown of ethnic communities, or decline in religious ritual practice and Jewish education, they view the history of Jews in 20th century America as a declension from their own definitions either of first-generation immigrant life in this country or the traditional East European Jewish shtetl life those immigrants left behind.[5]

Even American Jewish devotion to Israel is no substitute for more meaningful expressions of Jewish identity. As Arthur Hertzberg most recently put it, while American Jews contribute money to Israel, they "are less inclined to visit . . . or to endorse its occupation policies. . . ." As he sees it, the situation is analogous to the religious commitment of third- and fourth-generation families who join synagogues, attend high holiday services and hold Passover seders. "Some attention is paid to these observances," he notes, "but the commitments are relatively loose ones. Neither love of Judaism nor love of Israel can rest for very long on such unfirm ground."[6]

More concerned with their American identity than their Jewish one, American Jews, Hertzberg believes, are at a crossroads. Ethnic identity may well last several more generations, but more and more, he argues, it will depend solely on "evoking the past." And for him, history is not a sufficient base for the future. "A community," he insists, "can hardly survive on memory; it lives only because of what it affirms, believes, and practices." In the end, only a "spiritual revival," "theological grounds" for which are "not discernible," can save American Jews. "If it does not happen," Hertzberg concludes, "American Jewish history will soon end, and become part of American memory as a whole."[7]

Viewing Jewish history in the context of a worldwide transition from traditionalism to modernity, Charles Silberman, Calvin Goldscheider, and others more optimistic about the future of American Jewry certainly would welcome a spiritual revival. Some would even claim that it is already under way. With or without it, however, they find abundant evidence that assures them of a vibrant American Jewish future. Undismayed by statistics of increasing intermarriage, declining Jewish school enrollments, and diminishing ritual observance, they offer their own interpretations of the data that point to Jewish vitality rather than decline. Rather than bemoaning the disintegration of tightly knit ethnic first- and second-generation neighborhoods distinctively Jewish by sight, smell, and sound, they applaud the Jewish move to the sub- urbs—itself one of many signs of the incredible economic and social progress American Jews have experienced. Here, as Calvin Goldscheider and Sidney Goldstein argue, new Jewish subcultures are critical to Jewish continuity and survival.[8] For them, confident American Jews, no longer embarrassed by who they are and able to partake fully in the opportunities of American capitalism, look forward to increasing vitality and growth as Americans and as Jews.

My own views about the 20th-century American Jewish experience, understood through the prism of sport, embrace much of this optimistic view. Still, I must confess some ambivalence about what at times appears to be an almost Pollyannish view of what lies ahead for American Jews or for Ameri- can society. American Jews today live in a world without traditional anchors, available even as recently as a generation ago. For all the progress many have personally experienced in the last 40 years, it has not been without real cost. Much of it has been impelled by an acquisitive, materialistic ethic, and a desire, both as individuals and as a nation, to win at all costs. This mentality has produced the fears of doomsday and nuclear winter, environmental chaos, and an increasingly visible division between the haves and the have-nots in American society that legitimately call into question the very soundness of American values. Recent American politics marked by Vietnam, Watergate, and Irangate, and a less-than-unequivocal global stand on basic issues of human dignity and freedom—be they in Latin America, China, South Africa, or the Persian Gulf, hardly encourages security and faith in them.

Moved by these concerns, Anne Roiphe, journalist and novelist of the American Jewish experience, suggests that modern American society, for all its benefits, poses real problems for young Jewish Americans. In a world full of frightening prospects which offers them little in the way of stability, they are left alone to shape their own identity and beliefs. Even loyalty to Israel, certainly a basic foundation of American Jewish faith since World War II, that provided some anchor in a changing world, has become more ambiguous in the face of that country's internal politics and the Palestinian question that has divided not only Israelis themselves but American loyalties to them. The specter of the Holocaust even fills many with doubts about belief in God as much as it compels them to remain Jews. Whatever its shortcomings, absent too is the familiarity and closeness of tightly knit ethnic communities, that either by acceptance or rejection provided a baseline for determining who one was. No wonder she sees young American Jews as a troubled generation, one crying out for new ports of calm in the storm of the modern world.[9]

Although hardly calling for rejection of all that world has provided or some nostalgic return to the suffocating limits of some romanticized traditional orthodox Jewish past, Roiphe hopes that we can find some balance between what the future offers and what Jewish tradition contains and that Jewish par- ents can "build a humane and intelligent Jewish tradition as a way of giving our children something to hold on to." Eloquently, she speculates on the possibility that a traditional Jewish idealism full of concern for oppressed people might become a way that Jewish people create a new source of identity for future generations of American Jews. Through story and memories, Roiphe attempts to capture and make available that tradition for today's generations of American Jews and to help them feel connected to a rich Jewish past.[10] So too does this story of the Jewish experience in American sport.

In simplest terms it does so by reaffirming that redefining what it is to be Jewish and searching for new meanings relevant to the times in which we live is a Jewish tradition in itself, one exemplified by the second-generation American Jewish experience. Without minimizing the importance of keeping alive religious and ritual practice or instilling the teachings of Torah and mitzvoth through formal Jewish education, it is essential to recognize that these are not the only ways of expressing Jewish identity nor the only basis for its development. Fiercely Jewish as they were American, often in conflict with their parents' world, and growing to maturity at a time when real threats at home and abroad challenged Jewish survival, those who watched and participated in sport, often as part of the familiar ethnic world in which they lived, developed their own sense of Jewishness both relevant and important to their lives. The very fact that they did so should provide some reassurance for American Jews facing similar needs today.

Equally important is the specific legacy they offer about what it is to be Jewish. The first American Jewish generation to take advantage fully of American freedom and opportunity, their actions and their words affirmed a Jewish identity that included assertion of Jewish physical strength and pride in the service of Jewish survival. For many of the second generation, it still serves as an important part of American Jewish identity today, tied most often to defense and support of Israel as the symbol of Jewish peoplehood.

Not everyone applauds the persistence of this Jewish persona. Most recently, Paul Breines argues that American Jews, materially comfortable and fully assimilated by the 1950s and early 1960s, felt diminished, weak, and guilty because of their lack of attachment to anything Jewish in their lives. Convinced that most American Jews thought that "real Jews either vanished in Nazi crematoria or [were] soldiers in the Middle East," he suggests that to purge their own lack of Jewishness, they rallied in support of Israel's defense, first in 1948, and more significantly during the 1967 Six-Day War and the Yom Kippur War seven years later. Determined to make sure that the Holocaust would never happen again, American Jews glorified the image of the Israeli commando as tough Jew and offered uncritical support and acceptance of Israeli foreign policy, no matter its course. The consequences, Breines concludes, have been tragic. Uncritical support of Zionism has complicated the possibility of peace in the Middle East, ignored the human suffering and political rights of the Palestinians, and encouraged American Jews to accept "hostile and often racist depictions of Arab" men and women.[11]

I too share many of Breines's misgivings about Israeli foreign policy and the response of many American Jews to it. But being tough does not exclude the possibility of also being thoughtful and critical. Concern for Jewish sur-

vival tied to the existence of the state of Israel does not require blind acceptance of Israeli policy, either by American Jews or, as we know, by Israelis
themselves. Nor does being tough in response to legitimate challenges to
either collective or individual Jewish identity automatically require one to
hold racist attitudes toward Arabs. Most critically, as this story of Jewish muscle and American sport makes clear, Jewish admiration for tough, strong
landsmen has not always required Zionism or the protection of Israel as its
source.[12] Henry Ford, Father Coughlin and Adolf Hitler more than justified its
importance to American Jews living in the midst of economic depression and
world war.

   Indeed the tradition of the tough Jew, shaped by a particular set of historical circumstances, is an important part of the legacy of the second generation.
Struggling to find their own balance between their immigrant roots and the
promise of American life, many of them found in sport a middle ground that
eased the journey. This story, to be sure, is hardly as dramatic as knowledge
of Russian pogroms, the Holocaust, the struggle for Israeli independence, or
the Six-Day War, familiar historical touchstones, that, as Herbert Feingold
argues, connect American Jews to a corporate historical memory of the struggle for Jewish survival and help define their Jewish identity.[13] But historical
memory as a part of an American Jewish future also has room for recollections
of the rich everyday experiences of immigrants and their children. By shaping
a community and family life in which sport and physical activity played an
important role, the second generation became Americans without giving up
their Jewishness. In that spirit, Arthur Hertzberg's doubts that a meaningful
American Jewish future "can hardly survive solely on memory" has merit
only if the act of remembering is limited to bathos and wallowing. Efforts to
rekindle Jewish spirituality and to provide a more rigorous religious foundation for American Jewish children today may be for some the best means of
guaranteeing an American Jewish future. But memory and story that help
American Jews connect to particular traditions and attitudes also have an
important place in the own struggle for Jewish survival.

I began this chapter by asserting that my overriding purpose has not been to
idealize and mourn worlds lost but to marvel at and appreciate new worlds
created. It's also clear, however, that I do miss the world of Sammy Kaplan's
Dux and Bernie Reisman's Trojans, a world encapsulated temporally by my
parents' childhood as well as my own with them. Although not the same in
1908, the year my father was born, or 1944, when I arrived on the scene, it
was a world of Jewish people eager for assimilation who experienced that process in the texture of an ethnic family and community fabric that simply no
longer exists in the shuffle of contemporary urban and suburban American
life.

   Clearly the loss of that rich existence is not just a Jewish theme. If presidential politics are any indication of national tendencies, the nostalgic appeals
to pristine family life that so marked the 1988 Bush and Dukakis campaigns

suggest a general longing for a return to a more simple, well-defined family and community life. What I remember personally, however, and what I hope I have evoked in this book, is a richness there defined not only by love and warmth but by intense conflict and occasional resolution.

Surely it was not a world without shortcomings. Adolescents who came of age during the Depression became parents whose concern for economic success for themselves and their children at times denied them full emotional connection with them. Proud of their own ability to assimilate and to advance well beyond their own parents' dreams, they often became unabashed celebrants of American capitalism—unable and unwilling to consider its inequities or the plight of others deprived of its fruits. Many of these same people who experienced American anti-Semitism, European fascism, and the Holocaust, not surprisingly also became fierce and uncritical defenders of the American way and of the state of Israel—ready and eager to fight their wars and contribute in other ways to their causes. Many of them still hold these beliefs today, despite the fact that changing realities make both positions problematical and hinder efforts to rethink and deal creatively with current crises.[14] Even so, it was also a world of family, community, and sport that served as a generative source of growth for individual human beings and for the definition and redefinition of group identities. The fact that subsequent generations have been able to participate in those processes on their own terms and in the context of their own times offers comfort that the process of redefinition and adaptation so critical to Jewish survival continues apace.

Remembering that second-generation world as evoked through the Jewish experience in American sport transforms mourning into celebration. It does so by encouraging us to accept the past for what it was and not for what we might like it to have been, by putting it in its proper historical perspective, by learning from it what it has to offer about how to be Jewish, and by demonstrating the possibilities of making our own lives more meaningful and worthwhile both as Americans and as Jews.

Postscript:
The Jewish Experience in
Comparative Perspective

ALTHOUGH this book focuses on the Jewish experience in American sport, its meaning for understanding the process of assimilation, the shaping of identity, and the possiblities of an American Jewish future, it clearly has been influenced by the good work of others also interested in the connections between ethnicity, assimilation, and sport. While the Jewish experience, like that of any other group, certainly had its own unique elements, appreciation of their work makes clear the significance of sport in the everyday life of other ethnic groups as they came to terms with American life.[1]

Students of the 20th-century American black experience pay special attention to sport's role, both as experience and symbol, in that group's struggle for assimilation and full acceptance. In Pittsburgh between the wars, for example, Rob Ruck argues that a black community expanded by southern migrants, asserted control over parks, playgrounds, and organized sport first offered by white settlement-house workers, local industry, and the organized play movement, and shaped them to their own purpose. Through sandlot organizations, support of the Pittsburgh Crawfords and Homestead Grays, professional baseball teams in the National Negro League, and with the help of black entrepreneurs who controlled the numbers racket, sport permitted blacks control of some portion of their lives, encouraged a sense of community and self-esteem, and provided opportunity for "self-organization, expression, and creativity."[2] Recent books about Jackie Robinson, Jesse Owens, Jack Johnson, and Joe Louis emphatically underline their importance, for both blacks and whites, as symbols of racial pride and of the possibility for American acceptance, much the same way that Hank Greenberg served Jews. Indeed, in his impressive account of the integration of professional major-league baseball, Jules Tygiel even suggests that the efforts of Robinson, other black ballplayers, and black newspaper editors and activists to break the color line in 1947 influenced the ideas and tactics of the civil rights movement of the 1950s and 1960s.[3]

Place these studies alongside the obvious progress blacks have made in sport since World War II and it appears that black success in this very visible area of American popular culture represents real movement toward meaningful integration, full opportunity, and the diminishment of racism in not only the sports world but society at large. From segregated participation in intercollegiate athletics and virtual total exclusion from organized professional team sport, blacks have moved to the forefront of positive attention. Annual college and professional all-star teams in football, basketball, and baseball are dominated by black athletes who earn huge amounts of money. Although hardly as visible behind the scenes in coaching and administrative capacities, there is definitely movement at every level to increase the number of blacks in such positions. While more white athletes than black serve corporate America as spokespersons and role models, increasingly accomplished black performers and multi-millionaires like Earvin "Magic" Johnson, Michael Jordan, Hank Aaron, and Walter Payton sell Wheaties, Nikes, and Nissans with élan and style.

Unwittingly, however, these men who, in the value warp of contemporary America, certainly deserve what they earn, also sell something far more pernicious than the visible artifacts of a capitalist consumer culture. For some critics, their prominence as highly visible symbols of black success obscures the extent to which this society denies real opportunity for the large majority of American blacks, especially lower-class residents of neglected, deteriorating, burnt-out, drug-infested inner cities. Despite the positive role black sport played in Pittsburgh prior to the desegregation of major-league baseball, Rob Ruck concludes that as black control of community and professional sport in that city diminished after 1950, young blacks cut off from other vocational and educational opportunity still see sport as their lifeline to a better life. Armed with statistical studies of the exploitation of black college athletes and of exactly how illusive that lifeline is even for those who beat the odds and become professional athletes, Harry Edwards goes one step further. In his mind, a racist white society consistently reluctant to allow blacks full economic and political freedom channels blacks into sports—an area where black accomplishment does not especially threaten a dominant white power structure. For him, success in sport, divorced from comparable achievement elsewhere, does not signify assimilation and acceptance but rather the corrupt, racist, oppressive nature of American capitalist society.[4]

Certainly it is possible to challenge such positions. Edwards himself, it might be pointed out, is a very successful member of the academy, a sociologist at the University of California at Berkeley who has gone beyond his public image as the radical agitator who attempted to organize a black boycott of the 1968 U. S. Olympic team. Today he appears as a distinguished public servant who talks to Ted Koppel on "Nightline," helps major-league baseball find qualified black managers and executives, and serves as an advisor to the National Football League's San Francisco 49ers. Nor, it could be added, is he simply a token. Increasingly since World War II, blacks attend colleges in greater numbers, have made real gains in terms of economic and social mobility, exhibit real political clout on both the national and local level—indeed show every sign of achieving the kind of success that has been the basis of the American Dream for all racial and ethnic minorities in this country. Comparing the black experience of assimilation since the onset of formal segregation at the turn of the century with the experience of East European Jews and their children, some might even be tempted to argue that although it has taken them a little longer to overcome a racism ingrained since the days of slavery, blacks, like other minority groups throughout American history, are finally seeing the light of day. And in both cases, the visible success of black and Jewish athletes and the involvement of local community in sport positively served those larger ends.

For both blacks and Jews, sport did offer opportunities for self-esteem, group pride, and American accomplishment, especially in the years between the wars. For Jews, however, accomplishment in sport paralleled and ultimately was replaced by increased economic and social mobility; hardly the case for the majority of black Americans since World War II despite the very real gains made by the civil rights movement. Racism, the dynamics of capitalism, and historical context explain why.

Certainly second-generation American Jews, both as children and as adults, faced anti-Semitism, street violence, and discrimination in their struggle to succeed. Without minimizing what they confronted first-hand or the pain and horror they felt over the loss of family and friends in the Holocaust, nevertheless their collective personal experiences did not approach the violence, death, and discrimination faced by American blacks during the same period of time. Moreover, racism in a variety of forms clearly inhibited opportunity for blacks more so than anti-Semitism did for American Jews, denying them access to education and vocational training that might have facilitated their full integration into American society.

As Jews and other European ethnics, in their own ways, successfully escaped their working-class roots for middle-class suburban comfort, blacks took their place—becoming the major part of an exploited, impoverished underclass that is as integral a part of the American capitalist scene as Wall Street. Unlike Jews, Italians, and even their own forebears who lived in vital, urban working-class neighborhoods between the wars, they now live in cities marked by deteriorating urban infrastructures, by problems of crime and drugs far beyond anything ever imagined by an Arnold Rothstein, Gus Greenlee, or Al Capone, and by the collapse of public housing and health care. Complicating matters, as Mark Naison suggests, they are unable to escape urban poverty and its attendant ills because of major shifts in a post-industrial economy that less and less provides job opportunities based on "physical strength and mechanical skill." As he puts it:

> Young people hardened by a poverty not that different from generations before them can no longer use their street smarts and physical strength in construction, mining, transportation, or the production of basic commodities on the scale of the past; rather they must somehow transform themselves into

computer programmers, word processors . . . and advertising copywriters, exchanging the verbal jousting of street corners and school yards for the soft tones of office discourse. Needless to say, for people whose families have been locked into poverty for generations, whose neighborhoods have been abandoned by the literate, the civic-minded, and the upwardly mobile, this transition seems unlikely.[5]

No wonder, Naison concludes, despite the false promise it offers, sport fills the life of young blacks in America's urban ghettos today. Given the choices of "welfare, drugs, hustling and sports" it represents the only avenue, however elusive, that "combines glamour with resources and respectability." More than ever, even though sport is far less likely than it was in the past to provide escape and opportunity, it has taken on a "new and special poignancy" in the face of both racism and the imperatives of the marketplace, as a metaphor for achieving the American Dream.[6]

Everyday people's involvement and interest in sport, then, still tells us a good deal about the way in which ethnic and racial minorities come to terms with American life, but not always with the same results for all groups. It also cautions us to be careful in any assessments we might offer about assimilation or other social developments if seen too narrowly through the prism of sport.

Obviously, only a dramatic reordering of priorities and values and a willingness to recognize the bankruptcy of our acquisitive ethic and the damaging social and economic inequities it fosters will ultimately provide full opportunity for all Americans and make obsolete the notion that sports, as Naison puts it, should "serve as a primary repository of the hope of upward mobility." Such prospects, entailing a crisis of capitalism on the scale of the Communist upheaval now taking place in Eastern Europe, hardly seems likely in the near future. Indeed, American misperception of recent European events appears to be diminishing self-criticism in favor of self-congratulation about the triumph of capitalism and the American Way. The end of the Cold War is not likely to initiate a reordering of budgetary priorities that might deal humanely and constructively with the problems of today's poor and dispossessed. In such a society, where sport still offers a sense of empowerment, it may be possible to use it as a temporary, short-term avenue for improving the chances of black youth today. Ironically, the experience of other ethnic minorities, including Jewish immigrants and their children, provides some possibilities here.

Although with mixed intention, turn-of-the-century settlement-house workers, organized play reformers, and YMHA advocates truly believed that participation in sport taught positive values that would help immigrants, and especially their children, become solid, functioning American citizens. Like Mark Naison, I agree that such values as discipline, hard work, teamwork, fairness, and "endurance in the face of adversity" can "serve as powerful counterweights to the hustling culture and the welfare cycle."[7] Reinvigoration of community-based sport, run by caring coaches, social workers, and community leaders, has the potential to offer some counter to the obstacles poor black urban youth encounter every day. Without the opening up of opportunity and a shift in mainstream priorities, however, reason to adhere to such values will quicly wane. In that respect, organized sport for all children, middle- and upper-class whites as well as poor blacks, can play an important role in introducing them to new attitudes about society and their place in the world that in the long run may help bring about the kind of social change required to make American a more equitable society.

In short, as I have argued elsewhere, it does make a difference who coaches Little League, who runs Jewish Community Center or CYO athletic teams, or who manages organized athletic programs in our elementary schools, high schools, and colleges. Do these people encourage a win-at-all costs mentality replete with racism, sexism, and a disregard for others that may be used to legitimate the continual repression of opportunity and hope for those less fortunately situated because of class and race? Or do they serve as positive role models in helping to reshape American priorities and values?[8] Too often, in recent years, the evidence suggests domination by the former. It would be foolish, of course, and indeed a sign of the true bankruptcy of our system to place so great a burden of reform on sports. But, since sport will always serve as an agency of socialization, let's at least make sure that those who have in the past emphasized some of our society's worst tendencies in the process of doing their job no longer maintain a monopoly over it in the future.

Bibliographic Note

MY intention is not to provide a complete listing of all materials consulted, nor to repeat discussions already undertaken in chapter notes. Highlighted instead are those primary and secondary sources most important for understanding particular parts of the story I have told.

From Morris Raphael Cohen's "dreamer's journey" to Sammy Kaplan's 73-page letter to me about his life, this book depended upon the personal reminiscences of both well-known individuals and everyday people. The acknowledgments and chapter notes of this book already recount the names of those people who shared their stories with me either through interviews or through published accounts of their lives. The collection of transcribed interviews with Jewish sports figures and other Jewish personalities, located in the William E. Weiner Oral History Library at the American Jewish Committee in New York, however, deserves special note.

So too do certain authors whose work on the American Jewish experience and the connection between sport and the life of everyday people contributed to the conceptual substance of my work. Although I read more widely than represented here and although I did not necessarily agree with all that I read, the following works were most important in helping me formulate my own thoughts.

The literature that touches on the American Jewish experience is incredibly large and diverse. Most important to me were Ira Berkow, *Maxwell Street* (New York, 1977); David Biale, *Power and Powerlessness in Jewish History* (New York, 1986); John Bodnar, *The Transplanted: A History of Immigrants in Urban America* (New York, 1976); Paul Breines, *Tough Jews: Political Fantasies and the Moral Dilemma of American Jewry* (New York, 1990); Stephen Brumberg, *Going to America, Going to School: The Jewish Immigrant Public School Encounter in Turn-of-the-Century New York City* (New York, 1986); Naomi Cohen, *Encounter with Emancipation: The German Jews in the United States, 1830–1914* (Philadelphia, 1984); Steven M. Cohen, *American Modernity and Jewish Identity* (New York, 1983), and *Jewish Assimilation or Jewish Revival?* (Bloomington, 1988); Neil M. and Ruth Schwartz Cowan, *Our Parents' Lives: The Americanization of Eastern*

European Jews (New York, 1989); Leonard Dinnerstein, *Uneasy at Home: Anti-Semitism and the American Jewish Experience* (New York, 1987); Lucy Dawidowics, *On Equal Terms: Jews in America* (New York, 1982); Herbert Feingold, *A Midrash On American Jewish History* (Albany, 1982), and "Jewish Life in the United States: Perspectives in History," in Joseph B. Gittler, ed., *Jewish Life in the United States: Perspectives from the Social Sciences* (New York, 1981), and *Zion in America: The Jewish Experience from Colonial Times to the Present* (New York, 1974); Albert Fried, *The Rise and Fall of the Jewish Gangster in America* (New York, 1980); Neal Gabler, *An Empire of Their Own: How the Jews Invented Hollywood* (New York, 1988); Herbert J. Gans, "Symbolic Ethnicity: The Future of Ethnic Groups and Cultures in America," in Herbert Gans, ed., *On the Making of Americans: Essays in Honor of David Riesman* (Philadelphia, 1979); David A. Gerber, ed., *Anti-Semitism in American Life* (Urbana and Chicago, 1986); Calvin Goldscheider, *Jewish Continuity and Change: Emerging Patterns in America* (Bloomington, 1986); Sidney Goldstein and Calvin Goldscheider, *Jewish Americans: Three Generations in a Jewish Community* (Englewood Cliffs, 1960); Albert I. Gordon, *Jews in Suburbia* (Boston, 1959); Milton M. Gordon, *Assimilation in American Life* (New York, 1964); Sherry Gorelick, *City College and the Jewish Poor, Education in New York, 1800–1924*(New Brunswick, 1981); Andrew Heinze, *Adapting to Abundance, Jewish Immigrants, Mass Consumption, and the Search for American Identity* (New York, 1990); Arthur Hertzberg, *The Jews in America, Four Centuries of an Uneasy Encounter* (New York, 1989); Irving Howe, *The World of Our Fathers* (New York, 1976); Jenna Joselit, *New York's Jewish Jews* (Bloomington, 1990), and *Our Gang: Jewish Crime and the New York Jewish Community, 1900–1940* (Bloomington, 1983); Thomas Kessner, *The Golden Door: Italian and Jewish Immigrant Mobility in New York City, 1880–1915 (New York, 1977); Judith Kramer and Seymour Leventman, Children of the Gilded Ghetto: Conflict Resolutions of Three Generations of American Jews* (New Haven, 1961); Deborah Dash Moore, *At Home in America: Second Generation New York Jews* (New York, 1981); Jacob Neusner, *Stranger at Home* (Chicago, 1981); Marc Lee Raphael, *Jews and Judaism in a Midwestern Community, Columbus, Ohio* (Columbus, 1979); Moses Rischin, ed., *The Jews of North America* (Detroit, 1987); Rischin, *The Promised City: New York's Jews, 1870–1914* (Cambridge, 1962); Charles Silberman, *A Certain People: American Jews and Their Lives Today* (New York, 1985); Howard Simons, *Jewish Times: Voices of the American Jewish Experience* (Boston, 1988); Marshall Sklare, *The Jews: Social Patterns of an American Group* (Glencoe, 1958); Sklare and Joseph Greenblum, *Jewish Identity on the Suburban Frontier* (New York, 1967); Gerald Sorin, *The Nurturing Neighborhood: The Brownsville Boys Club and Jewish Community in Urban America, 1940–1990* (New York, 1990); Stephen Steinberg, *The Ethnic Myth: Race, Ethnicity, and Class in America* (New York, 1981); and Jonathan S. Woocher, *Sacred Survival: The Civil Religion of American Jews* (Bloomington, 1986).

Only in the last 15 years have American social historians begun to apply the insights and approaches of Warren Susman, Herbert Gutman, Eugene Genovese, and Lawrence Levine to the exploration of the leisure culture of everyday people. Especially useful are William Baker, *Jesse Owens, an American*

Life (New York, 1986); Cary Goodman, *Choosing Sides: Playground and Street Life on the Lower East Side* (New York, 1979); Elliott Gorn, *The Manly Art: Bare Knuckle Prize Fighting in America* (Ithaca, 1986); Michael Isenberg, *John L. Sullivan and His America* (Urbana, 1988); John Kasson, *Amusing the Millions* (New York, 1978); David Nasaw, *Children of the City: At Work and at Play* (Garden City, 1985); Steven Riess, *City Games: The Evolution of American Urban Society and the Rise of Sports* (Urbana, 1989); Randy Roberts, *Papa Jack: Jack Johnson and the Era of White Hopes* (New York, 1983); Donn Rogosin, *Invisible Men: Life in Baseball's Negro Leagues* (New York, 1983); Roy Rosenzweig, *Eight Hours for What We Will: Workers and Leisure in an Industrial City* (New York, 1983); Rob Ruck, *Sandlot Seasons: Sport in Black Pittsburgh* (Urbana, 1987); and Jules Tygiel, *Baseball's Great Experiment: Jackie Robinson and His Legacy* (New York, 1983).

Books that focus on the Jewish experience in American sport have not been of this sort. For the most part celebrations and compilations of Jewish sporting achievement, nevertheless they provide useful information. See Ken Blady, *The Jewish Boxers' Hall of Fame* (New York, 1988); Stanley Frank, *The Jew in Sport* (New York, 1936); Erwin Lynn, *The Jewish Baseball Hall of Fame* (New York, 1987); Bernard Postal, Jesse Silver, and Roy Silver, *Encyclopedia of Jews in Sports* (New York, 1965); Harold Ribalow, *The Jew in American Sports* (New York, 1948); Harold and Meir Ribalow, *Jewish Baseball Stars* (New York, 1984); and Robert Slater, *Great Jews in Sports* (Middle Village, N. Y., 1983). Important exceptions include Tilden Edelstein, "Cohen at the Bat," *Commentary* (Nov. 1983), 53–56; Steven Riess, "A Fighting Chance: The Jewish-American Boxing Experience, 1890–1940," *American Jewish History* 74 (March 1985), and William Simons, "The Athlete as Jewish Standard Bearer: Media Images of Hank Greenberg," *Jewish Social Studies* (Spring, 1982), 95–112.

Without rehearsing in detail the rich variety of material utilized in the writing of this book and elaborated upon in chapter notes, certain sources deserve mention. Whether trying to understand Jewish community response to the problems of immigrants or to the attention given to Jewish athletes, the American Jewish press is a vital source. Particularly useful were the *American Hebrew*, the Detroit *Jewish Chronicle*, the Cleveland *Jewish Independent*, the California *Jewish Voice*, and the Los Angeles *B'nai B'rith Messenger*. Haskell Cohen's numerous articles on Jews and sport, both in transcript and in published form, written for and syndicated by the Jewish Telegraphic Agency, were also important. Although I was unable to fully exploit the Yiddish press, the microfilm collection of the English translation of Chicago's ethnic newspapers, undertaken by the Works Project Administration (WPA) in the 1930s, provided some insight into Chicago's Yiddish newspapers.

Another WPA project, a study of the New York Jewish community, located in New York City's Municipal Archives, provided a variety of information, including the way in which Jewish community organizations participated in sport and recreation. Along with material provided by Jewish historical societies, libraries, and other organizations scattered throughout the country, it helped provide much of the information on Jewish community life and Jewish participation in sport. Other important collections here include the New York Public Library's Jewish division, the archives of New York City's 92nd Street YMHA, the Chicago Historical Society's material on the Jewish People's Institute, the YIVO Center for Jewish Studies holdings on the Educational Alliance, the Irene Kaufman Settlement House records located in the Jewish Archives at the Historical Society of Western Pennsylvania, and the Tamiment Labor collection for materials on the Workmen's Circle, located at New York University.

Certain collections, individuals, and books proved especially helpful in providing information on Jewish participation in particular sports. On basketball, see player files and yearbooks located in the Hickok Library at the Basketball Hall of Fame in Springfield, Massachusetts. For the Philadelphia SPHAs see material at the Philadelphia Jewish Archives located at the Balch Institute for Ethnic Studies. The archives of New York's 92nd Street Y provide similar information on that institution's varsity basketball team while the Jewish Historical Society of New Haven has a good collection of material on the Atlas Club. A microfilm collection called Jews and Sports, consisting primarily of Philadelphia newspaper clips from the 1930s and 1940s and located at the American Jewish Archives, also proved helpful for coverage of basketball and other sports. Robert Peterson, *Cages to Jump Shots: Professional Basketball's Early Years* (New York, 1990), and Charles Salzberg, *From Set Shot to Slam Dunk: The Glory Days of Basketball in the Words of Those Who Played It* (New York, 1987), provide respectively a useful history of professional basketball's early days and interviews with some of its early stars. Stanley Cohen, *They Played the Game* (New York, 1977), and Charles Rosen, *Scandals of '51* (New York, 1978), recount the story of the 1950–51 basketball scandals.

Player files and other collections at the library of the Baseball Hall of Fame in Cooperstown, New York, provided biographical information and newspaper stories on Jewish major-league baseball players. Harold Seymour, *Baseball: The Early Years* (New York, 1960), and David Voigt, *American Baseball: From Gentleman's Sport to the Commissioner System* (Norman, Okla., 1966), provide good general histories of the game. Jeffrey T. Sammons, *Beyond the Ring: The Role of Boxing in American Society* (Urbana, 1988), offers a useful history of American boxing.

For college and university life see Burton Bledstein, *The Culture of Professionalism: The Middle Class and the Development of Higher Education in the United States* (New York, 1976), and Paula Fass, *The Damned and the Beautiful: American Youth in the 1920s* (New York, 1977). On anti-Semitism in colleges see Heywood Broun and George Britt, *Christians Only: A Study in Prejudice* (New York, 1931), and Stephen Steinberg, "How Jewish Quotas Began," *Commentary* (Sept. 1971), 67–76. For the Jewish college experience in particular settings see Sherry Gorelick, *City College and the Jewish Poor: Education in New York, 1880–1924* (New Brunswick, 1981); Jeffrey Gurock, *The Men and Women of Yeshiva: Higher Education, Orthodoxy, and American Judaism* (New York, 1988); Daniel Oren, *Joining the Club: A History of Jews at Yale* (New Haven,

1985); and S. Willis Rudy, *The College of the City of New York: A History* (New York, 1949).

Much has been written about the 1936 Olympic games, the setting for a significant part of Marty Glickman's story. Most helpful were Moshe Gottlieb, "The American Controversy Over the Olympic Games," *American Jewish Quarterly* 61(March 1972), 181–213; Allen Guttmann, *The Games Must Go On: Avery Brundage and the Olympic Movement* (New York, 1984); and Richard Mandell, *The Nazi Olympics* (New York, 1971).

Notes

Introduction

1. *Sporting News,* 12/6/23.
2. Bernard Postal and Jesse Silver, *Encyclopedia of Jews in Sports* (New York, 1965), vii; Mordecai Richler, *Hunting Tribes Under Glass* (London, 1969), 54–57.
3. John Hoberman, "Why Jews Play Sports," *Moment* (April 1991), 39, contains the Henry Ford quotation.
4. Abraham Cahan, "The New Writers of the Ghetto," *Bookman* 39 (Aug. 1914), 631.
5. Irving Howe, *World of Our Fathers* (New York, 1976), 180–81.
6. Hoberman, "Why Jews Play Sports," 37.
7. This account of East European Jewry comes from a reading of a wide range of sources. Most useful were John Bodnar, *The Transplanted: A History of Immigrants in Urban America* (Bloomington, 1985); Steven M. Cohen, *Jewish Assimilation or Jewish Revival?* (Bloomington, 1988), 47–48; Lloyd Gartner, "Jewish Migrants en Route from Europe to North America: Tradition and Realities," in Moses Rischin, ed., *The Jews of North America* (Detroit, 1987), 26–32; Sidney Goldstein and Calvin Goldscheider, *Jewish Americans: Three Generations in a Jewish Community* (Englewood Cliffs, 1960), 6–7; Sherry Gorelick, *City College and the Jewish Poor, Education in New York, 1800–1924* (New Brunswick, 1981), 6–8; Andrew Heinze, *Adapting to Abundance, Jewish Immigrants, Mass Consumption, and the Search for American Identity* (New York, 1990); Arthur Hertzberg, *The Jews in America, Four Centuries of an Uneasy Encounter* (New York, 1989); Howe, *World of Our Fathers;* Stephen Steinberg, *The Ethnic Myth: Race, Ethnicity, and Class in America* (New York, 1981), 77–168; Jenna Joselit, *New York's Jewish Jews* (Bloomington, 1990); Rischin, *The Jews of North America,* 15–16. Population figures come from *American Jewish Yearbook, 1934–35* (New York, 1935), 389–90.
8. Howe, *World of Our Fathers,* 181, makes clear that many second-generation Jewish youth loved sport, especially baseball, and that this love often became symbolic of the conflict between parents and children about how to adjust to life in America. Focused on the experience of the first generation, however, he does not pursue this subject.
9. I am indebted to Richard White's development of the concept of the middle ground. See his *The Middle Ground: Indians, Empires, and Republics in the Great Lakes Region, 1650–1815* (New York, 1991). Although I am rarely describing a parallel situation,

White's insights very much influenced my own sense of the middle ground as part of a mediating culture.

Chapter 1. The Promise of Sport

1. Edward Ross, *The Old World and the New* (New York, 1913), 289–90.

2. Particularly useful here are Donald Mrozek, *Sport and American Mentality, 1880–1910* (Knoxville, 1983); T. Jackson Lears, *No Place of Grace: Antimodernism and the Transformation of American Culture, 1880–1920* (New York, 1982); Peter Levine, *A. G. Spalding and the Rise of Baseball: The Promise of American Sport* (New York, 1985), 97–122; Daniel T. Rodgers, *The Work Ethic in Industrial America, 1850–1920* (Chicago, 1978). On the organized play movement see Dominic Cavallo, *Muscles and Morals: Organized Playgrounds and Urban Reform, 1880–1920* (Philadelphia, 1981); Lawrence Finfer, "Leisure as Social Work in the Urban Community: The Progressive Recreation Movement, 1890–1920" (Ph.D. diss., Michigan State Univ., 1974); Cary Goodman, *Choosing Sides: Playground and Street Life on the Lower East Side* (New York, 1979); and Joel Spring, "Mass Culture and School Sports," *History of Education Quarterly* 14 (Winter, 1974), 483–98. Also see Allen Davis, *Spearheads for Reform: The Social Settlements and the Progressive Movement, 1890–1914* (New York, 1967).

3. Naomi Cohen, *Encounter with Emancipation: The German Jews in the United States, 1830–1914* (Philadelphia, 1984), and Arthur Hertzberg, *The Jews in America, Four Centuries of an Uneasy Encounter* (New York, 1989), 177–95.

4. See Introduction, note 7.

5. Works Project Administration Study of New York, Box 3633, Report on Recreational Centers, 3/26/42, p. 7, New York City Municipal Archives (hereafter WPA Study of New York).

6. Educational Alliance Records, Folder 21, 4/7/05, statement from Special Committee of Reorganization, YIVO Archives.

7. *Clubs and Club Leading in the Educational Alliance* (New York, 1903).

8. Benjamin Rabinowitz, *The Young Men's Hebrew Associations, 1854–1913* (New York, 1948). Also see WPA Study of New York, Report on Recreational Centers, p. 4. July 1912 *YMHA Bulletin* quotation cited in Michele Pavin, "Sports and Leisure of the American Jewish Community, 1848–1976" (Ph.D. thesis, Ohio State University, 1981, p. 183). Also see Irving Lehman's remark in *Bulletin of the 92nd Street YMHA of New York,* April 1917 (hereafter cited as 92nd Street YMHA Bulletin) and Abraham W. Rosenthal, "Objectives in Physical Education for the Jewish Center," in *Jewish Center* 1 (May 1923), quoted in WPA Study of New York, Box 3627, Jewish Center File. Another organization that expressed similar sentiments in regard to sport was the Hebrew Educational Society of Brooklyn. See its Minutes of Annual Meeting, 1903, pp. 9–10; Minutes of Annual Meeting, 1904, p. 3, New York Public Library (hereafter NYPL).

9. Steven Riess, *City Games: The Evolution of American Urban Society and the Rise of Sports* (Urbana, 1989), 165–66.

10. *American Citizen,* May 1913.

11. Atlas Club to William Mitchell and Board of Directors of YMHA, 3/20/07, 92nd Street YMHA Archives; New York *Globe,* 4/16/07; *New York Times,* 4/14/07; New York *Press,* 4/14/07; *American Hebrew,* 4/19/07; *Hebrew Standard,* 4/27/07.

12. 92nd Street YMHA Bulletin, May 1907; 92nd Street YMHA Annual Report, 1908. (Material related to the 92nd Street YMHA, unless otherwise noted, is located at 92nd Street YMHA Archives.)

13. *The Jewish Messenger*, 11/1/09.

14. Chicago Hebrew Institute *Observer*, 1/19/18.

15. Chicago *Daily Jewish Courier*, 4/23/23.

16. The critical figure for the notion of 19th-century muscular Judaism and its connection to the Maccabee movement and Zionism was Max Nordau. An interesting perspective on his thought was presented in an unpublished paper by John Hoberman, "Sport and the Myth of the Jewish Body," presented at a conference of the North American Society for Sport History, Clemson, South Carolina, May 1989. Subsequent chapters develop the idea of the tough Jew.

17. Chicago *Daily Jewish Courier*, 4/5/23.

18. *American Hebrew*, 5/11/17, 12/27/28.

19. Cohen, *Encounter With Emancipation*, 301–334.

20. *American Hebrew*, 3/23/17.

21. Ibid., 9/7/17. Also see Detroit *Jewish Chronicle*, 6/16/17; Chicago *Jewish Chronicle*, 9/8/33; and *Souvenir Program of the Town in Review*, published by the Seattle, Washington, YMHA, 1/25/14.

22. *American Hebrew*, 11/7, 11/28/24, 11/15/29. For expansion of facilities see *American Hebrew*, 5/16/24, 10/29/26, 8/31/28, 4/5/29.

23. These prescriptions varied in intensity and choice depending upon time and circumstance. Geography and Jewish settlement patterns were important here. Generally, the further removed individual Jewish organizations were from large enclaves of East European immigrants, the less likely they felt the need to announce didactic purpose. For example, in Dallas, with almost no immigrant population, the move to build a new YMHA gym had little in common with the intentions of men like Stroock or Proskauer. See Dallas Jewish Community Center Dedication Book, 1980, p. 10, which reprints a 1922 promotion flyer on the gym.

24. WPA Study of New York, Box 3633, Rewrite of draft of essay, "Jews and Sport," 8/20/41.

25. 92nd Street YMHA Annual Report, 1900, pp. 16–17, 54–55. The Y was rebuilt and expanded on the same spot in 1929.

26. 92nd Street YMHA Annual Report, 1901, p. 17, 42; Annual Report, 1908, p. 21.

27. A full account of the Y varsity basketball team appears in Chapter 3.

28. Pages of the 92nd Street YMHA Bulletin for these years are replete with such information. Also see 3/21/24 Bulletin for article on "The Gymnasium Dept. of the YMHA." 92nd Street YMHA Bulletin, January 1912.

29. Constitution of 92nd Street YMHA Athletic Council, Dec. 1932.

30. 92nd Street YMHA Athletic Council Monthly Reports, Sept., Dec. 1930.

31. Ibid., Dec. 1930.

32. Voluminous press releases from the Athletic Dept. and reports in 92nd Street YMHA Bulletin for 1920s and 1930s confirm this. For example, see releases from 2/22, 2/24/36 and Bulletin from 4/20, 6/29, 10/12/28, 1/10, 6/5/36. Physical Education Department Budgets, 1931–32, 1932–33, 1938–39.

33. Full description of settlement-house activity appears in subsequent chapters on boxing, basketball, and baseball. For general observations about sport there see WPA Study of New York, Box 3632, Report on Jewish Centers and also a Report on Recreation Centers. Also see "Jewish Recreation in New York," *The Survey*, 1/29/21.

34. Paula Fass, *Outside In: Minorities and the Transformation of American Education* (New York, 1989), 240. According to Fass's statistics, of all Jewish youth participating in the entire range of scholastic extracurricular activity, 24% did so in sport. Italians

participated at a slightly lower rate (23%), Germans and native-born slightly higher (32 and 29%), and the Irish most fully (40%). Extensive reading in newspapers bears this out. Subsequent chapters make ample use of this material.

35. Chicago Hebrew Institute, Superintendent's Report, 1918, p. 41. Also see Chicago Hebrew Institute *Observer,* Nov., Dec. 1912; Chicago *Journal,* 7/6/17.

36. Chicago Hebrew Institute *Observer,* Nov., Dec. 1912; *Daily Jewish Courier,* 8/23/12; Chicago *Jewish Courier,* 8/28/12; *Daily Jewish Courier,* 11/2/09. Summer camps for immigrant youth sponsored by Jewish organizations and settlement houses also were another dimension of efforts to utilize sport and leisure as a way of encouraging assimilation. For one description of these programs see *American Hebrew,* March 2, 1928.

37. Jewish People's Institute (hereafter JPI) Scrapbooks, unnamed clip, 2/3/28; Chicago *News,* 2/9/28; Chicago *Daily News,* 11/28/28.

38. Chicago *Jewish Daily Forward,* 5/5/26; Detroit *Jewish Courier,* 7/21/27; Chicago *Journal,* 8/5/29. Quotation is in Chicago *Jewish Courier,* 9/25/27.

39. For information on the Irene Kaufman Settlement House, including issues of the *I.K.S. Neighbors,* see Irene Kaufman Settlement House Records (hereafter IKS), located at the Jewish Archives of the Historical Society of Western Pennsylvania. For examples see *I.K.S. Neighbors,* 2/15/23; *Pittsburgh Press,* 4/18/28.

40. Los Angeles references come from a reading of California *Jewish Voice* and *B'nai B'rith Messenger* for 1920s and 1930s. Glantz quotation is from the *Messenger,* 1/16/31. Also see *American Hebrew,* 3/23/17; Detroit *Jewish Chronicle,* 6/23/16, as well as in numerous issues of the paper in the 1920s and 1930s. A similar story appears for Philadelphia from reading its *The Jewish Exponent* in 1920s. Also see Marc Raphael, *Jews and Judaism in a Midwestern Community, Columbus, Ohio, 1840–1975* (Columbus, 1979), 215.

41. Irving Howe, *World of Our Fathers* (New York, 1976), 315; 92nd Street YMHA schedule of basketball games, 1939; *Advance,* 8/3/21, 8/15/24, 7/10, 8/28/25; *Justice,* 7/29/27.

42. *Advance,* 1/15/20. There was for a brief time a Worker's Sports League of America that reported its sportive activities in behalf of creating a socialist America in a monthly magazine called *Proletarian Sports.*

43. Judah J. Shapiro, *The Friendly Society: A History of the Workmen's Circle* (New York, 1970), 26–46, 86–88.

44. Ibid., 92.

45. Based on my reading of the *Call of Youth* for 1933–36. *Call of Youth,* June 1935, Jan., Feb., April 1933.

46. Ibid., Jan. 1936, June, July, Aug. 1933; June, July 1934; Shapiro, *Friendly Society,* 96–97.

47. Red Sarachek Interview, American Jewish Archives.

48. Goodman, *Choosing Sides,* unsuccessfully argues this position; John Bodnar, *The Transplanted: A History of Immigrants in Urban America* (Bloomington, 1985), 210.

Chapter 2. Basketball and Community

1. Bernard Postal, Jesse Silver, and Roy Silver, *Encyclopedia of Jews in Sport* (New York, 1965), 78 (hereafter referred to as *Encyclopedia*).

2. Stanley Frank, *The Jew in Sport* (New York, 1936), 49–50.

3. Here and elsewhere, unless otherwise cited, information on Moskowitz comes from my interview with him, 12/12/87, referred to as Moskowitz interview, or from newspaper clips in his scrapbooks, referred to as Moskowitz scrapbooks. Material on Nat Krinsky comes from information provided by his son Ed Krinsky as well as scrap-

3. Robert Peterson, *Cages to Jump Shots: Professional Basketball's Early Years* (New York, 1990), 3–46, provides a good description of the early game.

4. Material in Sedran, Friedman, and Holman player files at Basketball Hall of Fame provide information on their careers. For Holman's comment on Sedran see Nat Holman, *Scientific Basketball* (New York, 1922), 110–12.

5. Bernard Postal, Jesse Silver, and Roy Silver, *Encyclopedia of Jews in Sports* (New York, 1965), 83 (hereafter *Encyclopedia*).

6. Ibid., 92.

7. Ibid., 93.

8. Carbondale *Times*, 2/6/72; *Encyclopedia*, 83–84.

9. *Encyclopedia*, 87.

10. Ibid., 83, 87, 96.

11. Peterson, *Cages to Jump Shots*, 70–72.

12. Undated, unnamed newspaper from Northhampton, Mass., in Friedman player file, Basketball Hall of Fame; Peterson, *Cages to Jump Shots*, 75.

13. *Reach Basketball Guide*, 1925, p. 151; ibid., 1926, p. 215; Peterson, *Cages to Jump Shots*, 73–76.

14. Peterson, *Cages to Jump Shots*, 76–77, 89.

15. *Encyclopedia*, 87, contains quotation from a 1947 *Sport Magazine* story on Holman.

16. Basketball Fraternity questionnaires.

17. Irving Weiner, "Nat Holman, Athlete and Intellectual," *National Jewish Monthly* (July 1928), 370.

18. Ibid.

19. *American Hebrew*, 6/6/24.

20. The following account of Jammy Moskowitz's career comes from my interview with him (12/26/87) and from newspaper clips in his scrapbooks. The clips do not always provide exact names of papers or dates but they are arranged chronologically.

21. Although hardly an exact science, I identified Jewish players by the obvious spelling of their names similar to the procedure used by Paula Fass, *Outside In: Minorities and the Transformation of American Education* (New York, 1989). Club rosters were provided by William F. Himmelman, the historian for the National Basketball Association.

22. League statistics in Moskowitz scrapbooks.

23. Peterson, *Cages to Jump Shots*, 119–23; Philadelphia *Jewish Exponent*, 6/25/82; Harry Litwack interview, 12/26/87; Moe Goldman interview, 12/26/87.

24. Bill Ordine, "A Better Team Than Money Could Buy," Philadelphia *Inquirer*, 4/17/77; Harry Litwack interview, 12/26/87.

25. Robert Slater, *Great Jews in Sports* (Middle Village, N.Y., 1983) 81–82; *Encyclopedia*, 84, Ordine, "A Better Team Than Money Could Buy"; *Reach Basketball Guide*, 1925, pp. 190–93; Frank Deford, "Eddie the Mogul," *Sports Illustrated*, 1/22/68.

26. Peterson, *Cages to Jump Shots*, 119–23; *Reach Basketball Guide*, 1926, pp. 219–23.

27. Peterson, *Cages to Jump Shots*, 119–23.

28. Litwack quotation in Robert Straus, "Oy How they Played the Game," untitled magazine (Feb. 1989), 40, in SPHAs file, Philadelphia Jewish Archives Center, Balch Institute for Ethnic Studies; Harry Litwack interview, 12/26/87; Moe Goldman interview, 12/26/87; Shikey Gotthoffer interview conducted by Robert Peterson and loaned to me.

29. Slater, *Great Jews in Sports*, 82–83; Ordine, "A Better Team Than Money Could Buy."

30. Philadelphia, *Jewish Exponent*, 6/25/82.

31. Peterson, *Cages to Jump Shots,* 108–83, describes the history of the American Basketball League, the National Basketball League and the coming of the Basketball Association of America and then the National Basketball Association.

32. American Basketball League (ABL) File, Basketball Hall of Fame.

33. Peterson, *Cages to Jump Shots,* 195–98; Compilation of League scorers, 5/14/41, ABL File, Basketball Hall of Fame. William Himmelman again provided roster names.

34. Ordine, "A Better Team Than Money Could Buy"; Harry Litwack interview; Moe Goldman interview; Harold Judenfriend interview, 6/28/87.

35. Peterson, *Cages to Jump Shots,* 183, contains Miletzok's quotation. Jules Tygiel, *Baseball's Great Experiment: Jackie Robinson and His Legacy* (New York, 1983); Rob Ruck, *Sandlot Seasons: Sport in Black Pittsburgh* (Urbana, 1987); Randy Roberts, *Papa Jack: Jack Johnson and the Era of White Hopes* (New York, 1983); and William Baker, *Jesse Owens, An American Life* (New York, 1986), all discuss the black experience in American sport. See Postscript for a fuller discussion.

36. Charles Salzberg, *From Set Shot to Slam Dunk: The Glory Days of Basketball in the Words of Those Who Played It* (New York, 1987), 2–3.

37. Ibid., 3–5; and Moe Goldman interview, 12/26/87.

38. Robert Peterson's Shikey Gotthoffer interview.

39. Sonny Hertzberg interview, 8/7/87; Salzberg, *From Set Shot to Slam Dunk,* 17–18.

40. Sammy Kaplan interview, 6/22/87, and copy of political broadside he provided.

41. Peterson, *Cages to Jump Shots,* 108–83. For American Basketball League Statistics see ABL file, Basketball Hall of Fame, which contains financial statements for late 1940s and early 1950s. The file also contains correspondence of Maloney. See especially Joseph Maloney to John O'Brien, 12/23/51, 1/11, 1/19, 1/26/52. Also see Red Sarachek interview, 8/5/87.

42. Chapter 12 contains more detailed discussion of Jewish involvement in professional basketball after World War II. The first BAA championship team of 1946–47, the Philadelphia Warriors, was coached by Eddie Gottlieb and fielded three Jewish players. Basloe's account of his days in basketball promotion and barnstorming can be found in Frank Basloe with D. Gordon Rohman, *I Grew Up in Basketball* (New York, 1952).

43. Salzberg, *From Set Shot to Slam Dunk,* 19.

44. See Chapter 12 for a full discussion of these developments.

45. Neal Gabler, *An Empire of Their Own: How the Jews Invented Hollywood* (New York, 1988).

46. Ibid., 4, 201, 215.

Chapter 4. The College Game, CCNY, and the Scandals of 1950

1. Detroit *Jewish Chronicle,* 12/26/35.

2. *American Hebrew,* 1/15/17.

3. Unnamed newspaper clips, 12/13/19, 2/28, 3/3, 3/14/20, Krinsky file.

4. Staten Island *Advance,* 3/3/39.

5. *American Hebrew,* 3/7/21.

6. Heywood Broun and George Britt, *Christians Only* (New York, 1931), and Sherry Gorelick, *City College and the Jewish Poor, Education in New York, 1800-1924* (New Brunswick, 1981), provide estimates of Jewish enrollments.

7. On Dec. 11, 1976, Nat Holman was honored at a testimonial dinner in New York by the United States Committee Sports for Israel. *Nat Holman Book of Honor,* handed out at the dinner, contains the rosters of all Holman-coached CCNY teams from which these statistics were compiled, using name identification process used previously.

8. *The Campus,* 1/3/20, another unnamed, undated newspaper clip; Krinsky file.

9. Ed Krinsky, Nat's son, told me of the poem that appeared in *Microcosm.* Willie was Nat Krinsky's teammate at Boy's High School in Brooklyn.

10. At this time Brandeis University did not exist and Yeshiva University had not yet begun fielding basketball teams. See Chapter 12 for a discussion of basketball there.

11. Los Angeles *B'nai B'rith Messenger,* 1/30/31.

12. Ibid., 1/1/32, contains this quotation. Numerous examples of such columns appear regularly in the Anglo-Jewish press for all major cities. See examples cited throughout this book.

13. Los Angeles *B'nai B'rith Messenger,* 6/7/29.

14. Editorial quoted in *CCNY Basketball Guide,* 1950–51, p. 5.

15. Stanley Cohen, *They Played the Game* (New York, 1977), and Charles Rosen, *Scandals of '51* (New York, 1978), both provide full coverage of the scandal. Unless otherwise cited, all details about actual games and events come from these two accounts.

16. Cohen, *They Played the Game,* 31–32.

17. Rosen, *Scandals of '51,* 93, contains the *New York Times* quotation.

18. Cohen, *They Played the Game,* 34–35.

19. Ibid., 45–46.

20. Rosen, *Scandals of '51,* 95–97.

21. Ibid.; Bobby Sand interview, 12/26/87.

22. Nat Holman to Ed Hickcox, 5/3/50, Nat Holman file, Basketball Hall of Fame; *CCNY Basketball Guide,* 1950–51.

23. Thomas Evans Coulton, *A City College in Action: Struggle and Achievement at Brooklyn College, 1930–1955* (New York, 1956), 173–83, contains the story of the Brooklyn College scandal.

24. Bobby Sand interview. Also see Rosen, *The Scandals of '51,* 105–6.

25. *New York Times,* 2/19/51. Also see Cohen, *They Played the Game,* 63–65.

26. Cohen, *They Played the Game,* 203.

27. *New York Times,* 3/4/51.

28. Cohen, *They Played the Game,* 206–9.

29. See Chapter 6 for a discussion of Jewish involvement in the Black Sox scandal. Both Cohen and Rosen discuss the Borscht Belt connection at length. So does Stefan Kanter, *A Summer World* (New York, 1989), 210–20. Even at small hotels like Jaffe's Evergreen Manor in Liberty, New York, where I spent my summers between 1949 and 1955, college ballplayers waited on tables during the day and played basketball at night.

30. Cohen, *They Played the Game,* 97–100; Rosen, *The Scandals of '51,* 118–30; *New York Times,* 2/21/51.

31. *New York Times,* 2/19/51.

32. *Sport Magazine,* Nov. 1951, pp. 13, 78. Also see Nat Holman to Ed Hickcox, 10/31/51, Nat Holman file, Basketball Hall of Fame; *New York Times,* 2/21/51.

33. Cohen, *They Played the Game,* 225; *New York Times,* 11/21, 11/22/51.

34. Robert Slater, *Great Jews in Sports* (Middle Village, N.Y., 1983), 106; Harold Judenfriend interview, 6/28/87; Sonny Hertzberg interview, 8/7/87.

35. *Program of the United States Committee Sports for Israel Dinner, December 11, 1976.* Both the USCSI and the Maccabiah games are discussed in Chapter 12.p-m

36. *Program of the B'nai B'rith Max Kase Sports Lodge Dinner, 1976.* Jewish sports lodges are discussed in Chapter 12.

Chapter 5. America's National Game

1. Irving Howe and Kenneth Libo, *How We Lived, 1880–1930* (New York, 1979), 51–52. Also see Cary Goodman, *Choosing Sides: Playground and Street Life on the Lower East Side* (New York, 1979), 89.

2. Abraham Cahan, *Yekl and the Imported Brideroom* (New York, 1970), 5.

3. There is a vast literature here, summarized most recently in Michael Kimmel, "Baseball and the Reconstitution of American Masculinity, 1880–1920," in Peter Levine, ed., *Baseball History 3* (Westport, Conn., 1990), 98–112. Also see Peter Levine, *A. G. Spalding and the Rise of Baseball: The Promise of American Sport* (New York, 1985), 97–122.

4. Levine, *A. G. Spalding and the Rise of Baseball,* 118, 99 for quotations.

5. Steven Riess, *City Games: The Evolution of American Urban Society and the Rise of Sports* (Urbana, 1989), 25–26.

6. Steven Riess, *Touching Base: Professional Baseball and American Culture in the Progressive Era* (Westport, 1980), spells out gaps between baseball rhetoric and reality.

7. George Burns, *The Third Time Around* (New York, 1980), 9–10.

8. Morris R. Cohen, *A Dreamer's Journey: The Autobiography of Morris Raphael Cohen* (Boston, 1949), 80–81.

9. Ibid.

10. Rich Marazzi, "Al Schacht, 'The Crown Prince of Baseball,'" *Baseball History* 1 (Winter, 1986), 35–36.

11. Ibid. Also see Al Schacht, *Clowning Through Baseball* (New York, 1941).

12. Charles Alexander, *John McGraw* (New York, 1988), 102.

13. Marrazi, "Al Schacht," 36.

14. Harry Danning interview, 8/7/85.

15. Andy Cohen interview, American Jewish Committee. All Cohen quotations are from this interview.

16. Tilden Edelstein, "The American Dream and the National Game: Andy and Syd Cohen Play Professional Baseball," paper presented at the Organization of American Historians Meeting, 1983, the best account of Cohen's major-league career, also contains this material. A shorter version appeared as "Cohen at the Bat" in *Commentary* (Nov. 1983), 53–56.

17. Mel Allen and Esther Kaufman interview, American Jewish Committee, is the source for the following account.

18. Phil Weintraub interview, 1/16/85.

19. Louis Kaufman, Barbara Fitzgerald, and Tom Sewell, *Moe Berg: Athlete, Scholar, Spy* (Boston, 1974), is the main source for this account of Berg.

20. Ibid., 42

21. "This Week," unnamed newspaper, 5/31/39; New York *Tribune,* 3/23/44; unnamed Cleveland newspaper, 4/16/31, all located in Moe Berg file, National Baseball Hall of Fame. Also see Harold and Meir Ribalow, *Jewish Baseball Stars* (New York, 1984), 158.

22. Ribalow, *Jewish Baseball Stars,* 155–56.

23. Kaufman et al., *Moe Berg,* 112.

24. Ibid., 111.

25. Ibid. traces this story.

26. Irwin Shaw, *Voices of a Summer Day* (New York, 1965), 142.

27. For examples see Jewish People's Institute scrapbooks, Chicago Historical Society; 92nd YMHA Bulletin, 6/22/28; Dallas YMHA Bulletin, 6/25.

28. Bernard Reisman, *Trojan's 50th Anniversary Book,* Sept. 1987.

29. *Sporting News,* 4/25/51; Cal Abrams interview, American Jewish Committee.

30. Marc Raphael, *Jews and Judaism in a Midwestern Community, Columbus, Ohio* (Columbus, 1979), 334.

31. Philip Roth, "My Life as a Boy," *New York Times Book Review,* 10/10/87. Be it Chaim Potok, Bernard Malamud, or Roger Kahn, virtually every modern Jewish fiction writer has touched on baseball. Eric Solomon of San Francisco State University is currently completing a book on Jewish writers and baseball. See his "The Boys of Summer Grows Older: Roger Kahn and the Baseball Memoir," in *Baseball History* 2 (Summer, 1987), 27–46.

Chapter 6. Cohen at the Bat

1. Rod Carew, a recent convert, did not make my list. Identification was easy when players signified their religious preference on the questionnaires located in their player files at the Baseball Hall of Fame Library at Cooperstown, N.Y. Occasionally I found that names listed in the various catalogues did not belong and so I excluded them. The 115 figure is of a rough estimate of some 10,000 names listed in the *Baseball Encyclopedia.* Special thanks to Jack Lipson who helped me go through the player files. Also helpful is Erwin Lynn, *The Jewish Baseball Hall of Fame* (New York, 1987).

2. *New York Times,* 1/26/88. Comparisons to the rosters of three major-league squads chosen at random suggest the tenure of Jewish ballplayers was less than others. The average career for a 1929 Detroit Tiger was 11 seasons and 98 games, for a 1938 New York Yankee, 12 seasons and 103 games, and for a 1956 Chicago Cub, 10 seasons and 90 games.

3. Harold and Meir Ribalow, *Jewish Baseball Stars* (New York, 1984), 13–20; Bernard Postal, Jesse Silver, and Roy Silver, *Encyclopedia of Jews in Sports* (New York, 1965), 42–44, 54–55 (hereafter *Encyclopedia*).

4. Lynn, *Jewish Baseball Hall of Fame;* Al Schacht, *Clowning Through Baseball* (New York, 1941).

5. *Encyclopedia,* 42–44, and Ribalow, *Jewish Baseball Stars,* 13–20, for example, refer to Kling as Jewish; Mrs. Johnny Kling to Lee Allen, Feb. 12, 1969, Kling player file, Baseball Hall of Fame.

6. Aside from Ribalow, *Jewish Baseball Stars,* and *Encyclopedia,* also see Stanley Frank, *The Jew in Sports* (New York, 1936); Harold Ribalow, *The Jew in American Sports* (New York, 1948). For further explanations of this tendency see Chapters 7 and 12.

7. *Sporting News,* 11/1/1890.

8. Eliot Asinof, *Eight Men Out* (New York, 1979).

9. The following story of the fix relies heavily on ibid.

10. For discussion of Arnold Rothstein and also of Jewish gangsters in general see Albert Fried, *The Rise and Fall of the Jewish Gangster in America* (New York, 1980); Leo Katcher, *The Big Bankroll* (New York, 1958); Jenna Joselit, *Our Gang: Jewish Crime and the New York Jewish Community, 1900–1940* (Bloomington, 1983).

11. F. Scott Fitzgerald, *The Great Gatsby* (New York, 1925), 88.

12. Asinof, *Eight Men Out,* 247–48.

13. These observations come from reading a variety of Jewish and regular newspapers including the Chicago *Tribune, New York Times,* San Francisco *Chronicle, Washington Post,* St Louis *Post Dispatch, American Hebrew,* and Detroit *Jewish Chronicle.*

14. *New York Times,* 7/23/22, for reference to Ford as one of 12 greatest Americans. My interpretation of Ford lies heavily on Warren Susman, *Culture and History: The Transformation of American Society in the 20th Century* (New York, 1984), 122–49.

15. Ibid. Also see John Higham, *Strangers in the Land: Patterns of American Nativism, 1860–1925* (New York, 1967), 228–330.

16. Higham, *Strangers in the Land,* 280–84; *Aspects of Jewish Power in the United States,* 4 vols. (Dearborn, 1920, 1921, 1922). Quotation from vol. 1, p. 6.

17. *Aspects of Jewish Power,* vol. 3, pp. 37–63, contain the various quotations.

18. Ibid.

19. Higham, *Strangers in the Land,* 285.

20. Joselit, *Our Gang,* 145–46.

21. *New York Times,* 2/16, 3/2, 3/3, 5/27, 11/2/21, 1/6/22 for examples of Jewish opposition to Ford.

22. David Voigt, *American Baseball,* vol. 2 (Norman, 1970), 132–33.

23. Leverett T. Smith, Jr., *The American Dream and the National Game* (Bowling Green, 1975), 200–201.

24. Susman, *Culture and History,* 122–49, and Ken Sobol, *Babe Ruth and the American Dream* (New York, 1976), provide the most interesting interpretations of Babe Ruth.

25. *Baseball Magazine,* Jan. 1926, p. 341. Tilden Edelstein, "The American Dream and the National Game: Andy and Syd Cohen Play Professional Baseball," paper presented at Organization of American Historians meeting, 1983, pp. 1–2.

26. Andrew Heinze, *Adapting to Abundance: Jewish Immigrants, Mass Consumption, and the Search for American Identity* (New York, 1990).

27. *American Hebrew,* 10/5/23; *Sporting News,* 9/6/23, 7/23/66. Also see Louis Jacobson, "Will the Real Rabbi of Swat Please Stand Up?," *Baseball Research Journal* 18 (1989), 17–18, for Solomon's brother's remembrances.

28. *American Hebrew,* 6/18/26.

29. Edelstein, "The American Dream and the National Game," p. 4. My own analysis of Cohen owes much to Prof. Edelstein's work.

30. Andy Cohen interview, American Jewish Committee; Edelstein, "The American Dream and the National Game," 5. *New York Times* quotation from Harold Ribalow, *The Jew in American Sports,* 23.

31. *American Hebrew,* 4/20/28; New York *Herald Tribune,* 4/12/28; Chicago *Tribune,* 4/13/28.

32. Edelstein, "The American Dream and the National Game," 4, contains the poem, found by Edelstein as an undated, unnamed newspaper clip in Andy Cohen's scrapbooks.

33. Ribalow, *The Jew in American Sports,* 23.

34. Edelstein, "The American Dream and the National Game,", 6.

35. Advertisement, Andy Cohen file, Baseball Hall of Fame; Andy Cohen interview, American Jewish Committee.

36. Andy Cohen interview, American Jewish Committee.

37. *Sporting News,* 11/23/29; *New York Post,* 3/29/60.

38. Edelstein, "The American Dream and the National Game," 8. This view has been expressed by many recent students of the black experience in American sport, most prominently by Harry Edwards.

39. Edelstein, "The American Dream and the National Game," 6–7.

40. Ibid, 6; Los Angeles *B'nai B'rith Messenger*, 1/22, 4/12/29.

41. Andy Cohen interview, American Jewish Committee.

42. *New York Post*, 3/29/60; Andy Cohen interview, American Jewish Committee.

43. Edelstein, "The American Dream and the National Game," 8.

44. Ibid., 9.

45. Irving Howe, *World of Our Fathers* (New York, 1976), 180–81.

Chapter 7. Jews and Major League Baseball

1. Stanley Frank, *The Jew in Sports* (New York, 1936), 23–29.

2. Ibid., 50.

3. Ibid., 77–79.

4. Such coverage is apparent in reading the American Jewish press for these years.

5. New York *World Telegram and Sun*, 3/19/42; *Washington Post*, 1/20/44. Also see *Sporting News*, 2/26, 3/26/42.

6. New York *World Telegram and Sun*, 3/19/42.

7. Unnamed 7/10/30 newspaper clip, Harry Rosenberg file, Baseball Hall of Fame Library. Perhaps McGraw would have done better with Harry's older brother, Lou, who played four games at second base for the White Sox in 1923 and went 1 for 4 at the plate.

8. New York *World Telegram and Sun*, 9/7/33; *Sporting News*, 6/28/34; New York *World Telegram and Sun*, 5/20, 8/7/34, 3/1/35; and unnamed 8/23/34 newspaper clip, Phil Weintraub file, Baseball Hall of Fame Library.

9. For examples see New York *World Telegram and Sun*, 7/19/33, 2/16, 7/14/34, 3/20, 5/5/39, 5/21/40; *Collier's Magazine*, 7/23/38; New York *Daily News*, 3/6/41.

10. Sandy Koufax joined the Dodgers in Brooklyn in 1955 but did not emerge as a prominent player until the Dodgers moved to Los Angeles. See Chapter 12 for his story.

11. New York *World Telegram and Sun*, April 1949, in Cal Abrams file, Baseball Hall of Fame Library.

12. *Sporting News*, 6/13/36.

13. Ira Berkow, "Introduction," in Hank Greenberg, *The Story of My Life* (New York, 1989), 8.

14. *American Hebrew*, 7/18/30; California *Jewish Voice*, 9/1/33, 8/3/34.

15. California *Jewish Voice*, 5/2/35.

16. The American Jewish Archives has two reels of microfilm called Jews and Sports Collection. It consists of newspaper columns, mostly unnamed and undated but apparently from Philadelphia newspapers. The Henry Levy quotation is from this collection, hereafter referred to as Jews and Sports Collection, AJA. Virtually every American Jewish newspaper I examined, including the *American Hebrew*, provided year-end reviews of Jewish amateur and professional sports celebrities.

17. New York *World Telegram and Sun*, 4/27/37.

18. *American Hebrew*, 5/21/37.

19. California *Jewish Voice*, 10/3/30, 8/14/31.

20. Examples from interviews with Jewish ballplayers and American Jewish newspapers already cited provide innumerable instances.

21. James Isaminger column, Jews and Sports Collection, AJA.

22. *Sporting News*, 7/20/39; Stan Baumgartner column, Jews and Sports Collection, AJA.

23. Undated, unnamed newspaper clip, Jewish and Sports Collection, AJA.

24. Cal Abrams interview, American Jewish Committee.

25. Bernard Postal, Jesse Silver, and Roy Silver, *Encyclopedia of Jews in Sport* (New York, 1965), 51.

26. *New York Times,* 10/2/86.

27. Deborah Dash Moore, *At Home in America: Second Generation New York Jews* (New York, 1981).

28. Peter Golenbock, *Bums: An Oral History of the Brooklyn Dodgers* (New York, 1984), 477, contains the *New York Times* quotation. Cal Abrams to Peter Levine, 3/10/85, details Cal's "proudest moment."

29. Harry Danning interview, 8/7/85; Phil Weintraub interview, 1/16/85; Cal Abrams interview, American Jewish Committee.

30. Haskell Cohen, sports publicist and longtime syndicated sports columnist for the Jewish Telegraphic Agency, graciously gave me access to his files of stories. Some were photocopies of actual newspaper pages; others were typescripts of articles that were also published. Here and elsewhere, reference to this material will be either exact newspaper reference or, if from a typescript, noted as Cohen typescript and date. Cy Block quotation is from an undated, unnamed newspaper clip.

31. *Sporting News,* 10/16/41.

32. *Washington Post,* 4/26/33.

33. Ibid., 4/27/33.

34. Harold Ribalow, *The Jew in American Sports* (New York, 1948), 52.

35. *American Hebrew,* 2/15, 4/12/46; Goody Rosen interview, 4/1/85.

36. Goody Rosen interview, 4/1/85.

37. Al Rosen interview, American Jewish Committee.

38. Roger Kahn, "The Jewish Education of Al Rosen," in Cleveland *Magazine,* no date, in Al Rosen file, Baseball Hall of Fame Library.

39. Ibid., *Saturday Evening Post,* 8/11/51.

40. Greenberg, *Story of My Life,* 217.

41. Saul Rogovin interview, American Jewish Committee.

42. Al Rosen interview, American Jewish Committee, and Kahn, "The Jewish Education of Al Rosen."

43. Kahn, "The Jewish Education of Al Rosen."

44. Unnamed 11/10/53 newspaper clip, "Baseball Free of Prejudice," in Al Rosen file, Baseball Hall of Fame Library.

45. Anglo-Jewish newspapers prior to 1940 invariably referred to Jewish players in these ways.

46. *Sporting News,* 7/11/40.

47. William Baker, *Jesse Owens, an American Life* (New York, 1986); Jeffrey Sammons, *Beyond the Ring: The Role of Boxing in American Society* (Urbana, 1988), 96–129; Christopher Mead, *Champion, Joe Louis: Black Hero in White America* (New York, 1983).

48. Jules Tygiel, *Baseball's Great Experiment: Jackie Robinson and His Legacy* (New York, 1983).

49. Ribalow, *The Jew in American Sports,* 3–4.

50. *American Hebrew,* 10/15/48, 3/10/50.

51. New York *World Telegram and Sun,* April 1949, in Cal Abrams file, Baseball Hall of Fame Library.

52. Carl Levin, *Congressional Record,* S1866, 9/17/86; Greenberg, *The Story of My Life,* 189–91.

53. *Sporting News,* 9/12/35; Detroit *Jewish Chronicle,* 9/21/34.

54. See Hank Greenberg interview, American Jewish Committee, and Greenberg, *Story of my Life*, for details of his childhood. Quotation from Greenberg, *Story of My Life*, 3.

55. Greenberg, *Story of My Life*, 10.

56. "How to Hit a Home Run," *Collier's Magazine*, 4/22/39.

57. *Sporting News*, 11/7/40.

58. Detroit *Jewish Chronicle*, 4/12/35.

59. California *Jewish Voice*, 3/7, 3/21/30, 5/8/31.

60. *American Hebrew*, 8/3/34.

61. Robert Slater, *Great Jews in Sports* (Middle Village, N.Y., 1983), 85, has the gefilte fish story; Haskell Cohen typescript written after Greenberg's death.

62. Greenberg, *Story of My Life*, 18–19; *New York Times* obituary, 9/5/86; and M. David Mogeloff, "A New Star of the Diamond," undated, unnamed newspaper article, Jews and Sports Collection, AJA.

63. Detroit *News*, 9/11/34. For examples of rabbinical debate see Detroit *Jewish Chronicle*, 9/14, 9/21/34. William Simons, "The Athlete as Jewish Standard Bearer: Media Images of Hank Greenberg," *Jewish Social Studies* (Spring, 1982), 95–112, tells this story although his interpretation is different than mine.

64. Detroit *Free Press*, 9/11/34.

65. Greenberg, *Story of My Life*, 59.

66. Detroit *Free Press*, 9/11/34; Cleveland *Press*, 9/11/34. Also see Robert L. Cohen, "Home(Plate) for the Holidays?", *Moment* 9 (Sept. 1984), 54–57.

67. Detroit *Jewish Chronicle*, 9/21/34.

68. Alan Brinkley, *Voices of Protest: Huey Long, Father Coughlin and the Great Depression* (New York, 1982), 119, on Coughlin's popularity. Brinkley suggests that Coughlin did not become overtly anti-Semitic until late 1930s but I disagree here.

69. Detroit *Jewish Chronicle*, 10/5/34, reprinted the poem.

70. Ibid., 9/21/34.

71. Detroit *News*, 9/12/86.

72. Greenberg, *Story of My Life*, 59–60; Detroit *Jewish Chronicle*, 9/14/34.

73. Ibid., 10/12/34.

74. Ibid., 4/12/35. Also see 9/21/34, 11/13/36 for further involvement in Jewish affairs.

75. Greenberg, *Story of My Life*, 78. See Chapter 9 for a discussion of Baer.

76. Greenberg's disengagement from religion is clear in his own words and in those of his wives, children, and friends as presented in Greenberg, *Story of My Life*.

77. Carl Levin, *Congressional Record*, S1866, 9/17/86.

78. The full text of Matthau's eulogy is in Greenberg, *Story of My Life*, 282–84.

79. *New York Times*, 9/7/86.

80. Greenberg, *Story of My Life*, 117.

81. *New York Times*, 9/7/86.

82. Greenberg, *Story of My Life*, 116.

83. Haskell Cohen, undated, unnamed newspaper clip, Jews and Sports Collection, AJA.

84. Greenberg, *Story of My Life*, 103.

85. Charles Silberman, *A Certain People: American Jews and Their Lives Today* (New York, 1985), 60, 47–73.

86. Greenberg, *Story of My Life*, 213, 217–19.

87. Cohen, "Home(Plate) for the Holidays."

88. *Sporting News*, 12/18/41.

89. Stanley Frank, "Hank Made Greenberg," *Saturday Evening Post,* 3/15/41; *Sporting News,* 9/29, 11/17/38, 9/7/39, 10/3, 3/7/40, 1/9, 1/23/41 for examples.

90. Greenberg, *Story of My Life,* 110.

91. Detroit *Jewish Chronicle,* 9/21/34; *Sporting News,* 9/28, 10/6/38.

92. Greenberg, *Story of My Life,* provides details on Hank's career after he retired from baseball. Also see *National Jewish Monthly* (Sept. 1948), 13.

93. Levin, Congressional Record, S1866, 9/17/86.

94. See Chapters 8 and 9 for a discussion of boxing.

Chapter 8. Boxing and the American Jewish Experience

1. Cleveland *Press,* 1/12/24.

2. Steven Riess, "A Fighting Chance: The Jewish-American Boxing Experience, 1890–1940," *American Jewish History* 74 (March 1985), 234, and Ken Blady, *The Jewish Boxers' Hall of Fame* (New York, 1988), are the sources for this information.

3. Abraham Cahan, *Yekl and the Imported Bridegroom* (New York, 1970), 2.

4. Ibid., 2–5.

5. Eliot Gorn, *The Manly Art: Bare-Knuckle Prize Fighting in America* (Ithaca, 1986), 132–41, 224–49.

6. Unless otherwise noted, information on Choynski's family and career comes from William Kramer and Norton B. Stern, "San Francisco's Fighting Jew," *California History* 53 (Winter, 1974), 333–45. Also see Blady, *The Jewish Boxers' Hall of Fame,* 27–38. On San Francisco, see Irena Narell, *Our City: The Jews of San Francisco* (San Diego, 1981).

7. Kramer and Stern, "San Francisco's Fighting Jew," 336.

8. All Fields quotations are from Ira Berkow, *Maxwell Street* (New York, 1977), 142–43.

9. 1934 unnamed newspaper clip by Frank Menke called "Benny Bass Started as Pug by Beating Up Irish Kids," Jews and Sports Collection, AJA.

10. Blady, *The Jewish Boxers' Hall of Fame,* 112–13.

11. Ibid.

12. Bernard Postal, Jesse Silver, and Roy Silver, *Encyclopedia of Jews in Sport* (New York, 1965), 154 (hereafter *Encyclopedia*); Ruby Goldstein, *Third Man in the Ring* (New York, 1959), 6, 16–18, 23.

13. Cleveland *Press,* 3/22/24; *Encyclopedia,* 171; Cleveland *Jewish Independent,* 10/30/25; Marc Raphael, *Jews and Judaism in a Midwestern Community, Columbus, Ohio* (Columbus, 1979); Detroit *Jewish Chronicle,* 11/2/34.

14. Blady, *The Jewish Boxers' Hall of Fame,* 81–90, covers Cross's career. Also see Riess, "A Fighting Chance," 230, and *Encyclopedia,* 152.

15. Jeffrey T. Sammons, *Beyond the Ring: The Role of Boxing in American Society* (Urbana, 1988), provides an overview of the history of boxing in the United States.

16. Riess, "A Fighting Chance," 230.

17. For information on Attell see Blady, *The Jewish Boxers' Hall of Fame,* 39–48. Also see Riess, "A Fighting Chance," 232–34.

18. Blady, *The Jewish Boxers' Hall of Fame,* 41–42.

19. *Jewish Tribune,* 10/5/23; Nat Fleischer, *Leonard the Magnificent* (Norwalk, Conn., 1947), 96; *Encyclopedia,* 162–65; Blady, *The Jewish Boxers' Hall of Fame,* 109–28, all provide information on Leonard and repeat this story.

20. Fleischer, *Leonard the Magnificent,* 87.

21. Riess, "A Fighting Chance," 233. For connections between Jewish gangsters and boxing see Albert Fried, *The Rise and Fall of the Jewish Gangster in America* (New York, 1980), and Jenna Joselit, *Our Gang: Jewish Crime and the New York Jewish Community, 1900–1940* (Bloomington, 1983).

22. Goldstein, *Third Man in the Ring*, 31–35.

23. Philadelphia *Jewish Exponent*, 4/25/47.

24. New York *Jewish Daily Bulletin*, 3/25/25, reprints the column.

25. Ibid.

26. Budd Schulberg, "The Great Benny Leonard," *Ring Magazine* (May 1980), 32–37, is the source for the following account and the quotations.

27. Neal Gabler, *An Empire of Their Own: How the Jews Invented Hollywood* (New York, 1988), 283.

28. Los Angeles *B'nai B'rith Messenger*, 10/7/32.

29. Irving Rudd interview, 7/5/88.

30. Benton Rosen, "Some Outstanding Jewish Athletes and Sportsmen in Rhode Island, 1916–1964," *Rhode Island Historical Society Notes* 5 (Nov. 1968), 153–67; Chicago *Jewish Chronicle*, 3/30/29; Morrie Bloom Scrapbooks, Chicago Jewish Archives, Spertus College of Judaica; Chicago *Tribune*, 6/21/25; *American Hebrew*, 1/20/28. Extensive reading of the Detroit *Free Press*, Detroit *Jewish Chronicle*, the Chicago *Tribune*, the *New York Times*, the *American Hebrew*, and the Los Angeles *B'nai B'rith Messenger* provide abundant examples.

31. Irving Rudd interview, 7/5/88.

32. Ruby Goldstein, *Third Man in the Ring*, 45–46.

33. Riess, "A Fighting Chance," 230. *Encyclopedia*, 152.

34. Nat Fleischer, *Fifty Years at Ringside* (New York, 1958), 163.

35. Chicago *Herald American*, 3/3/41; Chicago *Tribune*, 11/18/82.

36. Blady, *The Jewish Boxers' Hall of Fame*, 111; *Jewish Tribune*, 10/5/23.

37. Riess, "A Fighting Chance," 239–40. Broun quotation in New York *World*, 7/23/23.

38. *American Hebrew*, 7/31/25; Chicago *Tribune*, 7/22/25. For other examples see Los Angeles *B'nai B'rith Messenger*, 10/25/29, 8/28/31, 11/29/35, 6/26/36; Ruby Goldstein, *Third Man in the Ring*, 90–91.

39. Blady, *The Jewish Boxers' Hall of Fame*, 185–89.

40. Ibid, 99–104.

41. Berkow, *Maxwell Street*, 141–42.

42. *New York Times*, 7/19, 7/20, 7/21/40.

43. Irving Rudd interview, 7/5/88.

44. *American Hebrew*, 6/6/19.

45. *American Israelite*, 6/30/1885.

46. Ibid., 12/16/1887.

47. Kramer and Stern, "San Francisco's Fighting Jew," 336.

48. *Jewish Independent*, 7/30/26.

49. Los Angeles *B'nai B'rith Messenger*, 11/20/31.

50. Detroit *Jewish Chronicle*, 3/15/35.

51. Los Angeles *B'nai B'rith Messenger*, 6/23/33.

52. *Jewish Tribune*, Oct. 5, 1923.

53. *American Hebrew*, 6/4/26.

54. Chicago *Daily Jewish Courier*, 2/16/23.

55. John Hoberman, "Sport and the Myth of the Jewish Body," paper presented at North American Society for Sport History Conference, May 27, 1989.

56. Fleischer, *Leonard the Magnificent*, 1–2; *Jewish Tribune*, 10/5/23; Cleveland *Press*, 1/11/24. Johnny Ray quotation is in Christopher Mead, *Champion, Joe Louis: Black Hero in White America* (New York, 1985), 180–81.

57. *Encyclopedia*, 138, has *Jewish Daily Forward* quotation.

58. Clifford Odets, *Six Plays of Clifford Odets* (New York, 1933), 252.

59. Ibid., 305.

60. E. L. Doctorow, *Billy Bathgate* (New York, 1989), 94–95.

Chapter 9. Jewish Champions and American Heroes

1. *American Hebrew*, 9/22/33.

2. Barney Ross and Martin Abramson, *No Man Stands Alone: The True Story of Barney Ross* (Philadelphia, 1957), is the major source for this discussion of Ross. Although clearly at times an overly sentimental account, it does depict one man's sense of his own mission and Jewish connections. Unless otherwise noted, information on Ross comes from this source, with quotations duly noted. Also useful is Ken Blady, *The Jewish Boxers' Hall of Fame* (New York, 1988), 227–36.

3. Ross, *No Man Stands Alone*, 35–36.

4. Ibid., 28.

5. Ibid., 13–14.

6. Ibid., 34–35.

7. Ibid., 21.

8. Ibid., 42–43.

9. Ibid., 21.

10. Ibid., 18.

11. Ibid., 50.

12. Ibid., 55.

13. Ibid., 82; Chicago *Tribune*, 11/11/32.

14. Ross, *No Man Stands Alone*, 79; *American Hebrew*, 7/21, 9/22/33.

15. Ben Bentley interview, 5/12/88.

16. Ross, *No Man Stands Alone*, 86.

17. Ibid., 115.

18. Ibid., 122.

19. Ibid., 128.

20. Los Angeles *B'nai B'rith Messenger*, 11/30/33.

21. Ross, *No Man Stands Alone*, 130–31.

22. Blady, *The Jewish Boxers' Hall of Fame*, 233.

23. Los Angeles *B'nai B'rith Messenger*, 4/27, 5/25/34.

24. Steven Riess, "A Fighting Chance: The Jewish-American Boxing Experience, 1890–1940," *American Jewish History* 74 (March 1985), 246; Ross, *No Man Stands Alone*, 140, 150–53.

25. Blady, *The Jewish Boxers' Hall of Fame*, 232; Ross, *No Man Stands Alone*, 151, 154–55; Los Angeles *B'nai B'rith Messenger*, 6/8/34.

26. Detroit *Jewish Chronicle*, 9/21, 10/12/34.

27. *American Hebrew*, 4/19/43; Marty Glickman interview, 9/10/85.

28. Blady, *The Jewish Boxers' Hall of Fame*, 235.

29. Aron quotation on undated, unnamed newspaper clip, Jews and Sports Collection, AJA.

30. Los Angeles *B'nai B'rith Messenger,* 1/12/34.

31. Baer is not listed in Blady, *The Jewish Boxers' Hall of Fame,* or in Robert Slater, *Great Jews in Sports* (Middle Village, N.Y., 1983). He does appear in Bernard Postal, Jesse Silver, and Roy Silver, *Encyclopedia of Jews in Sport* (New York, 1965), 146 but here doubts are raised about his Jewish credentials. Also see Detroit *Jewish Chronicle,* 7/5/35. Ray Arcel interview, American Jewish Committee.

32. *American Hebrew,* 6/16/33; Detroit *Jewish Chronicle,* 7/5/35.

33. John D. McCallum, *The World Heavyweight Boxing Championship, a History* (Radnor, Penn., 1974), 158–72, for account of Carnera's career. Quotations are from 161, 169.

34. Los Angeles *B'nai B'rith Messenger,* 6/22/34; undated and unnamed column by Abner Phillipson titled "Max Baer Wins Heavyweight Crown" in Jews and Sports Collection, AJA; Detroit *Jewish Chronicle,* 7/5, 9/27/35.

35. Los Angeles *B'nai B'rith Messenger,* 6/22/34; also see Nat Fleischer, *Max Baer, Glamour Boy of the Ring* (New York, 1942).

36. For background on Mike Jacobs see Steven Riess, "A Fighting Chance," 251–52; Christopher Mead, *Champion: Joe Louis, Black Hero in White America* (New York, 1985); and Jeffrey Sammons, *Beyond the Ring: The Role of Boxing in American Society* (Urbana, 1988), 96–145.

37. Sammons, *Beyond the Ring,* 97–98. On Jack Johnson see Randy Roberts, *Papa Jack: Johnson and the Era of White Hopes* (New York, 1983).

38. For account of Carnera-Louis fight and the quotation see Sammons, *Beyond the Ring,* 101–2. Sammons notes that southern sportswriters were less enthusiastic about the meaning of Louis's victory.

39. Ibid., 103. Mead, *Champion,* 65–72; quotation is on p. 73 of Mead and comes from Shirley Povich of the *Washington Post.*

40. Mead, *Champion,* 75–97, has full account of background and the first fight of Louis-Schmeling.

41. Ibid., 100–101.

42. Sammons, *Beyond the Ring,* 109; *American Hebrew,* 7/10/36.

43. *American Hebrew,* 7/3/36.

44. Mead, *Champion,* 108–12, provides a good account of these machinations but I found his descriptions of Jacobs and Gould as money-grubbing Jews bordering on anti-Semitic.

45. Ibid., 134–41; Sammons, *Beyond the Ring,* 109–17, for account of fight and popular reaction to it.

46. Mead, *Champion,* 133.

47. Sammons, *Beyond the Ring,* 116.

48. Ibid.

49. Ibid., 117.

50. For example see Maya Angelou, *I Know Why the Caged Bird Sings* (New York, 1977), 111–13, and Lawrence Levine, *Black Culture and Black Consciousness: Afro-American Folk Thought from Slavery to Freedom* (New York, 1977), 420, 433.

51. *American Hebrew,* 6/14/46.

52. Riess, "A Fighting Chance."

53. Paul Breines, *Tough Jews: Political Fantasies and the Moral Dilemma of American Jewry* (New York, 1990), offers a fascinating discussion of the historical tradition of the tough Jew and its significance in today's world. See Chapters 12 and 13 of this book for further discussion of this issue.

54. Philip Roth, "My Life as a Boy," *New York Times Book Review,* 10/10/87.

Chapter 10. College Life and College Sport

1. *American Hebrew,* 12/18/31.

2. Burton Bledstein, *The Culture of Professionalism: The Middle Class and the Development of Higher Education in the United States* (New York, 1976).

3. Paula Fass, *The Damned and the Beautiful: American Youth in the 1920s* (New York, 1977) 124.

4. Heywood Broun and George Britt, *Christians Only: A Study in Prejudice* (New York, 1931), 72. Also see Stephen Steinberg, "How Jewish Quotas Began," *Commentary* (Sept. 1971), 67–76.

5. Steinberg, "How Jewish Quotas Began," 68–69.

6. Brown and Britt, *Christians Only,* 73.

7. Bledstein, *The Culture of Professionalism,* 203–332; Fass, *The Damned and the Beautiful,* 168–221; Daniel Oren, *Joining the Club: A History of Jews at Yale* (New Haven, 1985), 17–111.

8. Oren, *Joining the Club,* 29–36; Steinberg, "How Jewish Quotas Began."

9. Broun and Britt, *Christians Only,* 72–124; Steinberg, "How Jewish Quotas Began." Also see Oren, *Joining the Club,* 38–63.

10. Oren, *Joining the Club,* 38–56, describes the imposition of quotas at Yale. The Jones quotations are on p. 43 and the Harvard references on p. 46. See p. 54 for Oren's own comments.

11. Ibid., 45–48. Also see Steinberg, "How Jewish Quotas Began."

12. Steinberg, "How Jewish Quotas Began", Broun and Britt, *Christians Only,* 72–124.

13. Broun and Britt, *Christians Only,* 89–93.

14. Ibid., 100–101.

15. Ibid., 91–92.

16. Ibid., 93–94.

17. Ibid., 72–124, is full of examples, at times giving information school by school. The quotation is on p. 78.

18. Oren, *Joining the Club,* 71–88.

19. Broun and Britt, *Christians Only,* 72–78.

20. Ibid., 115–18; *American Hebrew,* 12/19/30. Both sources contain accounts of Kelson's views that are in the text. All quotations from Kelson are from his *American Hebrew* article.

21. Jewish athletes, when interviewed about their college days, rarely talked about anti-Semitism. Allie Sherman interview, 6/29/87; Marshall Goldberg interview, 7/26/90; Marshall Goldberg interview, American Jewish Committee; Benny Friedman interview, American Jewish Committee.

22. Cleveland *Jewish Independent,* 10/30/25, 7/23/26; Los Angeles *B'nai B'rith Messenger,* 8/8/30, 2/13/31.

23. Los Angeles *B'nai B'rith Messenger,* 3/22/29; Cleveland *Jewish Independent,* 7/16/26.

24. Los Angeles *B'nai B'rith Messenger,* 1/16/31.

25. Chicago *Daily Jewish Courier,* 4/5/23.

26. *American Hebrew,* 12/19/24.

27. Ibid., 11/13/25.

28. Ibid., 12/20/29.

29. Ibid., 8/3/28, 3/25/32. For other of the *Hebrew*'s annual surveys see 12/1/22, 12/19/24, 12/4/25, 12/16/27, 12/20/29, 12/18/31, 12/16/32, 12/21/34, 12/11/36, 6/4/37, 1/12/40.

30. Ibid., 12/16/32.

31. Except when noted the following discussion of Yale basketball and all quotations are from Oren, *Joining the Club,* 78–80.

32. *American Hebrew,* 6/30/22.

33. Ibid., 6/15/28, contains this story and all quotations cited.

34. California *Jewish Voice,* 10/15/37.

35. Donald Mrozek, *Sport and American Mentality, 1880–1910* (Knoxville, 1983), 3–67, is one of a number of pieces that spell out the popularity and symbolic role of college football. On professional football as a minor spectator attraction see Steven Riess, *City Games: The Evolution of American Urban Society and the Rise of Sports* (Urbana, 1989), 233–34.

36. *American Hebrew,* 12/16/27, 12/21/28.

37. California *Jewish Voice,* 11/14/30, 3/27/36. Any of the many Anglo-Jewish newspapers located in major cities contains innumerable references.

38. Detroit *Jewish Chronicle,* 11/4/30, 12/13, 12/20/35, 12/4/36. Although Kupcinet refused to alter his 1935 selections, he did offer his readers another "all-star" team that he knew would not generate any "letters of indignation"—his professional Jewish team. Kupcinet's self-assurance was based on the fact that there were only 11 Jews playing in the NFL in 1935. For other examples of all-star team selection, see *American Hebrew,* 11/26, 12/17/37; Los Angeles *B'nai B'rith Messenger,* 12/4/31, 12/16/33; California *Jewish Voice,* 12/12/30, 12/11/31.

39. *American Hebrew,* 11/26/37.

40. Pittsburgh *American Jewish Outlook,* 11/19/37.

41. Cleveland *Jewish Independent,* 12/2/27.

42. Ibid.

43. Unless otherwise noted, all quotations and information about Friedman come from Benny Friedman interview, American Jewish Committee.

44. Chicago *Tribune,* 11/24/35; Bernard Postal, Jesse Silver, and Roy Silver, *Encyclopedia of Jews in Sports* (New York, 1965), 245 (hereafter *Encyclopedia*).

45. *American Hebrew* 12/4, 12/18/25; *Jewish Digest* (Dec. 1940), 84. In his American Jewish Committee interview, Friedman suggests that during his sophomore year, the varsity coach, a man named Little, denied him the opportunity to play because of anti-Semitism. Michigan's athletic director, Fielding Yost, replaced Little midway in the season and Friedman's fortunes turned for the better. *American Hebrew,* 12/18/25, mentions Friedman's frustration in his sophomore year but blames it on the fierce competition he faced among his teammates for playing time. Los Angeles *B'nai B'rith Messenger,* 12/2/32, also reiterates Friedman's comments that he did not experience prejudice as an athlete.

46. Except where noted, all information and quotations about Goldberg come from Marshall Goldberg interview, 7/26/90, and Marshall Goldberg interview, American Jewish Committee. Also helpful about his career is promotional literature provided by the University of Pittsburgh.

47. *Encyclopedia,* 264.

48. Unnamed magazine clip, 1938, in University of Pittsburgh Archives; *American Hebrew,* 10/2, 10/16, 11/6, 12/11/36, 10/15/37, 1/12/40; Pittsburgh *American Jewish Outlook,* 1/14, 2/11, 9/23/38.

49. The quotation is from Marshall Goldberg interview, American Jewish Committee, but the message was the same when I interviewed him 10 years later.

50. *American Hebrew,* 12/11/36.

51. Justin Kestenbaum interview, 1/4/91. Although Luckman played in New York, his Columbia teams were at best mediocre and never received the kind of national attention accorded Friedman's Michigan and Goldberg's Pittsburgh teams. Of the three, Luckman had the most successful professional career as quarterback for the Chicago Bears. For example, see *American Hebrew,* 1/24/36, that named him and Hank Greenberg as the two outstanding Jewish athletes in the United States. Also see *American Hebrew,* 1/13/39. For a recent account of his football exploits see Jacqueline Dutton, "The Legendary Sid Luckman, '39," *Columbia College Today* 17 (Fall, 1990), 24–27.

52. S. Willis Rudy, *The College of the City of New York: A History* (New York, 1949), 397; Sherry Gorelick, *City College and the Jewish Poor: Education in New York, 1880–1924* (New Brunswick, N.J., 1981). As Jeffrey Gurock points out in his recent history of Yeshiva University, Jewish students at institutions specifically Jewish in design at times looked with disdain at the notion that City was a "Jewish" school. Sports did not become part of the Yeshiva University scene until well into the 1950s. See Jeffrey Gurock, *The Men and Women of Yeshiva: Higher Education, Orthodoxy, and American Judaism* (New York, 1988). Brandeis University was not founded until 1948. Development of its sports programs therefore took place outside the scope of this discussion.

Chapter 11. Marty Glickman's American Jewish Odyssey

1. Southern California *Jewish Historical Society Newsletter* (Summer, 1984), 1.

2. With noted exceptions, all direct quotations from Marty Glickman interview, 9/10/85. As cited, other material on Glickman comes from Marty Glickman interview, American Jewish Committee.

3. Marty Glickman interview, American Jewish Committee.

4. Moshe Gottlieb, "The American Controversy Over the Olympic Games," *American Jewish Quarterly* 61 (March 1972), 181–213, traces the boycott movement in detail. Broun quotation reported in *American Hebrew,* 8/9/35, from a syndicated column in Scripps-Howard newspapers.

5. Gottlieb, "The American Controversy Over the Olympic Games," and also Allen Guttmann, *The Games Must Go On: Avery Brundage and the Olympic Movement* (New York, 1984), 68–73. Also see various Anglo-Jewish newspapers. Holman reference is in 92nd Street YMHA Bulletin, 1/10/36. Reference to Polish soccer player in *American Hebrew,* 9/27/35. For expressions of the *Hebrew*'s editorials on the boycott see 6/16/33, 10/5, 12/14/34, 8/2, 8/27, 9/27, 10/4, 10/18, 10/25, 12/13/35, 1/3/36. Also see Detroit *Jewish Chronicle,* 8/16/35.

6. *American Hebrew,* 11/18/36.

7. Arnd Kruger, "'Fair Play for American Athletes': A Study in Anti-Semitism," *Canadian Journal of History of Sport and Physical Education* 9 (May 1978), 43–57. For other accounts of the boycott controversy see William Baker, *Jesse Owens: An American Life* (New York, 1986), 63–66, and Richard Mandell, *The Nazi Olympics* (New York, 1971), 68–82.

8. 92nd Street YMHA Athletic Council minutes, 7/31/35; 92nd Street YMHA Bulletin, 3/13/36, 92nd Street YMHA Archives; Howard Simons, *Jewish Times: Voices of the American Jewish Experience* (New York, 1988), 332–33.

9. California *Jewish Voice,* 4/17, 4/24, 7/17/36; *American Hebrew,* undated 1936 clip.

10. Louis Jacobson, "Herman Goldberg: Baseball Olympian and Jewish-American," in Peter Levine, ed., *Baseball History 3* (Westport, 1990), 71–72.

11. Marty Glickman interview, American Jewish Committee.

12. Frederick W. Rubien, ed., *Report of the American Olympic Committee: Games of the XIth Olympiad* (New York, 1936), 111–21.

13. Besides Glickman's account, see Baker, *Jesse Owens,* 102.

14. Ibid., 102–5; *New York Times,* 8/5/36.

15. Glickman recounts the same story in his interview with me and in his American Jewish Committee interview. See also Baker, *Jesse Owens,* 102–5.

16. Baker, *Jesse Owens,* 102–5; William O. Johnson, Jr., *All That Glitters is Not Gold: The Olympic Game* (New York, 1972), 178–82.

17. Johnson, *All That Glitters,* 182–84, contains excerpts from Stoller's diary.

18. Ibid.

19. *New York Times,* 8/10/36.

20. Detroit *Jewish Chronicle,* 9/4/36.

21. Ibid., 8/14/36.

22. John Kieran, *The Story of the Olympic Games, 776 B.C.–1936 A.D.* (New York, 1936), 267.

23. *New York Times,* 8/8/36.

24. Ibid. The Brundage quotation is in his final report of the games in Rubien, ed. *Games of the XIth Olympiad,* 35.

25. *American Hebrew,* 12/11/36; California *Jewish Voice,* 8/14/36, also see 7/10/36.

26. Mandell, *The Nazi Olympics,* 165–66; Johnson, *All That Glitters,* 177–84; Baker, *Jesse Owens,* 105–6.

27. Marty Glickman interview, American Jewish Committee.

28. Ibid.

29. This story and the quotations appear in Glickman's own incomplete autobiography, a copy of which he gave to me.

30. This important debate is engaged more completely in Chapter 13.

31. Herbert Feingold, "Jewish Life in the United States: Perspectives from History," in Joseph B. Gittler, ed., *Jewish Life in the United States: Perspectives from the Social Sciences* (New York, 1981), 271, provides this definition of historical memory. Also see Steven Cohen, *American Modernity and Jewish Identity* (New York, 1983), and Charles Silberman, *A Certain People: American Jews and Their Lives Today* (New York, 1985).

Chapter 12. Sport and the American Jewish Experience Since World War II

1. *New York Times,* 12/19/57.

2. Ibid., 6/2/73.

3. *The Jewish Transcript,* 3/23/72.

4. Ibid., R. D. Rosen "What Sports Needs Is More Jewish Athletes," *Inside Sports,* Baseball Hall of Fame Library.

5. Charles Silberman, *A Certain People: American Jews and Their Lives Today* (New York, 1985), 223; Philip Roth, *Goodbye Columbus* (New York, 1959), 15.

6. *Sporting News,* 1/17/70; Hank Greenberg, *The Story of My Life* (New York, 1989), 233.

7. Statistics on baseball players are drawn from the same sources used previously in Chapters 5, 6, and 7.

8. Especially useful here are players' files at the National Baseball Hall of Fame

Library, and information from published and unpublished interviews in innumerable newspapers and magazines.

9. Unless otherwise noted, information and quotations from Mike Epstein interview, 8/18/87.

10. Larry and Norm Sherry who both played in the major leagues, also grew up in the Fairfax neighborhood.

11. *American Hebrew,* 2/18/48.

12. Ibid., 4/23/48.

13. *New York Times,* 6/7/67, 8/8/71; Boston *Record American,* 8/21/71; *Sporting News,* 12/3/77; quotation from "Boom-Boom Blomberg," in *Sunday News,* 6/17/73, Ron Blomberg file, Baseball Hall of Fame Library.

14. *New York Times,* 6/7/67.

15. *Sporting News,* 11/10/66.

16. *Binghamton Sunday Press,* 5/9/71.

17. King's reminiscences are in Howard Simons, *Jewish Times: Voices of the American Jewish Experience* (Boston, 1988), 126–39. Koufax's reminiscences, cited here and elsewhere, are from Sandy Koufax with Ed Linn, *Koufax* (New York, 1966). Koufax declined to be interviewed.

18. New York *World Telegram,* 12/16/54.

19. George Vecsey, "Koufax Makes Yankees True Believers," n.d., *New York Times,* in Sandy Koufax file, Baseball Hall of Fame Library; Melvin Durslag, "Sandy Koufax, the Strikeout King," *Saturday Evening Post,* 7/14/62; "I'm Only Human," *Look Magazine,* Dec. 1963.

20. Mordecai Richler, "Koufax the Incomparable," *Commentary* 42 (Nov. 1966), 87–89.

21. Koufax, *Koufax,* 258.

22. Robert Cohen, "Home(Plate) for the Holidays?," *Moment* 9 (Sept. 1984), 54–57.

23. Story told to me by Sharon Liebhofer, 4/14/91.

24. *New York Times,* 9/20/86.

25. Edward Tivnan, *The Lobby: Jewish Political Power and American Foreign Policy* (New York, 1987), 26. Virtually every book on the contemporary American Jewish experience makes this connection. For other examples, see Paul Breines, *Tough Jews: Political Fantasies and the Moral Dilemma of American Jewry* (New York, 1990); Arthur Hertzberg, *The Jews in America: Four Centuries of an Uneasy Encounter* (New York, 1989), 372–76; Charles Silberman, *A Certain People, American Jews and Their Lives Today* (New York, 1985) 181–85. The importance of definitions of Jewish identity and their connection to this issue and to the issue of toughness and strength will be discussed in Chapter 13.

26. Breines, *Tough Jews,* brings this evidence to bear in provocative ways. See Chapter 13 for a discussion of his work.

27. In the 1920s, as various issues of the *American Hebrew* make clear, German Jews built their own golf courses and country clubs, often as palatial as those from which they were restricted. There were also any number of Jewish youngsters who excelled at tennis and handball on city parks and playgrounds. Most notable in handball was Vic Hershkowitz, a Brooklyn-born fireman who dominated the sport in the 1940s and 1950s.

28. All information and quotations from Dick Savitt, unless noted, come from Dick Savitt interview, American Jewish Committee.

29. Philadelphia *Jewish Exponent,* 7/20/51. The Jews and Sports Collection, Amer-

ican Jewish Archives, contains a good many newspaper clips on Savitt, but few mention anything about his Jewishness.

30. *Time,* 8/27/51.

31. Robert Slater, *Great Jews in Sports* (New York, 1983), 197–98.

32. USA Cable Network coverage of U.S. Open, Sept. 7, 1989; *New York Times,* 9/8/89; *American Jewish Life,* 6/27/86.

33. Haskell Cohen graciously gave me access to his files on stories written for the Jewish Telegraphic Agency and syndicated for many years to the American Jewish press. Some were photocopies of actual newspaper pages. Others were typescripts of published articles. Here and elsewhere, reference to this material will be either the exact newspaper reference or, if from a typescript, noted as Cohen typescript, and the date. Cohen typescripts, 5/24/76, 2/22/79.

34. Nancy Lieberman confirmed this for me in an interview on 8/6/87. Material in her press kit, which includes copies of numerous articles about her, underlines that public discussion of her career centers on her role as a pioneering woman athlete, with virtually no mention of her Jewish background. *Sports Illustrated,* 12/3/79; *Women's Sport and Fitness,* 9/86; *Sporting News,* 7/28/86; *Glamour,* Aug. 1987.

35. From time to time in this book I have made mention of Jewish entrepreneurs and sport. This subject would make a book in itself, especially if the focus was on assimilation in terms of mobility and economic opportunity. but because my focus is on assimilation in the context of identity and community and because of space limitations, I chose to limit attention to this subject.

36. For details of Spitz's career see Slater, *Great Jews in Sports,* 210–13. Spitz declined to be interviewed.

37. *New York Times,* 8/29/72.

38. Ibid., 9/3/72. Also see Slater, *Great Jews in Sports,* 210–11.

39. *New York Times,* 8/24, 9/29, 9/4, 9/5/72.

40. Ibid., 9/6, 9/9, 9/10, 9/11/72.

41. Ibid., 9/6/72.

42. Ibid., 9/16/72.

43. Jerry Kirshenbaum, "On Your Mark, Get Set, Sell," *Sports Illustrated,* 5/14/73, contains much of this information. Spitz quotation on p. 36. Also see Joseph Bell, "Mark Spitz, What Now?," *Seventeen,* May 1973; *TV Guide,* 6/2/73, 12/27/75.

44. Susan Lydon, "All That Gold Waiting to Glitter," *New York Times Magazine,* 3/11/73.

45. Slater, *Great Jews in Sports,* 213.

46. *New York Times Magazine,* 4/8/73.

47. *U.S. Committee Sports for Israel Newsletter,* Spring/Summer, 1985; 1987 U.S. Committee Sports for Israel Spitz solicitation letter, 1987. ABC-TV broadcast of "Insport," 11/18/89. Spitz returned to the water competitively in April 1991 on ABC's Wide World of Sports. Commentators made no mention of his Jewish background. Also see *The National,* 4/19/91.

48. Unnamed newspaper clips sent to me by Ed Krinsky, Nat's son, from his father's scrapbooks.

49. Bernard Postal, Jesse Silver and Roy Silver, *Enclyclopedia of Jews in Sport* (New York, 1965), 114 (hereafter *Encyclopedia*); Slater, *Great Jews in Sport,* 99–101.

50. *Encyclopedia,* 111–12, 114, 118–19; Slater, *Great Jews in Sports,* 235, 244. Also see Art Heyman, Lenny Rosenbluth, and Larry Brown files, Basketball Hall of Fame, and Jesse and Roy Silver, "The Fifth Man: Art Heyman," *Jewish Digest* (Jan. 1964), 67–71.

51. *1958 National College Basketball Blue Book.*

52. *Encyclopedia,* 118.

53. *New York Times,* 6/14/88; Curry Kirkpatrick, "A One Man Show," *Sports Illustrated,* 4/11/88; *Lansing State Journal,* 2/28/88.

54. Jeffrey Gurock, *The Men and Women of Yeshiva: Higher Education, Orthodoxy, and American Judaism* (New York, 1988), 170–79, is the major source for this story of Yeshiva basketball.

55. Gurock, *The Men and Women of Yeshiva,* 173–74.

56. Ibid., 173, 176–78. Also see Gay Talese, "Mighty Mites of Yeshiva," *New York Times,* 11/25/56.

57. Gurock, *The Men and Women of Yeshiva,* 178.

58. Unless otherwise noted, all information on Dolph Schayes comes from Bill Simons, "An Interview with Adolph Schayes," *American Jewish History* 74 (March 1985), 287–307.

59. Unless otherwise noted, all information on Danny Schayes comes from Danny Schayes interview, 1/3/88.

60. Statistics on Danny Schayes compiled from *The Sporting News NBA Guide, 1987–88 Edition* (St. Louis, 1987). For Dolph Schayes see Slater, *Great Jews in Sports,* 199–201.

61. Lansing *State Journal,* 7/31/88.

62. Boston *Jewish Advocate,* 2/13/58.

63. For sampling of articles in *Jewish Digest* see those by Jesse Silver, "The Earliest Jewish All-American" (March 1970), 65–67; "Notable Jewish Athletes of Today and Yesterday" (July 1975), 58–62; "All-Time, All-Jewish Nine" (May 1963), 17–22. Also see Bernard Postal, "Johnny Kling, Baseball's Forgotten Hero" (April 1956), 45–49. For other articles see George Castle, "The All-Time, All-Jewish Team, *JUF News,* Aug. 1989, which also included an excerpt from Hank Greenberg, *The Story of My Life,* and another story on Ken Holtzman. Louis Schoenfeld in 1986 organized the Jewish Sports Information Center, a one-man show that collects information on Jewish baseball players and cards and distributes it to interested parties; some 150 according to a 11/2/89 letter from him to members. A story on the organization is Neal Karlen, "Jews on First," *Spy* (Aug. 1989), 95–96. A newsletter called the *Sports Collectors Digest,* 6/12/87, contains news of interest in collecting Jewish baseball cards as does another undated issue that contains a story by Art Kellerman on his collection. Also see Neal Karlen, "The Boychiks of Summer," *New York Magazine,* 4/20/87.

64. *Program of 36th Annual B'nai B'rith Sports Awards Dinner, Max Kase Lodge, June 28, 1987* contains information on the New York lodge. Records of the Chicago lodge are in Chicago Jewish Archives, Spertus College of Judaica, Chicago, Illinois.

65. Michigan Jewish Sports Hall of Fame letter and invitation to 1988 dinner and commemorative dinner books from 1985 and 1990; Mike Rosenbaum, "One Handed Wizard," *Detroit Jewish News,* 10/9/87. Extremely helpful was an interview I had with the founders of the Hall on April 26, 1991. Information about halls in other cities comes from a variety of correspondence with hall organizers. A brief story on the Western Pennsylvania (Pittsburgh) hall appeared in *The New Yorker,* 1/7/91.

66. Interview with founders, 4/26/91. Heller's quotation from *Program of Chicago Jewish Sports Hall of Fame Dinner,* 11/21/82.

67. The history of the Maccabiah games is well told in George Eisen, "The Maccabiah Games: A History of the Jewish Olympics" (Ph.D. diss., University of Maryland, 1979); *The Maccabi Movement* (World Maccabi Union, 1979).

68. *USA Commemorative Journal of 12th Maccabiah,* 12, contains Walker quotation. Detroit *Jewish Chronicle,* 11/2/34, 4/12, 3/22/35.

69. Detroit *Jewish Chronicle,* 10/2/36.

70. *USA Commemorative Journal of 12th Maccabiah,* 18. Also see newsletters and solic-itation letters from U.S. Committee Sports for Israel.

71. Robert Spivak, President of U.S. Committee Sports for Israel (USCSI), 1987 solicitation letter and accompanying advertisement for Hall of Fame. Also see *Jewish Messenger,* [1987], on formation of Hall of Fame and Cohen typescript on Hall, 1980. Aside from USCSI, another organization known as Maccabai Union, USA, also raises money to send American Jewish athletes to the Maccabiah games and to foster sport in Israel. It also maintains a Jewish sports hall of fame there. Information on it comes from my interview with its founder Paul Berns on 3/12/87 and from newsletters and pamphlets he sent me.

72. Cohen typescript, 9/9/77; Haskell Cohen interview, 8/7/87.

73. Cohen typescript, 9/9/77.

74. Mordecai Soltes, "A Program of Jewish Activities for Community Centers," *The Jewish Center* 3 (Sept. 1925), 42–43.

75. For history of JWB see Morris Janofsky, *JWB Survey* (New York, 1946).

76. Information on the mission and expansion of Jewish community centers after World War II can be found in Janofsky, *The JWB Survey,* and also in the *American Jewish Yearbooks,* 1956, pp. 262–70; 1965, p. 261. Also see Hillel Ruskin, "Competitive Sports in Jewish Community Centers," *Journal of Jewish Communal Service* 53 (March 1977), 268–77. Harold Zimman, longtime promoter of the role of sport in JCC life was instru-mental in urging the formation of a committee on Health and Physical Education in the JWB as a result of its 1946 survey. See my phone interview with him, 7/30/90.

77. David Sorkin interview, 6/18/87.

78. Information on the Detroit JCC comes from its 1989 annual report, member-ship packet, and Morton Plotnick interview, 12/29/89.

79. Cohen typescript, 1974.

Conclusion

1. John Bodnar, *The Transplanted: A History of Immigrants in Urban America* (Bloo-mington, 1985), xx.

2. Meyer Liben, "Athletic Jews," *Commentary* 43 (Feb. 1967), 80–81.

3. Invitation to Dux 65th reunion, 3/18/90.

4. Bruce Kuklick, *To Everything a Season: Shibe Park and Urban Philadelphia, 1909–1976* (Princeton, 1991), speaks eloquently on this subject.

5. Steven Cohen, *American Assimilation or Jewish Revival?* (Bloomington, 1988), pro-vides a more complete summary of this debate. He uses the term "assimilationist" to describe those who are pessimistic about an American Jewish future and the term "transformationist" to describe those more optimistic about what lies ahead. As Cohen points out, Arthur Hertzberg and Herbert Gans articulate important components of the pessimist position. See Arthur Hertzberg, *The Jews in America: Four Centuries of an Uneasy Encounter* (New York, 1989); Herbert J. Gans, "Symbolic Ethnicity: The Future of Eth-nic Groups and Cultures in America," in Herbert Gans, ed., *On the Making of Americans: Essays in Honor of David Riesman* (Philadelphia, 1979).

6. Hertzberg, *The Jews in America,* 383–85, and a slightly different version of the conclusions of his book that appeared in the *New York Review of Books,* 10/26/90.

7. Ibid.

8. The most popular expression of the optimist position is Charles Silberman, *A Certain People: American Jews and Their Lives Today* (New York, 1985). Also see Sidney Goldstein and Calvin Goldscheider, *Jewish Americans: Three Generations in a Jewish Com-*

munity (Englewood Cliffs, 1968), and Calvin Goldscheider, *Jewish Continuity and Change: Emerging Patterns in America* (Bloomington, 1986).

9. On 1/18/90 Anne Roiphe spoke at Shaarey Zedek synagogue, East Lansing, Michigan, about these concerns. Earler that day I had sketched out a draft of my conclusions for this book that spoke to many of the same concerns and issues. It was both surprising and comforting to hear her eloquent commentary that evening.

10. Ibid.

11. Paul Breines, *Tough Jews: Political Fantasies and the Moral Dilemma of American Jewry* (New York, 1990).

12. Breines himself admits persistence of tough imagery throughout Jewish history tied to matters other than Zionism and Israeli survival. In terms of American traditions, while he discusses American Jewish gangsters, he omits any discussion of American Jewish athletes.

13. Herbert Feingold, "Jewish Life in the United States: Perspectives in History," in Joseph B. Gittler, ed., *Jewish Life in the United States: Perspectives from the Social Sciences* (New York, 1981), 271. Also see Herbert Feingold, *A Midrash on American Jewish History* (Albany, 1982), and Steven Cohen, *American Modernity and Jewish Identity* (New York, 1983).

14. I am grateful to David Nasaw, *Children of the City: At Work and at Play* (Garden City, 1985), who offers a similar appraisal of the children of immigrants.

Postscript

1. Most helpful have been Roy Rosenzweig, *Eight Hours for What We Will: Workers and Leisure in an Industrial City* (New York, 1983); William Baker, *Jesse Owens, an American Life* (New York, 1986); Elliott Gorn, *The Manly Art: Bare Knuckle Prize Fighting in America* (Ithaca, 1986); Jules Tygiel, *Baseball's Great Experiment: Jackie Robinson and His Legacy* (New York, 1983); David Nasaw, *Children of the City: At Work and at Play* (Garden City, 1985); Cary Goodman, *Choosing Sides: Playground and Street Life on the Lower East Side* (New York, 1979); Steven Riess, *City Games: The Evolution of American Urban Society and the Rise of Sports* (Urbana, 1989); Rob Ruck, *Sandlot Seasons: Sport in Black Pittsburgh* (Urbana, 1987); Randy Roberts, *Papa Jack: Jack Johnson and the Era of White Hopes* (New York, 1983); Christopher Mead, *Champion: Joe Louis, Black Hero in White America* (New York, 1985); Donn Rogosin, *Invisible Men: Life in Baseball's Negro Leagues* (New York, 1983), and Michael Isenberg, *John L. Sullivan and His America* (Urbana, 1988).

2. Ruck, *Sandlot Seasons,* 206–9.

3. Tygiel, *Baseball's Great Experiment.*

4. Harry Edwards, *The Revolt of the Black Athlete* (New York, 1969), and "The Olympic Project for Human Rights: An Assessment Ten Years Later," *Black Scholar* (March–April 1979), also in Peter Levine, *American Sport: A Documentary History* (Englewood Cliffs, 1989), 136–43. Edwards's views are better known from his public speeches and television appearances on these issues.

5. Mark Naison, "A Failed Game Plan: Shooting for Lasting Goals," *Commonweal,* 4/10/87.

6. Ibid., 199–200.

7. Ibid., 200.

8. Peter Levine and Peter Vinten-Johansen, "Sports Violence and Social Crisis," in Donald Spivey, ed., *Sport in America: New Historical Perspectives* (Westport, Conn., 1985), 219–38.

Index

Aaron, Hank, 282
Abrams, Cal, 97, 124–25, 131, 240
Addams, Jane, 14
Adler, Babe, 47–48
A. G. Spalding and Brothers, 55
Ah Chung, 144
Albert, Marv, 231
Alcott, Amy, 250
Alderman, Harry, 36
Alger, Horatio, 92, 100
Allen, Mel, 92–93, 263
Alston, Walt, 246
Amalgamated Clothing Workers, 22
Amateur Athletic Union, 19–20, 28, 220–21
American Basketball League, 60–61, 63, 65–70
American Jewish Committee, 187, 219–20, 233
American Jewish future, 275–79
American Jewish identity, 7, 46, 48–50, 119, 125–29, 138–43, 145–46, 153, 162–69, 179–89, 191, 208, 217, 229–34, 237, 242–43, 247, 260–61, 264–69, 270–79
American Labor Party, 69
American Olympic Committee, 220–22
Amerks, 258
Anderson, David, 235
Angell, James, 206
Anti-Nazi League, 187
anti-Semitism, 6–7, 9, 16, 50, 55–56, 85–87, 102, 106–8, 112, 115–16, 125–29, 138, 146, 149, 162, 166, 176–81, 185–86, 193–200, 210, 212, 219–22, 224, 226–29, 233–34, 242, 249, 251, 256, 261–62, 272, 279, 283
Arcel, Ray, 181
Armstrong, Henry, 171
Arnovich, Morrie, 122–23, 129

Aron, Milt, 179
Aronowitz, Joseph, 83
Arum, Bob, 188
assimilation, 46, 71, 270–74; and colleges, 200–215; and sport, 3–52, 72–73, 75, 77, 86–99, 110–16, 121, 141, 147, 151, 162–69, 188–89, 200–215, 218–19, 232, 240, 266–67, 270–74. *See also* baseball; immigrants; Jewish; middle ground; sport.
Atlantic Coast Conference, 256
Atlas Athletic Club (N.Y.), 15
Atlas Club (New Haven), 35–36, 49, 71, 96, 205–6
Attell, Abe, 103–4, 147, 151–53, 174–75
Atz, Jacob, 102
Auerbach, Red, 43–44, 265, 273
Auker, Eldon, 139–40

Baer, Max, 137, 170, 180–85, 189
"Bagel Twins," 250
Bailey, Maurice, 36
Baker, Macyln, 28, 76
Baker, William, 229
Ball, Willie, 75, 77
Balter, Sam, 78, 221
Baltimore, Md., Jewish baseball fans in, 124
Baltimore Orioles, 243, 240
Banks, Davey, 60–61, 63
Bar Mitzvah. *See* Jewish, religious observance.
Barber, Red, 124
Barzell, David, 165
baseball, 87–143; as America's National Game, 3, 9, 87, 103, 106, 116, 127, 130, 138, 143; and assimilation, 88–95, 129–31, 118–43; and Hispanics, 239–40; and Jewish community, 88–99, 118–43; and Jewish participation in, 9, 100–143, 238–

baseball (*continued*)
   239; and Jewish unsuitability for, 118. *See also* blacks; *specific teams and players.*
baseball cards, 262
Baseball Hall of Fame, 132, 245
basketball, 14, 24, 26–86, 236; and assimilation, 26–51; and colleges, 74–86; and 1950–51 college fix scandal, 78–86, 255; and Jewish community, 26–73; and Jewish participation in 8–9, 255–57; as professional sport, 52–73; and rules, 53, 69; and salaries in, 54, 59, 68–69, 260. *See also* blacks; *specific teams, players.*
Basketball Association of America, 69–70
Basketball Fraternity, 47–50, 57, 68–70, 234
Basketball Hall of Fame, 29, 82, 259
Basloe, Frank, 70
Bass, Benny, 149
Baum, Harry, 28
Beckman, Johnny, 57
Bee, Clair, 77
Behr, Louis, 207, 209
Behr, Sammy, 209
Belsky, Abraham, 83
Benjamin, Ruby, 30
Bentley, Ben, 175
Berg, Bernard, 93–94
Berg, Moe, 93–95, 132, 273
Berg, Samuel, 95
Berger, Jay, 250
Berkow, Ira, 121
Berlin, 224
Berman, Bob, 101
Bernstein, Irving, 49
Bernstein, Joe, 151, 158–59
Bidane, Abe, 47–48
Bierman, Steve, 236
Billingkoff, Maurice, 157
"Billy Bathgate," 168–69
Bingay, Milton, 136
"Bintel Brief," 87–88
Birnbaum, Kenny, 236
Black September, 251
Black Sox scandal, 83–84, 103–8, 156. *See also* baseball.
blacks, 17, 167, 182–88, 281–85. *See also* specific sports.
Block, Cy, 125–26
Blomberg, Ron, 235, 241
Bloom, Lou, 150
Bloom, Morrie, 157
B'nai B'rith, 125, 262–63
Bodnar, John, 24
Body and Soul, 179

Bohne, Sammy, 102, 109
Bonaparte, Joe, 167–68
Borchmeyer, Eric, 227
"Borscht Belt," 47, 84
Borten, Alvin, 31
Botwinik, Mickey, 36
boxing, 143–89; and assimilation, 144–89; and blacks, 158–59, 183–89; and crime, 153, 168–69; and the Irish, 146–47; and Italians, 158–59; and Jewish champions, 144–45; and Jewish community, 153–61; and Jewish stereotypes, 162–69. *See also* blacks; *specific boxers.*
Braddock, Jimmy, 137, 182–83, 186
Bradley, Bill, 26
Bradley Braves, 79–80, 85
Breines, Paul, 277–78, 318n
Brisbane, Arthur, 159
Britt, George, 194, 196–99
Bronx, 143. *See also* Jewish, neighborhoods.
Bronx YMHA, 48
Brooklyn, 124–25. *See also* Jewish, neighborhoods.
Brooklyn College, 26, 35, 47–48, 82
Brooklyn College of Pharmacy, 60, 62
Brooklyn Dodgers, 90, 120, 127, 140–41, 239, 241, 244
Brooklyn Jewels, 65–67, 71
Brooklyn Visitations, 66
Broun, Heywood, 160, 194, 196–99, 220
Brower, Lou, 101
Brown, Larry, 255–57
Brown, Nathan, 83
Brown, "Newsboy," 45
Brownsville, 26, 41, 46, 70, 89–90
Brownsville Boys Club, 296n
Brownsville YMHA, 69
Brundage, Avery, 219–21, 228–29
Buchwald, Art, 187
Buffalo Bisons, 111
bull-fighting, 190
Burns, George, 89, 95

Cahan, Abraham, 4, 5, 23, 87–88, 146–48, 159
Callahan, Mushy, 157, 161
Cantor, Eddie, 90, 93, 95, 179
Cantor, Hymie, 150
Canzoneri, Tony, 170, 175–76
capitalism, 283–85
Capone, Al, 174–75, 283
Carnera, Primo, 33, 180–81, 184
Catskill mountains, 47
Celler, Emanuel, 220

Chamberlain, Wilt, 256
Chapman, Ben, 126–27
chess, 252
Chicago, 157. *See also* Jewish, neighborhoods.
Chicago Bears, 213, 241
Chicago Cardinals, 213
Chicago Cubs, 101, 123, 125
Chicago Hebrew Institute, 15–16, 21
Chicago Jewish Sports Hall of Fame, 264
Chicago Stadium, 175–76
Chicago Stags, 45, 53
Chicago Studebakers, 33
Chicago White Sox, 84, 94, 96, 103–8, 139, 142
Choynski, Isadore, 147–48, 162–63
Choynski, Joe, 147–48, 163
Christians Only, 194–96
Cicotte, Eddie, 105
Cincinnati Reds, 84
City College of New York, 20, 27, 29, 33, 42–44, 47–48, 51, 56, 67–68, 74, 78–86, 192, 254–55
civil rights movement, 281
Cleveland, 211
Cleveland Indians, 128, 142–43
Cleveland Rosenblums, 60–61, 63
Clifton, Sweet Water, 26, 217
Cohen, Andy, 91–92, 100, 108–16, 119, 123, 235, 243, 248, 271
Cohen, Haskell, 86, 139, 210, 236–37, 255, 263, 266, 269
Cohen, Herb, 79, 83
Cohen, Hy, 4
Cohen, Morris Raphael, 89–90, 100
Cohen, Stanley, 79–81
Cohen, Steven, 10, 317n
Cohen, Syd, 92
Cohen at the Bat, 112
Cold War, 85–86, 251–53, 284
colleges, 190–215; and admissions policies, 193–96; and anti-Semitism at, 195–200; and Jewish involvement in, 190–215. *See also* assimilation; *names of specific institutions.*
Columbia University, 196
Columbus (Ohio), 97, 150
Comiskey, Charles, 103
communism, 284
Coney Island, 229
Conerly, Charlie, 217
Conn, Billy, 166–67
consumer culture, 109
Cooney, Phil, 102
Copeland, Lillian, 190, 265
Corbett, Jim, 146–47

Cornell University, 48, 199–200, 248
Coughlin, Father Charles, 125, 130, 135, 165, 278. *See also* anti-Semitism.
Cromwell, Dean, 224, 229
Cross, Leach, 150–52, 159, 161
Cunningham, Billy, 26
Cy Young award, 243

Dallas YMHA, 96
Dambrot, Irwin, 79, 83, 255
Daniel, Dan, 114, 119–20, 122, 130, 244
Danning, Harry, 91, 118, 120, 122, 125, 129–32, 141, 243, 273
Danning, Saul, 273
Davidson, William, 70, 263
Davis Cup, 249
Davis-Elkins College, 213
Day, Davey, 159, 161
Dayan, Moishe, 247
Debs, Eugene, 23
Dehnert, Dutch, 57
Dempsey, Jack, 154
Denver Nuggets, 257–60
Depression (1930s), 39–46, 71, 121, 204, 215, 264, 279
Detroit Jewish Community Center, 263, 268–69
Detroit Pistons, 263
Detroit Tigers, 132–43, 242
Dibbs, Eddie, 250
Dimaggio, Joe, 123
Doctorow, E. L., 168–69
Dodd, Lora, 136
Dorfman, Sammy, 150
Draper, Foy, 223–29
Drebinger, John, 235
Dreyfuss, Barney, 142
Drucker, Norm, 48
Drysdale, Don, 244, 246
Duke University, 255
Dukes, Walter, 26
Dux, 30–34, 48–49, 62, 69, 71, 75, 96, 255, 268, 271, 274

East European Jews, 4, 13, 270. *See also* assimilation; Jewish.
Eastern District Soccer League, 23
Eastern Jewish Center League, 20, 22
Eastman, Monk, 104
Ebbets Field, 97, 120, 124
Ebner, Michael, 124–25
Educational Alliance, 14, 30, 150, 271

Edwards, Harry, 114, 282–83
Einstein, Albert, 154, 189
Eisenstat, Harry, 133, 140
El Paso, 7
Elkins, West Va., 212–13
Emanuel Cohen settlement house, 36–37
Epstein, Jack, 239
Epstein, Mike, 239–43
Erasmus High School, 48, 219
Evening Recreation Center 184, 26
Ewing, Reuben, 102
Exodus, 247

Fairfax, 239
Fass, Paula, 293n
Feingold, Herbert, 10, 234, 278
Felix, Ray, 26
Ferris, Dan, 221
Fields, Jackie, 145, 148–50, 157, 161, 175, 190, 252–53, 265
Fischer, Bobby, 252–53
Fitch, Gil, 65
Flam, Herb, 248–49
Flatbush, 48
Fleischer, Nat, 159, 166, 188–89
Fogarty, Joseph, 206
football, 203, 207–15. *See also individual players and teams.*
Ford, Henry, 4, 56, 106–8, 125, 202, 278
Frank, Stanley, 27, 117, 127, 142
Franklin, Sidney, 190–91
Free Sons of Israel, 26
Freed, Paul, 209, 228
Freedman, Andrew, 142
Frieberger, Isadore, 29
Friedkin, Bernie, 158
Friedman, Benny, 201, 208, 210–11, 234, 263, 265, 311n
Friedman, Max, 27–29, 53–56, 60, 61
frontier, 11–12
Fullerton, Hugh, 89

Gabler, Neal, 72–73
Gallatin, Harry, 26, 217
Gallico, Paul, 27, 114, 182
gambling, 177, 182. *See also* basketball, 1950–51 college fix scandal; Black Sox scandal.
Gandil, Chick, 103–4
Gans, Herbert, 10
Gard, Eddie, 83–84
Gehrig, Lou, 119, 134
Gellman, Rabbi Marc, 247

Gentile, perception of Jews, 53, 56, 67, 99, 112, 115, 129–31, 136, 200, 204–7. *See also* anti-Semitism; assimilation; middle ground.
Gerchick, Abe, 8, 47
German-American Jews, 8, 12–18, 97, 191
Germany, 222
Gershon, Herb, 48
Gilbert, Brad, 250
Gimbel, Carol, 142
Glantz, Harry, 22, 38, 114, 123, 134, 201–2, 209
Glickman, Harry, 38, 40, 70
Glickman, Harry (father of Marty), 217–19, 232–33, 273
Glickman, Marty, 9, 79, 179, 191, 216–34, 263, 273
Goldberg, Herman, 222
Goldberg, Jeffrey, 236
Goldberg, Marshall, 208–9, 212–15, 234, 272–73
Goldberg, Saul, 212–13
Golden Boy, 167–68, 178
"Golden Medinah," 5
Goldman, Jonah, 123
Goldman, Moe, 42–43, 47–48, 52, 64, 66–68, 71, 84, 86
Goldscheider, Calvin, 275–76
Goldstein, Abie, 150, 160
Goldstein, Jonah, 83
Goldstein, Ruby, 150, 153, 158, 160, 175, 263, 271
Goldstein, Sidney, 276
golf, 248, 250
Goodbye Columbus, 237
Gordon, Sid, 120, 240, 243
Gordon, Waxie, 153
Gorn, Elliott, 98, 146–47
Gotthoffer, "Shikey," 47, 64, 66, 68, 71
Gottlieb, Eddie, 37, 63, 66–68, 70–71
Gould, Ben, 52
Gould, Joe, 186
Gould, Paul, 241
Grant, Madison, 202
Great Gatsby, 105
"Great White Hope," 184
Greenberg, David, 133
Greenberg, Glen, 238
Greenberg, Hank, 9, 33, 68, 86, 118, 121, 126, 128, 131–43, 162, 180, 182, 214, 234, 237–38, 240–47, 262, 263, 265, 272–73, 281
Greenberg, Steven, 238
Greenlee, Gus, 283
Greenspan, Clara, 204, 248

Grossinger's Hotel, 84
Guest, Edgar, 136
Gurock, Jeffrey, 257

Hammerman, Kenny, 26
Hank Greenberg's All-Stars, 142
Hannah Schloss Jewish Center, 263
Harlem Rens, 34–35, 60, 63, 67
Harris, Harry, 147
Harris, Sheriff, 94
Harvard University, 192, 195, 201–2
Harwell, Ernie, 263
Hawkins, Connie, 26
Haymarket riot, 12
HBO, 231
"Heavenly Twins," 54, 71
Hebrew Cyclones, 33
Hebrew Educational Society, 32, 48, 59
Heller, Harry, 264
Henry Street, 14
Hertz, Steve, 4
Hertzberg, Arthur, 10, 275, 278
Hertzberg, Sonny, 50–51, 68–70
Heyman, Art, 255–56
Hickcox, Ed, 82
hillels, 263
historical memory, 51, 189, 233–34, 265,
    278
Hitler, Adolph, 138, 165, 180, 182, 185, 214,
    215, 278
Hoberman, John, 166
Hobson, Howard, 81
Hofstra University, 48
Hogan, Frank, 83, 85
Hogan, Frank "Shanty," 113
Hollander, H. P., 164
Holman, Nat, 20, 27, 29, 34, 54, 56–59, 60–
    62, 71, 73, 81, 85–86, 220, 254, 271
Holocaust, 51, 125, 188, 233–34, 262, 276
Holtzman, Ken, 243
Holzman, Red, 70
Homestead Greys, 281
Hope, Bob, 252–53
Hornsby, Rogers, 111, 236
Horween, Arnold, 201, 211
Houk, Ralph, 235
House of David, 33
Houston Astros, 4
Howe, Irving, 4, 10, 291n
Huggins, Miller, 134
Hull House, 14
Hunter College, 192
Husing, Ted, 224

immigrants, 12
immigration, 5–7, 192. *See also* assimilation;
    East European Jews; Jewish.
Immigration Restriction League, 195
integration, 239, 282–83. *See also* blacks.
International Jewish Sports Hall of Fame, 265
International Ladies Garment Workers Union,
    22
International Olympic Committee, 219
Inter-Settlement Athletic Association, 14
Irish, 17, 98, 146–47
Irish, Ned, 81
Israel, 51, 125, 179, 234, 237, 241, 261, 275–
    76
Israel, Julius, 93
Israeli Olympic team, 251

Jackson, Joe, 105
Jackson, Levi, 241
Jacobs, Joe, 180, 185–88
Jacobs, Mike, 183–88
Jaffee, Irving, 190
Jaffe's Evergreen Manor, 84, 299n
James Madison High School, 28, 47, 60, 62,
    219
"Jazz Singer," 177
Jeby, Ben, 145
Jeffries, Jim, 184
Jersey City Hebrews, 33
Jersey City Reds, 33
Jew in American Sports, 127
Jew in Sports, 117
Jewish: athletes as heroes, 59, 60–62, 71–73,
    86, 111–16, 118–43, 153–69, 170–89,
    202–3, 211–15, 245, 260–64, 272–77;
    attitudes about sport, 3–5, 127, 173, 175,
    245–46, 272; community centers, 236–37,
    263, 267–69; economic success, 71, 81,
    88–89, 233–37, 240–43, 245–46, 248, 259,
    271; entrepreneurs, 70, 142, 159, 183–89,
    250–51, 259; gangsters, 104;
    neighborhoods, 46, 48, 145, 171–73, 243;
    religious observance, 38, 137, 142–43,
    170–74, 217–18, 234, 242–43, 245, 258,
    269, 275–79; sports halls of fame, 261–64;
    stereotypes about weakness, 12–18, 117,
    130, 132; survival, 262–69; toughness, 117,
    138, 162–69, 180–89, 214, 262, 272, 277–
    78. *See also* American Jewish future;
    American Jewish identity; anti-Semitism;
    assimilation; second-generation Jews.
Jewish Basketball League, 37
Jewish People's Institute, 21
Jewish Relief Fund, 36

Jewish studies program, 256–57. *See also*
  Yeshiva University.
Jewish Telegraphic Agency, 209, 266
Jewish Welfare Board, 254–55, 264, 267
Jewishness: decline of, 234, 261, 269, 275;
  optimism about, 261–62, 269, 276–79
Joel, George, 210
Johnson, Earvin "Magic," 26, 253, 282
Johnson, Jack, 167, 183, 281
Johnson, William O., Jr., 229
Jones, Frederick, 195
Jordan, Michael, 73, 253, 282
Judenfriend, Harold, 44–45, 67, 273
Judenfriend, Morris, 273

Kadison, Bill, 165
Kahn, Roger, 128–29
Kaplan, "K.O." Phil, 160
Kaplan, Louis, 157
Kaplan, Sammy, 30–35, 39, 41, 47–48, 50,
  52, 69, 71, 84, 234, 271, 273–74, 278
Kaselman, Cy, 37, 64
Kaufman, Esther, 92
Kaye, Eli, 83
Kelly Park, 26
Kelson, Saul, 199–200
Kenneth Sterling Day Award, 207
Kentucky Miners Defense Fund, 23
Keren Ami Fund, 38
Kerner, Ben, 70
Kestenbaum, Justin, 215
Kieran, John, 228
King, Larry, 243, 245
Kinsbrunner, Mac, 66
Kinsella, Dick, 110
Kiviat, Abel, 190
Kling, Johnny, 101–2, 132
Klonsky, Milton, 39
Klotz, Babe, 63
Knights of St. Anthony's, 58, 60
Koppel, Ted, 282
Koufax, Sandy, 4, 132, 243–47, 255, 265, 269
Krickstein, Aaron, 250
Krinsky, Nat, 28, 30, 52, 60, 75–76, 219, 254
Ku Klux Klan, 3, 106
Kupcinet, Irv, 209
Kutsher, Milton, 84–85

Lafayette High School, 243
LaGuardia, Fiorello, 186, 220
Landesman, Meyer, 32
Landis, Kenesaw Mountain, 108
Lane, Floyd, 79, 82–83
Lapchick, Joe, 57
Lasker plan, 107–8

Lasky, Art, 160
LaSorda, Tommy, 239
Lautman, "Inky," 37
Lazzeri, Tony, 109, 123
Lefcourt, Louis, 51
Leiner, Gershon, 152
Leonard, Benny, 9, 16, 144–45, 149, 152–57,
  159–62, 165–67, 170–71, 173–74, 188–
  89, 234, 265, 271
Leonard, Chris, 57
Levey, Jim, 123
Levin, Carl, 138, 143
Levine, Jon, 236
Levine, Sam, 26, 243, 278
Levinsky, "Battling," 145, 160–61
Levinsky, David, 6
Levinsky, "Kingfish," 180
Levy, Ed, 119
Levy, Henry, 122, 170–71, 181, 185–86,
  191–92, 203, 209
Levy, Mannie, 198–200
Liben, Meyer, 272
Libhofer, Sharon, 246
Lieb, Fred, 132
Lieberman, Elias, 75, 162, 206
Lieberman, Nancy, 250
Litwack, Harry, 29–30, 40, 46, 50, 59, 63–64,
  66–67, 71
Litwhiler, Danny, 131
Long Acre Athletic Club, 150–51
Long Island Jewish Basketball League, 269
Long Island University, 47, 77, 83
Los Angeles Dodgers, 239, 244–46
Lou Gehrig's All-Stars, 59–61
Louis, Joe, 130, 167, 170, 182–88, 281
Lowell, Lawrence A., 195
Lower East Side, 5, 7, 13, 28, 89, 146, 150,
  158, 183, 265
Luckman, Sid, 208–9, 211, 213, 215, 219,
  243, 265, 312n
Lurie, Al, 153
Lydon, Susan, 253
Lynn, Dudie, 31, 59, 69

Maccabi Union, 317n
Maccabi World Union, 264
Maccabiah Games, 50, 86, 263, 264–66
MacPhail, Larry, 120
Madden, Owney, 182
Madison Square Garden, 79–80, 82–83, 156,
  183
Mager, Norm, 79–80
Mahoney, Jeremiah, 220
Maloney, "Speed," 69–70
Mandell, Richard, 229

Mann Act, 184
Marks, Marcus, 18
Martin, Billy, 242
Mathewson, Christy, 88, 91, 100
Matthau, Walter, 138
Max Kase Sports Lodge, 86
Maxwell Street, 46, 95, 148–50, 171–75, 177, 180
Mayer, Erskine, 103
Mayer, Louis B., 72
McCarthy, Joseph, 85
McGraw, John J., 109–16, 119, 134, 244
McGuire, Frank, 256
McLarnin, Jimmy, 156–57, 170–71, 177–78, 180
Meekin, Jouett, 90, 100
Melchiorre, Gene, 80
Mendoza, Daniel, 163
Merriwell, Frank, 232
Metcalfe, Ralph, 223–28
Metropolitan League, 60, 63
Metropolitan YMHA League, 19, 20
Miami Beach, 47
Michigan Jewish Sports Hall of Fame, 263, 269
middle ground, 30–38, 44–46, 64, 78, 88, 115–16, 129–31, 145, 162–69, 191, 203, 215, 237, 240, 255–56, 270–73, 278. *See also* assimilation; sport.
Miletzok, Nat, 67, 70
Miller, Bill, 164
Milwaukee Bucks, 257, 259–60
Minnesota Twins, 246
Mitchell, Richie, 156
Mitchell, William, 15
Monkey on My Back, 179
Moore, Deborah Dash, 124
Morgan, Dan, 161
Moses, Wally, 121
Moskowitz, Jammy, 28, 41, 47, 52, 59–62, 64, 71, 73, 219, 273
movies, 72–73
Murder Incorporated, 45
"muscular Christians," 208
"muscular Jews," 16, 162, 264
Mussolini, 182
Myer, Buddy, 119, 126–27

Nadel, Jack, 221
Naison, Mark, 283–84
name-changing, 56, 77, 93, 102, 119, 160–62, 190–91, 232
Nasaw, David, 32
Nash, Billy, 103

Nathanson, Norm, 47
National Basketball Association, 29, 63, 69–70, 257, 259
National Collegiate Athletic Association basketball championships, 79–81, 255
National Football League, 213, 231
National Invitational Tournament, 79–81, 255
National League, 244
National Negro League, 281
Nazism, 130, 181, 185–87, 220, 272–73
Nelson, Robert C., 194–95
Neugass, Herman, 221
New York Athletic Club, 229
New York Celtics, 56–57, 60, 63
New York Giants, baseball, 91–93, 109–16, 120–21, 235
New York Giants, football, 231
New York Hakoahs, 57, 59, 62
New York Jewels, 33, 68
New York Knickerbockers, 26, 45, 52, 230, 246
New York Mets, 246
New York University, 33, 67–68, 75, 83, 134, 192, 255, 258–59
New York Whirlwinds, 54, 56
New York Yankees, 109, 119, 235
Newark Hebrews, 62
Newman, Harry, 208, 263
Ninety-second Street YMHA, 15, 19–20, 34–35, 221, 268
No Man Stands Alone, 171
Nonpariels, 57, 60–61
Non-Sectarian Anti-Nazi League, 186
Nordau, Max, 162, 166, 264, 293n
North Carolina State University, 80
Notre Dame University, 209
Nuremberg laws, 164, 187, 220, 222, 229

Oakland Athletics, 242
Odets, Clifford, 167–68, 178
Ohio State University, 201
Olin, Bob, 145
Olympics, 190–91, 216; 1924 games, 148, 161; 1932 games, 265; 1936 games, 117, 191, 216, 219–29, 232–33, 251; boycott of, 185–86, 219–21; trials, 222–24; 1964 games, 256; 1968 games, 282; 1972 games, 216, 251–54
O'Malley, Walter, 244
Orde Wingate Institute, 265
Oren, Daniel, 195, 197–98
Owens, Jesse, 130, 223–29, 232, 281
Ozanam Oradales, 34

Palestine, 36
Palmer, A. Mitchell, 106
Passon, Chick, 37, 63
Passover, 38
Payton, Walter, 282
Pearl Harbor, 178
Pegler, Westbrook, 111, 185
Pelley, William Dudley, 186
Pelty, Barney, 103
Phi Beta Kappa, 195, 199
Philadelphia, 46, 123, 159–60
Philadelphia Jewish Basketball League, 49
Philadelphia League, 63
Philadelphia 76ers, 259
Philadelphia SPHAs, 62–67, 71, 255
Pian, Sam, 175
Pike, Lipman, 100
Pilgrim, Paul, 230
Pitler, Jake, 121, 124, 241
Pittsburgh Crawfords, 281
Pittsburgh Pirates, 131
Platt, Natey, 35
Playground Association of America, 12, 14–15
Plitnick, Sidney, 269
Plotnick, Mort, 268–69
Podoloff, Maurice, 70
Polo Grounds, 112
Portland, Oregon, 7, 38
Portland Trailblazers, 38
Poster, William, 39
Povich, Shirley, 119, 126
Prinstein, Meyer, 190
Proskauer, Joseph, 18
Protho, "Doc," 123
Protocols of the Elders of Zion, 106
Providence, R.I., 157

racism, 182–83, 186–88, 282–83
Randall's Island, 223
Rasofsky, Isadore, 171, 176–77
Rasofsky, Sarah, 171–76, 189
Ray, Johnny, 166–67
red scare, 106
Reese, Jimmy, 119
Reisman, Bernie, 96, 98, 278
Retton, Mary Lou, 231
Reulbach, Eddie, 109
Ribalow, Harold, 127, 130, 142
Rice, Grantland, 111, 211
Richler, Mordecai, 4, 245
Rickard, Tex, 56, 156, 183
Rickey, Branch, 120
Ring, 159, 189
Risewerg, Rube, 29

Robertson, Lawson, 225, 229
Robinson, Jackie, 120, 130–31, 140, 143, 239–41, 281
Robinson, Mack, 223
Rogovin, Saul, 128
Roiphe, Anne, 276–77
Roman, Eddie, 79, 82–83, 255
Roosevelt, Theodore, 16
Rose Bowl, 202
Rosen, Al, 126, 128–29, 140, 143, 234, 240, 244, 273
Rosen, Goody, 126–29
Rosen, R. D., 236–37
Rosenberg, Charlie Phil, 160
Rosenberg, Harry, 120
Rosenberg, Petey, 66
Rosenbloom, "Slapsie" Maxie, 145, 150, 160, 189
Rosenbluth, Lenny, 255–56
Rosenhouse, Charlie, 153
Rosenthal, Louie, 104
Rosh Hashonah, 245; and baseball playing on, 124, 134–36, 140–41
Ross, Barney, 9, 145, 170–80, 182, 188, 189, 234, 237, 254, 262, 265, 272–73
Ross, Edward, 11, 19
Rotblatt, Marv, 96
Roth, Al, 79–80, 82–84
Roth, Philip, 97–98, 236, 273, 188–89
Rothstein, Arnold, 100, 103–8, 153, 156, 283
Roxborough, John, 183–84
Ruck, Rob, 281–82
Rudd, Irving, 157–58, 161–62, 263
Rupp, Adolph, 79
Ruth, Babe, 88, 108–11, 113, 119, 132–33, 139, 141, 154, 251

Saint John's University, 45; "Wonder Five," 66, 77
Sallazzo, Salvatore, 83–84
Salsinger, H. G., 135
San Francisco Giants, 128, 243, 256–57
Sand, Bobby, 82, 85
Saperstein, Abe, 70
Sarachek, Red, 24–25, 30, 69–70, 256–57
Savage School of Physical Education, 28–29, 60
Savitt, Dick, 248–50
Schacht, Al, 90–91, 93, 100, 102, 263
Schayes, Danny, 257–62, 269
Schayes, Dolph, 70, 257–62, 265, 269
Schmeling, Max, 170, 180, 182, 184–88
Schulberg, B. P., 155–57, 188–89
Schulberg, Budd, 154–58
Schultz, Dutch, 168–69, 182

Schwartz, "Corporal" Izzy, 145
Scranton Miners, 67
Scully, Vin, 124
Seaman, Philip, 21
Sears, Kenny, 26
second-generation Jews, 6–7, 17–18, 24–25,
    49–51, 62, 70–73, 86, 258–59, 271. *See also*
    assimilation; Jewish; *individual sports.*
Sedran, Barney, 27–29, 54–55, 60, 62, 68
settlement houses, 22, 30, 150–51, 266–68.
    See also assimilation; Jewish; *individual*
    houses; individual sports.
Shaary Zedek synagogue, 135
Shapiro, David, 83
Sharkey, Jack, 181–82
Shaver, Bud, 135, 137
Shaw, Irwin, 95
Shawn, Dick, 270
Sherill, Charles, 219
Shields, Frank, 249
Sierens, Gayle, 231
Silberman, Charles, 10, 140, 143, 275
Six-Day War, 247, 277–78
Smith, Alec, 101
Solomon, Harold, 250
Solomon, Mose, 110
Soltes, Mordecai, 267
Sonny and Cher, 251
Sorin, Gerald, 296n
Sorkin, David, 268–69
South Philadelphia High School, 63
Spalding, A. G., 88, 107, 251
Spink, John, 133, 141
Spitz, Mark, 216, 251–54, 265, 269
sport: as artificial frontier, 12; and Jewish
    renewal, 266–69; parental attitudes toward,
    39–46, 88, 90–95, 127, 133, 151–52, 163,
    174–75, 218–19, 232, 236, 239–40, 258–
    59, 273; women in, 250. *See also*
    assimilation; blacks; Jewish; middle
    ground; *individual athletes and sports.*
sports broadcasting, 217, 230–32
sportswriters, 191. *See also individual names*
Star of David, 161, 175, 180–81
Stark, Abe, 66
Starobin, Mordecai, 203
Staten Island Jewish Community Center, 33
Stearns, Dan, 103
Steinberg, Richie, 236
Stein, Bill, 232
Stern, David, 70
Stevens, Harry M., 112
Stoller, Sam, 221, 223–29
Stone, George, 101
Stone, Steve, 100, 243

Straus, Isidore, 14
Streit, Saul, 83–84
Stroock, Sol, 18
suburbanization, 236, 248, 258
Sugerman, Lou, 63
Sullivan, George, 52
Sullivan, John L., 113, 146–47, 163, 167
"SuperJew," 241–42
Sutherland, Jock, 213
swimming, 251–54
Syracuse Nationals, 257–59
Syracuse University, 196, 203, 219, 230, 259

Talmud Torah Athletic Club (Minneapolis),
    36–37
Tannenbaum, Sid, 243
Temple University, 29, 67
Tendler, Lou, 159–60, 204–5, 248–50
Tevye, 5
Thornton, Frank, 82
Torgoff, Irv, 47
track, at Olympics, 223–29
Trojans, 96, 278
Twentieth Century Sporting Club, 183–84
Tygiel, Jules, 281
tzedakah, 38, 48, 160

United Jewish Appeal, 128
United States Committee Sports for Israel, 86,
    265
United States Maccabi Committee, 214
United States Maccabiah Association, 264
United States Maccabiah teams, 254, 260–61.
    See also Maccabiah Games.
United States National Tennis championships,
    248–49
University of California at Los Angeles, 78
University of Cincinnati, 244
University of Iowa, 201
University of Kansas, 256
University of Kentucky, 79, 85
University of Michigan, 211–12, 263
University of Minnesota, 36
University of Missouri, 82
University of North Carolina, 255–56
University of Pennsylvania, 198–99
University of Pittsburgh, 213
University of Southern California, 223–24
University of Wisconsin, 207
University of Wyoming, 85
University Settlement House, 14, 28
Untermyer, Samuel, 220
Uris, Leon, 247
Utah Jazz, 259

vaudeville, 113
Veeck, Bill, 121, 142
Vietnam, 276
Voices of a Summer Day, 95

Walker, Jimmy, 264
Wallach, Chaim, 151
Warner, Ed, 79–84
Washington Senators, 119, 126–27
Watergate, 276
Weinberg, Jack, 209
Weiner, Irving, 57–58
Weiner, Joseph, 35–36, 205
Weiner, Morris, 178, 209
Weintraub, Phil, 93, 120, 122, 125, 130, 132, 243, 273
Welsh, Yock, 64
Western Reserve University, 29
White, Richard, 291n
Whitehall, Earl, 126
Whiteman, Burton, 236
Willard, Jess, 184
Williams, Claude, 105
Wimbledon, 248–49
Winch, Al, 175
Wineapple, Ed, 77
Winograd, Sam, 82
Wise, Isaac Mayer, 147
Wise, Rabbi Joseph, 124
Worker's Sports League of America, 294n

Workmen's Circle, 23–24, 45
Works Project Administration, 19
World Athletic Labor Carnival, 222
World Series, 120, 153, 242, 244, 246
World War Two, 85–86
wrestling, 14
Wright, Harry, 80–81
Wykoff, Frank, 223–29

Yale University, 36, 194–96, 205–6, 241
Yekl, 6, 87–88, 143, 146, 148, 158, 167–68
Yekutieli, Yosef, 264
Yeshiva University, 30, 256–57
Yiddish, 157, 217
Yom Kippur, 260; baseball playing on, 124, 128, 134–36, 245–47
Yom Kippur War, 277
Young Circle League, 23–25
YMCA, 12
YMHAs, 14, 18–19, 22, 30, 150, 254, 266–68, 271, 284. *See also individual YMHAs.*
Young People's Socialist League, 23

Zarakov, Isadore, 201
Zaslofsky, Max, 44–46, 52, 70
Zelig, "Big" Jack, 104
zionism, 277–78
Zinkoff, Dave, 65, 71
Zukor, Adolph, 72